TACITUS

CLARENCE W. MENDELL

TACITUS

THE MAN AND HIS WORK

ARCHON BOOKS
1970

SBN: 208 00818 7
Library of Congress Catalog Card Number: 70-95027
Printed in the United States of America

I F IT were still the nineteenth century, this book might be called "Prolegomena to an Edition of the Works of Tacitus." There are, however, plenty of editions of Tacitus,' and amongst them are adequate ones. New discoveries may render them less adequate; in the meantime people (some at least) will continue to read, study, and use the great Roman historian. It is for them that this book is compiled, to make their approach to Tacitus not merely easier but more immediately rewarding. Four hundred and fifty years have produced an enormous mass of literature about Tacitus and what he wrote, more than anyone should try to master in less than a generation, and much of it is now out of date. The present volume is the result of an effort to gather together the chief results of these Tacitean studies and either to present them concisely or to indicate where they may most readily be found.

In addition, it makes some attempt at a revaluation of the man and his methods, not to estimate his greatness but to try better to understand it. Tacitus was an historian. To read and use his histories the modern scholar must know something of his approach to history, his conception of the historian's function, and the methods and spirit with which he sought out and handled his historical material. Tacitus was also a lawyer, which meant at Rome that he was presumably engaged, to some extent at least, in politics. The modern student should be able to understand what his legal equipment was and in what lines it was applied, what his political tendencies and prejudices may have been, and to what extent he was in a position to exercise them. Furthermore, Tacitus was consciously a man of letters. Anyone who wishes to appreciate him must know something of his literary tastes and qualities, for Roman history and literature were not divorced and the former cannot be evaluated without an understanding and appreciation of the latter. Finally, Tacitus was a man of strong individual personality. Into everything that he wrote this personality entered, and his modern reader will best understand and appreciate what he reads if he knows, insofar as he can, what sort of man the writer was, in what sort of social group he moved, what he believed, and how he reacted to the events of his own day and his own environment.

The present book will attempt in its first part to furnish something of this necessary background, in its second to give a more factual account of what posterity has done with the works of Tacitus.

C.W.M.

New Haven
January 1957

CONTENTS

Preface   v

PART I

1. Life and Qualifications   3
2. Historiography before Tacitus   31
3. Religious and Philosophical Position   50
4. Tacitus' Political Theory   64
5. Literary Style   71
6. Technique of Composition   96
7. Character Delineation   138
8. Tacitus As Historian of Military Affairs   166
9. Digressions in the Historical Works   189
10. Sources   199
11. Credibility of Tacitus' History   219

PART II

12. From Publication to Discovery   225
13. Discovery of the Works   239
14. Manuscripts of the Minor Works   256
15. Manuscript Affiliations of the Minor Works   279
16. Manuscripts of the Major Works   294
17. Manuscript Affiliations: Books XI–XXI   325
18. Titles   345
19. History of the Printed Text   349

Selected Bibliography   379

Index   387

PART I

1. LIFE AND QUALIFICATIONS

O F ALL the literary figures in Roman antiquity scarcely any has left a more vivid impression of personality than Tacitus, in spite of the fact that astonishingly few of the external events of his life are definitely known. There is not even any dependable evidence about his family. The name Cornelius signifies nothing because of the vast number of freedmen and their descendants bearing it. There was a Cornelius Tacitus, a Roman *eques,* procurator of Belgic Gaul, known personally to the elder Pliny (*N.H.* 7. 16. 76), but no further information exists concerning him. The only value of this bit of information vouchsafed by Pliny lies in the support it gives to the probability that Tacitus, the historian, was a new man in the senate and came from a family of the equestrian order. There is nothing to prove this hypothesis, but there is no evidence of the family in the senate before the time of the historian and it is tempting to find in the fiery partisanship of Tacitus for senatorial prerogative the zeal of a newcomer. The great champion of the senate in the days of Caesar was a *novus homo.*

The question of Tacitus' full name is still unsolved. By Pliny and the few later writers who refer to him he is usually called either Cornelius or Tacitus, or Cornelius Tacitus. The first use of a praenomen is by Sidonius Apollinaris, who twice (*Ep.* 4. 14, 22) uses the name Gaius. In the second of these instances, the juxtaposition of the name Gaius Plinius might have led to an error, but in the earlier citation Gaius Tacitus stands alone. In the Medicean MS of the first six books, our oldest MS, the praenomen is Publius. That the reading is genuine and not a modern addition is shown by a letter of Cardinal Soderini, who saw the MS in Rome in 1509.[1] The only other MSS earlier than the fifteenth century, the Aesinus of the minor works and Medicean II of Books 11–21, have Cornelius Taci-

1. *Eos, 1* (1894), 223 ff., 243 ff.

tus. This is also the reading of most of the fifteenth-century
MSS, though some few have Gaius Cornelius Tacitus. It is
hardly possible that they took the Gaius from Sidonius.
An inscription from Mylasa in Caria was reported in the
Bulletin de correspondance hellénique (1890), p. 621, which
for the moment seemed to settle the question in favor of Publius, but in 1895 Edward Hula and Emil Szanto reported in
the *Sitzungsberichte* of the Vienna Academy [2] that on a trip
through Caria they had read with care this inscription and that
what had been reported as πο was actually ΤΩ. This was then
in reality the final syllable of ᾽ΑΝΘΥΠΑΤΩ—the title and not
the praenomen of Cornelius Tacitus.

The question is therefore still unsettled. There is perhaps
some slight justification for giving weight to the evidence of
Medicean I on the ground that there is no possible confusion
of the abbreviation P with the C of Cornelius or with the praenomen of Seutonius or Pliny, whose works are so often associated with those of Tacitus.

The same uncertainty exists with regard to the birthplace of
the historian. Interamna has frequently been claimed because
of a confused and worthless rumor of late date relative to the
emperor Tacitus, who considered himself a descendant of the
writer (Vopiscus, *Tac.* 10).

The date of Tacitus' birth can be approximately determined
as A.D. 54–56. In the first place, Pliny speaks of himself as
adulescentulus cum iam tu fama gloriaque floreres (*Ep.* 7. 20).
At the same time, however, he refers to himself and Tacitus
as *aetate, dignitate propemodum aequales*. Pliny was born in
61 or 62. This evidence gives us nothing precise, but the phraseology would indicate that Tacitus was surely not more than
ten years older than Pliny, probably less. He held the consulship either two or three years before Pliny, the praetorship
five years before his friend.

A second approach to the problem is furnished by Tacitus
himself in the *Dialogus*. But before discussing this it will be
necessary to consider briefly the claim which has from time to

2. *Philosophisch-historische Classe, 132* (1895), Treatise 2, p. 18.

time been made that the *Dialogus* is not a work of Tacitus. Ettore Paratore has recently raised the question again, and his presentation, being most comprehensive, may be taken to represent the position.[3] He insists that the argument from the supposed lack of an author's name in the title of the archetype is not of great importance, but he carefully elaborates that argument which is really basic. He cites the memorandum of Niccoli which presents Tacitus as author of the *Germania* and *Agricola* but gives no author for the *Dialogus*. He also cites the letter of Panormita about the same series of finds. But Panormita's letter is based on Niccoli's memorandum or its source and furnishes no independent evidence. Niccoli obtained his information from Poggio, who got it from the Hersfeld monk whom we now know to have been Heinrich von Grebenstein [4] and who produced for Poggio only an inventory. Paratore does not indicate that the journal of Decembrio is the first evidence we have from anyone who *saw* the MS and that Decembrio gives Tacitus as the author without any question: *Cornelii Taciti Dialogus de Oratoribus*. This should dispose of the claim that the Hersfeld (really the Fulda) MS left the authorship in doubt. Only one existing MS of any value fails to name Tacitus as author of the *Dialogus:* the Leiden MS, which almost surely derives from a copy made hastily for or by Enoch of Ascoli of a German original and brought independently to Rome by Enoch.[5] The MSS, therefore, do not give any ground for doubting the Tacitean authorship of the *Dialogus*.

Bilde von Rheinau did, as Paratore notes, question the Tacitean authorship on the grounds of style, but the matter was not taken seriously until Justus Lipsius came out in violent protest against the idea that Tacitus could have written an essay so completely different in style from his other works. Rather disingenuously, Paratore fails to mention the fact that in later editions Lipsius very decidedly softened his assertion.

3. "Tacito," in the *Biblioteca Universitaria*, 2d ser. *3*, n.d.
4. Ludwig Pralle, *Die Wiederentdeckung des Tacitus*, Fulda, 1952.
5. See below, pp. 248 f.

Paratore rests his case largely on his own interpretation of readings in the *Dialogus,* chiefly from chapters 3 and 4. The discussion in these chapters, he claims, clearly alludes to the martyrdom of Maternus and therefore makes a date previous to A.D. 91 impossible for the essay. The claim is unconvincing and is not strengthened by an accumulation of interpretations of other passages equally unconvincing.

With no sound MS evidence against Tacitean authorship, the burden of proof clearly lies on those who question it. Hendrickson and others have clearly demonstrated that the difference in style between the *Dialogus* and the other works of Tacitus is no argument against the Tacitean authorship. Up to the present time no other convincing arguments have been adduced to warrant the arbitrary removal of the *Dialogus* from the Tacitean canon.

Tacitus fixes the assumed date of the discussion held in the *Dialogus* as A.D. 75, the sixth year of Vespasian's principate (*Dial.* 17. 10 ff.), and in the dedicatory introduction addressed to Justus Fabius he says that he was *iuvenis admodum* at the time. The natural interpretation of this phrase is "just a young man" or "a very young man." It could hardly be used of one under fifteen or over twenty-five. Like the evidence from Pliny, this indicates a date of birth in the fifties and points to the early or middle fifties.

In *Ann.* 11. 11. 3 Tacitus tells us that he was praetor in 88, presiding over the *ludi saeculares* of Domitian. This adds little to our evidence, but in *Hist.* 1. 1. 4 he makes the following statement: "Dignitatem nostram a Vespasiano inchoatam, a Tito auctam, a Domitiano longius provectam non abnuerim." Obviously *dignitatem* is used in its ordinary sense of "career of office," but there may be some doubt as to whether *inchoatam* refers to the quaestorship or to his first political committee appointment; in the latter case *auctam* would refer to the quaestorship. This office would normally be closed to anyone under twenty-five. To be twenty-five under Vespasian, Tacitus must have been born by A.D. 54. If he were quaestor under Titus, the date might be two years later at the most. The conclusion that he was born about A.D. 55 cannot be far from right.

From *Agric.* 9 we know that Tacitus became engaged to the daughter of Cn. Julius Agricola in 77 and was married to her after Agricola's consulship, which he held some time during that year. From the letters of his friend Pliny it is clear that he must have had the regular training in rhetoric and law and that he was perhaps the most eminent lawyer of his day. His political success carried him at an early age into the senate. In 88 he was not only praetor (*Ann.* 11. 11) but also a member of the college of quindecemviral priests specially charged with the conduct of the saecular games. It is clear from *Agric.* 45. 4 that he was absent from Rome from 89 to 93, when he may have been governor of a Caesarian province (assignment to a senatorial province would have been for a shorter term) or, less probably, a *legatus legionis.* As consul, probably in 98, he pronounced the eulogy over Verginius Rufus (Pliny, *Ep.* 2. 1). In the year 100 he was associated with Pliny in the prosecution of Marius Priscus for maladministration of the province of Africa. The inscription from Mylasa cited above indicates that he was subsequently governor of Asia. The date of his death can be only approximately determined. It must have come after 116, when the *Annals* seem to have been published. In *Ann.* 2. 61. 2 and 4. 4. 6 he mentions Trajan's eastern extension of the Empire without noting the subsequent withdrawal by Hadrian in 117.

The letters of Pliny furnish ample evidence of Tacitus' active legal career and of his diligence in the field of publication. Of his surviving works (and we know of none that has been completely lost, unless it be the eulogy of Verginius Rufus and such of his speeches as he may have published in accord with a common Roman practice) the *Dialogus* was in all probability the earliest, although competent opinion has been sharply divided on the question of its date. Since the understanding of Tacitus' character is dependent largely on the impression which he himself leaves in his writings, it is important to determine as far as possible the relation of these in time to one another. All except the *Dialogus* are datable within narrow limits, the *Germania* and *Agricola* appearing in about 98, the *Annals* in 116, and the *Histories* at some date between these two. It is generally agreed that the *Dialogus* is his earliest production and also that it could hardly have been published during the more despotic years of Domitian's reign. But there is sharp disagreement as between the reign of Titus, the early years of Domitian, and the reign of Nerva.

The question depends in part on the assumed date of the conversation recorded in the essay but more specifically on the interpretation of Tacitus' statement that he was *iuvenis admodum* at the time and remembers the conversation. Aper in *Dial.* 17 gives what appears to be a meticulously accurate dating for the scene. He states that there have been 120 years since the death of Cicero, and he specifies the periods—Augustus, Tiberius and so on—which make up his total. But he gives fifty-nine years instead of fifty-six for the period from the death of Cicero to that of Augustus. At any rate, the assumed date is somewhere between A.D. 75 and 77. According to Aper it is the *sexta statio* of the *principatus* of Vespasian. The simplest interpretation of this is that the conversation is supposed to take place in the sixth year of Vespasian's principate, or 74–75. This use of *statio* is difficult but not impossible, as Peterson points out in his edition, if we take each year of the reign as a "watch," remembering that the tribunician powers were renewed each year and that the renewals were regularly noted on the coins, largely for the purpose of dating.

The date of the imaginary scene is therefore fixed within a period of two or three years. The most probable year is 75. All the internal evidence is satisfactory if we accept this date. To justify Tacitus in saying that he was *iuvenis admodum* at the time (he would presumably have been just under twenty), we must assume that he is writing some years later. At this point we meet with a real difficulty, for in the introduction to the *Agricola* Tacitus says that he has survived fifteen years of enforced silence under Domitian—in other words that he did not publish between 81 and 96. That this is not merely a general or vague statement is borne out by evidence which makes it impossible to accept the argument that there was no repression during the early years of Domitian and that the *Dialogus* might have been written then. The effect of the fifteen years is emphasized by describing its effect on both *iuvenes* and *senes*, and the *per silentium* is made emphatic by its position. Also it is of the year 85 that Tacitus says (*Agric.* 39): "frustra studia fori et civilium artium in silentium acta, si" etc. It was in 85 that Agricola was recalled from Britain, and Tacitus depicts the jealous character of Domitian as well developed by that time. The praise of imperial security expressed in the *Dialogus* which can be accepted as honest during the reigns of Titus or Nerva or Trajan can hardly be so considered if written during the reign of Domitian by one who held this opinion of that emperor.

This leaves the choice then between the periods before and after the reign of Domitian. Gudeman considers the earlier date proven, but his proofs consist too much of exclamations and rhetorical questions. Leo and Hendrickson are equally sure of the later date and present sound argument for at least one important point. They have forever eliminated the old assumption that the Ciceronian style of the essay marks it necessarily as an early production and that Tacitus developed from this style to his later one progressively. The style of the *Dialogus* is the conventional one for the particular type of literature. They also consider that the defense of poetry is in a way Tacitus' defense for leaving his oratory for history, another form of *eloquentia*. This reasoning is persuasive and the conclusion cannot be disproven. On the other hand its sponsors lay no claim to absolute proof. Under these circumstances there can probably be no general agreement.

First of all the phrase *iuvenis admodum* must be considered. It would be perfectly suitable if the essay were written in 96 or later. But it is also possible that in 81 a man of twenty-six might look back six years and use the phrase of himself at the earlier date even if it were in a tone of self-conscious whimsicality. The decisive evidence to me is the whole tone and spirit of the essay. It is written in a buoyant spirit in unmistakable contrast with the grim point of view that pervades the *Agricola* and the longer historical works. The *Germania,* too, while not conspicuously grim, has touches of a pessimistic attitude toward contemporary Roman society that sharply differentiate it from the *Dialogus.* The latter is not merely a dramatic tour de force by which Tacitus revives the more hopeful days when he was *iuvenis admodum.* The fifteen years of Domitian had bitten so deep that even the tempered optimism of the opening chapters of the *Agricola* cannot drown the bitterness that breathes through the whole. As Tacitus himself says, to forget is not so much in our power as to keep silent. It would be little short of a literary miracle if the man who said that by the nature of human infirmity remedies are slower than evils and you can more readily crush than revive intellectual pursuits could, almost in the same breath, present the vigorous literary argument in which Aper and Mesalla discuss the right models and methods for the orator to follow. For they do not give the impression of men arguing in a vacuum. The question has contemporary vitality. Tacitus is still young enough to appreciate the thrill of the younger generation in its innovations; oratory for him still has a future as well as a past.

By the time of Nerva, Tacitus would have been far more concerned with the equipment of the historian than of the orator. The *Dialogus* deals constructively with forensic oratory. It deals with it in a pleasant, discursive, yet well organized fashion. There is no tension. Even Maternus, who is abandoning oratory, has no bitterness, and there is no compulsion or even pressure upon him to withdraw. The scope of the orator's activity is admittedly reduced, but there is no personal danger involved in his profession. Such a situation could be only a hope in 96.

Another indication of the early date of the *Dialogus* is the use of earlier literature by the writer as compared with that made in the *Agricola,* for example. The *Dialogus,* based on a Ciceronian model, frequently echoes Cicero, especially his *De oratore*, material which was familiar to Tacitus from his school studies. But of that wide reading, especially in the historians, which is constantly evidenced in the *Agricola* there is no trace in the *Dialogus*. Granted the difference in genre, it is hard to believe that one who reworked and made his own the phrases of Nepos, Velleius Paterculus, Sallust, and Livy in his eulogy of Agricola would have meticulously avoided all such reminiscences in a contemporary essay on oratory. The *Dialogus* reads like the enthusiastic output of a young but extremely able, well educated, thoughtful lawyer, the by-product of a man in active practice. The writer was the product but not the devotee of the popular training and practice of the day. The essay was a courteous protest against much of the contemporary fashion, but it was not a disheartened or despairing protest, nor by any means a sweeping or devastating condemnation of that fashion. It has a buoyancy and openmindedness that does not characterize the product of the older Tacitus. No decisions are arrived at; there is no partisan tension or dogmatism. The *Agricola,* on the other hand, with all its brilliance is brittle with nervous tension wholly understandable after the experience of fifteen years under Domitian. Tacitus was by this time already at work on his *Histories,* and the essay might win or forfeit the favor of the literary public toward his larger work. It gives evidence as the *Dialogus* does not of a striving after the approval of his contemporaries. The one essay breathes the enthusiasm of youth, the other the disillusionment of middle age.

To complete then what we know of Tacitus' career, the evidence seems to indicate that his active life at the bar reached its peak in about 81 and that it led him to the quaestorship and the senate, only to be thwarted to a large extent by the attitude of the emperor. After fifteen years, in which he must have done a vast amount of reading and research, he published the *Germania* and the *Agricola* in about 98. These were followed after some years by the *Histories* and, probably in 116, by the *Annals.* Beyond that date we know nothing of the facts of Tacitus' life.

In spite of the meager nature of this biographical material, there is small reason to regret that the facts are so little known. The man's character and point of view and his qualifications as an historian and a man of letters are abundantly evident. This is due in part to the letters of his friend Pliny, but largely to his own self-revelation. The evidence from Pliny may be most conveniently studied first. The dominant character in the letters of Pliny is Pliny himself. Here is a man depicted presumably as he wished to be depicted, presented as a man of self-conscious integrity and real devotion to the public welfare. He was one of the best lawyers of the day, with a supreme passion for writing, perhaps largely because by writing he hoped to win immortality. This desire to win a name among posterity was the sincere and unconcealed motive for almost everything that Pliny did, nor should it be lightly dismissed as unworthy. He tells Tacitus of the part he played in an important case (against Massa Baebius—*Ep.* 7. 33), hoping that the historian may use it in his great work and thus make immortal his example of old fashioned integrity. He revised his speeches for publication after delivery (9. 28), he published the speech he made in presenting the library to Comum (1. 8), he longed to write history in order to extend not only the fame of the characters that he depicted but also his own (5. 8), and even from lighter verse he hoped to acquire some glory (9. 25). If this ambition for fame was more naive and outspoken in Pliny than in most of his contemporaries, it would seem to have been no more real. A glance through his published correspondence gives an almost appalling picture of the amount of publication, usually following upon public recitation, that the end of the first century witnessed. The evidence of Juvenal and Martial is not necessary to confirm this picture, but the satiric and the humorous touch seem to demand less of our credulity after a study of the letters of Pliny. The more reticent Tacitus set about winning the glory that Pliny craved, but he referred to it only indirectly in his remark (*Agric.* 46) that while many great men had gone down to oblivion, Agricola, thanks to his eulogy, would always survive. What Tacitus sought to bestow upon his father-in-law as the best gift in his power, he can hardly have scorned for himself.

Pliny must not, however, be thought of as living for fame in any light sense of the word. Notoriety he scorned; he wished to be remembered for service to the state. For he was not typical of his age except as a conservative minority is typical of any age of materialism. The age of Pliny and Tacitus was an age of the individual. The old community of interest, the old all-embracing sufficiency of the state, was a thing of the past and the individual devoted to that anachronism was decidedly rare. A later age has preserved the literature of protest, and one might think that the attitude of Tacitus and Juvenal and, in fact, of most of the surviving writers, was the prevailing attitude. Such was not the case. As the power of the emperor became more solidified, the senate became more and more of a debating society, and even within the senate the advocates of the old senatorial government with all that went with it—the reactionaries who bemoaned the defunct republic—were a minority submerged by the increasing horde of contented modernists who, like Ovid, were glad that they had not been born before they were. Pliny was no fiery obstructionist or potential revolutionary. The bitterness had been largely extracted from the situation under the Ulpian regime, and Pliny was not only a gentleman but an even-tempered gentleman. Juvenal might rage in satire and no one ever know whether his bitterness was personal or inherent in his literary type. Tacitus, writing the history of the darker days, might flay the outrages of Tiberius and Nero and Domitian. But Pliny lived in the present and in the future. His arraignment of the new regime (to the senatorial opposition it was still new after a century of development) was urbane and a trifle plaintive, the polished expression of a preference, rather than any belligerent effort to effect a change. In the more dangerous days of Domitian, Pliny would probably never have voiced even his preferences. As it was, he merely expressed keen regret at the low estate of education, deplored the existence of a Regulus and the informers, and reserved his real admiration for those who had, with more heroic natures than his, faced the emperors in open opposition. Occasionally (he liked to think) he had himself risked much for his old republican principles, but this deliberate inducement of vicarious terror was the luxury of an imaginary danger and no stern reality. I should be inclined to think that his was exactly the type of character that belonged to Agricola and which Tacitus commended (*Agric.* 43), the character of those who do not brave the lightning or gain fame by a melodramatic end with no advantage to their country but arrive at a higher plane of true glory by self-controlled discipline combined with energy and patient effort. Tacitus himself, in spite of his admiration for the Paetus Thraseas of the century, did not, as a senator, follow their example, nor does he wholly commend Paetus Thrasea, certainly not Asinius Gallus. They were in the ranks of the righteous but they made some of the righteous most uneasy.

The net service to the state on the part of Pliny must have been very great. His devotion to his principles went so far as to keep him in town in the summer and often when he wished to be elsewhere. He was the generous patron of his native commune. The pressure of legal demands upon his time and strength can hardly be the figment of his imagination: he was actually engaged in too many important cases to have had an excess of leisure. As is so often the case, the conservative minority, helpless to stem the tide of what seemed to them a fatal heedlessness, and unheard in the councils of government, nevertheless, from a deep-rooted sense of loyal devotion to the country of their dreams, did the necessary work of everyday government, carried on the routine of the senate and the courts, and in an unappreciative generation played the unpopular but useful role of elder statesmen.

It would not be right to leave an impression of Pliny as a martyr to the modernism of his day. Undoubtedly he enjoyed life, but he enjoyed it consciously and in the fashion of an earlier generation as he himself conceived that generation. The world about him had given way to the mania for speed; respect for ancient standards of worth had largely disappeared; money was perhaps the greatest test of greatness; and in business and in government and in society there was prevalent an irresponsible levity. At least that was the belief of the old guard, of which Pliny represented the moderate wing.

Pliny would probably have fixed on the senate as the weak spot in the governmental set-up of his day, and to the restoration of the power and dignity and prestige of that body he would have pinned his faith as the panacea for the troubles of Rome. There were plenty of minor difficulties in the life of his generation, irritations which drove Juvenal into vehement vituperation and Martial into lighter but more effective raillery. But to Pliny these were rather the incidentals, the more external symptoms of the central disease, the ill-judged displacement of that class whose god-given function it was to govern Rome and civilize the world.

Much more of course might be said about Pliny, but this is not primarily a sketch of Pliny. It is an effort to understand one side of the one man that we positively know to have been a close friend of Tacitus. It is surely safe to assume from the letters of Pliny that the two men had many similarities of taste in addition to being politically in complete harmony. Pliny resorts to rapturous exclamations over their harmonious intimacy (7. 20), and it should be noted that the familiar story of the man at the circus games who knew that his seatmate must be either Tacitus or Pliny came from Tacitus (9. 23), that the historian was in the habit of sending his manuscripts to Pliny for criticism, and that he himself begged for the product of Pliny's pen (7. 20, 8. 7, 9. 10). It was not a one-sided friendship. Different as the two men undoubtedly were, their fundamental point of view about the state of empire will prove, I think, to have been almost identical.

There is no questioning the opinion which Pliny held of Tacitus. As a young man he picked him out as a model and he was never disappointed: in the prime of life he still looked upon Tacitus as the first man in the world in their profession (7. 20). His authority as a critic Pliny does not question (1. 20); his histories are assured of immortality (7. 33); even

Verginius Rufus is extraordinarily fortunate to have Tacitus to pronounce his eulogy (2. 1). And obviously Tacitus is one of the senatorial group that Pliny approves: they are associated in the public mind, selected together for the important task of prosecuting Marius Priscus, and regularly included in the wills of the same people and with similar bequests (*Ep.* 7. 20). On this last point Pliny is not left without confirmation. In 1820 and 1830 two pieces of an inscription were found in Rome which together form a fragmentary copy of the will of one Dasumius.[6] After provision for Dasumia, a considerable section contains names with a decidedly familiar sound and amongst them, in juxtaposition, "— *Secundo / Cornelio* —."

There can be practically no doubt that these two beneficiaries are Plinius Secundus and Cornelius Tacitus. The will and the persons mentioned in it become therefore of some interest. It seems to be the will of Lucius Dasumius, who was proconsul of Asia under Trajan. According to T. Mommsen, Dasumius was consul after 103.[7] The will seems to date from 108 or 109, and the testator to have adopted the son of P. Tullius Varro, who became L. Dasumius Tuscus and was consul under Antonius Pius. The names are in many cases fragmentary, and some that are preserved entire have no longer any significance. The presence, however, of such a name as Minicius Iustus is most interesting. He was the husband of Corellia and sister of Corellius Rufus, one of Pliny's older friends and one whom Pliny admired most among his acquaintances. Corellia was an intimate of Pliny's mother. Minicius Iustus is highly praised by Pliny (7. 11). Tacitus goes out of his way to tell in *Hist.* 3. 7 how Minicius was sent to Vespasian during the civil war of 69 because he was too strict in his standards to be safe in command of the camp of the seventh legion. It would certainly seem that he was in all probability one of the older members of the circle of Pliny and Tacitus. Fabius

6. *CIL*, *6*, 1350, No. 10, 229; cf. Wilmanns, *Exempla Inscr. Lat.*, *1*, 101, No. 314.
7. "Zur Lebensgeschichte des Jüngeren Plinius," *Hermes*, *3* (1869), 45 n.

Rusticus is presumably the historian of that name whom Tacitus rates (*Agric.* 10) as best of all the modern historians and the Rusticus to whom Pliny writes (9. 29) in familiar tones on literary matters. Junius Avitus receives the highest eulogy of which Pliny is capable (8. 23), serving as a model contrast with the typical youth of the day as seen by the conservative Pliny ("Statim sapiunt, statim sciunt omnia, neminem verentur, imitantur neminem atque ipsi sibi exempla sunt. Sed non Avitus" etc.). The whole letter is marked by a genuine admiration and affection. A kinsman of the testator seems to be L. Iulius Ursus Servianus, who was born in 47, according to Dio (69. 17), married Domitia Paulina, the sister of Hadrian, and was consul under Domitian and again in 102. In this latter instance his colleague was the friend of both Pliny and Tacitus, L. Fabius Iustus. In his earlier consulship his colleague was L. Licinius Sura, one of the older type of statesman, admired by Martial, partly because he came from Spain and was generous, but also because his oratory was fit to rival that of the ancients (7. 47. 1). There is not in all this very much more than an indication of the type of men with whom Tacitus is associated, at least in this particular instance. They are all men who have served the state, and all, so far as we can judge, incline strongly toward the conservative side. Cornutus Tertullus, the colleague and intimate friend of Pliny, for example, is spoken of by him as *exemplar antiquitatis* (5. 14), and Pliny says that he and Cornutus shared all the same personal friends. Certainly this flavor of olden days would have appealed to Tacitus.

This impression of the group within which Tacitus moved is strengthened if we extend it by including the other friends of whom we have any indication. Corellius and Pliny had a friend Claudius Pollio (Pliny, *Ep.* 7. 31) whom Pliny recommends cordially to the friendship of Cornutus. He speaks of Pollio as unusual in his solid worth and mentions his loyalty as shown by his "Life of Annius Bassus." Bassus is spoken of by Pliny as *gravissimus cives* and receives somewhat similar praise from Tacitus (*Hist.* 3. 50). Minicius Fundanus, proconsul in Asia —as were Dasumius and Cornutus and Tacitus himself—was the friend of Pliny, of Tacitus and of Plutarch (Pliny, *Ep.* 4. 15; Plut., *de. tr. an.* 1). Asinius Rufus and his son Asinius Bassus also figure as highly valued friends of Pliny and Tacitus, recommended to Minicius Fundanus by the former. Of the Stoic philosopher, C. Musonius Rufus, Pliny speaks (3. 11) in the very highest terms and says in addition: "quantum licitum est per aetatem cum admiratione dilexi." In Tacitus (*Hist.* 4. 10, 40) much is made of Musonius' attack on Publius Celer, and he is brought into *Ann.* 14. 59 to urge Plautus to die bravely. On the other hand the account of his approach to the troops, in *Hist.* 3. 81, is less enthusiastic, and Tacitus even speaks of his *intempestivam sapientiam.* Here is a curious echo of the early chapters of the *Agricola* and a reminder that Tacitus stood for moderation in opposition. A number of his friends were evidently Stoics, but of the extremists he was somewhat wary. This is well illustrated by his attitude toward some of the traditionally great names in the annals of Stoic republicanism.

Pliny (*Ep.* 3. 11) speaks of a group of his friends who have suffered martyrdom under Domitian. They were all opponents of the imperial regime and eulogists of the republic: Herennius Senecio, Arulenus Rusticus, Helvidius Priscus, all three of whom were put to death, and Junius Mauricus, banished by Domitian but still alive in 97. Mauricus and Arulenus Rusticus were brothers, and Pliny's letter to the former (1. 14) about choosing a husband for the daughter of the latter gives ample evidence of his intimate friendship with both. Helvidius Priscus was the son-in-law of Paetus Thrasea, whose obstinate opposition he and his wife Fannia perpetuated. Fannia afterwards persuaded Herennius Senecio to write the life of her husband, and this labor of love was his undoing.

Now this same group of four is singled out by Tacitus in *Agric.* 45. It is their fate under the tyranny of Domitian, while men like himself sat helplessly watching in the senate chamber, that seems to Tacitus some consolation for Agricola's early death. There is, furthermore, a note of personal bitterness in the chapter about these men, almost, I believe, a bitterness that came from the knowledge that he had somehow failed his friends—the feeling that tempts him more than once to condemn at least mildly the violence that he admires (*Agric.* 42; *Hist.* 3. 81; *Ann.* 2. 35). Obviously these four are his heroes if not his friends, and the presumption is all in favor of a close friendship. The character of the group is further illustrated by the fact that according to Juvenal (5. 36), Helvidius and Thrasea had indulged in the same gesture as Titinius Capito (Pliny, *Ep.* 1. 17), the paying of honors to the memory of Brutus and Cassius. Martial (5. 28)' uses the two brothers, the Maurici, as types of *aequitas,* and Pliny describes Junius Mauricus as a senator, *quo viro nihil firmius, nihil verius* (4. 22) and again (1. 5) as *gravis, prudens, multis experimentis eruditus et qui futura possit ex praeteritis providere.* There can be no question of the conservative solidarity of this group with which Tacitus and Pliny felt themselves spiritually one. It is interesting to note that the name Senecio appears also in the will of Dasumius.

In *Agric.* 17 Tacitus speaks with enthusiasm of Julius Frontinus, *vir magnus quantum licebat,* who was not overshadowed even by such a predecessor as Petilius Cerialis. To Pliny (*Ep.* 4.8) it was his chief joy in becoming augur to succeed Julius Frontinus, who had ever been his real patron. Pliny considered (5. 1) Frontinus and Corellius the most eminent men of their generation and felt for the engineer a real affection as well as admiration, comparing him in this respect with Verginius Rufus (*Ep.* 9.19). To Fabius Justus, Tacitus addressed his first work, the *Dialogus,* and to the same Fabius Justus, Regulus turned, knowing him as an intimate friend of Pliny's, when he sought reconciliation with the latter. Pliny wrote him two very trifling but rather intimate notes (1. 11, 7. 2). Finally, a word should be said about Verginius Rufus, who bulks large in the *Histories,* winning the highest admiration of Tacitus, who pronounced the encomium at his funeral. To Pliny, Verginius Rufus was not merely the greatest man of his day, but a father, patron, and intimate friend (cf. *Ep.* 2. 1).

It is tempting to explore further the possibilities of friendships shared by Pliny and Tacitus. It seems impossible that Quintilian was not a teacher or friend of Tacitus, as he was of Pliny. Pliny had at least some acquaintance with Martial, whose real friends seem to have been of the conservative group. Martial and Juvenal were certainly acquaintances if not friends, and it is tempting to bring them both into touch with Tacitus. But that would be to enter the field of conjecture. In the group of common friends as we find it we are able to get the personal background of Tacitus, married to the daughter of a moderate conservative of consular rank, admiring the heroes of the republican tradition, and on friendly terms with the senatorial group that found it impossible wholly to reconcile themselves to the ways of the Empire.

Almost as evident from the letters of Pliny as his admiration for the past and its standards, real or assumed, is his preoccupation with literary matters. Even the actual cases which he conducted seem to have been of as much interest to him because of the material they furnished for publication as for their inherent importance as legal processes. Again and again he tells of working over some speech to put it into form for preservation; he sends his manuscripts to friends, of whom Tacitus is perhaps the most favored, to receive their advice and criticism; he tells of the success which some of his productions have had. Pliny did not by any means confine his publication to these oratorical productions; he published a eulogy of the son of Vestricius Spurinna, (*Ep.* 3. 10); a eulogy of the emperor (3. 13); a speech of thanks to the emperor (3. 18) which he first prepared and delivered as a speech, then amplified and recited, and finally published; a book of hendecasyllabic verse (4. 14, 9. 13); and a book of miscellaneous light verses (8. 21); and he contemplated the writing of some work of history, but presumably abandoned the project (5. 8). He recited his own writings and attended faithfully the recitations of others. A large part of his correspondence deals with the writings of his friends as well as his own. He and Tacitus exchanged speeches for criticism (7. 20; 8. 7; 9. 10) and discussed the question of style (1. 20). Tacitus turned to Pliny for first-hand material for his *Histories* (6. 16, 20), and Pliny submitted some unsolicited (7. 33). In one letter (4. 13) Pliny asks Tacitus to select a candidate for a teaching position in the school which Pliny has inspired and largely endowed in Comum. He suggests that the teacher be chosen "ex copia studiosorum, quae ad te ex admiratione ingenii tui convenit." The picture of this following of students in attendance on Tacitus is reminiscent of Tacitus' own description of the ideal training of earlier days (*Dial.* 34) which he was evidently trying to maintain.

A passion for literature, a reverence for the traditional senatorial past, a sense of obligation to one's self, to one's friends, and to the state—these seem to have been the most effective characteristics of the group in which Tacitus moved.

To estimate the trend of Tacitus' writings, not on the basis of probabilities indicated by his social and political milieu but by means of the indications which he himself provides within those writings, requires a sharp distinction between the evidence which bears on the formal type to which each particular publication belongs, with such variations in each as may turn out to be Tacitean, and the evidence of those more personal elements which must have exercised a general influence on all of his works alike. It is the latter that are of prime importance in the present study.

A treatise on the decline of oratory done in the manner of Cicero is not the most promising material in which to search for a personal point of view. But even in his twenties Tacitus was a man of definite characteristics, which emerge even through the paragraphs of a formal treatise. The leading role in the dialogue is assigned to Maternus, who characteristically has recited and is preparing to publish a Cato, a drama which places him pretty definitely in the general group of those *laudatores temporis acti* whose heroes were Brutus and Cassius and Cato. He is not of the violent type. The principate of Domitian had not yet made its indelible impression upon the souls of those who loved most the earlier days. But he is not wholly pleased with the political life of his day and is contemplating a withdrawal into the groves of pure literature. He is a polished critic of contemporary life but not a favorable one. And he has obviously the sympathy of his literary creator. Again, Aper, who undertakes to argue with him, is no extremist, no raucous modernist. He believes in his own day and resents the habit which leads the others to assume a lowering of standards in the modern age. He advances materialistic arguments, he scorns or pretends to scorn, the literary life. But he is in reality a cultured gentleman making a courteous and persuasive plea for his own belief. Tacitus does not make Aper disagreeable or grotesque as a satirist might have done, but he gives him no possible chance of winning his case. The group as a whole rather cavalierly assumes that oratory has sadly declined and that Aper is the delightful but misguided champion of a lost cause. While, for literary purposes, Aper is presented as a provincial and a modernist, the artist who created him either knew only the cultured group of senatorial families within which already he seems to have moved, or else he deliberately chose to present only that group. Aper is a dissenter within his class, not a deserter from it or an assailant from without. Tacitus is not merely the young rhetorician making a studio study in the Ciceronian manner; the form is congenial; he is of the school of Cicero in a double sense; he identifies himself completely with the senatorial class, and he finds in the world of letters an appeal which rivals the call of practical politics. It is worth remembering in passing that Cicero, the master champion of the senate, was a new man; of Tacitus' family we know nothing, but there is no inconsistency in his devotion to the aristocracy, whether he was a member of the group by birth or only the aspiring protégé of some Maternus.

But there are also *individual* traits to be observed in the *Dialogus*. When Aper arraigns the tedium of old-fashioned oratory and pictures the modern judge as ever in advance of the advocate and requiring some rhetorical decorations to win his favor, there is, to be sure, a suspicion of irony, but there is also at that point and throughout the speeches of Aper a wholeheartedness of appeal that betrays the man of broad gauge who in spite of his devotion to the old is prepared to use the best of the new. With this point of view Tacitus deals sympathetically and to some extent follows Aper's principle in writing the *Dialogus*. Even in this Ciceronian study there are un-Ciceronian qualities which foreshadow the trend of the young lawyer's development. Commentators have been at great pains to point out in the *Diagolus* reminiscences of the rhetorical works of Cicero, and such there are in abundance. Tacitus himself indicates this by not infrequent references to Cicero, ample acknowledgment according to the convention of the day for any borrowing that he saw fit to make. But his borrowings are not in the nature of the direct transfer even of slight phrases. No idea, no expression, is taken over without remodeling, nothing is borrowed except with an attempt by improvement to make it the borrower's own. Many years later, in the biography of his father-in-law, Tacitus showed to what an extreme he could carry this process. The *Dialogus* is certainly no collection of rhetorical gems. It does, however, furnish enough illustration of this sort of workmanship to prove the scholastic interests of its author. Gudeman calls attention to Cicero's *Brutus* 56. 204: "atque in his oratoribus illud animadvertendum est, posse esse summos qui inter se sunt dissimiles" as the probable source of Tacitus' *Dial.* 18: "non esse unum eloquentiae vultum sed in illis quoque . . . plures species deprehendi nec statim deterius esse quod diversum est." The parallel is not compelling, but in view of the fact that Tacitus specifically cites the Brutus elsewhere in the essay, it is probably sound. Twenty years later there would have been no final *est,* and *nec statim deterius esse quod diversum* is a truly Tacitean phrase forged from a Ciceronian, the touch of the ironical giving it the hallmark.

This irony, which we associate instinctively with the mature Tacitus, plays no great part in the *Dialogus*. There is a fine touch of it in the reference to the poetry of Caesar and Brutus in chapter 21: "fecerunt enim et carmina et in bibliothecas rettulerunt, non melius quam Cicero, sed felicius, quia illos fecisse pauciores sciunt," and in chapter 8 there is a phrase that might well have come from the later works: "divitiae et opes quas facilius invenies qui vituperet quam qui fastidiat." Again there is a flash in chapter 25: "Nam quod invicem se obrectaverunt . . . non est oratorum vitium sed hominum." The writer is not a conspicuous master of the mordant phrase, but he has the talent.

In the same way there is no conspicuous criticism of the morals and manners of the day after the fashion of the satirists —and this, too, in an essay which maintains the superiority of ancient oratory—but there is enough of it to suggest a point of view which might easily be modified in either direction by the experiences of life. One of the most noteworthy examples is the arraignment of home training in chapter 29: "Iam vero propria et peculiaria huius urbis vitia paene in utero matris concipi mihi videntur, histrionalis favor et gladiatorum equorumque studia; quibus occupatus et obsessus animus quantulum loci bonis artibus relinquit? quotum quemque invenies qui domo quicquam aliud loquatur?" This has a familiar sound to one who has read any of the satiric literature of the century and even more in conformity with that type is the picture of contemporary rhetorical training given in chapter 35, a chapter less vigorous than Petronius' on the same subject but identical in point of view. So in chapter 13 there is the mild satire of a less furious Juvenal written before the nerves had become too jaded for restraint: "non me fremitus salutantium nec anhelans libertus excitet, nec incertus futuri testamentum pro pignore scribam, nec plus habeam quam quod possim cui velim relinquere."

Finally, it should be noted that from the purely political side there is very little indication in the *Dialogus* of what position the future historian will be likely to take. When Maternus urges Messalla "utere antiqua libertate qua vel magis degeneravimus quam eloquentia" (27), there is really no serious political bearing in the remark. He is bewailing the loss not of so-called freedom of speech but rather of the old-fashioned habit of blunt outspokenness. Perhaps the closest approach to any expression of political feeling is in chapter 13, when

Maternus, in answer to something said by Aper, expresses thorough disapproval of Vibius Crispus and Eprius Marcellus. It is really, however, disgust at the character of the informer rather than anger at his political influence that prompts the severe words of Maternus, so that the case is more an example of satiric than of political expression: "quod adligati adulatione nec imperantibus umquam satis servi videntur nec nobis satis liberi? Quae haec summa eorum potentia est? Tantum posse liberti solent."

On the whole, the *Dialogus* presents us with a young author, well trained not only in the old-fashioned, apprentice method but also in the latest rhetorical school of which he does not wholly approve, a man with an admiration for the earlier days of his country, a member of the senatorial class, armed with an ability to write trenchantly but without strongly developed political feelings to call out the irony at his command, a young lawyer of the aristocracy, still a student and possessing a highly developed taste for literature.

It was the fifteen years following the publication of the *Dialogus* that really determined the evolution of these traits into the ultimate character of Tacitus the historian, and it is to the *Agricola* first of all that one must turn to understand the processes and to discover the results. To the casual first glance the biography presents itself as just another product of the age of rhetoric, better to be sure than the average that we are led by the critics to expect but typical nevertheless and even exaggerated in its rhetorical artificiality. There is a tremendous straining after verbal effects which reaches more than one climax in phrases that have been ever since accepted as beyond improvement. *Omne ignotum pro magnifico* may stand as the example of this sententious quality. Quintilian, who worshiped at the shrine of Cicero, complained that the modern writers "non multas plerique sententias dicunt, sed omnia tamquam sententias." Tacitus, trained first in the Ciceronian style—but even in the Ciceronian product of his own youth speaking a less scornful word for the newer style—embraced it warmly and made it his effective tool. It is scarcely exaggeration to say that every Latin author, to say nothing of many a Greek writer, was ransacked by Tacitus to find material that could be re-molded into the brilliant "sentences" of the *Agricola*. Further-more, so far as the form of the essay is concerned, he wrote according to the book. The *Agricola* belongs definitely to the type of the eulogistic biography. But here again, as with the phrases that he culled from other men's gardens, Tacitus changed the form in detail, improved on what he found, and, in the matter of execution, brought to the task consummate work-manship. Stylistically he traveled far between the time of the *Dialogus* and that of the *Agricola;* his individualism led him to abandon the overconservative and to forge something of his own out of the still unstandardized new. But the possibility of such a change was already evident in the earlier work; even there he showed a willingness to explore new areas. During fifteen years he explored them so thoroughly that he emerged almost unrecognizable. Almost but not quite—for there is still the meticulous workmanship; the mastery of the phraseology that was dimly foreshadowed has developed strikingly; and in spite of the "new" style it is entirely within the realm of the possible that Tacitus considered that he was really going back to something older and sounder than Cicero and that this is why the opening line of the *Agricola* re-echoes the sonorous organ note of Cato: *clarorum virorum atque magnorum.*

When we turn from the formal matter of style to the more fundamental question of the point of view from which Tacitus scanned the moral, social, and political world in the late nine-ties, we find fully as marked a change. There is still the love for the earlier age, grown stronger in fifteen years, and in addition there has entered in a bitterness toward his own day only partly soothed by the promise of better things under the Ulpian re-gime. The very opening of the biography hits savagely at the times *tam saeva et infesta virtutibus.* He announces his histor-ical works to come as being a memorial of the slavery through which they have passed, with the implication that the present work, the life of his father-in-law, is not an arraignment of the times. But the eulogy of the past and of characteristics worthy of the past and the bitter vituperation of the days of Domitian furnish the dominant tone throughout. It reaches its first high point in the speech of Calgacus and its final terrific force in chapters 45 and 46, but it is never absent. In the *Germania* there is less scope for the indulgence of this tendency, but it is sufficiently in evidence to have led more than one critic to put the *Germania* in the category of satiric writings and to believe that its chief object was to show the contrast between the degenerate Roman and the noble savage. This theory can hardly be accepted: the fact is that Tacitus no more than states the case as it was when he tells of sitting year after year in the senate and seeing the foremost of his conservative friends persecuted by the emperor while worthless upstarts flourished on the pickings. During those years, the polished aristocratic scholar of the *Dialogus* became the bitter foe of the imperial system which had stripped the senate of its high position and large prerogatives. The rather poetic idealization of the past became hardened into an *idée fixe* which presented the era of the republic as an age of sound and disinterested government by a dignified, honest, and able senate. That the picture was largely a figment of the imagination made it no less potent, and there was undeniable reality in the power of a princeps who could throttle all but the most rash of the senators for fifteen years. Tacitus believed that his father-in-law had been poisoned by Domitian; he knew that many of the outspoken champions of liberty like Arulenus Rusticus and Herennius Senecio had been silenced forever by the same hand; to him it was all the result of the system which took from the senate and gave to the emperor, and when the opportunity offered he put into the mouth of the Caledonian chieftain the most terrific arraignment of the Roman Empire and of imperialism in general that has ever been penned.

The *Agricola* is an essay directly concerned with Roman public life and politics only insofar as the chapters on Britain give the writer an opportunity to present these against a background of simpler and different character. In the *Germania* the interest is centered on the life of the people in general and, without pushing the point too far, it is safe to say that the emphasis is on moral rather than political characteristics and that the Roman life is suggested only by comparison or contrast. But the *Germania* adds very materially to the understanding of Tacitus' tendencies as a writer and his qualifications as an historian. Even the descriptive geographical sections contain such remarks as "Argentum et aurum propitiine an irati dii negaverint dubito," and when he reaches the subject of morals the reader's attention is at once riveted by similar ironic implication in many a pregnant phrase. The most familiar, "nemo illic vitia ridet, nec corrumpere et corrumpi saeculum vocatur," is also one of the most significant, for here is a touch of the satirist, the moral critic defending the stoic virtues of the past, long since identified with the virtues of the primitive Roman. The moral criticism is also hand in hand with epigrammatic expression which is characteristic of the satirist. There is a considerable degree of seriousness about this presentation of a morally superior people and a brilliancy of phrase, but there is not the intense bitterness that the political criticism of the *Agricola* called forth. The young historian is not a moralist of Juvenal's type; his burning wrath is reserved for other ends. But neither is he Horatian, for the burning wrath is there and the easy pose of lazy indifference is not. The *Germania* shows us a serious side of Tacitus that will surely affect his writing of history, even though it is less dominant than his political emotions.

After another fifteen years Tacitus completed his great history of the first century: the memorial of past servitude, with little enough to fulfill the other half of his promise, the testimonial of present blessings. The opening sentences of the *Annals* strike a keynote: "Urbem Romam a principio reges habuere. Libertatem et consulatum L. Brutus instituit." It is a natural opening for a history of Rome, but the wording is significant and becomes more so when we find in chapter 2 the contrast "tuta et praesentia" with "vetera et periculosa," and when chapter 3 ends "quotus quisque reliquus qui rem publicam vidisset?" and 4 begins: "Igitur verso civitatis statu nihil usquam prisci et integri moris." The *vetus aetas* and *libertas* are the ideals against which as a constant background he paints the new age of tyranny. His is a legal and political opposition. His indignation, expressed with the mature irony that was already so far developed in the *Agricola,* is not primarily if at all a moral indignation. It is noteworthy that in the prologue to the *Annals* when quite naturally the vices that caused degeneration are enumerated, he cites vices familiar in Stoic satire but not *all* the cardinal vices—only those that apply to politics, that are the vices of public rather than private life.

We are dealing, then, with a man thoroughly trained in legal methods and the art of rhetoric, a staunch believer in the superiority of the republic, the relentless foe of imperialism, a bitter partisan of the emasculated senate, member of a social circle that comprised the best of conservative Rome, seriously devoted to literature, rather skeptical of philosophy, opposed to violence, yet well nigh hopeless of any other cure for the ills of empire.

When such a man turns to the writing of history we may properly expect from him certain well defined qualities. We may certainly look for marked individuality. The man who wrote the *Agricola* could never be expected to write in a calm and disinterested fashion, no matter how determined he might be to tell the truth without fear or favor. His interest will be centered on the great political question which had affected his whole life and that of his friends. He will be a partisan. To the presentation of his own political beliefs he will bring his supreme skill as an orator, and everything that he writes will presumably be charged with the emotion engendered by his career as an oppositionist. Yet we may expect the emotion to be handled with the adroitness of the politician whose position in the minority has taught him discretion. These are some of the qualities we have a right to expect from Tacitus the historian. From his generally conservative point of view we should look for reasonable conformity with the traditional Roman beliefs and the convictions of an earlier day. In the form of presentation which he might adopt, if we could judge from his earlier essays, we should expect him to accept the conventional type but to introduce such variations as his own genius might suggest. This is what he did even in the *Dialogus,* to a greater extent in the *Germania,* and most notably in the *Agricola.* It is essential therefore to recall as clearly as possible the conventional type of historical narrative as it existed in Tacitus' time after a long period of development from the days of the first chroniclers of Roman history.

2. HISTORIOGRAPHY BEFORE TACITUS

THE EARLY WRITING of history at Rome was firmly conditioned by the national habit of year-by-year record keeping. Lists of events dated by the names of the annual consuls were religiously preserved. These lists included important events at home and abroad—especially wars, victories and defeats, triumphs, laws passed, and cases decided, but also all kinds of supernatural occurrences and unusual weather conditions. Beyond any doubt the *Annales Maximi* were the most important single factor in the determination of the form which Roman history writing was to take.

The influence of this chronological method, however, may easily be exaggerated. It is fundamentally a natural method of recounting events. The Romans merely had more complete records accessible than had the Greek writers at the corresponding stage of development. But they also had the example of Thucydides and Xenophon in the year-by-year arrangement of events. For their earliest history they had no formal records and were forced to give more summary accounts, which presumably resembled those of the Greek logographers. Nevertheless the annalistic type is significant, especially as regards the summary listing of omens and miscellaneous events at the close of each year's account.

For the story of Rome's origin and early days the annalists found already at hand the epic treatment of Naevius, which probably drew on Timaeus as a chief source. The first historians took the myths as they found them, for the early story of Rome was largely a traditional background for the more nearly contemporary history which they wished to record. That their efforts were consciously literary must be emphasized, for the tendency has always been strong to represent the Roman annalists as crude reproducers of the records preserved in the public files. Undoubtedly one of the foremost reasons for writing annals was to make it easier for senators or magistrates to perform their duties. But the very fact that down to the time of Cato all the writers of Roman history—Fabius Pictor, Cincius Alimentus, C. Acilius, A. Postumius Albinus—wrote in Greek indicates an attempt to present to the cultivated class at Rome the first prose productions to compete with the Greek models. The son of Scipio the Great wrote a history in Greek, *dulcissime* according to Cicero. All of the annalists were members of the aristocracy, men of action in the state, and certainly not the sort who would do the hack work of mere recording. Their efforts at literary distinction were undoubtedly somewhat crude (Cicero went so far as to say *abest historia litteris nostris*). But equally without doubt they aimed at winning literary distinction for themselves and for the state.

It was Cato who first set himself to combat the idea that to attain this distinction, prose literature must be in Greek. He also expanded to some extent at least the conception of history. For he introduced speeches into his narrative and also described the things he thought of interest which he had encountered in Spain and Italy. Much of his book was concerned, too, with the origins of various Italian states and cities. In all of this, despite his traditional anti-Hellenic attitude, he must have been following the methods of Greek historians. One fragment shows clearly the literary purpose of Cato (77, ed. Peter): "non lubet scribere quod in tabula apud pontificem maximum est, quotiens annona cara, quotiens lunae aut solis lumine caligo aut quid obstiterit." Following the lead of Cato, annalists such as L. Cassius Hemina, L. Calpurnius Piso, and Fabius Maximus Servilianus wrote their histories in Latin for a somewhat larger audience than that of their predecessors.

Meanwhile the impetus of Greek culture was increasing among the Roman aristocracy at a rapid rate. While poetry was still in the hands of the grammatici and a few favored freedmen, prose was taken up enthusiastically by the group that gathered around the younger Scipio, who had become the possessor of the library of King Perseus. From this circle emanated the second great formative influence on Roman history writing.

The Scipionic circle was largely dominated by Polybius the historian and Panaetius the Stoic philosopher. To it can be attributed directly several of the main trends in later historiography: the sharp differentiation between prose history and epic, the Stoic tone of moral instruction, the plain style which that philosophy endorsed as best suited to didactic purposes, and the political objectives of history writing. Primarily, the group, aristocratic and devoted to the public service, was interested in philosophy. To them the Stoic creed appealed as giving a rational basis to the Roman standards. It was they who merged the Stoic ideal with the Roman ideal of *virtus* until they were hard to distinguish. They set up the standards of public ethics which were accepted theoretically for generations to come, the duty of service to the state, to family, to friends, and only last to self. They developed grammar as an essential tool, history as a source of useful examples, and the plain style as essential for the expression of truth with clarity and propriety.

From this coterie of self-conscious literati emerged a new group of narrators who wrote in Latin and began to pride themselves on being historians rather than mere annalists. The publication of the records in the Gracchan period made unnecessary the old type of annals. These later annalists did not produce any great history which has survived but they learned from Polybius to aim at a high standard of historical truth and to go beyond the facts of material history to the reasons behind them and to the methods of accomplishment. The names of Cn. Gellius, Sempronius Asellio, Quadrigarius, Valerius Antias survive. They introduced speeches freely to indicate the motivation of an action and even documents to confirm their facts. There is some indication of the use of Stoic tags of proverbial wisdom. At least one of the group wrote the history of a short period, Coelius Antipater on the Second Punic War. Also it was at the same time, although perhaps not by members of the circle, that autobiographies began to appear in Roman literature. The writing of biography had been a natural Roman tendency from the earliest days, eulogistic in tone, deriving from the funeral orations carefully preserved in all the great families, and presumably the charge against the annalists that they tended to eulogize members of their own families had some ground. Cato in omitting names from his narrative may have been exercising his genius for destructive criticism. Stoicism fostered the biography as one of the best methods of preserving examples of the virtuous life. Under the pressure of political strife the autobiography is by no means a surprising development. Aemilius Scaurus, Sulla, Marius, and Catulus wrote apologia that were autobiographical, and Licinius Macer and Cornelius Sisenna wrote factional histories of short contemporary periods.

By the time of Cicero the pattern of Roman history had been set but in the opinion of the great orator no history had been written. The answer to this paradox is not far to seek. Cicero held that history was *opus unum oratorium maxime*. In other words the field had not yet been developed under the rules of oratorical style derived from Greek sources. It is a narrow point of view but an important one to grasp. For the new line of Greek influence implied in the criticism was destined to have great influence on the writing of history even though it did not essentially change the pattern. *Oratorium* meant to Cicero "stylistically polished," for to him the rules of oratorical style were the only literary rules.

It was not only through the rhetorical manuals that Greek influence reached the historians. Through Polybius first and then directly, Greek historiography was a strong molding force on the Roman writers that followed the annalists. The discussion by Polybius in 2. 56 of the relative merits of Aratus and Phylarchus as historians is highly illuminating. It is true that the latter was hostile to the Achaean league and so was an unsympathetic source for Polybius, but the criticism is none the less interesting. Phylarchus, says Polybius, presented clinging women with hair disheveled and breasts bare to thrill his readers with exaggerated pictures. For the same purpose of fascinating his audience Phylarchus, like the tragic poets, gives imaginary utterances of his characters as genuine, seeking to endow them with verisimilitude. In contrast with this, Polybius claims that the historian should record only what was actually done and said. Yet he himself inserted in his histories many speeches, including those of Hannibal, Scipio, and Aemilius, which were certainly not recorded and preserved for him to use. He would seem to be arguing for the method of Thucydides as against the more florid and imaginative school which like Herodotus sought to entertain rather than to instruct. He insists always on this duty of the historian to instruct and dwells on the consequent necessity of accuracy. It is the inaccuracy of Fabius that offends him. He discusses his own sources and his own thoroughness, illustrated by his visit to the Alps to study the route of Hannibal. In 3. 57 he attacks the writers who embellish their writings with imaginary accounts of the unknown.

A second point of emphasis in Polybius is the duty of the historian to deal not only with events but with causes. This is again an obvious echo of Thucydides, and it is a second point in which Polybius finds Phylarchus wanting.

Polybius introduces considerable geographical and historical background and obviously considers it important. He gives also summary accounts of important characters at the crucial point in their careers.

It will never be possible to say to what extent later Roman historians went back to Polybius as a model and how far they may have gone more directly to the source of this type of history in Thucydides. The latter's handling of chronology by a division of the year into summer and winter activities suggests an influence on the historical part of Tacitus' *Agricola* but by no means proves it. There is, however, in the Athenian writer much that can hardly have failed to exercise an effect on the Roman writers. His introduction states concretely his subject, expounds its important significance, sketches previous Greek history, promises a faithful and accurate account of what was said and done, with emphasis on the causes of all events, and stresses the fact that his history will be a permanently useful gift rather than a transitory bit of entertainment. This is all matter that is unknown in the earlier Roman annalists but familiar in the later historians. Thucydides uses speeches freely: more than a quarter of the first book is composed of speeches and five of these are by unnamed envoys which confirms the impression that their purpose is to present not characters but situations.

One thing is notably lacking in Thucydides. Neither by general statement nor by specific example does he introduce any of the moralizing that characterized the later productions under Stoic influence.

Such in brief was the formative period of Roman historiography. It had from the beginning an annalistic character. In its earlier phases it was factual insofar as it had recorded facts at its disposal. For earlier periods it was credulous in its acceptance of the traditional myths. The "facts" which it accepted from the records included omens and divine interference in human affairs. During the second century B.C. it was wrought on by the influence of the first self-conscious study of literary production, by the imported Stoicism absorbed by the Romans both consciously and unconsciously, and by the beginnings of the newer and more formal education. By the end of this period it had to some extent foresworn its unlimited range and confined itself to shorter periods. It had adopted some devices for holding the reader's attention. Temporary influences had led to an emphasis on partisan presentation and a concentration on personalities.

The following period shows these various elements of the tradition at work in varying degrees on four noteworthy historians. They no longer show as great uniformity of pattern as did the early annalists. Training in formal rhetoric affected all of them, as did the battle over the styles, Asian versus Attic, with its Ciceronian compromise. Caesar, Nepos, Sallust, and Livy all represent an age of greater sophistication than that of the republic before the days of the Gracchi and civil war. Political bias had developed and the new trends in poetry have begun to influence prose style. This poetical element is strong in the case of Livy, who lived through and beyond the age of Augustus. These four writers mark the culmination of the long development of historical prose in republican Rome.

In the composition of his *Commentaries,* as in almost everything that he did, Caesar shows definitely individual characteristics. He follows the simple chronological method of the annalists and he carries the development of the plain style well nigh to perfection. Otherwise his work is practically unique in the surviving literature, for it is written with the definite purpose of defending his own career. Under the guise of notes on the campaigns he produced an *apologia pro vita sua* in the form of history. Sketches of the geographical settings with digressions on customs, fauna, and the like are in line with historical practice but in general the *Commentaries* lie outside the field of tradition. They are a unique tour de force. It is therefore the remaining three historians of the period who require consideration here, and before that is given it is essential to recall briefly the oratorical practices and theories that had developed in the first half of the century.

In the field of rhetoric Cicero is our great source of information, for he was at once the historian of oratory at Rome and the greatest formulator and practitioner of the doctrine as it existed in his day. When Cato defined the orator as *vir bonus dicendi peritus,* he reflected in the first place the unquestioned belief of his own day that the orator was essentially a public servant: *vir bonus* meant to him a good citizen. In the second place *dicendi peritus* meant experienced in speaking, trained in the school of practice rather than equipped with the doctrines of the schools of rhetoric. These schools can hardly have developed greatly before the time of Cicero, in whose day the apprentice method of training for legal practice was still in vogue.

If it were not for the two facts that all advanced education at Rome was rhetorical—that is, primarily aimed at the making of a public speaker—and that history was looked on as, in a way, a branch of oratory or at least as the branch of literature which had most of the oratorical in it, there would be little need of considering the school rhetoric. The influence of school training would be no more effective on the historian than on any other writer. But *narratio* was an essential element in a speech and at this point the Roman rhetorical authorities stretched their tentacles to include history as a parallel type of *narratio,* and every writer of history at Rome who attained any importance at all was trained for public service in the regular school of the orator.

In the first place the doctrine which the rhetor applied to the exordium was accepted by the historian. His introduction must serve to make his audience attentive, tractable, and sympathetic. He must, if possible, gain their interest by showing that what he has to tell is either novel or of supreme importance. Now this principle, applied directly to the proemium, must of course with the orator be extended to the remainder of his speech. In other words he cannot make his point once and for all and then neglect the duty of maintaining the interest and sympathy of the audience. To an even greater extent, without the help of voice and gesture, the historian must, by every device, maintain the interest of the reader. This was not necessary to the same extent when the early annalists were writing bald chronological narratives of events that were in themselves to a considerable extent unfamiliar. But there is plenty of evidence to show that even they felt the need of some attention to the reader's interest. Now, under specific training, the effort to sustain sympathetic interest became the object of definite rules and practices. Variety, pungency of expression, neat phraseology, dramatic narrative, the introduction of relatively extraneous matter for its own interest—all these and many other characteristics of the later historians have their origin in the attempt to appeal to the reader's interest. The increased tendency toward the profession of careful respect for the truth may well stem in part from the oratorical training. And certainly the habit of inventing, collecting, and reworking sententious phrases affected history as well as all other forms of literature. The Scipionic circle had read avidly the literature of Greece and had eagerly sought to produce a Roman counterpart. Now the Roman need of success in oratory as a practical political tool had led to the formulation of a systematic doctrine of speech which could apply to written as well as spoken matter, and the second step was under way, the elaboration and conscious perfection of the Roman counterpart. The Greek influence was not abandoned. The Greek models were studied and even the rhetorical manuals probably followed Greek archetypes. But the effort was applied to the Roman product and artificiality entered the picture—the conscious art which may either remain obvious and repellent or be carried to the perfection which conceals art. The earlier education of each Roman of the class from which literature derived was largely concerned with reading and memorizing and paraphrasing the works of Homer, the dramatists both Greek and Latin, and Ennius, with such selections from other poets as the teachers might choose. His mind was stocked with quotations. In the school of the rhetor he had to study prose and practice composition, again with a considerable amount of memorizing and adaptation. The whole education tended to produce a particularly Roman type of imitation but without restricting the powers of invention. Finally the Roman writer of the Ciceronian Age and later had at his command a series of informational manuals which had sprung from the Stoic appetite for knowledge, manuals on law, grammar, antiquities, usage, and also concise biographies. The stage was set for a new advance in prose writing.

What we have left of the work of Nepos can hardly be considered as much more than a manual of biographical information. And yet the lives of Atticus and of the foreign notables show definitely with their phrases that even Tacitus honored by imitation the influence of the rhetorical education, and it would seem probable that Nepos' *Universal History*, admired by Catullus, was a new departure in the field.

It is Sallust who most clearly illustrates the trends that we have been following. The elaborate detachable introductions to the *Catiline* and the *Jugurtha* are clearly intended to win the sympathetic interest of the reader. Both essays bristle with *sententiae* largely culled from Stoic collections, and the traditional Stoic attacks on luxury and ambition are conspicuous. The style, too, is definitely of the Stoic tradition, going back of the normal plain style to the more archaic fashion of Cato. Situations are handled dramatically, the narrative is vivid, speeches are introduced directly and indirectly both for the purpose of clarifying situations and for that of illuminating the characters of the tales. There is a unity to each essay which is the result of deliberate artistic composition. We have enough fragments of the five books of his *History* to know that within an annalistic framework the same characteristics were in evidence. A definite period was selected for narration, with sufficiently marked political trend to give over-all unity. The style is the same, rugged, intense, concise, and packed with sententious phrases and Stoic criticism of wealth and ambition. Letters and speeches are quoted in full. Obviously, Sallust wrote with the bias of a man possessed by a thesis, but he asserts unhesitatingly his devotion to truth alone. His is the rhetorical product of an age of unrest and revolution.

Quite different and yet the later product of the same literary background and training is the work of Livy. He was well out of the political confusion that surrounded Sallust. He had mildly republican enthusiasms, but they were rather those of a somewhat nostalgic recluse than of a warm partisan or a participant in the active struggle. He enjoyed the aura of peace with which Augustus surrounded his period of reconstruction, and like Vergil he went slowly and deliberately at the task of recording the grandeur of the Roman past, which without great conviction he hoped might be revived by the new regime. His was the same adherence as Sallust's to the old tenets of the Stoic faith, the same belief in the degeneracy produced by luxury and ambition, but he expressed them less raucously. His was a vastly broader canvas presenting the whole range of Roman history. Such unity as it possessed came from Livy's conception of Rome as an entity and the grandeur of his belief in its predestined role. That the unity was incomplete was due to the fact that he could not, as Vergil did, look upon the Augustan regime as the climax of that long development. In Livy's *History* we find still the traditional uncritical treatment of the story of Rome's beginning and early days. For more recent times he adopted the familiar annalistic method. He, too, introduces speeches and documents freely rendered. His style, in keeping with his times, approximates the Ciceronian rather than the Sallustian, but it has an additional coloring. This, too, is the product of his age, for it is poetic in character and derives in part at least from Vergil. This poetical enrichment is perhaps his greatest individual contribution to historical prose style. From it rather than from the Stoic commonplace spring such phrases as are sufficiently notable to be adopted by later writers. He avoids the striking effects of rhetoric, but he is none the less a product of the normal rhetorical training. His prologue is a detachable essay on Stoic lines. He, too, can summarize the character of a man in effective if not trenchant phrases. He never fails to hold the interest of the reader, if necessary by unsubstantiated stories or incidents of doubtful authenticity. And yet where possible he discusses his sources, to give a sense of authenticity to his narrative. Without any fanatical devotion to a cause to be defended, he is comparatively unconcerned with the need to be persuasive. He assumes the soundness of his central theme without argument and devotes his powers to producing intelligent pleasure for his readers, with only such didactic moral element as emerges naturally from the presentation of his great prose epic.

At this point begins a period of rather different development in all fields of literature, including history. It is not that the establishment of the empire produced a literary "silence of the graveyard." The great writers of the Augustan Age mark the climax of a long development: Vergil, Horace, and Livy became "classics" almost upon publication. Such an achievement does not, as is sometimes assumed, discourage the further production of literature, creating a temporary vacuum. But the immediate successors are either imitators who are presently ignored and lost, or pioneers in some new line which, until it attains a certain stature, is scorned and forgotten. Far from being silent in awe before the great writers of Augustus' day, a profusion of writers appeared in the early empire, and literature was even artificially fostered. Tiberius himself wrote, and so did Claudius and Nero. Literature was fashionable in the smart set. The product, however, was not, for numerous reasons, of a distinction to give it immortality.

Chief among these reasons was the changed character of the Roman aristocracy, in whose hands now as always lay the fate of literature. There was never at Rome a great reading public or any outlet for mass publication. The old families of the republican aristocracy were wholly depleted by civil war and proscription. New families dominated the senate and society. The men who brought these families into prominence did so either by the power of money or by rising from the ranks of the freedmen and foreigners through abilities that had no relation to the old Roman qualities that had won the empire. The widespread dictum of the Stoic opposition, that degeneracy came to Rome with the influx of wealth after the fall of Carthage, was not merely the wail of the dispossessed: it had a sound core of truth. Money was one of the leading titles to social position in the first century of our era. The novel of Petronius is a satire on middle-class life, but it leaves an unavoidable conviction of the materialistic character of the aristocracy which these small folk aped. In such an age the lasting literature is almost certain to be the literature of protest. The dominant class of the newly rich have for the most part neither the inclination nor the ability to write anything destined to live.

A second reason for change is in a way a product of this social revolution. But it, like the change in the character of the dominating class, had its beginnings in the earlier epoch. The writers in the time of the Scipionic circle, those of the Age of Cicero and even the groups that gathered around Maecenas and Messalla in the days of Augustus, all wrote not merely with a justifiable human desire for fame and glory but also with some idea of contributing to the glory of Rome. It is not wholly impossible that the ostracism by the old guard of the more personal poets of love, the neoteroi, was due in large part to their lack of contribution to the public honor, to their self-centered attitude toward their art. At any rate, while the older Roman always accepted personal glory as a legitimate and worthy aim, he definitely insisted that such glory should in some way come through service to the state. In the new Rome which Augustus founded, in spite of every insistence that it was a restoration of the old republic, the fact remained that it was no longer possible for the individual Roman to be identified as he had been with the essential life of his country. Under an increasingly business-like form of government the individual must more and more find himself leaving to the professional the conduct of the state and motivating his own career by his own self-centered interests. The effect of this on literary production was to require of authors the brilliance and glitter that would demonstrate the cleverness of the writer.

The point may be best appreciated perhaps by considering the innovation attributed to Asinius Pollio, himself an historian. Pollio was by no means one of the newly rich. He served the state throughout its most troubled times and maintained the respect of all sides. He was orator, poet, historian, and literary critic. But if Seneca is right, it was he who first opened his house for public literary recitations. It had already been a familiar tradition to invite audiences to listen to students and teachers as they declaimed the speeches they had prepared in the schools. Great orators had long since been in the habit of "declaiming" at home, in practice for court appearance. And writers of all sorts of literature had read their products to their friends for mutual pleasure and to obtain criticism. But the beginning of public recitation as a social entertainment was a new departure and fraught with unforeseen consequences. The custom spread rapidly, as is clear from the evidence of Seneca, Persius, Petronius, and Pliny. Naturally the effects were not wholly bad, but in general the result was to put an enormous premium on superficial cleverness and brilliance. The verdict came no longer from experts but from a social jury whose judgment was of the weakest. The aim of the average writer came almost inevitably to be to win the applause of an audience quite incompetent to judge with authority and too often looking forward to return favors on a later occasion. Emphasis on novelty, on a show of learning, on striking antithesis and compelling phrase overshadowed the traditional pride in solid achievement and honest workmanship. Again, this is not wholly a new phenomenon. The "singers of Euphorion" had followed this vein in imitation of a similar desperate assault on fame by certain Alexandrian poets. But for the time being it became the general practice, and in an increasingly materialistic and culture-conscious society the effects were enormous. It is not often remembered that one of the favorite poets of the grim Tiberius was Euphorion.

While history in general may have been less directly affected by the increasingly artificial standards of the day, it can hardly have escaped their influence. In one branch, that of the eulogistic biography, it was peculiarly vulnerable. It is noteworthy also that the treatment of specific periods became increasingly popular. In all its phases, history was influenced as almost no other branch of literature by the change of government from aristocratic democracy to monarchy. We do not have to accept without reservation Tacitus' statement that all writers of history during the first century were dominated either by fear or hatred, but complete freedom of expression was certainly impossible for the greater part of the century. Vituperation and eulogy would tend to bulk large; historians and biographers hostile to the emperors or too enthusiastic for liberty might be eliminated and their books burned; enthusiastic encomiasts like Velleius Paterculus could hardly be accepted at face value. But while little has survived much was written, and it is essential to try to get some idea of its trends.

Asinius Pollio was a contemporary of Livy. We are led by the evidence, however, to believe that he was very different as an historian. If his narrative style was like that of his oratory as described by Tacitus through the mouth of Aper in the *Dialogus,* he was stiff and dry, a worthy follower of Menenius Agrippa and Appius Claudius. Messalla, in the same essay, is made to rate him among the great orators of the age of Cicero and to grant him some rhythmical qualities. Horace expected mighty things of him. Quintilian grants him a degree of greatness but inclines toward Aper's opinion of his archaism. It is to be noted that he was an admirer of Brutus in a day when that attitude was still safe. He wrote a history of his own period, from 60 B.C. to the close of the century. His style was presumably more akin to Sallust's than to Livy's, with a tinge of archaism and an abundance of sharp epigrammatic and caustic sentences.

Meanwhile Corvinus (*ca.* 70–8 B.C.) was contemporary with Livy and Asinius Pollio. He wrote a history of events from 44 on, speaking well of Brutus. Nothing more of it is known.

The republican bias which these writers showed and which was tolerated by Augustus at the time proved fatal to the works of T. Labienus, whose books were burned in A.D. 12, the first instance of this penalty applied to an historian. The same fate was in store for Cremutius Cordus, who wrote a history of his own generation in which he commended Brutus and Cassius. He was driven to suicide in A.D. 25 and his books burned. Copies survived, however, and they were brought out again by his daughter Marcia. Tacitus speaks of them as *annales* (*Ann.* 4. 34), which may indicate a year-by-year treatment.

On the other side of the political alignment were Bruttidius Niger and Velleius Paterculus, both known to Tacitus. Of the former, all that we can be sure of is that he wrote about the death of Cicero and that he was involved in the fall of Sejanus. The latter is one of the two historians of the first century whose work has come down to us. Unfortunately his preface has been lost, together with much of the first book, which gave the history of the world down to the fall of Carthage. But Velleius was a military man not too skilled in writing, and his history illustrates all the more clearly the trends of the day. Badly proportioned as it is, it reveals the writer's intention of making the reign of his hero, Tiberius, the climax of the story, giving to it such unity as it has. Sallust rather than Livy is his stylistic model and he exhibits many characteristics of the rhetorical schools: word pictures of his characters, poetic coloring, sententious moralizing, exclamations, and rhetorical questions— sometimes successfully but usually in too obvious a fashion. The extravagant eulogies of the characters which he approves, especially of Sejanus and Tiberius, are heavily overdone.

Finally, during this age of Tiberius, there is indication that the elder Seneca wrote a history of the period from the Civil Wars to his own time, spoken of by Seneca the younger as still unpublished in his time. Of the character of this work nothing is known.

Obviously, the shorter historical monograph had, for the time being at least, superseded the long annalistic history. Rhetorical treatment and political bias had become more important than the search for and presentation of the unvarnished facts. But it should not be forgotten that many of the annalists had been accused of family bias and that from the days of Cato the rhetorical habit of each age had had a determining influence on style. We are not dealing with new characteristics; we are recognizing their effect on the history writing of a period in which the authors are largely from a new class in society and in which a new type of rhetorical training has an extraordinary influence, and the political tension is confined to the stress between a new monarchial power and a vanishing "democracy."

Except for the lost autobiography and general history of Claudius, about which we have no information, there is no book of history after A.D. 25 that can be positively dated before A.D. 50 and only two before the age of the Flavians. Aufidius Bassus and Servilius Nonianus both died at about the middle of Nero's reign and must have written their histories in the fifties. They are cited together in the *Dialogus* by Aper as examples that would be generally accepted as representing the best of the modern *eloquentia*. Quintilian confirms this in the case of Nonianus and describes him as "creber sententiis sed minus pressus quam historiae auctoritas postulat." To Quintilian, the dignity of history would not admit as much adornment or color as Aper would have approved. What period his history covered is unfortunately never stated. We do know, on the other hand, that Aufidius Bassus wrote a general history of which the elder Pliny thought sufficiently well to make his own history a continuation of it, entitled *A fine Aufidii Bassi Libri XXXI*. The history of Aufidius Bassus contained an account of Cicero's death and, since Pliny speaks of his own history as an account of his own times, it probably came down to the death of Claudius. He also wrote a history of the German wars.

Pliny, too, wrote an account of the wars in Germany as well as the history of his own times, and Tacitus cites it as a source along with the works of Cluvius Rufus and Fabius Rusticus. It is generally assumed that these men wrote period histories, as did Vipstanus Messalla, who covered the time of Nero and the subsequent Civil War. All four authors presumably wrote under Vespasian, although Fabius Rusticus, whom Tacitus rates highest of "modern" historians, lived on into the Ulpian regime.

In addition to the strictly historical works, this period saw the production of many eulogistic biographies, such as the lives of Thrasea and Helvidius, written by their admirers, Arulenus Rusticus and Herennius Senecio, with fatal results. The writing of the *Exitus virorum illustrium* seems to have had a definite vogue.

Curtius Rufus is hard to place in the analysis of the historiography of the first century. No dates for his life or for the publication of his *History of Alexander the Great* are known. The best evidence that he did write during the first century lies in the apparent imitation by Tacitus of many of his phrases, especially from the speeches which Tacitus introduces into his history. It might be of course (and it has been so argued) that the borrowing was in the opposite direction, but in the first place the bulk of it is in the *Agricola*—which in its most carefully constructed sections, the prologue and epilogue and the speeches of Agricola and Calgacus, is a composite of such borrowing from Sallust, Nepos, Livy, and Cicero—and in the second place it is almost always Tacitus and not Curtius who gives the vital, effective turn to the phrase. That the history cannot go back as far as the Augustan age seems certain from the fact that an emperor is taken for granted by Curtius and in one digression (10. 9. 3 ff.) he speaks in glowing terms of a new emperor who has saved the state from dissolution *cum sine suo capite discordia membra trepidarent*. This is certainly vague but may best be applied to the accession of Vespasian after the year of the four emperors, or rather of revolution, in A.D. 69. This would put Curtius into the era when history was flourishing again, the age of Cluvius and Fabius Rusticus, Pliny and Vipstanus Messalla. His expressed hope that Rome may long flourish under the same family is consistent with the fact that Vespasian's two sons might give ground for such a hope. The only other important Curtius Rufus that we know of was awarded the insignia of a triumph in 47. Tacitus devotes a chapter to him, implying that his birth was most humble and mentioning no literary tendencies. His son may well have flourished under Vespasian. A rhetorician, Q. Curtius Rufus, is named in the index that has come down with the *De rhetoribus* of Suetonius, between Porcius Latro and L. Valerius Primanus, who in turn is followed by Virginius Flavus, the tutor of Persius. This would put the rhetorician Curtius Rufus too early for him to have been the same as the historian, even if we were to accept the most generally held opinion that it was Claudius rather than Vespasian whose reign Curtius hailed with extravagant hope. Certainly the phrase quoted above is more applicable to Vespasian. There was no interval between the reign of Gaius and that of Claudius comparable with the Civil War of 68/69, nor does it seem too fanciful to see in *sine suo capite* a reference to Vespasian's delayed return to Rome.

The question is not one of major importance: the *History of Alexander* was written some time in the first century. It deals not with the history of a country or a period but with that of a hero. It is not annalistic in form. It has many of the qualities taught by the rhetors. Curtius frequently begins the account of an incident with a general truth which that incident seems to illustrate. He is always interested in men, but in events only as they are romantic or dramatic. He introduces many speeches but does not have the knack of making them characteristic of the speakers; they are all cut from the same cloth. It has been widely held that Curtius follows very closely some Greek biographer of Alexander. Unfortunately his introduction is lost and we have nowhere any statement by the writer himself of his purpose or plan.

The century on which Tacitus could look back as he approached his historical work saw the disappearance to a large extent of the annalistic type of general history. Shorter and more unified epochs had become the more favored subjects. Character depiction was popular. Rhetorical appeal of every sort prevailed. The convention of Stoic moralizing would seem to have persisted, although the evidence is extremely slight. Biography was on the whole more popular than history proper, and in spite of imperial censorship there was almost a cult of intransigent eulogistic biography whose product was surreptitiously preserved. It is safe to say without exaggeration that so far as the particular field of history is concerned, the first century was largely concerned with the problem of life under a one-party absolutism, involving considerable high emotional tension, and that the means used to present the problem were the means provided by the rhetorical education developed at the turn of the century. That there was no great historian between Livy and Tacitus does not therefore seem surprising. Adjustment to many different changes was necessary before conditions would permit of another great canvas. This first century saw a new social class in power with comparatively small cultural background, a new form of government which affected all departments of life, a changed religious outlook along with a new cosmopolitan atmosphere—and to express all this, if it were to be expressed, a new, feverish, superficial, literary taste and habit which surely needed the hand of time to mold it into something that could hope to endure.

3. RELIGIOUS AND PHILOSOPHIC POSITION

I N HIS first statement with regard to omens (*Hist.* 1. 3),
Tacitus at least recognizes definitely the existence of supernatural powers and even of gods who are actively concerned in human affairs. A more exact analysis of his belief as
expressed in his introductory words is harder to make with confidence. But the presence of this acknowledgment in the opening of his historical work is important to note. The first three
chapters of the *Histories* are a general introduction stating not
only the field to be covered but the spirit in which the subject
matter is to be treated. The historian defines—partly by contrast, in part directly—his program of candor. He expects to recount events of which he disapproves strongly, horrors from
which he recoils, but also examples of nobility and fortitude,
and with these "over and above the vicissitudes of human affairs, the prodigies in heaven and earth, the lightning bolts with
their warnings, the hints of events to come, omens happy and
evil, obscure and obvious." There seems to be no ground for
taking these words in anything but a literal sense or for questioning the faith of their author in the signs of which he speaks.
Only in the next sentence does the slightest question of any
irony enter and this has to do with definite events rather than
with omens. "Never has it been proved" he says "by more
frightful disasters to the Roman people or by more downright
evidence that while our security is not of concern to the gods,
our punishment is."

This remark is an epigrammatic climax to the first section of
the introductory matter before his summary of the *status quo*.
If taken wholly literally it forces us to assume that the *monitus*
and *praesagia* were warnings only in the sense of advance information given without any idea of saving the recipients. Like
many of the Delphic oracles, they prophesy the coming events
without the purpose of forestalling them. And perhaps that is
the intent of the climactic epigram with its hint of irony. Or

possibly the irony is suggested only by a knowledge of its appearance elsewhere in Tacitus, and the effort to make an epigram has led him into a slight inconsistency. Only a study of
his use of omens and of his attitude toward them and toward
the gods in the rest of his work can determine the answer to
this doubt.

Of no real use as evidence are the instances in which Tacitus
presents one or another of his characters under the influence
of signs and omens unless he makes some comment on their
behavior or attitude. In 2. 50 he does step out of his rôle as
objective historian to comment briefly on his method. He has
just finished his account of Otho's death and begins a digression on his character in familiar form: *Origo illi e municipio
Ferentio.* He does not, however, go far with what promises to
be a summary of his life. Instead he proceeds: "Ut conquirere
fabulosa et fictis oblectare legentium animos procul gravitate
coepti operis crediderim, ita vulgatis traditisque demere fidem
non ausim." He goes on to recount the story told by the inhabitants of Regium about the strange bird that appeared there
and could not be frightened away until, at the moment which
turned out to be that of Otho's death, it vanished. Obviously
this is a sign and not an omen. There is no warning involved
nor, so far as we can see, any other real significance. But for
some reason Tacitus wanted to include it, and he made the
apology which I have quoted, which serves only to emphasize
the story. When Tacitus says that he would not venture to
question the story he does not commit himself, but he does
stress the incident and thus enhance whatever dramatic effect it has on the story as a whole. The result is much like that
of the alternative reasons which he so frequently gives for
events in his narrative, the more sinister or dramatic ones, for
which he is not quite willing to vouch, coming last and therefore lingering effectively (and undenied) in the mind of the
reader.

Early in the first book of the *Histories,* at chapter 10, Tacitus speaks for himself with a decidedly sophisticated skepticism
toward omens: "Occulta fati et ostentis ac responsis destina-

tum Vespasiano liberisque eius imperium post fortunam credidimus." Surely there is a touch of irony here, and surely the writer more than hints that it is hindsight which creates at least belief in ominous signs if not indeed the signs themselves. But again he does not by any means deny the existence of supernatural signs.

In 1. 27 Tacitus recounts the unfavorable omens obtained by the haruspex and reported to Galba. Otho is standing by and hears what are to him happy indications, and almost immediately departs to put into effect the conspiracy against Galba. Once more there is no definite belief or disbelief expressed by the writer, but there is again the presentation of a dramatic prelude to a striking event.

Not dissimilar is the situation in 2. 78. Vespasian is presented as in doubt with regard to attempting the throne. Mucianus delivers a speech urging him to action, and others press around reminding him of favorable omens and prophecies. "Nor was he unaffected by such superstition, as was to be expected from one who presently when master of the world maintained openly one Seleucus, an astrologer, as his adviser and prophet. Old prodigies came back to mind." Here is the same touch of ironical skepticism, but the rest of the paragraph is taken up with the story of rather unusual omens which have a certain antiquarian interest of their own. After the suspense of this paragraph, the beginning of Vespasian's active revolt follows rapidly. Whether Tacitus believed at all in this supernatural background or not, he appreciated fully its dramatic value.

Vitellius' scorn of tradition in the matter of lucky and unlucky days (2. 91) is left equally without any expressed opinion on Tacitus' part of belief or disbelief in the superstitious side, except that he definitely ascribes such belief to the people. He uses the situation, however, to suggest the arrogance of Vitellius as well as to create dramatic suspense.

Similar pauses in the narrative occur in Book 4. At chapter 53 the restoration of the Capitol under Vespasian's orders is carried out with scrupulous observance of the prescriptions of the haruspices. Tacitus passes no judgment on this action, but the dramatic effect is as favorable as it was unfavorable to Vitellius in the preceding instance. To make a contrast the following chapter recounts the effect which the destruction of the Capitol had had on Rome's enemies. The whole is a bit of dramatic suspense before the final struggle of the year of civil war.

Toward the end of Book 4 (81) Tacitus tells of two miraculous cures effected by Vespasian and (82) of a miraculous omen experienced by him. Some effort is made to authenticate each. In the two following chapters an account is given of the Egyptian god, Serapis. Here again, Tacitus has searched his authorities, but his interest is not in the power of Serapis but in his tradition. This antiquarian interest has probably some weight in his whole treatment of the Egyptian affair. At any rate, the miraculous cures are not actually omens and the miraculous vision is reported mainly on the authority of Vespasian himself. The whole incident is more difficult to interpret than the earlier ones but it can at least be said that dramatic suspense and dramatic character drawing both have their influence, and that at most Tacitus shows a slightly more credulous attitude than he does elsewhere.

I have reserved till the end of this discussion what is perhaps the most significant account of prodigies. Toward the end of Book 1 Otho is about to set forth against the Vitellian forces. For once there is (86) an accumulation of *prodigia* which is reminiscent of the end-of-the-year summaries in Livy and the older annalists. But now they are presented at a crucial juncture in the course of events, not merely at the turn of the year. The reins fall from the hands of the statue of Victory, a superhuman form is seen emerging from the temple of Juno, a statue of Julius Caesar turns on its pedestal, a bull speaks in Etruria, there are strange animal abortions, and many other occurrences "such as in ruder ages were observed even in days of peace, but now are rumored only in times of terror." All of these are reported and not vouched for by Tacitus. What he does accept as beyond doubt is the flood of the Tiber, and he points out its material damage to the cause of Otho, adding that "a fortuitis vel naturalibus causis in prodigium et omen imminentium cladium vertebatur." The ironical skepticism is, I think, obvious, but the situation offered dramatic possibilities of suspense and foreshadowing which Tacitus seized upon.

Such is the major evidence from the *Histories* on the matter of omens and auguries. But there are several smaller bits which contribute something, especially those instances in which characters in the history are presented consulting or interpreting omens. Titus consults the Paphian Venus (2. 4) and departs with increased spirit to join his father. Fabius Valens and his army (1. 62) proceed with new courage because of an auspicious eagle. Otho uses the weather as an omen to impress his troops (1. 38). Otho takes heart from the prophecies of the astrologers (1. 22). Galba's scorn of the traditional observance of omens (1. 18) has already been noted. The superstitious character of the Jews is illustrated by their observance of prodigies (5. 13). All of these instances are recounted without comment by Tacitus, who seems to accept the general attitude toward the supernatural because of its dramatic value in presenting his characters.

One final instance sums up what has appeared in the others. In 3. 56 Tacitus recounts what followed a speech by Vitellius. Cremona had fallen and things looked black for Vitellius, who is presented throughout as an incompetent leader, chiefly because of his inertia. He has at last aroused himself "as from sleep" and with his senatorial following has entered the camp "uncertain in mind and a prey to treacherous counsels." Tacitus continues: "Contionanti, prodigiosum dictu, tantum foedarum volucrum supervolitavit ut nube atra diem obtenderent. Accessit dirum omen, profugus altaribus taurus disiecto sacrificii apparatu, longe, nec ut feriri hostias mos est, confossus. Sed praecipuum ipse Vitellius ostentum erat, ignarus militiae, improvidus consilii, quis ordo agminis, quae cura explorandi, quantus urgendo trahendove bello modus, alios rogitans et ad omnis nuntios vultu quoque et incessu trepidus, dein temulentus." This whole incident seems to bring out the dramatic use of omens to foreshadow coming events and to create suspense and at the same time the rational good sense of the author, expressed with the typical force of his ironical skepticism.

In the *Histories,* then, Tacitus takes no definite stand either as a believer or disbeliever in omens. On the whole he seems to have the attitude of an intelligent man who realizes that there is fairly general acceptance of the fact that the future may be indicated by omens, that his own intelligence finds such acceptance difficult, but that, whether omens are genuine signs or mere coincidences, they may properly serve his dramatic purposes as a writer of vivid historical narrative. At the same time he allows his skepticism and his feeling for the ironical to have considerable play in creating epigrammatic comment on the unreasoning acceptance of omens.

If Tacitus' deepest belief in the matter of omens is discreetly hidden, it is hardly to be expected that he would put forward a sharply defined theology. If his reason forbade him to yield wholly to a belief in omens, consistency would require him to refuse allegiance to a faith in divine supervision of human affairs. The first presentation of gods as of omens, in the prefatory chapters (1. 3), gives to the gods a respectable if restricted standing: "nec enim umquam atrocioribus populi Romani cladibus magisve iustis indiciis adprobatum est non esse curae deis securitatem nostram, esse ultionem." These are jealous gods and grim, not the gods of early agricultural Rome, but rather the gods of Sophoclean tragedy. The conception was not new: the Stoic Lucan had expressed much the same idea in 4. 807–9: "Felix Roma quidem civesque habiture beatos, / si libertatis superis tam cura placeret / quam vindicta placet."

In speaking of the destruction of the Capitol (3. 72) Tacitus condemns the act most violently because done "nullo externo hoste, propitiis, si per mores nostros liceret, deis." In a digression on the Roman Civil Wars from Marius to Vitellius (2. 38), he says, "eadem illos deum ira, eadem hominum rabies, eaedem scelerum causae in discordiam egere." There is more irony in the comment in 4. 26: "apud imperitos prodigii loco accipiebatur aquarum penuria, tamquam nos amnes quoque et vetera imperii munimenta desererent: quod in pace fors

seu natura, tunc fatum et ira deum vocabatur." In 4. 78, on the
contrary, there seems to be nothing but a direct statement of
fact: "nec sine ope divina mutatis repente animis terga victores
vertere." In telling of Vespasian's visit to Alexandria, Tacitus
states explicitly, "multa miracula evenere, quis caelestis favor
et quaedam in Vespasianum inclinatio numinum ostendere-
tur." He proceeds to give details and does not question the
evidence or treat the affair with irony. The subjunctive *osten-
deretur* may have significance.

Beyond these quotations, the *Histories* present no statements
about the gods which are given on Tacitus' own authority, representing his own belief. He tells of other people's attitudes,
gives others' statements and tells of religious procedure. It
need hardly be said that the gods of the foreigner are creatures
of superstition (4. 54, 5. 13). The Roman gods are perhaps
little more than conventional beings to Tacitus save as disaster
deepens the belief in them as avengers. In this rôle they serve
a dramatic part not unlike that of the omens.

From the account of what amounts to contemporary history
Tacitus turned to the annals of the Julio-Claudian dynasty.
In the first six books of the *Annals* as we have them there is
even less of a definite attitude toward omens and toward the
gods from whom these presumably come than there was in the
Histories. Tacitus continues to be the objective historian, telling of new religious rites and orders (1. 10, 1. 54, 2. 41), of
the effect of prodigies on the popular mind (1. 28), and once
or twice discussing superficially the metaphysical. When an
eclipse of the moon helped Germanicus to quell a mutiny
(1. 28), he says that it was chance that brought it on oppor-
tunely, but he makes it clear that he knows the cause to be a
natural one and ascribes *formido caelestis irae* to the soldiers
only. A modern materialist might have written the account.
The return of the phoenix to Egypt is stated as a fact (6. 28)
with real antiquarian interest on the part of the historian, and
he uses the term *miraculum* for the event. He speaks with some
scorn of the popular belief in magic (2. 69). There is no list
of prodigies, in fact no further mention of them. In 1. 35 the

words *faustis in Germanicum ominibus* have the modern connotation. But there is some discussion of fate, chance, and providence.

The most elaborate instance is 6. 22. The story of Thrasyllus and his prophecy about his own imminent danger has just been told. Tacitus proceeds: "Sed mihi haec ac talia audienti in incerto iudicium est, fatone res mortalium et necessitate immutabili an forte volvantur." Elaborating his doubt he points to the divergence between the ancient philosophers and between their sects in his own day. Some have the fixed belief "non initia nostri, non finem, non denique homines dis curae." Others believe that fate rules men's lives "sed non e vagis stellis, verum apud principia et nexus naturalium causarum." These grant to men the original choice of life, which is then immutable. This second group, even without the safe assumption that the first were Epicureans, are obviously Stoics, for, says Tacitus, they do not view the goods and ills of life as do the common folk but hold that man can be happy in the midst of misfortune, or miserable even when endowed with great wealth. The majority of mankind, he continues, are not freed from the belief that their future is determined at birth, although the signs may sometimes be wrongly interpreted by ignorant or even false practitioners. He winds up: "ita corrumpi fidem artis cuius clara documenta et antiqua aetas et nostra tulerit. Quippe a filio eiusdem Thrasulli praedictum Neronis imperium in tempore memorabitur, ne nunc incepta longius abierim." It can hardly be questioned that Tacitus here declares definitely his own belief in the art of astrology.

In 4. 20, after telling of the wise moderation of M'. Lepidus, Tacitus says: "unde dubitare cogor fato et sorte nascendi, ut cetera, ita principum inclinatio in hos, offensio in illos, an sit aliquid in nostris consiliis liceatque inter obruptam contumaciam et deforme obsequium pergere iter ambitione ac periculis vacuum." The *ut cetera* confirms his general belief; the rest is special pleading for the course of action which he had long since approved in the case of Agricola (*Agric.* 42).

The departure of Tiberius from Rome gave rise to a proph-

ecy which confirmed Tacitus' distinction between correct signs
and faulty interpretation. 4. 58 reads: "Ferebant periti caele-
stium iis motibus siderum excessisse Roma Tiberium ut reditus
illi negaretur. . . . Mox patuit breve confinium artis et falsi,
veraque quam obscuris tegerentur. Nam in urbem non regres-
surum haud forte dictum: ceterorum nescii egere [i.e. those
who assumed his immediate death] cum propinquo rure aut litore et saepe moenia urbis adsidens extremam senectam com-
pleverit." This is explicit language: *artis et falsi* and even more
definitely *vera*. It cannot be questioned that Tacitus here holds
the same position which Iokaste had defended in the *Oedipus
Tyrannus* half a millennium earlier.

One more comment by Tacitus on the events of his narrative
is noteworthy in this connection, 6. 6. He has just quoted verbatim the opening of a letter from Tiberius to the senate, including the words: "di me deaeque peius perdant, quam perire
me cotidie sentio, si scio." Tacitus' comment is: "Adeo facinora
atque flagitia sua ipsi quoque in supplicium verterant. Neque
frustra praestantissimus sapientiae firmare solitus est, si reclu-
dantur tyrannorum mentes, posse aspici laniatus et ictus,
quando, ut corpora verberibus, ita saevitia libidine malis con-
sultis animus dilaceretur." Tacitus does not express any agreement or disagreement with Tiberius' implication that the tor-
ture is from the gods (Tiberius' phrase may be purely conventional), but he evidently does accept the dictum of Socrates.

At the opening of Book 4 there seems to be a deliberate effort to give the tone of tragic drama to the turn in the tide of
Tiberius' affair. "Nonus Tiberio annus erat, compositae rei
publicae, florentis domus . . . cum repente turbare fortuna
coepit, saevire ipse aut saevientibus vires praebere. Initium et
causa penes Aelium Seianum." The characterization of Sejanus
follows with an account of how he won the confidence of Tiberius, "non tam sollertia (quippe isdem artibus victus est)
quam deum ira in rem Romanam, cuius pari exitio viguit
ceciditque." If only for dramatic effect, Tacitus accepts the
possibility of divine interference in the affairs of men, though
once again for the purpose of punishment not of reward.

A final observation by the historian is to be noted in 3. 18. In a motion by Messalinus to pass a vote of thanks for the avenging of Germanicus the name of Claudius was first omitted and then added at the last minute. This action brings from Tacitus the following comment: "Mihi quanto plura recentium seu veterum revolvo, tanto magis ludibria rerum mortalium cunctis in negotiis obversatum. Quippe fama spe veneratione potius omnes destinebantur imperio quam quem futurum imperatorem fortuna in occulto tenebat." The irony of the situation undoubtedly appealed to Tacitus, but the acceptance of *fortuna* or fate as controlling affairs is definite.

The writer's own irony is probably behind the method of narration in 1. 10. He has been outlining the comments on Augustus after his death, both favorable and unfavorable. Amongst the latter was the remark that in accepting worship for himself with all the accompanying paraphernalia he left nothing to the honors of the gods. The paragraph winds up: "Ceterum sepultura more perfecta templum et caelestes religiones decernuntur."

The evidence of the first six books of the *Annals* would seem to confirm that of the *Histories:* Tacitus was not primarily concerned with metaphysical theory. He assumes the conventional attitude, accepting the gods and fate, accepting the validity of astrology if properly understood, and accepting also the commonplace philosophy of conduct without any strict knowledge of or interest in the schools of philosophic thought. He would not seem to have studied philosophy more deeply than was proper for a Roman and a senator (cf. *Agric.* 4).

Before turning to the later books of the *Annals,* one phase of the composition of Books 1–16 must be considered. In the *Histories* Tacitus dealt with one long year of revolution. The five books, as they exist for us today, would indicate that the first half at least of the *Histories* dealt with a single large situation: they furnish little opportunity to study the annalistic method of composition. It is quite otherwise with the books dealing with Tiberius, Claudius, and Nero. The beginning of each year is marked by the naming of the consuls for the year.

Ordinarily at the end of the account of each year's events there is a summary of happenings during the year which do not fall readily into the direct narrative, including the deaths of distinguished persons, religious rites, construction or repair of buildings, legations from outside nations, odd bits of legislation, prodigies and disasters, and an occasional bizarre event told for its own interest. It is almost the invariable practice of Tacitus to introduce these miscellaneous items by such phrases as *eodem anno, isdem consulibus, fine anni, eo anno,* or slight variations of these. One particular formula is noteworthy: *obiere eo anno insignes viri.* The practice is a well recognized one with annalistic writers; the important thing to notice in the particular case of Tacitus is the selection which he makes out of all the possible items to include in the annual summaries. In the first six books the lists of deaths are the most prominent single category, some twelve years presenting these, although the specific formula occurs only four or five times. This formula appears but once in the last six books, where only four years end with an account of distinguished deaths. On the other hand, prodigies are listed seven times during the reign of Nero but never before that. The formula corresponding to that cited above for the early books is *multa eo anno prodigia evenere* (12. 43) or *fine anni volgantur prodigia* (15. 47).

With the exception just noted, namely that prodigy lists do not occur except in the reign of Nero, there is no real differentiation between the end-of-year summaries in the first six books and those in the last six. Since so much of the account of Tiberius deals with cases tried in the senate, it is natural that these should play a less prominent part in the summaries. The dramatic struggle in the reign of Nero between the powers working to control him relegated the cases of one sort and another to the miscellaneous summaries. Almost all the material for these summaries could have come from the records of the senate, and an unprejudiced reading definitely leaves the impression that Tacitus followed these records from year to year, selecting the material that he considered important or pertinent. A curious incident in Spain in the year 25, the return of the phoenix in 34, and possibly the story of the impostor who pretended to be Agrippa Postumus in 16, are matters foreign to the records of the senate and may have come from the *acta diurna* which Tacitus as a rule considered rather beneath his notice.

This use of annalistic tradition may account for some of the increased use of prodigies in Books 11–16. His selective method, however, would seem to exclude the conclusion that their use was purely conventional. Furthermore, omens (in Books 11–16) are not infrequent outside the summary lists, and in both uses the implication is usually that they are valid. For example 12. 64: "mutationem rerum in deterius portendi cognitum est crebris prodigiis." A list follows. Or again, after Nero had violated tradition by swimming in the source of the Aqua Marcia (14. 22): "secutaque anceps valetudo iram deum affirmavit." There are omens before the disaster in Britain (14. 32) and similarly in Mesopotamia (15. 7), and omens which warned Nero in 15. 34, 36. In the latter case it should be noted that Tacitus leaves the impression that Nero's violent shaking may have been not an ordinary omen but rather the direct result of a guilty conscience. Omens foreshadow the revolt of Vindex (15. 74). In 16. 13 the conviction is explicit: "tot facinoribus foedum annum etiam dii tempestatibus et morbis insignivere. Vastata Campania" etc. Almost as explicit is 15. 47: "Fine anni volgantur prodigia imminentium malorum nuntia: vis fulgorum" etc.

The tragic tone of the Neronian history foreshadowed by the omens in 12. 64 is summarized in 16. 16 as the reign draws toward its close: "Ira illa numinum in res Romanas fuit, quam non, ut in cladibus exercituum aut captivitate urbium, semel edito transire licet." The dramatic withering of the Ruminal fig tree just before the murder of Agrippina (13. 58) is hardly more than a melodramatic flourish, and the same is probably true of the statement in 14. 5: "Noctem sideribus illustrem et placido mari quietam quasi convincendum ad scelus dii praebuere."

Irony leads Tacitus into what might be considered a contradictory attitude in at least one instance, 14. 12: "Prodigia quoque crebra et inrita intercessere . . . Quae adeo sine cura deum eveniebant, ut multos post annos Nero imperium et scelera continuaverit." Both irony and pessimism operated to produce the famous dictum in 16. 33: "exutusque omnibus fortunis et in exsilium actus, aequitate deum erga bona malaque documenta." Even so, this last is hardly inconsistent with the earlier statement that the gods were interested not in rewarding us but only in punishing. It is simply more bitter. Their grim attitude leads them to look complacently on the suffering of the righteous so long as their rôle of avengers continues.

In Books 11–16 there is but one definite reference to philosophy. It indicates an unquestioning acceptance of the Stoic virtues, in fact takes them for granted. Tacitus speaks of an act of extreme disloyalty (16. 32) and of the perpetrator says: "auctoritatem Stoicae sectae praeferebat, habitu et ore ad exprimendam imaginem honesti exercitus, ceterum animo perfidiosus subdolus, avaritiam ac libidinem occultans" etc.

In the latest work of Tacitus, then, the author's attitude is not wholly changed but strengthened and embittered. He accepts the interference of supernatural powers. They are malignant powers on the whole. What there is of good in the universe would seem to be furnished by the exceptional human. He has not become more of a philosopher. He is certainly not a rationalist. But he cannot fairly be called either mystic or romantic. He is an intelligent Roman in a desperately pessimistic mood. His irony and dramatic sense lead him into minor inconsistencies, but this is less significant because he is never writing with a religious or philosophical intent either explicit or implicit. His interest was personal and political and to a minor extent moral, but as an historian his metaphysical assumptions were the conventional ones of his own class shaded by his own skeptical irony, made too effective for strict consistency by his power of mordant expression.

In one or two details it is possible to make more specific this conventional attitude of Tacitus. His gods are never the individual gods of the old Roman religion. Fortuna is the only

individual god that acts to influence events, and Fortuna is not
the goddess from Antium but either fate or luck as the situation determines. She furnishes dramatic motivation, like the
Moira of the Greek tragedians (cf. *Ann.* 4. 1, 16. 1; *Hist.*
2. 1), but she has no individuality. She is a force, the abstract
fate of conventional Stoicism. In the great majority of instances
in which Tacitus uses *fortuna,* the word means good luck rather
than bad luck or fate. *Fatum* is used in the same way for luck
in *Hist.* 3. 84, and *fors* in *Ann.* 1. 28, 49, as is also *sors* in *Hist.*
2. 70. It is the language of the layman, not of the theologian
or the philosopher. In his philosophic position as in his historical, Tacitus was content to follow the intelligent majority.
Insofar as he diverges at all from the conventional Stoicism of
his day which had displaced early Roman religion, it is under
the influence of his dramatic conception of historical events.

4. POLITICAL THEORY

TACITUS divided the old order from the new by the battle of Actium, in other words by the event that left Octavian supreme. In his conception of government, therefore, the *vetus res publica* was the Roman state without the Julio-Claudian emperors and their successors. This is a theoretically defensible position, but it seems to assume that the *vetus res publica* was actually functioning in the years preceding Actium and makes difficult any clear-cut definition of what Tacitus thought it to be. For obviously a large element in his conception of the old republic is an active and efficient senate in the driver's seat. In cold fact the senate had not really functioned freely for more than a generation, certainly not since Pompey, Caesar, and Crassus had combined to dictate its actions. It would seem, however, that in the course of time the stubborn resistance of Cato and the eloquence of Cicero had given to their day an aura of independence and greatness which was hardly deserved. The word *libertas* seems to have characterized the *vetus res publica* in the mind of Tacitus, and the fact that he dates the life span of *libertas* from the fall of the kings to the success of Augustus indicates that he did not wholly realize the changes that had occurred in the period following the Gracchi. Their attempt to use the tribunician power and their appeal to the assembly against the senate was not a great success, but Cicero's frantic efforts to maintain senatorial rule were equally ineffective. Between the two assaults the traditional *res publica,* a senatorial government under the constant check of a possible appeal to the assembly, collapsed into a state of anarchy that could not fail to result in one man control. Probably, however, there is no greater example of the persistent appeal of an idea than the survival of the wholly visionary conception of the *res publica populi Romani*. Perhaps the idea had never actually corresponded to any existing reality but it was in itself an almost concrete reality. It was

what the Gracchi and Marius and Caesar claimed to be fighting for. So, too, Sulla and Pompey and Cicero were its champions. It was what Augustus claimed to have restored, and
each of his successors did at least lip service to the great idea.
To Tacitus it seemed to have disappeared with Actium. And
around it for him had gathered a glory that he would have
found hard to define. While he still used the term *res publica*
for the Roman state, he did not do so in the sense of the old
symbol. The new state was an *imperium* into which Augustus
as its personification had absorbed the powers of senate, magistrates, and laws. No one opposed this move, Tacitus says, because the most spirited of the *nobiles* had disappeared and the
rest were lured by Augustus' inducements to prefer the new in
safety to danger in championing the old. It is worth noting that
the only possible opposition of which Tacitus conceives is that
from the *nobiles*. Few men have ever been more unconcerned
with—it may almost be said, unconscious of—the common
man than Tacitus. But as far as politics is concerned he is
merely realistic in this attitude. The senate and its supporting
class, the *nobiles,* had for centuries ruled Rome, so entrenched
in their position that only revolution could break their power.
These *nobiles* were not merely the members of the old families
of early Rome. The dignity and tradition of the senate was as
much a myth in its way as the *res publica populi Romani.*
There is a natural decline in old families by mere abrasion;
moreover, a definite change in the composition of the senate
began with the compromise which preserved its power by admitting the *equites,* the commercial element of the population.
This was politically wise and in fact necessary, but it was no
less galling to the conservative *nobiles*. Perhaps the conventional belief that moral and political weakness entered Roman
life with the wealth of Carthage and Corinth was given vigor
and long life by the fact that the *equites* rode into power on
this flood of new wealth. The civil wars and the proscriptions
completed the deflation of the old families as the real power of
the state, socially and politically. But the new senators clung
to the old watchwords, and Tacitus seems to have the same

respect for the senatorial concept that Cicero had. The old republic was to him therefore in the first instance the government of an idealized senate unhampered by an emperor.

In the *Dialogus* he seems to recognize the fact that the great day of oratory was a day of political confusion. Maternus, the poet, definitely prefers the peace and security of the empire to the confusion and lawless independence that produced such orators as Gracchus and Cicero. What seems of immediate importance is the fact that Tacitus really thinks of the republic as the century with Cicero at its center but surrounded with an aura that came from the vague traditions of an earlier day.

Another ideology that enters into the question, to confuse the issue still further, is that of the Stoic school of thought. From the time of Panaetius and the Scipionic circle a sort of popular Stoicism had become conventional among the Romans. It might be more correct to say that a moral tone or a moral standard had come to be accepted as orthodox, expressing in Stoic terms the general ideas of old-fashioned integrity which the Romans liked to believe had once been the hall mark of their leaders and to some extent of the whole people. Much of the literature gives evidence of this, especially in the conventional attacks on luxury and degeneracy. It naturally figured also in political oratory and formed such a large element in the program of the so-called opposition under the emperors as to lead some writers to speak of a Stoic opposition. It is quite true that many of the victims of Nero were men of Stoic character and belief, but it is probably a mistake to speak of a Stoic opposition. These victims, with the exception of Seneca, were not in any sense philosophers, nor was any philosophic sect in active opposition to Nero. The most respectable characters of the day were Stoic in the sense that a man might be called Christian today, without thought of any organization or any particular dogma. So far as the Stoic sect had any political tenets, it believed in the absolute rule of a philosopher king. It is a well known fact that in spite of his nostalgic reverence for the old republic, Tacitus welcomed enthusiastically the reign of Trajan, while his close friend Pliny eulogized that emperor in the most extravagant terms. Tacitus presumably accepted his own fundamental Stoicism without any critical analysis, and, as mentioned before, he certainly never studied philosophy beyond the point that was advisable for a senator.

The fact remains that as the historian looked back on those who came to be considered the defenders of the old order, he found in Cato and Brutus at least men who were recognized as outstanding Stoics. These men, with Cassius, became the heroes of people like Thrasea and Helvidius, who came into clashes with the emperors. Hence the myth of Stoic opposition. But Cato and Brutus had themselves become symbols like the *res publica populi Romani* and the incorruptible senate of old Rome. It is easy to indicate the later progress of this symbolism. Augustus, as he states in the summary of his reign, punished those who had murdered his father, but his policy with their followers was one of conciliation. He avoided identifying them with the senate. He respected L. Sestius in spite of his devotion to Brutus and Cassius. He did not move against Livy or Asinius Pollio or Messalla when they spoke a good word for the tyrannicides. In A.D. 25, however, under Tiberius, Cremutius Cordus becomes the first victim of the charge of eulogizing Brutus and Cassius and commits suicide during his trial. Junia, the wife of Cassius and sister of Brutus, as well as niece of Cato, had been allowed a public funeral, although she pointedly left Tiberius out of her will and Tacitus comments that the effigies of Brutus and Cassius were conspicuous by their absence from the funeral procession. He says nothing of Cato. Under Nero, C. Cassius was charged with having an image of Cassius in his house inscribed *duci partium*. He was exiled. Juvenal speaks of the secret toasts to the tyrannicides on their birthdays by Thrasea and Helvidius. Meanwhile, Cato under the same emperors could be well spoken of: his philosophy rose above his republicanism. What is indicated is, on the part of the emperors, a growing fear of revolution and assassination and a somewhat sentimental parlor "republicanism" on the part of those who hated the particular rulers for their characters and actions. Under Trajan, Pliny tells us, images of

Brutus, Cassius, and Cato could be safely exhibited in the home.

This background of Tacitus has perhaps been sketched at too great length. It seems, however, to account for much of his anti-imperial attitude. As an ambitious young man he had started on a normal career full of enthusiasm for the newer oratory without being an extremist. As a senator his career was circumscribed by Domitian's rough handling of that body. In his private life he had seen, as he believed, the subtle destruction of his father-in-law by the same emperor. He had witnessed the downfall under Domitian of the men he most admired in the senate and the preferment of others whom he considered to be venal renegades from his own profession. He had more and more resented the influence with the emperor of men of low origin while men of his own social position and higher were wholly passed over. His hatred for Domitian is well founded. Then as he looks back over the previous reigns he finds, or believes he finds, ample evidence of the same things happening. His conviction grows that liberty has been lost with the advent of the emperors. The conviction does not blind him to the possibility of a good emperor, but it enhances his somewhat vague and not too well informed idealization of the old republic. Its heroes and those of the Empire that he admires seem to him to have been the men of good principles—Stoic principles of course—men of standing, men of integrity. And they appear most consistently in opposition to men who have seized or inherited inordinate and even illegal power, usually with the support of men of no standing, no principles. His position is hardly that of a political theorist; it is that of a good citizen shocked at the abuse of power, disgusted with the influx of unprincipled upstarts into a society and a government with a glorious and unsullied past. We should be as far astray in trying to pin Tacitus down to a political theory as in asking of him a consistent philosophical outlook. As with Juvenal, it is indignation that makes him a writer.

There is plenty of evidence in the volumes of Tacitus' published works to confirm this general conclusion. The great arraignment of imperialism incorporated in the speech of Calgacus in the *Agricola* strikes far more effectively at the conquests of the republic than at those under the emperor. It pictures in the large the cruelty of conquest, the sort of inhumanity which Horace glimpsed in detail on the personal side when he drew his vignette of the poor farmer dispossessed by the senseless building mania of the rich. It does not involve the political principle of senate versus emperor or republic versus empire. It attacks not empire but imperialism, which was at its height when the senate was in power. That is why there is always involved in such attacks a moral judgment, and that is why Stoicism, which stood fast against avarice and lust for power, even from the time of Lucilius, entered into all such attacks on those who profited, to another's injury, by the results of conquest.

The implications of the *Germania* are similar. We find the normal reaction of the average decent citizen toward the moral laxity of the Roman society, as it is made evident by contrast with the simpler and hence (by the conventional line of reasoning) more idealistic social behavior of the Germans. The noble savage is no modern invention; he is the natural corollary of the Stoic age of gold against which the embryonic evolution of Epicureanism never made any substantial headway. No political theory is involved.

In the major works the personal antagonism of the author against individual emperors is clear and undisguised. In the *Dialogus* it had already been suggested that *libertas* could easily turn into *licentia* and that it had done so in the days of Cicero. It is this *licentia* of the emperors rather than the faults of a system that Tacitus abhors. When he digresses to give the history of some element of the Roman political system, there is no attempt to show that the change from republic to empire had been a turning point. His summary of the history of laws and lawmaking (*Ann.* 3. 26–28) is a good example, which incidentally shows that Tacitus actually realized that the last years of the republic were years of anarchy in spite of the sentimental aura with which he might surround them under pressure of his disgust with the present.

It would be foolish to look for political theory in Tacitus'
writings. He was not a theorist. He was a lawyer and in that
sphere his freedom of action had been curtailed and he had
seen lawyers of unscrupulous character highly rewarded by
emperors. He was a writer and had been prevented from writing freely by the oppression of an emperor. He was a senator
and felt strongly that the dignity of that body had been lost by
the despotic action of succeeding emperors. He was a decent
citizen of high integrity and was concerned with the immoral-
ity and outrageous luxury rampant in the court of one emperor
after another. It is, then, a human and on the whole commendable indignation which rouses him to flay Tiberius and Nero
and Domitian. A later age spoke of his works as Lives of the
Caesars and such in reality they were, lives wrought into a unified history but lives nonetheless. For it is to the presentation
of the characters on the throne that Tacitus bends all his en-
ergies. On them rather than on the progress of the state or the
development of the constitution are focused all his accounts of
the years from Tiberius to Domitian.

5. LITERARY STYLE

TACITUS' literary style is unique. His history can hardly be thought of apart from the style in which it is written, and that style, unlike Cicero's, is so difficult to imitate that it stands alone in Latin literature. Sallust comes nearest, and from Sallust, Tacitus drew much, but in his mature style he had advanced far from his earlier approximation to that of his predecessor, so far as to justify a claim of unique independence. Subsequent writers show little effort to imitate, certainly no success. It would seem that Tacitus, trained in the school of Quintilian which produced a brief Ciceronian revival, had first discarded the rotund periods of Cicero as unsuited to his day and subject. The extreme Attic simplicity which had made convincing the special pleading of Caesar did not lend itself to the more general and dramatic theme of Tacitus. The popular colloquial style of Seneca lacked the dignity required by the historian's subject. Sallust offered the best model. Here was a writer who abandoned the active life of public affairs and deliberately attempted to win a reputation as historian. To a limited extent he had a thesis to maintain, a thesis at variance with the accepted conclusions of his own generation and class. He was, as a man of affairs, interested in men and their reactions to each other, and in the dramatic turns of fortune which marked the periods which he treated. He was a man well trained in oratory and endowed with some sense of irony. It is unnecessary to point the parallel: Tacitus could hardly have failed to find in Sallust the best point of departure for developing his own literary weapons. But fortunately we are not left wholly to conjecture in trying to understand how he came to turn to the writer of the *Catiline* and *Jugurtha* for guidance. His earliest literary product furnishes the clue.

It does not require any extensive study of the *Dialogus* to realize that it is more than a mere school exercise in the manner of Cicero. Cicero is the obvious model and the style is generally agreed to be largely Ciceronian. Such a style is suitable to the leisurely, polished discussion of a literary subject, a discussion in the most decorous manner, without polemic purpose and resulting in no dogmatic conclusion.

It is customary among editors to assume that Maternus, in whose home the scene of the *Dialogus* is laid, represents the ideas and conclusions of the author. This is an assumption which is not wholly borne out by a study of the essay. It is undoubtedly true that Tacitus, whether willingly or not, did reconcile himself, after an early career as an orator, to the withdrawal from active pleading that he found necessary under Domitian and did retire to the literary life. It is not at all clear that this was his intention at the time he wrote the *Dialogus*. In the same way it is true that he eventually reconciled himself to the idea that the Republic could not be revived and that under a good emperor the principate was the best solution. But this again cannot be proved for the earlier date.

In the prologue to the *Dialogus* Tacitus states definitely that he followed the activities of Aper and Secundus with youthful enthusiasm and he defends them against current criticism. He furthermore forestalls any decision throughout the essay. He makes Aper a most appealing character in his defense of the modern point of view even as he does Maternus in his eulogy of the literary life. Messalla, too, with his arraignment of contemporary education and his appeal for more fundamental preparation, is on the whole convincingly eloquent. The final speech of Maternus, presenting the changes in the life of Rome which make for practical efficiency but not for polished oratory, is left without refutation.

If one were to try to draw a general conclusion from the arguments of the essay, it might be something like this. The old days of the Republic encouraged great oratory in the grand style, leisurely, learned and somewhat rotund. The times have changed. One who would succeed today in the forensic area must pursue new methods. These are possible and they are exciting as well as profitable. But for one who does not wish to adapt himself to them, a rich field of enjoyment is open in the realm of pure literature. The criticism of old and new, developed by well drawn partisans of each, is, in the large, descriptive and scholarly rather than polemic and is not pointed toward a judgment in favor of one or the other. Differences are noted between periods of oratory as well as between kinds.

All of this seems to present a perfectly consistent position for a young man, trained in a conservative school but surrounded by men in active life, many of whom were of a definitely different school. Presumably there had been a meager survival of Ciceronian tradition throughout the earlier years of the principate, a survival represented in the *Dialogus* by Maternus and especially by Messalla. But there was also a distinct revival of Ciceronianism led by Quintilian, a revival that implies the ascendancy of a different style. His chief purpose seems to have been to combat the growing popularity of the Senecan style, but he sought to accomplish this by a reinstatement of the authority of Cicero. He wrote at some time an essay on the causes for the degeneration in oratory, indicating his own belief in the general thesis on which the *Dialogus* is based, namely that the Ciceronian age was the great day of oratory and Cicero its master.

Quintilian took up his official position as state-supported lecturer in 68. The general assumption that Tacitus studied under him as did his friend Pliny is a reasonable one. The extent of Tacitus' knowledge of Cicero in the *Dialogus* would suggest this, although it does not furnish proof. Quintilian's teaching, while undoubtedly effective and possessing an added force because of his official position, was opposed to the tide. It was aimed against the popular prejudice in favor of Seneca's modern style. But Quintilian cannot have taught any slavish imitation of Cicero. His own style comprises modes of expression which were developed after the time of Cicero. In his eighth book he defines the proper *ornatus* of a speech, indicates the various types of appropriate *sententiae,* and in many ways proves that he wished the orator to exercise his own *inventio* to enrich his speech.

It was under this sort of training if not actually under Quintilian that Tacitus must have developed during the crucial years of his youth. When he wrote the *Dialogus* he was still under the influence of that training. The fundamental structure of his first publication was Ciceronian. The literary form, the sentence structure, the choice of words, all are fundamentally Ciceronian. This is wholly natural. But in all three areas there are non-Ciceronian traits. The dialogue characters are selected carefully for the sake of the argument and are for this purpose more dramatically introduced than those of Cicero. The dialogue has to be sure a single theme, which is developed without refutation once it has been launched; but before that point has been reached, the argument has been quite sufficient to indicate that there is an underlying difference of opinion which is never resolved. The periodic structure is also and not infrequently departed from in favor of something more brief and pungent. Finally, not a few words appear which are post-Augustan and, more often than not, drawn from the vocabulary of poetry. All of these characteristics appear to a minor degree only, but they are readily discernible.

Even more striking is the apparent restlessness of the writer under the restraint imposed by the Ciceronian training. He is more than ready to grant the greatness of the master but quite unwilling to admit that to attain greatness at the later date a mere imitation of the master will suffice. Aper's resentment of such a position is all too vivid; Maternus' withdrawal from public life, on the one hand, and on the other Messalla's admission of the impracticality under the empire of Ciceronian eloquence, both indicate a mind interested in finding the proper solution for its own day. At no point in the essay is there even the implication that Cicero's style could succeed in the days of Vespasian. Maternus, in his concluding paragraph, holds the position that the modern speakers could have mastered the requirements of Cicero's day and that Cicero, moved into their century, would have met successfully its peculiar demands.

To a considerable degree, therefore, the *Dialogus* is the platform of a young man not so much in rebellion against the conservative training that he has received as concerned with the best method of adapting what was sound and permanent in the old school to the requirements of the present. To this extent the *Dialogus* is more than a study of the decline of oratory. It is a study of literary trends in general. The author does not adopt the Senecan answer, for he accepts the implied criticism of Seneca's style, the extreme reaction against tradition, without questioning the fact that change is necessary. And as he feels his way toward a solution of the problem, even while he writes within the orthodox essay form of the earlier day, he makes certain tentative approaches toward a new and independent style. The Ciceronian character of the *Dialogus* is too generally accepted and appreciated to need any documentation. The signs of a new style, latent but recognizable, are not so universally understood.

That Tacitus should use many words that had come into general use since the time of Cicero is perfectly natural and does not constitute a change of style. But certain characteristics of the words he selected are to be noted as typical of his style, and the *Dialogus* furnishes examples of some of these which later did become characteristic. For example, in Tacitus' later works a tendency toward the use of words usually confined to poetry has often been noted. In the *Dialogus* (5) he uses *quatenus* as the equivalent of *quoniam, sacer* in the sense of *venerabilis* (10), *donec* for *quamdiu* (8), *quid* in an indirect question where the ordinary prose usage would be *cur* (17). Other words, used in a somewhat unusual sense, he seems to have employed for their striking effect, culling them especially from Livy and Sallust. Such are *ante* and *post* to indicate "better" and "worse" (26), *virium robore* (26), and *adeo,* "in addition," "besides" (14, 21, 23). Certain post-Augustan usages appealed to him in the same way: *spectanda haberemus* (8), *proeliator* (37), *errare* in an absolute sense (10), *paenitentiam ago* (15), *ex comparatione* for *prae* (23), and *conversatio* (9). There are frequent examples in the *Dialogus* of his practice, familiar in the major works, of using present participles as substantives and of preferring the combination of a preposition and adjective to an adverb.

The most significant factors of style, however, are those
which became his most characteristic qualities: variety, brevity, and the use of the pungent aphorism. It cannot be said that
these are greatly prominent in the *Dialogus,* but they are sufficiently noticeable to be significant in an essay which is pre-
dominantly Ciceronian in style. Such passages as the two following indicate a definite attempt at both brevity and variety
which is un-Ciceronian: from 12, "quod non in strepitu nec
sedente ante ostium litigatore nec inter sordes ac lacrimas
reorum componuntur sed secedit animus" etc.; from 22, "len-
tus est in principiis, longus in narrationibus, otiosus circa ex-
cessus; tarde commovetur, raro incalescit, pauci sensus apte
et cum quodam lumine terminantur." The use of two verbs
without a connective, like *fastidiunt oderunt* in 23, becomes a
mannerism in the later works. Examples of *sententiae* are the
following: "Prope abest ab infirmitate in quo sola sanitas
laudatur" (23); "divitiae et opes quas facilius invenies qui
vituperet quam qui fastidiat" (8); "nec statim deterius esse
quod diversum est" (18). The *sententiae* are not numerous,
but they are characteristic of Tacitus and can be supplemented
by brief ironic epigrams of satiric pungency: "nec incertus futuri testamentum pro pignore scribam, nec plus habeam quam
quod possim cui velim relinquere" (13); "non melius quam
Cicero sed felicius quia illos fecisse pauciores sciunt" (21).

These are not striking examples of a new style. The *Dialogus*
does little by itself to demonstrate the determination of its author to supplant the Ciceronian Latin. It is not a demonstration
but an exploratory essay, in which Tacitus suggests that he
would like to do something modern and that he does not mean
to follow Seneca.

Seneca's style must have been not only recognizably different from that of other writers but also definitely popular at
some period. *Accomodatum auribus temporis eius* would seem
to indicate its popularity in Seneca's own day. Quintilian confirms this statement of Tacitus. Seutonius' *tum maxime placen-
tem,* referring to the reign of Gaius, indicates that this popular-

ity came to Seneca at an early date. Fronto and Aulus Gellius furnish evidence that his reputation lived on with sufficient influcncc to arousc thcm to hostile criticism more scathing than that of Quintilian.

To understand the character of this style it would be well to start with Seneca's own statement of his faith: *oratio certam regulam non habet* (*Ep.* 114. 13). And he adds to this: *consuetudo illam Civitatis quae numquam in eodem diu stetit, versat.* Style reflects the manners of the day, and if "corrupted" either *inflata explicatio* or *infracta et in morem cantici ducta* may flourish. Faults are overlooked in those that truly represent their times, and these *vitia* are even admired. Seneca condemns alike the man who seeks to use only words sanctioned by old tradition and the one who uses only the words of contemporary colloquial standing. Quintilian was to accuse Seneca himself of abounding in pleasant vices and of enjoying his own faults. And the term *fractus* was to be turned against him. Presumably he represented well the taste of his own day, and his effort to reproduce the cultivated conversational style of that day would seem to have been immediately successful: *solus hic fere in manibus adulescentium fuit.* To this colloquialism he added, to win the popularity indicated, gleanings from the rhetor's school.

Let us consider the qualities of Seneca's style as listed by Quintilian and others. He is granted *ingenium facile et copiosum. Copia* is his special characteristic. Again, *multae in eo claraeque sententiae.* So far Quintilian, but Fronto also says that he was *copiosis sententiis.* He is credited by Tacitus with *ingenium amoenum.* There is doubtless irony in the adjective but no one denied him *ingenium.* Quintilian wishes that he had used his own *ingenium* but someone else's *iudicium.* Aulus Gellius avoids a specific judgment but says that some people deny him either worth-while content or commendable style, while others grant him to be a man of scholarly knowledge and a not unpleasing strictness and gravity in the ethical field. The criticisms against his style, as suggested by Gellius, are that

oratio eius vulgaris videtur et protrita, that his *sententiae* are
also cheap and superficial, and that his learning is *vernacula et
plebeia* and possesses neither grace nor dignity.

Quintilian was a Ciceronian; Gellius and Fronto were ar-
chaists; all three were naturally opposed to the easygoing style
of Seneca. For Seneca discarded the periodic sentence in large
degree. His sentences might be long or short, like those of ordinary conversation, but they were never constructed on the
basis of a literary formula. Terse and pointed phrases tending
to become sententious aphorisms are the constant means which
he employs to give life and color to his otherwise plain prose.
He would never have been called Attic, for purity of Latin
makes no appeal to him and brevity he does not understand.
He seeks naturalness relieved by sententious spice—no doubt
the qualities that marked the conversation of the court of Nero.
Smartness long drawn out is not only tiresome, it is annoying,
and that probably accounts for the bitterness of the critics toward Seneca. That and the inevitable tendency of humankind
to confuse moral criticism with literary. It is not easy to justify
Fronto in his statement that Seneca's style is engrafted with
soft and fever-producing plums. Caligula was far more accurate in his figure of speech when he called Seneca's writings
arena sine calce. This might fairly describe the colloquial style
which ignores the building force of periodic structure and conventional sentence connection. I am inclined to believe that the
same quality of disconnectedness may explain the use of *fractus*
in the criticism of Seneca, that it may mean abrupt, disjointed
rather than broken down, weak, effeminate, as it so often does
in the field of criticism. By the extreme critics of Seneca the
more disparaging connotation was probably intended. In the
Dialogus Tacitus quotes Brutus as charging Cicero with being
fractus et elumbis, referring presumably to the exuberant
Asianism of Cicero as compared with Brutus' style, *otiosus
atque disiunctus,* according to Cicero.

Seneca, who paid traditional tribute to Cicero as the master,
still believed that new times called for a new style, and this he
successfully established. He loosened the structure, deflated

the pomposity (as the ancient dignity appeared to be after a hundred years) and, to compensate, he added the decorations of the *rhetores,* who since Cicero's day had come into their own.

Tacitus, in his younger days, was imbued with the spirit of the Ciceronian revival, but his independent nature resisted the archaic control. Obviously he did not approve of Seneca's line of departure. He could not follow Cicero, but he would not accept Seneca. In the *Dialogus,* Aper's eulogy of modernism is left unanswered, but also Messalla's tirade against the rhetors of his day who teach their pupils to speak in everyday conversational Latin, not avoiding its *pudenda vitia,* and who confine oratory to a few commonplaces and cramped epigrams. This might well be the indictment of Senecan style by one of Tacitus' spokesmen.

The *Dialogus* does furnish us, as we have seen, some indication of Tacitus' style in the making. For the moment, let us scrutinize it, not for examples of stylistic peculiarities but for traces of the writer's theoretical position on style. Tacitus announces himself as an admiring follower of Aper and Secundus, who represent the new school in oratory, the modernists. Yet all have a keen admiration for Maternus, who is leaving oratory for poetry. Secundus, in particular, as a friend of Saleius Bassus claims a special interest in poetry, and Aper, while unwilling to allow any sort of extraneous profession, especially that of philosophy, to play a prominent part in the equipment of the orator, nevertheless is tolerant of poetry in its own sphere. In Secundus, Tacitus found a *sermo purus et pressus et, in quantum satis erat, profluens* which he obviously admired. Also he defended Aper against the charge that he was lacking in literary and scholarly culture by saying that he did not *lack* this culture but *chose* to trust rather to his *ingenium.* Aper himself makes much the same case that Seneca does: times change, the old style of Ciceronian oratory becomes tedious to a later, swifter age. But deflation is not sufficient: new allurements must hold the hearer's attention. The philosophy and literary allusion of Cicero's day is not attractive today. The philosophy in particu-

lar has become trite. The present-day listener demands more arresting means, which the modern rhetor teaches. Aper's position is not unlike that of Horace when he discussed Lucilius and
satire. He believed that Lucilius himself would have moved
with the times if his life had been prolonged and would have
written very differently in the days of Augustus. Aper does not
so much attack the ancients as criticize the blind worship of
them and the failure to see that times change and with them
the taste of the public and the requirements for the orator. In
his summing up he demands of the up-to-date orator (and this
demand he would extend, I think, to the historian) a considerable list of qualities: "gravitas sensuum, nitor et cultus verborum, electio inventionis, ordo rerum, ubertas (quotiens causa
poscit), brevitas (quotiens causa permittit), decor composi-
tionis, planitas sententiarum, adfectus, libertas temperata." This
is a program difficult to attack and one that seems to present the
beliefs of Tacitus as exemplified in his practice. There is even
a suggestion of the variety so dear to Tacitus, although this
element is not actually specified. The adornment that the poet
can furnish is rather surprisingly suggested by Aper. Even
Messalla, in urging the orator to study philosophy, wishes him
to taste all types but not to be a philosopher or companion of
the Stoics.

   None of the speakers in the *Dialogus* defends the sort of
thing that we associate with the term Senecan when we talk of
style. Messalla's references to the *calamistri* of Maecenas or
Gallio's *tinnitus* are left unanswered as well as his attacks on
lascivia verborum, levitas sententiarum, and *licentia composi-
tionis.* All of the speakers respect Cicero as the great orator
at least of his own day. The times have changed. The change
may be met in several ways. Maternus chooses to retire to the
realm of poetic creation. Aper would accept the new conditions
and create new means for dealing with them. Messalla would
like to go back to the old, recognizes the impossibility of that,
and would try to find a compromise. No conclusion is reached.
The young auditor who reports the discussion takes no definite
position but, unless I am much mistaken, he has from his edu-

cation a lingering hero worship for the days of Cicero, which he recognizes as futile. He would maintain the dignity and seriousness of the Ciceronian style but abandon its tedious monotony. He would attempt a modification which does not resort to the slack, conversational style such as had been popularized by Seneca, but which—by dramatic tension, brevity, variety and brilliant expression—compensates for the loss of that spacious amplitude of the Ciceronian periods. His quarrel with the schools was based largely on their superficiality, as was his real quarrel with the manners and morals of his day. To him the Senecan solution was itself superficial because it was in reality only a relaxation and not a true development. The future historian demanded a dignity commensurate with that which Cicero's day felt in his resounding periods but attained by means that appealed to his own generation. The silence imposed by Domitian gave ample time for Tacitus to study the historians that had preceded him and to develop his own inimitable style.

The *Dialogus* presents a writer interested in poetry and oratory and shows his knowledge of Cicero's literary productions as well as his speeches, and of the orations of a great number of the noted pleaders of Rome. But there is little evidence in the essay on which to claim any particularly wide general reading on the part of Tacitus. This is one of the most convincing indications of an early date for the *Dialogus*. When Tacitus wrote the *Agricola,* he showed constant reminiscence of the writings of Sallust, Livy, Nepos, Curtius, Vergil, and others, as well as Cicero. Also his own particular style was already well on the way toward its ultimate character. It would be almost impossible for him to have written the *Dialogus* as late as A.D. 98 without showing the results of his reading and of his stylistic studies. Even the *Germania,* exemplar of a specific literary type, objective and factual, betrays its author. The *Dialogus* shows the young student trained in the Ciceronian product but not captured by its out-of-date rotundity and only just beginning to develop something different of his own.

The *Agricola* presents this something new, not in its final form, but at a well advanced stage of development. The increased speed and concise brevity which Aper advocated in the *Dialogus* are already conspicuous, as well as a definite picturesqueness of phrase, and in many a piquant aphorism there is a distinct touch of irony. The author has done away with the ample periods of Cicero and replaced them, not with the loose, sometimes inarticulate sentences of Seneca, but with a style that is taut, concise, even elliptic at times, full of vigor and variety, less majestic than the Ciceronian but more arresting. These are qualities that had been associated with the writings of Sallust and it is often said that the *Agricola* represents the Sallustian period of Tacitus. The fact can hardly be questioned that the author of the *Agricola* was not only thoroughly acquainted with Sallust's work but in many points imitated it. The earlier writer was also rhetor-trained and a conscious rival of Cicero in the literary field. The important thing is to note the limitations within which Tacitus followed Sallust in building his own style.

In the first place, too much is often made of the fact that Sallust, in the *Catiline* and *Jugurtha,* and Tacitus in the *Agricola,* wrote short historical monographs. This is not a precise statement of the facts. Sallust wrote short historical monographs; Tacitus wrote a eulogistic biography. It is precisely in the historical section of the *Agricola* that the biography is least in the manner of Sallust. Tacitus, in these chapters, experiments with his own adaptation of the annalistic method, which may or may not have been helped by a study of Thucydides but which Sallust never attempted. The detachable prologues at first seem to be similar. Further analysis, however, shows that the Sallustian prologues are heavily laden with philosophical platitudes and self-justification. Tacitus' prologue is an introduction to a particular type of essay—biography—and in this sense is more strictly traditional. It explains not the philosophy of human history or the personal philosophy of the writer but, more concretely, the reasons for writing biography and particularly this biography. In this it resembles the prologue of Livy's history and that of Cato's *De agricultura* much more

closely than it does the two Sallustian introductions, and in this
connection it should not be overlooked that the opening words
of the *Agricola* suggest sharply the opening of Cato's *Origines*
as quoted by Cicero: *clarorum virorum atque magnorum*. Sallust himself went back to Cato and was accused of too close
an imitation. Tacitus went back to Cato both through the medium of Sallust and directly but he avoided the archaism which
gave offense in Sallust.

So, too, the ethnogeographic digression on Britain and its
people is traditionally compared with the similar digression on
Africa in the *Jugurtha*. There is much in common between the
two, but such digressions are commonplace in history. Tacitus
is unique in borrowing the device for use in a eulogy to enhance the glory of his subject, but the type of digression itself
was scarcely a characteristic feature peculiar to Sallust. Here
again Tacitus borrows not the larger unit but the effective word
and phrase.

The outstanding traits which combine to give speed and
color to the *Agricola* are perfectly familiar: brevity, variety,
and a brilliancy of phrase sometimes evinced in a terse description, sometimes in a pungent aphorism. Speed and concinnity
are combined in the description of the defeated Britons after
the great battle of Mt. Graupius (38). The tone is set by means
of contrast supplied by one concise statement about the Romans: *Et nox quidem gaudio praedaque laeta victoribus*. This
sentence by itself illustrates many of the methods by which
Tacitus made his style most effective. *Quidem* gives warning of
a contrast to come, and since this is sufficiently clear, Tacitus
does not follow it with a *sed* as Cicero would probably have
done but lets the contrast speak for itself, the next sentence beginning with *Britanni,* in clear contrast with *victoribus*. *Gaudio
praedaque,* an abstract and a concrete—not quite but very
nearly a case of hendiadys, and between them covering the
situation—is thoroughly Tacitean. The omission of the verb
adds both to the speed and to the vividness of the clause. With
this preparation there follows the more elaborate picture of
misery amongst the barbarians: "Britanni palantes mixto viro-

rum mulierum ploratu trahere vulneratos, vocare integros, deserere domos ac per iram ultro incendere, eligere latebras et statim relinquere; miscere in vicem consilia aliqua, dein separare; aliquando frangi aspectu pignorum suorum saepius concitari." The succession of "historical" infinitives plays its part in the creation of a vivid picture, as does the sparing use of conjunctions, but primarily the effect is gained by the poetically exact choice of detail to present, and the masterly selection of words to express, the details. With the genius of the poet, Tacitus follows this description with a final statement—compact, pregnant, and ironical—which says all that can be said: "Sattisque constabat saevisse quosdam in coniuges ac liberos, tamquam misererentur." Finally, the physical aspect completes the impression, nouns used to give the vivid static effect instead of the infinitives in the action picture: "Proximus dies faciem victoriae latius aperuit: vastum ubique silentium, secreti colles: fumantia procul tecta, nemo exploratoribus obvius." As used in this selection several words are wholly poetic in both source and connotation: *pignorum, vastum, secreti.* But the whole effect is poetic as well, and the sympathy with the wretched victims of Rome's victory is in the same character. One small and prosaic point should be noted. The last phrase, *nemo exploratoribus obvius,* is effective in itself, but it has also a practical purpose in the continuity of the swift narrative which has been delayed by the descriptive passage, concise as that is. For Tacitus continues: *Quibus in omnem partem dimissis* etc. Such care for transitions is typical of Tacitus and makes for rapidity of narrative.

One noticeable characteristic of the passage that I have used for illustration is the variety of expression throughout. This trait is conspicuous in every part of the essay but least so in the final peroration of chapter 46. In this conclusion something of the older style creeps in, along with the phraseology reminiscent of Cicero. Yet even here, Tacitus' own touch is clear. *Is verus honos, ea coniunctissimi cuiusque pietas* has the familiar brevity and force. Elsewhere the passion for variety has full play. *Pronum magisque in aperto* in the very first chapter is typical. In chapter 10, *non in comparationem curae . . . sed quia* is another phase of the same practice. Often the variety gives opportunity for suggesting more than could be expressed by the more familiar method, as is the case in chapter 12: *olim regibus parebant, nunc per principes factionibus et studiis trahuntur.*

On a larger scale the desire to give variety to his essay is equally apparent. In the lesser battle, the motives of the Britons are given in indirect discourse and the appeal of Boudicca is largely concrete. In the later situation Calgacus speaks directly and, combining concrete incentives with abstract motives, scarcely repeating an item of Boudicca's harangue, makes his great appeal to the principle of liberty. In the accounts of the various years of Agricola's governorship before the crucial climax, Tacitus makes the selection of his material on the basis of variety. This is in part because he wishes to demonstrate different qualities in his hero, but the interest of the reader is never lost sight of.

Contrast is a constant factor in the arresting phrases that distinguish the essay as well as in its larger elements. *Ita singuli pugnant, universi vincuntur* (12) may illustrate one type; the contrast between the fiery harangue of Calgacus and the dignified restraint of Agricola's essentially Roman address presents the other and larger phase.

In the Caledonian's speech, one phrase illustrates several characteristics of Tacitus' method: "Nam ut superasse tantum itineris, evasisse silvas, transisse aestuaria pulchrum ac decorum in frontem, ita fugientibus periculosissima quae hodie prosperrima sunt." The use of the present participle as a substantive is probably of poetic origin. Certainly it came to be almost a mannerism with Tacitus. The approach to the major contrast by an almost Ciceronian repetition followed by a sharp variation of construction is almost as typical, as is also the complete variation of expression in the last clause which prepares the way for what follows, introduced by *enim*.

Such characteristics could be illustrated to wearisome length, for they *are* characteristic and not casual. A word should be added about the brilliant phrases which are necessarily more occasional and yet frequent. These are not primarily *sententiae*. Such there are, as for instance the famous *omne ignotum pro magnifico est*. But the greatest are the result of the writer's emotion clothed in exactly the right words, which usually imply more than they say. *Ubi solitudinem faciunt, pacem appellant* has never ceased to be quoted. *Ut nesciret a bono patre non scribi heredem nisi malum principem* has the touch of the satirist, as has also *tamquam pro virili portione innocentiam principi donares*. Even when the epigrammatic quality is lacking, Tacitus' singular felicity of expression always rises to its height when his bitterness is aroused. One final example will suffice: "illud tempus quo Domitianus non iam per intervalla ac spiramenta temporum, sed continuo et velut uno ictu rem publicam exhausit." In a situation which Cicero would have met with an accumulation of balanced sentences, Tacitus relies on the trenchant phrase or on the single right word.

To turn from the *Agricola* to the *Germania* is to realize at once the influence of the literary type on the style of the writer. In the ethnogeographical essay there is none of the emotional tension and little of the rhetorical display of the eulogy. The style is plain to suit the objective subject matter. Even the tendency noticeable in the *Agricola* to move the verb from the end of the sentence to the most effective position for stylistic effect is rarely in evidence. But this does not mean a return to rotund periods. The sentences are on the average short, the effect is crisp and hard. Brevity is more conspicuous than variety or color. The most frequent practice contributing to this result is the omission of *est* or *sunt:* "Heredes tamen successoresque sui cuique liberi, et nullum testamentum: Si liberi non sunt, proximus gradus in possessione fratres patrui avunculi. Quanto plus propinquorum quanto maior affinium numerus, tanto gratiosior senectus; nec ulla orbitatis pretia." This usage leads often to the impression of an inventory rather than a narrative description even when infinitives replace nouns: "Duriora genti corpora, stricti artus minax vultus et maior animi vigor. Mul-

tum ut inter Germanos rationis ac sollertiae: praeponere elec-
tos, audire praepositos, nosse ordines, intellegere occasiones,"
etc. An average example of the nominal inventory is the following: "Fennis mira feritas, foeda paupertas: non arma, non
equi, non penates, victui herba, vestitui pelles, cubile humus:
sola in sagittis spes."

Occasionally the touch of the poetic shown in the *Agricola*
betrays the tendency of the writer though not to any great extent. As extreme as any case is the following: "et in proximo
pignora, unde feminarum ululatus audiri, unde vagitus infan-
tium. Hi cuique sanctissimi testes, hi maximi laudatores: ad
matres, ad coniuges vulnera ferunt: nec illae numerare aut
exigere plagas pavent, cibosque et hortamina pugnantibus ges-
tant." This use of the participle as a substantive is constant
throughout the essay.

The only further color that is at all noteworthy is the epigrammatic irony which is a more typical characteristic of Tacitus than perhaps any other. It is the touch of the satirist, the
urbanitas which intentionally restrains itself and never becomes more than suggestive. A few examples must suffice to
represent a quality which permeates the essay to such an extent
as to lead some critics carelessly to classify the *Germania* as a
satire instead of accepting for it the obvious classification and
recognizing the irony as typical of the author in all that he
wrote. In the fifth chapter Tacitus remarks dryly: "Argentum
et aurum proptiine an irati dii negaverint dubito." Other examples of the same attitude are: *Nemo enim illic vitia ridet,
nec corrumpere et corrumpi saeculum vocatur* (19); *Apud
ceteros impares libertini libertatis argumentum sunt* (25);
reverentius visum de actis deorum credere quam scire (34);
triumphati magis quam victi sunt (37); and *diu quin etiam
inter cetera eiectamenta maris iacebat donec luxuria nostra
dedit nomen* (45).

The *Dialogus* showed Tacitus, keenly interested in the problems of oratory and literature, writing a dramatic dialogue in
the general style of Cicero but with a definite suggestion of his
own individuality. In the *Agricola* he produced a eulogistic

biography, once more following in general the rules of the type but varying them in line with his own requirements. In this case it was Sallust whom he took in a large way as a stylistic model, partly because the work approached in some degree the monographs of Sallust, but even more because in this particular style Tacitus began to find the answer to his search for a modern substitute for the Ciceronian manner. In the *Germania* he tried his hand at a third type, the ethnogeographical essay. Here the basic model is not so easy to detect. There is something of Caesar, something more of Cato, and more than a suggestion of the Sallustian digression. But, while the demands of the type produce something very different from the *Agricola,* the essay is permeated, as was the biography, with Tacitus' own characteristic style. With marked success he would seem to have developed during fifteen years what he had indicated as his goal in the *Dialogus,* a method of expression to rival the Ciceronian, to be acceptable to his own generation, and yet to avoid the slipshod effect of Seneca's inadequate cohesion. There is no impresison of colloquialism in this style. By strict avoidance of the commonplace, by careful choice of the precisely appropriate word, by a compactness and speed which implies intelligence on the part of the reader, and by the frequent infusion of a dignified irony that rises above the captious criticism of the popular aphorism it attains the gravity and distinction which contemporary criticism generously recognized.

When Tacitus turned to the writing of his major histories he simply applied the same devices to another literary type on a much grander scale. It has been traditional to find stylistic differences between the *Histories* and the *Annals* and it is to be expected that the later work would show, as to a considerable degree it does, a greater mastery over the methods that we have been considering. The compact brevity perhaps reaches its peak in the *Annals,* as the variety and the highly charged irony undoubtedly do. But the point may readily be overstressed. The emotional tension of the *Annals* does not go beyond that of parts of the *Agricola.* We do not possess those chapters of the

Histories to which it would be most appropriate. The character of each work and the character of the various parts of each is more responsible for the variations of style than any change in the working methods of Tacitus. In the early books of the *Histories* the author had, as he tells us, material inherently exciting and full of important action. It is in the early part of the *Annals* that Tacitus feels the responsibility of the writer to make thrilling subject matter that might well, as he himself observes, either bore or repel the reader. Furthermore, in the later books of the *Annals,* when the drama of the Neronian tragedy grips the writer, it is only natural that his style should rise to the highest emotional tension of which it was capable.

It would be possible if it were necessary to illustrate at any length from the historical works the characteristics that have been traced in the shorter essays. The detailed work of scholars has provided ample material and this has been abundantly used by editors and essayists. Most recently Salvatore [1] and Martin [2] have considered the element of variety, while there have appeared more general appraisals of the style by Löfstedt,[3] J. Cousin,[4] and J. Perret.[5] All scholars must of necessity go back to the basic study of Draeger, *Über Syntax und Stil des Tacitus.*[6] Furneaux in the introduction to his edition of the *Annals*[7] gives a convenient summary of Draeger, with additional material.

A brief survey of the first thirty chapters of the *Histories* leaves no doubt that the development of a new style, suggested as a desirable end in the *Dialogus* and foreshadowed brilliantly in the *Agricola,* has been largely completed during the years following. One might expect that the traditional framework of history which Tacitus accepts would influence him to the ex-

1. *Stile e ritmo in Tacito,* Naples, 1950.
2. "Variatio and the Development of Tacitus' Style," *Eranos, 51* (1953), 89–96.
3. "On the Style of Tacitus," *JRS, 38* (1948), 1–8.
4. "Rhétorique et psychologie chez Tacite," *REL, 29* (1951), 228–47.
5. *REA, 56* (1954), 90–120.
6. 3d ed. Leipzig, 1882.
7. 2d ed. Oxford, 1896.

tent of reducing the individualistic trend that we have been following. This is not the case. He accepts the annalistic method familiar in Roman historiography. According to the prologue he accepts also the traditional approach: statement of subject, summary of situation and background, demonstration of importance of subject, and insistence on unbiased truth and even a claim for the moral value of history. With all of this he accepted also the traditional practice of inserting speeches by historical characters, intended to crystallize a situation or characterize the speaker, incidentally lending variety and vividness to the narrative. He accepted, too, the tradition of summary sketches of more or less important individuals, usually at the time of death but sometimes at their first appearance or at the moment of their greatest significance. Finally, he accepted the tradition of the digression, the device by which writers had lent interest to their narrative by furnishing relevant or merely interesting information or comments not directly concerned with the strict hisorical account. In all of this Tacitus follows tradition but by the devices which he had already developed in the earlier essays he attains an individualism in each which gives them new character and significance, while in the narrative proper the same qualities produce a speed and tension without loss of dignity which constitute a new literary style.

The stark brevity of the opening sentence of the *Histories* is in marked contrast with, for instance, the beginning of Livy's history, or with the involved rhetorical introductory sentence of Tacitus' own *Agricola:* "Initium mihi operis Servius Galba iterum Titus Vinius consules erunt." The *terminus ad quem* is not stated but is left to be inferred from the method which he adopts to guarantee his freedom from bias: "Mihi Galba Otho Vitellius nec beneficio nec iniuria cogniti. Dignitatem nostram a Vespasiano inchoatam, a Tito auctam, a Domitiano longius provectam non abnuerim: sed incorruptam fidem professis neque amore quisquam et sine odio dicendus est." (Note in passing the omission of auxiliaries, the participle used as a noun, and the *quisque* understood in the last clause, all contributing to the concise brevity and speed of the statement.) The intervening sentences exhibit practically every trait of style noted in the *Agricola*. The restrained but tense bitterness sets the key for the imperial history: "ita neutris cura posteritatis inter infensos vel obnoxios. Quippe audulationi foedum crimen servitutis malignitati falso species libertatis inest." The final promise at the end of the paragraph, introduced by Cicero's favorite *quod si*, would seem to violate the canon of brevity but is obviously a bow to the reigning house and justifies its position by the implication of the last clause: "rara temporum felicitate, ubi sentire quae velis et quae sentias dicere licet." The bitterness is implicit and retrospective but no less effective on that account. Chapters 2 and 3, which characterize the period he is to deal with, are composed very largely of nouns or their equivalent, with hardly a verb throughout. Abstract nouns are used for concrete; rhetorical plurals add picturesque exaggeration. There is a crescendo of horror from the opening sentence—"Opus adgredior opimum casibus, atrox proeliis, discors seditionibus, ipsa etiam pace saevum"—to the final one: "Nec enim umquam atrocioribus populi Romani cladibus magisve iustis indiciis adprobatum est non esse curae deis securitatem nostram, esse ultionem." The framework is that of tradition but the method and tone are Tacitus' own. Such a sentence as "Ita neutris cura posteritatis inter infensos vel obnoxios" could hardly come from another author, and it should not be overlooked that after the words *Opus adgredior* there are seventeen lines without a verb, nouns and participles alternating to produce a vivid, impressionistic picture of the confused period which is to be the subject of the first books.

There has come to be a general belief that Tacitus's style evolves progressively through the *Histories* and early books of the *Annals* but that in the later books his tendency has been to revert to a more conservative and conventional style. I think that Löfstedt has properly questioned this assumption. It will be enough here to note one striking piece of evidence to indicate that the devices which Tacitus employed were progressively employed even though their particular use was definitely influenced by the material which he was treating. I refer to the adoption of synonyms for ordinary words, which gave a certain weight or dignity to the style. The longer form *claritudo* is used for *claritas* almost exclusively in the *Annals,* although only the shorter form appears in the Minor Works and the use is evenly divided in the *Histories.* So *cuncta* gradually takes the place of *omnia, essem* gives way to *forem, possum* to *queo, magnus* to *ingens,* and so on.

It is equally true that the qualities of brevity, variety, and poetic coloring are just as pervasive in the later books of the *Annals* as in the *Histories. Per silentium aut modice querendo* (15. 1) is a mannerism already familiar, used frequently to avoid monotony. *Statim relictum Agrippinae limen: nemo solari, nemo adire praeter paucas feminas, amore an odio incertas* (13. 19) is as typical in its brevity and pungent cynicism and in its alternative reasons (of which the latter, unsupported by evidence, leaves the stronger impression) of the later books as of the earlier ones. And such poetical touches as *octavus ut imperium obtines* (14. 53), *quae adusque bellum evaluerunt* (14. 58), or *fessis rebus succurreret* are no less frequent in 11–16 than in the *Histories.* The same sharp lines etched with acid present the pictures of Poppaea in 13. 45, and of Calvia Crispinilla in *Hist.* 1. 73.

The following two paragraphs may be compared and will appear equally "Tacitean": "Sed sceleris cogitatio incertum an repens: studia militum iam pridem spe successionis aut paratu facinoris adfectaverat, in itinere, in agmine, in stationibus vetustissimum quemque militum nomine vocans ac memoria Neroniani comitatus contubernales appellando; alios agnoscere, quosdam requirere et pecunia aut gratia iuvare, inserendo saepius querellas et ambiguos de Galba sermones quaeque alia turbamenta vulgi" (*Hist.* 1. 23); "Versa ex eo civitas et cuncta feminae oboediebant, non per lasciviam, ut Messalina, rebus Romanis inludenti. Adductum et quasi virile servitium: palam severitas ac saepius superbia; nihil domi impudicum nisi dominationi expediret. Cupido auri immensa obtentum habebat, quasi subsidium regno pararetur. Die nuptiarum Silanus mortem sibi conscivit, sive eo usque spem vitae produxerat, seu delecto die augendam ad invidiam" (*Ann.* 12. 7).

Variety is pressed to the limit in many characterizations, of which the following from *Ann.* 15. 48 may serve as typical: "Namque facundiam tuendis civibus exercebat, largitionem adversum amicos, et ignotis quoque comi sermone et congressu; aderant etiam fortuita: corpus procerum, decora facies: sed procul gravitas morum aut voluptatum parsimonia: levitati ac magnificentiae et aliquando luxu indulgebat."

Pregnant phrases, with bitter, often ironical insinuation, are innumerable, such as: *Prima novo principatu mors Juni Silani* (*Ann.* 13. 1); *et maerens Burrus ac laudans* (14. 15. 7); *huic mulieri cuncta alia fuere praeter honestum animum* (13. 45. 2). Tacitus' habit (by no means confined to him) of making a general statement or even a *sententia* at the opening of a paragraph followed by the explanatory details becomes increasingly familiar through the historical works: *prodigia quoque crebra et inrita intercessere* (*Ann.* 14. 12); *Nihil rerum mortalium tam instabile ac fluxum est quam fama potentiae non sua vi nixae* (*Ann.* 13. 19. 1).

The "brevity" which with "variety" is most characteristic of Tacitus' mature style is not confined by any means to the omission of conjunctions, parts of the verb, and the like. In fact the more characteristic brevity is to be found in a compactness of whole clauses or sentences, witnessing to a compression which becomes evident in any attempt to translate a given passage into an English rendering which uses the same number of words. Typical of the less extreme examples is: "Et cepisse impetum Subrius Flavus ferebatur in scaena canentem Neronem adgrediendi, aut cum ardente domo per noctem huc illuc cursaret incustoditus. Hic occasio solitudinis, ibi ipsa frequentia tanti decoris testis pulcherrima animum exstimulaverant, nisi impunitatis cupido retinuisset, magnis semper conatibus adversa" (*Ann.* 15. 50. 6).

At the same time it is undoubtedly true that there is a difference, not easy to analyze, between the stylistic effect of the

Histories and that of the *Annals,* due largely, I believe, to the difference in subject matter. This might be less true if we had more of the *Histories.* What we have deals with a period of sufficiently exciting material to relieve the author of any great effort to control the attention of the reader. Furthermore, there is not the same amount of debatable material as in the *Annals,* which led Tacitus not merely to interest his readers but to persuade them—hence, perhaps, a slightly more conventional use of his medium combined with an increased employment of the cynical epigram. Such a generalization is, however, hard to prove, and the more fundamental difference will be found to lie in the more dramatic handling of the material in the *Annals* rather than in the stylistic details.

The impression seems to be general that the style of Tacitus represents the extreme in the omission of conjunctions. This is not actually true. In the total number of conjunctions used there is practically no difference between Cicero and Tacitus. Varro, Sallust, and Seneca use less than either. The significant feature is that Tacitus uses less than half as many *subordinating* conjunctions as Cicero. Of the simple copulative conjunctions (*et, -que, atque, neque*) Tacitus uses almost twice as many as Cicero. The result is that Tacitus puts the burden of the expression of relation between sentences and clauses on the nonconjunctional means and forces on the reader the interpretation of these relations. That the relations are rarely obscure to the attentive reader is due to the skill with which they are expressed. The largest single element in this skill is the choice of words and the order in which they are placed. Tacitus always assumes an intelligent and responsive reader, never relaxing the tension and dignity of his prose for the purpose of making it more easily comprehensible to the casual reader. It is this quality which chiefly distinguishes the style of Tacitus from that of Seneca.

Peterson, in the introduction to his *Dialogus,* is responsible for another misapprehension. He states: "Quintilian's mission at Rome then and afterwards was to recall the literature of the day from the studied affectation and empty elegance that were then held in repute to the purity, simplicity and naturalness of republican models." Cicero's periodic and fulsome style was neither simple nor natural. It was another type of rhetorical creation, different from first-century Latin but just as surely artificial. Seneca came nearer to simplicity and naturalness than did Cicero. Quintilian himself saw more clearly than Peterson what he was trying to do: *corruptum et omnibus vitiis fractum dicendi genus revocare ad severiora iudicia contendo.* Seneca sought to replace Ciceronian prose with a more literally colloquial type. To Tacitus this type lacked dignity. His own prose, opposed to what to him was the pompous and wearying style of Cicero, was not less rhetorical (in the technical sense) than that of his predecessor but differently rhetorical, more rugged and pungent, more concise and more varied—more suited to his own day, but made unique by his own skill in manipulation and his own compelling emotion.

6. TECHNIQUE OF COMPOSITION

THE *Annals* have always been considered by the critics as the culmination of Tacitus' historical style. I have already suggested in the preceding chapter that it is not so much the style, in the narrower sense, that makes the *Annals* different from that part of the *Histories* which we possess, as it is the difference of subject matter and the general method of treatment which Tacitus developed to meet the challenge of the different material. In brief this consists in applying much of the technique of the drama to the narration of historical events. It involves a presentation of characters through action and speech and through their reactions to each other. It involves a sense of compulsion or inevitability which drives the characters toward a climax and a catastrophe. It involves an analysis of the action into significant stages, with the use of suspense to enhance the tragic outcome. It is not merely a feeling of tragedy on the part of the writer conveyed in a general way to the reader: it is the conscious use of means familiar in the drama to give to the narration of historical facts the tension and enthralling interest of a great and serious play. It is important to understand because it goes far toward explaining the character of Tacitus' historical work and because there is involved in its understanding the question of Tacitus' integrity as an historian.

Tacitus' approach to the dramatic technique was gradual. In the *Dialogus* may be seen the qualities and proclivities which led him toward that particular technique, but as a young man Tacitus was obviously something of an enthusiast for the current movements and responsive to a wide range of influence. Few men of his day can have read more widely or more thoroughly than he and not many men have been so susceptible to the influences emanating from the authors read.

When he wrote the *Dialogus*, Tacitus was already master of the Ciceronian type of dialogue. That Cicero was his model can hardly be questioned, but it is equally obvious that there is no slavish imitation, no indication of an apprentice's awkward fumbling or lack of independence. His touch is sure, his procedure confident. Perhaps the most immediately noticeable difference between the work of Tacitus and that of Cicero is the extent to which the young writer represses his own function in the essay as compared with the older man. Tacitus plays just enough part in the opening of the dialogue to make a conventional dedication to Justus Fabius, to define his subject, and to introduce the characters and setting. After that, only a first person plural in the closing scene betrays the presence of the master of ceremonies. This difference is of course most obvious in comparison with the dialogues in which Cicero is frankly expounding his subject didactically, but the *Dialogus* has less of the writer than even the *Cato* and the *Laelius*. It should be noted in passing however that Tacitus *does* complete the dramatic framework by means of the closing paragraph. Maternus, Aper, and Secundus in the *Dialogus* are more effectively introduced than the characters of Cicero to this extent: Cicero assumes some acquaintance on the part of the reader with the prominent speakers. He does indicate, in the *Amicitia* and the *Senectute,* the appropriateness of the protagonists, but he does not attempt to individualize them. In chapter 2 of the *Dialogus,* by the briefest touches, Tacitus puts real people before us: Maternus, by implication an unregenerate admirer of Cato, absorbed in playwriting; Aper and Secundus, up-to-date pleaders in the court, objects of the youthful admiration of the young writer, the one somewhat self-restrained and cautious, the other exuberant and fiery. This impression is supported by a brief conversation in which each reveals his own characteristics, and then Aper is perfectly naturally off on a speech not wholly germane to the topic Tacitus indicated in the opening paragraph. This, too, is in character. The whole approach is much more in the real dramatic manner than in that of the dialogues of Cicero. The temptation is of course to look to Plato for this dramatic model. If it were necessary to indicate a source of inspiration I should be more inclined to turn to the

second book of Horace's *Satires,* itself perhaps a remote descendant of the Platonic dialogue, but it should not be necessary to go back of Tacitus himself. Acquainted with, in fact
definitely interested in, the drama, he writes here with an assurance that suggests originalty. His prologue is brief and effective; it introduces only those characters who appear in the first
act of the dialogue and these are presented as individuals, not
as merely appropriate mouthpieces for certain ideas. All this
is supported by character touches introduced in later parts of
the dialogue as well as by the conversational style of each
speaker, always appropriate but never descending to the quality of a dialect story. When Messalla enters, the prologue with
its opportunity for descriptive characterization is long since
over and the new character is presented through direct conversation. He is to be sure a better known character than the rest,
but Tacitus nonetheless individualizes him and leaves no room
for doubt as to his dignified courtesy or his open-minded admiration for the old and tried.

In the *Agricola* Tacitus turned his hand to the eulogistic
biography. His originality is again in evidence, so much so in
fact as to have deceived many a critic into the attempt to
classify the essay in a different category. But the originality
here lies in adapting the historical technique to the purposes of
the eulogy. The *Germania* also is an essay in a recognized
category. The irony and the satiric comment already noticeable in a minor way in the *Dialogus* appear in both essays, but
neither the eulogistic biography nor the geographical-ethnographical dissertation offers any opportunity for the dramatic
approach. In detail, however, the tendency of the writer
emerges in the highly characterized speeches of Calgacus and
Agricola and in the frequent foreshadowing of future events
in the biography.

So also in the *Histories* there are qualities that have been
called dramatic, but they are matters of detail and not of general technique. The *Histories* are Tacitus' first attempt at
straight history. His selection of the point at which to begin
provides him with a period sufficiently crowded with exciting

and fast-moving events to require no new literary device for holding the reader's attention. What he may have done when he came to the reign of Domitian we cannot say, but in what we have left of the *Histories* the movement of events carries the story swiftly without artificial support. And so we find his characters presented largely, not by carefully placed bits of characteristic action or speech or by indication of their effect on other characters, but by brief, direct, often epigrammatic characterizations. Speeches are more generally used to present a situation or the two sides of a problem than to depict the character of the speaker. The long digression on the Jews is of exaggerated length, but it is consistent with historical tradition; in the more dramatic *Annals* it could hardly have found a place. It is noteworthy that no such account of the Parthians is introduced into the *Annals*. It seems probable that the specifically dramatic method of presentation was the method devised by Tacitus to overcome the lack of great military achievements in the period covered by his latest work.

Tacitus, it is clear, was held in high esteem by his contemporaries. He filled with credit positions of trust and importance. His circle of friends was the most conservative and trustworthy group in the Rome of his time. His own moral standards appear to have been those of the conventional Stoic doctrine of the day. All in all, there can be no question of his integrity. He did not write history to deceive. And yet modern scholarship has found cause not only to modify but in some cases to reject the picture of first-century history which he presents. The question of how trustworthy we should consider the Tacitean history of the early empire has been argued in books and pamphlets innumerable. Some writers have gone so far as to question his integrity, but for the most part it is the results that have been attacked or defended. Perhaps too little attention has been given to the purpose of the works and the means used to attain that purpose. The fact should not be overlooked that the characters of whom Tacitus' judgment has been seriously questioned are the characters not of the *Histories* but of the *Annals*.

It must be remembered at the outset that there is small opportunity to test the accuracy of Tacitus' work as a whole.
Most of the books that would have afforded the chance of
comparative study have been lost. Details may be checked
against archaeological discoveries but such comparison merely
serves to confirm the integrity of the historian rather than his
conception of the age in which he lived. That conception has
become the generally accepted one and continues to be so in
spite of the skepticism of scholars. This is not merely the result of the fact that his is the only great history of the period;
it derives from the persuasive, convincing nature of his work.
This force in turn derives first from the strong conviction and
unquestioning belief of the writer himself and, second, from the
means which he uses to convey his own conviction.

Of the driving motive behind all that Tacitus wrote there
can be no doubt. He himself made no secret of it. He was determined to leave a record of the evil of tyranny as exemplified in the emperors from Tiberius to Domitian. Ostensibly
the contrasted form of government in which he believed was
that of the old senatorial republic; actually it was probably the
rule of a virtuous monarch guided always by a controlling senate. But it was the indictment of the tyrants that was throughout the driving force in all he wrote.

This conception of a great legal indictment has been one of
the favorite explanations of Tacitus' powers of persuasion. It
is argued that as a lawyer presenting his case to the jury of
mankind Tacitus did not scruple to use every means, fair or
unfair, to blacken the reputation of his victims. Those who take
this position refer constantly to the theories of Cicero as to the
methods to be employed in criminal processes. Cicero allowed
the use of deceit as a perfectly proper means of winning a case.
But Cicero did not apply his legal standards to the writing of
history and again and again we find evidence of a different
standard in the *narratio* of law and that of history. Tacitus'
standard of integrity in the use of facts is above question. His
legal training and experience taught him how to present his
facts effectively for his own purpose but not how to manufac-

ture evidence or falsify the facts. Selection and arrangement were to him legitimate tools but not creation or distortion. This of course at once raises the question of whether Tacitus was primarily a lawyer or an historian.

His earliest professional activity is generally assumed to have been that of a lawyer or perhaps more accurately that of an active senator. All that we actually know about this is that he did take his part in the senate, actively as long as it was possible, passively in the latter part of Domitian's reign, and that he was a lawyer of distinction as evidenced by the testimony of Pliny. It is not safe, on the basis of these facts, to assume that he adopted the rôle of historian only when he was estopped from active politics. Numerous men of action spring to mind who were at the same time prolific writers. Cicero, to be sure, published most profusely when under pledge to refrain from his oratorical practice, but his pen was at no time idle. Caesar wrote constantly during a life of increasing activity. It is altogether probable that Tacitus felt no sharp contrast between the life of an orator and that of a literary creator. For the poet, Tacitus would grant the need of seclusion from an active profession, but in the *Dialogus,* when he consigns the poet to the woods and groves, he notes that the active lawyer Secundus has published a life of Julius Africanus and that more such books are expected of him. In the introduction to the *Agricola* it is the *suppression* of historical writing of which he complains, and his appeal for a sympathetic hearing is in part based on the claim that it is lack of literary exercise that makes his style crude and inartistic. To be sure, the fifteen years of suppression gave him ample opportunity for research and writing, forcibly relieved as he was from the active political life, but it would be rash to assert that without this interval he would not have been an historian. The *Dialogus* presents an author already devoted to the field of letters.

Whatever may have been the first incentive that led him to write history, it is obvious that Tacitus read very widely the works of his predecessors before undertaking his own great project. One of the most striking characteristics of his first

quasihistorical publication, the *Agricola,* is the wealth of allusion to earlier writers by means of thinly veiled borrowings
of phraseology. Among the historians, he knew well the works
of Sallust, Nepos, Caesar, and Livy, and probably knew just
as well those of Pliny, Curtius Rufus, Cluvius Rufus, and
Fabius Rusticus. In other words, he was thoroughly familiar
with the traditional models.

Furthermore, there can be no doubt that Tacitus wrote with
a keen desire to win the approval of his audience, to gain fame
as a writer of history. The prologue and epilogue of the *Agricola* both bear evidence to this desire. The prologue of the
Histories has the same implication, with its insistence not only
that his work is to deal with a period full of interest but that his
approach will be new in its freedom from falsification. His
apologies for dullness (*Ann.* 4. 32, 33; 16. 16) prove the same
ambition, and throughout everything he wrote the conscious
artistry indicates an author thoroughly imbued with the desire
to win honest glory by his pen.

This ambition was perhaps a strong motive in Tacitus' selection of the specific subject for his first extensive history, the
year of the four emperors and the Flavian regime that followed. As he himself stated (*Ann.* 1. 1), the age of the Republic had been covered by famous historians and the age of
Augustus had been treated reasonably well. His own opportunity, he felt, was to deal fairly with the subsequent period. In
Ann. 4. 32, while apologizing for the monotony of his account
of case after case in the senate, he compares his material with
that of the writers of the Republic whom he envies. They had
great wars to write about, cities overthrown, and kings conquered and captured. Or, if their stories turned to civil affairs,
they found important struggles between consuls and tribunes,
weighty laws promulgated, crucial contacts between the popular forces and the aristocrats, all vital to the life of Rome. Such
events allowed free scope to the narrator, while the material
of Tiberius' reign made his own efforts a labor "in arto et
inglorius." He could and did select for his first effort, however,
that part of the century which came nearest to giving him the

scope he desired: "Opus adgredior opimum casibus, atrox proeliis, discors seditionibus, ipsa etiam pace saevum." This is a grim outlook but one calculated to hold the attention of his audience.

This challenge to attention in the prologue to the *Histories* is part of an introduction which aligns Tacitus with the tradition of historiography. The opening words, "Initium mihi operis Servius Galba iterum Titus Vinius consules erunt," indicate the annalistic framework. The surviving books of the *Histories* cover only a year and a half, but the first of January A.D. 70 is marked by the statement (4. 38): "Interea Vespasianus iterum ac Titus consulatum absentes inierunt." In spite of the individual traits which develop in his method of narration, Tacitus maintains through all of his work this traditional annalistic framework. In the *Annals,* which cover many years, he also adopts the tradition of summarizing at the end of a year's record the events of minor importance, and occasionally the prodigies recorded for that year. In the *Histories* especially he gives brief biographies of important characters, most frequently at the time of their deaths, but also on other occasions. He constantly presents condensed characterizations of the figures in his narrative. The ethnogeographical digression familiar from Caesar and Sallust and Livy appears in the *Histories,* most notably in Tacitus' longest digression, the account of the Jews in Book 5. There are at least twelve other digressions of considerable extent, usually of historical or antiquarian interest. The résumé of the *status quo* in the opening chapters is, like the prologue, traditional. It does not summarize early history after the fashion of more complete histories of Rome, but it closely parallels the practice of Sallust in his shorter monographs. Throughout the *Histories,* speeches are included as if reproduced verbatim.

In all of this, in spite of his own pungent style and his own characteristic methods of presenting characters and events, Tacitus is the conventional historian. He accepts the traditions of historiography and writes within the traditional framework. He would compete with Fabius Rusticus and Sallust and Livy on their own ground. But there is also a vital difference which goes beyond the brilliancy of his trenchant prose. There are variations from the conventional type of history even in his *Histories,* variations which became more pronounced in his later works. In these variations lay the convincing power of Tacitus' picture. The trenchant style contributed mightily, but it was a contribution to the over-all result and not the fundamental element. In a word, it was the use of techniques borrowed from the drama which finally enabled Tacitus to present his historical narrative in the vivid and enthralling manner which carried conviction.

Such a theory will require the support of much evidence if it is itself to be convincing. But first it requires some definition. It does not mean merely that Tacitus has dramatic power as a writer. That phrase has been much overused and has little precise meaning. This can best be seen by considering for a moment other similar phrases which have been used in describing the work of Tacitus. Eduard Courbaud sought in a brilliant book to prove that Tacitus was in reality a painter and worked with the technique of the brush artist. But his theory, however plausible and appealing, in reality gained its ends largely by confusing the terms of one art with those of another. Word-picture, broad, sweeping lines of narrative, rich color, character sketching—all of these are impressionistic phrases, useful for the understanding of Tacitus' style, highly suggestive, and all of them well supported with evidence by Courbaud. It takes but a moment's thought, however, to realize that these are the qualities (in their figurative sense) of the great writers of tragedy and of epic, as well as of history. They represent the mastery of his tools by the expert, and in the literary field they are all used in a figurative sense. The same is true of the term "dramatic," as frequently applied to Tacitus as to many other writers in nondramatic fields. It usually means little more than vivid, striking, or "alive." It is also used to mean something exaggerated or melodramatic in content or tone. In the latter sense it is applied to Lucan's epic, in the former to the history of Thucydides, because of the use of direct speech and the final reversal of fortune in the catastrophe as well as the vivid character of his whole narrative as compared with the more discursive Herodotus.

The present use of the phrase "dramatic technique" has to do with something much more objective and precise. Greek classical tragedy was sufficiently conventional to make possible certain broad statements about it with less danger of dogmatic inaccuracy than is usually involved in such generalizations. It presented normally the downfall of a character of importance, neither complete hero nor consummate villain, under the compulsion of fate by means of human actions, in themselves free acts arising from the inherent character of the persons involved. It presented these characters by means of dialogue and action. Only by the reaction of one person on another or by the comments of other persons does there enter into tragedy any discussion or analysis of character. By virtue of its historical development, orthodox tragedy presented the career of the hero in successive scenes or acts which raised him to a position of prominence and then, by a reversal of fortune, reduced him to an object of pity. The process is not consecutive but the stages are represented by significant incidents separated by choral interludes. It is this general method of presenting a narrative, the dramatic technique, quite capable of transfer in its chief characteristics to other literary types without recourse to figurative usage, that seems to have exercised a growing influence over Tacitus in the writing of historical narrative and which largely differentiated him from other writers of history and gave to his pages their power to convince posterity.

It should not be surprising to find in Tacitus a tendency to use the dramatic method. Tragedy was one of the favorite presentations at the social recitations of the day and many of Tacitus' friends were among the writers of drama. The fact should not be overlooked that in the setting of the *Dialogus*, his earliest production, Tacitus presented his hero Maternus on the day after he had recited his tragedy, *Cato*. Some offense was supposed to have been given by the reading of this play, and Maternus' friends go so far as to suggest that he might revise it for safety's sake. Maternus had no such purpose: indeed he asserted that the *Thyestes* which he was already composing would continue the same subject in the same vein. Both of these tragedies would deal with the tyrant. Seneca had already written a *Thyestes* with a ringing chorus on the contrast between king and tyrant. The theme was as familiar as it was dangerous. The conversation in the *Dialogus* turns on the conflict between the active life and public speech of the orator and the private activities of the poet. But it should not be forgotten that the poet immediately concerned is a tragic poet and that no matter how far afield the discussion goes it is dramatic poetry which is under consideration. Even Saleius Bassus, of whom Maternus speaks kindly and whom Quintilian rates as a minor epic poet, may well have written tragedy. Martial addresses an epigram (5. 53) to a Bassus, speaking harshly of his *Medea* and *Thyestes,* and since he is adapting an epigram of Leonidas it is quite possible that he is speaking not of a contemporary but of Saleius Bassus. Maternus cites also Pomponius Secundus, to whom Tacitus refers in *Ann.* 12. 28 as especially eminent, *gloria carminum,* the *carmina* being tragedies, according to Quintilian (10. 1. 98). The point should not be overstressed; Vergil is cited also. But the fact cannot be ignored that Tacitus in his earliest work shows himself most sympathetic with the writer of the *Cato* and *Thyestes.* His poetic coloring has always been stressed, his predilection for the tragedy has been perhaps too little considered. Tragedies seem clearly to have been one of the most prominent types presented in the *recitationes,* which were well established before the time of Persius and which burdened the life of Pliny in Tacitus' day. Even without the evidence of Martial and Juvenal we could be sure of the prevalence of tragedy in the literary production of the first century, if only from the number of titles surviving. The effect of this dramatic influence appears in Tacitus' method of character drawing, in his attitude toward Fate, and even in his selective use of digressions. For the moment it is cited only to indicate that the tendency toward a dramatic presentation of the struggle between Liberty and Tyranny is not wholly surprising.

It would seem that the tendency to follow dramatic technique, while not unnatural to Tacitus, grew as he developed his mastery of the writing of history. It is less evident in the earlier work than in the later; it reaches its climax with the Age of Nero. But even in the *Histories* there are indications of the tendency. The prologue is in two parts. The first is of the conventional type drawn by earlier historians from oratorical usage. The author speaks in his own person, citing his subject, his own qualifications and the shortcomings of those who have previously covered the field, promising freedom from flattery and venom, vouching for his own adherence to the truth, and stressing the inherent interest of his subject. The first part of the prologue has one striking variation from those of Livy and Sallust: it lacks the moralizing tone. The author is concerned with the political change in the Roman picture rather than with the degenerating influences which had changed the citizens. The second part of the prologue is the résumé of the *status quo*. In Livy and the annalists what corresponded with this part was the early history comprised within the narrative proper. Tacitus follows more nearly the model of Sallust, and he introduces some of his chief characters in advance of his narrative, marking the end of the prologue by a repetition of the names of the consuls. This is perhaps important only as it foreshadows the change by which, in the *Annals,* the character presentation becomes an integral part of the rhetorical prologue.

There is also a tendency in the *Histories* to build up the characters dramatically, presenting them in significant situations and actions and interpreting them through their speeches. These are only tendencies, but they become significant in the sequel. Finally, because of the situation in which events were developing simultaneously in Germany, Syria, and Rome, Tacitus is almost compelled to adopt a method of procedure which tends toward the dramatic. He develops one situation and then another up to a critical point where they meet in a

significant struggle. All in all, the *Histories* would seem to
be Tacitus' successful attempt to write history within the
traditional framework and without wide divergence from
the traditional methods.

When he turned to the *Annals* and the story of Tiberius, his
problem was different. There were no longer thrilling campaigns and violent rivalries to recount. He faced a period in
which there were no glorious frontier wars, no conquests, no
genuine triumphs. There were no great civil struggles, for the
day of political freedom was gone. It was a drab era of tyranny
(such it appeared at any rate to Tacitus), in which all that
was left for the Roman of the old aristocracy was endurance
and a smothered resentment. But in this smothered resentment
Tacitus found the solution for his. problem of how to vitalize
the story of such an era. Devoted himself to the lost cause of
the Republic and burning with a passionate hatred of those
who had mishandled the centralized government of the Empire, he conceived of his history of the years from Augustus
to the Revolution as the tragic struggle between Liberty and
Tyranny. From this point of view he considered his facts and
his characters. He modified his prologue in the *Annals* to fit
this point of view and made it dramatic as well as rhetorical.
He developed dramatic tension and let his characters emerge
more and more in action. They became more natural because
less static. The thumbnail sketches of the *Histories* are brilliant, but the characters of the *Annals* are no less vital and,
on the whole, they are more enduring.

It was in writing of the reign of Tiberius that Tacitus began
to diverge from traditional Roman history writing. He was
forced by the lack of strong characters with which to confront
the emperor to personalize to a large extent the cause of
liberty. In so doing he represented (on the whole fairly) such
opposition as there was. Stoicism had long since made familiar
the contrast between the ideal king and the tyrant. Stoicism
was only sentimentally republican, with its nostalgic worship of
the old heroes of the opposition, Brutus and Cassius and Cato.
By its doctrine it supported the king by divine right, that ideal

monarch, the wise and perfect man. This position was wholly consistent with Tacitus' own beliefs, for it is hardly conceivable that he really expected or desired a return to the republican form of government in spite of his eulogies of the past and bitter denunciation of imperial tyranny. His emotions, however, and his reason were often in conflict and so led inevitably to minor inconsistencies. His genius of expression, his unequaled ability to depict vividly both character and situation, served to emphasize these inconsistencies. And his dramatic power was no small part of his genius.

When he passed to the Age of Nero, fortune gave Tacitus far better dramatic material than had been provided by the earlier period. It is in these later books that the technique of the dramatist emerges clearly. To substantiate such a theory— namely, that from a more conventional historical presentation in the *Histories* Tacitus moved on toward a definitely dramatic technique in the later *Annals*—it will be necessary to analyze more in detail and at some length the methods of the historian, to discover if possible the elements that give these books the true atmosphere of tragic drama. The present thesis is consistent with the general agreement between Tacitus scholars that the "peculiarities" of his style are less prominent in the later half of the *Annals*. This is true not in regard to many verbal and syntactical mannerisms but insofar as some of the larger elements of style are concerned. Their place is taken by the dramatic devices.

The natural point at which to begin is the prologue, and a survey of the practice of historians, both Greek and Latin, does as a matter of fact bring out at least one important dramatic element present in the work of Tacitus but absent from that of his predecessors.

"All historians," announces Polybius in the preface of his *History*, "All historians, one may say, have insistently urged that the study of history is the soundest education and training for the political life." For this reason, he states, he will not himself urge the value of history as a corrective of political conduct, assuming that such value will be generally granted.

There is no chance adequately to check this statement of Polybius, for more of the Greek historians have been lost than survive. That the educational value was actually urged by some we can infer from the usage of such historians of Rome as Livy and Diodorus Siculus and from such later Greek writers as Procopius. But from the great predecessors of Polybius we do not get confirmation of his sweeping assertion. Perhaps it was Ephorus or Theopompus that he had in mind rather than Herodotus or Thucydides or Xenophon. Xenophon, of course, resolutely presents his *Hellenica* as a continuation of Thucydides and has therefore no place for a formal prologue. The other two have characteristic prefaces.

"This is the history of Herodotus of Halicarnassus." Such is the plain statement of the father of Greek history, to which he adds five lines covering his aim in writing: to see to it that great deeds of both Greeks and barbarians should not be lost to fame, and in particular how these two divisions of mankind came into mortal conflict. Thucydides is not so concise in spite of a similar opening sentence: "Thucydides, an Athenian, wrote the war between the Peloponnesians and the Athenians." These statements of name and subject matter are in reality no more than titles. Procopius copied the method closely; Josephus introduces his name less abruptly but brings it into the prologue. No Roman, I think, followed this tradition.

Thucydides did not, however, confine his prefatory words to a personal introduction of himself; he expanded at some length on the fact that he was to chronicle a war which was the greatest of all wars. After following this point far afield, he returns to add a last point; facts will be reported by him with meticulous accuracy; if he is less precise in reporting speeches, nevertheless he will always give the essential truth.

The type of prologue familiar from Herodotus and Thucydides seems to have been foreshadowed at least by writers that have been denied the honorable name of historian. The evidence is scanty, but from Demetrius, *De elocutione* 12, we gather the opening sentence of the *Genealogies* of sixth-century

Hecataeus: Ἑκαταῖος Μιλήσιος ὧδε μυθεῖται· τάδε γράφω, ὥς μοι ἀληθέα δοκέει εἶναι· οἱγὰρ Ἑλλήνων λόγοι πολλοί τε καὶ γελοῖοι, ὡς ἐμοὶ φαίνονται, εἰσίν. There is no mention preserved of any claim to special interest, but the name of the writer is given and the pledge of strict veracity, with a certain disparagement of what has gone before.

Polybius himself, after the somewhat disingenuous statement of what he will not mention, proceeds to show how very interesting his field is, the most important, in fact, that could be found. After a paragraph establishing his chronology, he states that Books 1 and 2 will give a summary of previous events. Polybius does not in the preface argue his own special competence and historical accuracy, although he does do so later more than once in the body of the book.

Josephus believes that *his* period is the greatest and gives his reasons. He then states that previous writers have been either too biased or too timid. He has been a personal observer of the facts and can and will give an accurate account. He outlines his subject (as did Herodotus also) and then announces a "brief" summary of previous history which in reality goes well into Book 2.

There would seem to be six things which are likely to appear in the preface of a Greek historian: the exposition of the utility of history in general; insistence on the unique importance of the subject matter of the particular history in hand; submission of the qualifications of the writer with assurances of his conscientious accuracy and freedom from bias; a résumé of the factual antecedents; a definition of the field to be covered; and perhaps the name of the writer. Of these various points, some are definitely connected with the particular piece of writing in hand and in a way part of the history rather than of the prologue. Such are the summary of what has gone before and the definition of the field. In part this is true of the glorification of the field to be covered, but such glorification cannot but recall the rhetorical instruction of the text books which bids the orator win the attention of his hearers by showing them that his case has something extraordinarily *important* about it or else something entirely *new*.[1] It seems pretty clear that the topic of subject interest and that of the practical value of history, as well as the assurance of perfect honesty, are all aimed at winning the interest and confidence of the reader. The point of personal qualification is often stretched to include the presentation of difficulties over which the writer has triumphed. So Diodorus Siculus emphasizes the thirty years of hard work that he has spent in preparation, and A. Postumius Albinus asks indulgence because of the difficulty of using an alien tongue.[2] This emphasis the rhetoricians urged as one means of making the audience benevolent. Possibly the vituperation of the other side in an oration has its counterpart in the insistence of many a historian on the inefficient or insincere work of those who had covered the ground before.

In this respect the preface to the Roman Archaeology of Dionysius of Halicarnassus is of interest. He begins with the assurance that while Anaximenes and Theopompus disparaged other historians in their prologues, he desires to avoid that practice as well as all the familiar things that other historians say: he is not going to boast of his own ability or disparage that of others. He must, however, say a few words about his choice of subject and his motive in writing. Whereupon he proceeds to prove that this is *the greatest* field of history and that furthermore it is *new* to the Greeks, for not much has been written for them and pretty nearly all that has been is inaccurate. He himself will write solely the truth. He has lived twenty-two years in Rome and knows all the facts. After defining his point of departure he winds up with the archaistic formula: ὁ δὲ συντάξας αὐτὴν Διονύσιός εἰμι Ἀλεξάνδρου Ἁλικαρνασεύς.

Livy is familiar with the claims made by historians. Usually, he says, they maintain that they are going to produce more authentic facts or else that they are going to embellish the old with better style. Very modestly he implies that it will be his effort to meet these demands, but he wins favor by stressing the

1. Cf. *Auct. ad heren.* 1. 4.
2. Aulus Gellius, 11. 8. 2.

difficulty of his task, deftly suggesting its importance. He shows that he is free from bias. He points out the value of history as a guide and injects at this point an idea which we have not met heretofore, the moral value of the study of history, the presentation of the effects of luxury, wealth, and all the fruits of prosperous empire. The phrases of popular philosophy appear, and there is a tone of moralizing, not oppressive but obvious.

This suggestion of a moral purpose, the possible improvement of the character of the individual, is not, I should say, primarily Greek. There is a suggestion of it, to be sure, in Diodorus Siculus, and what appears in Diodorus is apt to come fairly intact from his sources. But his prologue is his most original effort, and the emphasis in it seems to be on public virtues rather than on private. Stoicism he inherited and Stoic doctrines are prominent in his long history.[3] The Stoic moral, applied to private behavior, is not however in evidence. Furthermore, Diodorus was clearly familiar with Roman historians to whom the moralizing tone was congenial.

This tone appears first, so far as the *extant* historians are concerned, in the monographs of Sallust. There it is laid on with a heavier hand than Livy's and less artistically. Sallust, in fact, coming deliberately to the writing of history after a somewhat melodramatic and active life, is a decidedly self-conscious practitioner of the art of rhetoric. The prologue to his *Histories* is lost, but at the beginning of each of the well known essays he writes first a general rhetorical introduction entirely detachable from the particular production to which it is the preface, and, second, a specific introduction dealing with the subject matter to be treated. The *Catiline* opens with a eulogy of intellectual achievement as contrasted with physical, a condemnation of sloth, an encomium of public service by deeds or with the pen, an apology for his own life and the assertion of his freedom from ambition which will allow him to write the truth, free from hope, fear, or partisanship. Then follows a paragraph stating the importance of his subject because of its novelty, and a picture of Catiline's past and his character pre-

3. Cf. Busolt, in *Jahrbuch für Philosophie* (1889), 297 ff.

liminary to the narrative. Similarly the *Jugurtha* has an introduction discussing the contrast between mind and body and
granting the palm to intellectual pursuits over political, presenting an apology for his own retirement and an attack on the
degeneracy of the day. This is followed by the statement of his
subject, important because the war against Jugurtha was long,
bloody, and varied, and because it represented the first resistance to the nobility. It winds up with a summary of antecedent
facts.

The most striking points in Sallust's prologues are the philosophizing tone and the frequent use of the terms of Stoic
satire accompanying his attacks on the morals of the day. The
latter may be merely the Roman exaggeration of the argument
of the corrective value of history, but it is different from the
classical Greek practice in that it stresses the moral side and
is truly Roman in the chief point of attack, the malevolent
influence of wealth. But Sallust expressly places this argument
in its proper category when he says: *In primis magno usui
memoria rerum gestarum* (*Jug.* 4. 1). The detachable prologues are clearly defined also. In the *Catiline* there is something of a transition, for Sallust passes from the account of his
determination to write history to the history itself, but the body
of the essay proper begins: "Igitur de Catilinae coniuratione,"
about which there has been as yet no word. In the *Jugurtha* the
general introduction ends baldly: "Nunc ad inceptum redeo;
bellum scripturus sum." This suggests inevitably the first rhetorical prooemium that we have in Latin, the opening of Cato's *De
agricultura*. After a brave but not brilliant attempt to use the
rhetoric which he despised, Cato winds up: "Nunc ut ad rem
redeam."

There is little enough material for comparison when we try
to decide in a particular instance whether or not we are dealing
with typical Roman prologues to histories. Caesar definitely
avoided anything that would detract from the impression that
his histories were in fact *commentarii*. The opening chapters
of Velleius Paterculus, of Curtius Rufus, and of Ammianus are
lost. From a fragment of C. Fannius it looks as though he had

had recourse to a philosophizing vein, and L. Coelius Antipater is said by Cicero to have defended his own sincerity, at
least to the point of promising not to exaggerate except when
necessary. Sempronius Asellio may have considered his explanation of the difference between annals and history as a means
of showing that his work was great and new. But these fragmentary bits of evidence do not go far. We are forced to assume with some diffidence that the Greek model was before the
Roman historians when they composed their prologue but that
they transferred the name of the writer to the title and added
the moralizing and philosophic tone. This is entirely in keeping
with what we should expect.

Now, when we come to compare the prologues of Tacitus
with the tradition as we have reconstructed it, we must first of
all eliminate the minor works. The *Dialogus* and the *Germania*
are wholly outside the category of history, and while the *Agricola* has history included within it and begins with a very clearly
defined prologue, still it is orthodox eulogistic biography, and
of such are the introductory chapters.

The *Histories* begin with a statement refreshingly direct for
a Roman historian: "Initium mihi operis Servius Galba iterum, Titus Vinius consules erunt." This is followed by an
explanation: the period of the Empire has not been covered
impartially; fear and favor have been always in evidence; from
these the writer is free, and can and will give the truth. In the
next chapter, Tacitus expands on the striking interest which
the period holds and makes this evident by a summary. Violent
as the period was, it was not, he insists, *sterile virtutum:* it produced *bona exempla.* Finally he gives a summary of the state of
the Empire at the date which he has chosen for opening his history. This summary, however, is unlike those which we have
hitherto met in our survey of prologues. It is not a summary
of past history, the relic of the days when history to be history
had to begin with Aeneas or before. It is a picture of the *status
quo* at the moment, and it discusses characters who are to figure in the history proper. There is, then, an insistence on the
striking quality if not the importance of the subject matter, the

submission of credentials in proper form, a statement of the
ground to be covered, and a résumé (of a sort) of the factual
antecedents. The value of history is only hinted at in the suggestion of examples to be found in the period, and—true to
Roman custom—the author's name is not given. In terminology there is just a touch of the moral tone of Livy and Sallust. In addition there is a Tacitean element, the introduction
of characters, which will be more understandable if we exam-
ine the prologue to the *Annals,* which represent the Tacitean
style in its most advanced form.

   In the later work the opening is as abrupt as it was in the
Histories, but it bursts into a rapid summary of earlier history,
leaving the statement of specific subject to the end of the first
chapter. Into the chapter in the meantime are slipped the disparagement of other writers who covered the period and the
assurance of the present writer's freedom from fear or favor.
With the second chapter begins a summary of the immediate
background, the days of Augustus, which occupies four chapters, all the rest of the prologue, and effectively introduces
the chief characters of the history itself in its opening phase. In
the place of the old moral virtues and vices we find only political ones, and the great degeneracy is no longer in the character of the Roman people but in that of the government.
Libertas, vetus populus, priscus et integer mos, res publica are
contrasted with the new *servitium* and *principatus.* But chiefly
these chapters introduce with telling strokes not merely the
all-embracing struggle between old and new but Tiberius himself with the *insita Claudiae familiae superbia,* the *indicia
saevitiae,* and his *simulatio* and *secretae libidines;* Livia,
branded with the undenied rumor that she assisted the death of
Augustus as well as that of the princes, Lucius and Gaius;
Agrippa Postumus, destined to play but one short scene in the
great drama; and finally Germanicus, the son of Drusus, second in importance to Tiberius alone. Each is presented in a
clear-cut picture, partly by vivid characterization, partly by
the implication of facts recounted. And finally, more noticeable
than all beside, there is created the atmosphere of tragedy

surely and effectively, a thing hitherto unknown even to such tragic histories as that of Thucydides. For everything is spread on a background of suggested intrigue; tyranny is already supplanting liberty in spite of the specious cry of Roman peace. There is not an actually misleading statement in these chapters, but by suggestion, by grouping, by emphasis—in other words dramatically—the audience is prepared to witness the tragic struggle as Tacitus conceived it, and each fact in the exposition has the color which the writer would give it in order that it might play its part in the drama.

The prologue of the *Annals* combines the rhetorical introduction intended to win the interest and sympathy of the reader (and, in this connection, Tacitus' vocation of lawyer should be remembered) with the specific introduction proper to history and with the *prologos* of a tragedy. For here I think is to be found the explanation of the Tacitean variation from tradition. A good dramatic *prologos* established the atmosphere of the tragedy,[4] it gave the setting of the story with necessary antecedent facts, and it introduced at least some of the leading characters, making them as vital as possible within a limited space. This is exactly what Tacitus does, and it suggests a line of approach to his peculiar technique of history writing.

It would be foolish to think of the *Annals* of Tacitus as constructed in the form of a drama and to try to analyze it into acts and interludes. It is, however, a very different thing to look for the technique of the dramatist, which is so clearly suggested in this adaptation of the prologue. Courbaud, with his theory of Tacitus the painter,[5] notes the combination of stock rhetorical prologue and the historical summary. He does not note the additional element. And he weakens his chapter by trying to show a detailed resemblance to the prologue of Lucan. Here his presentation is not quite straightforward, for he uses evidence wholly outside the prologues and his nearest approach to con-

4. Roman tragedy, as we know it from Seneca, concentrated in the prologue on this atmosphere until it became something quite distinct from the Greek prologue.

5. Edmund Courbaud, *Les Procédés d'art de Tacite dans les "Histoires,"* Paris, 1918.

crete evidence, the fact that Lucan in 1. 72 uses the phrase *compage soluta* while Tacitus in *Hist.* 4. 74 uses the phrase *fortuna disciplinaque compages haec coaluit, quae convelli sine exitio convellentium non potest,* is far from convincing even when he presents it rather unfairly as the same phrase, *compage soluta, convulsa.* For Manilius, Seneca, Statius, and Silius had all used the figure as well as Lucan, and Courbaud by his method throughout indicates clearly that he is not distinguishing sharply between verbal echoes and true imitation of type.

Courbaud used the *Histories* for the development of his "artist" theory because, as he believes, they marked the height of Tacitus' literary power. Such a point is a matter of personal feeling and cannot be determined. One thing, however, will probably be generally admitted—for good or bad, the *Annals* show the ultimate development of the Tacitean historical style and type. Now the *Agricola,* of course, has a prologue different from those of the large historical works. It is wholly of the rhetorical type, tense, highly charged with emotion, highly personal. Except for the last sentence, of a transitional character, it is detachable. Obviously it has nothing in common with the tragic prologue except as the element of tone is normally common to the two types. In the prologue to the *Histories* are found the conventional elements plus the introduction of characters that are to continue beyond the prologue. But among the conventional elements the personal note is still present, a note antagonistic to a dramatic presentation. In the *Annals* the change has gone a step further and the personal, first-person address is gone. In other words, the narrative has jettisoned one large element which was undramatic. This, in ancient history writing, is I believe unique. Herodotus, in his six-line prologue, assumed the third person but did not thereby avoid the undramatic quality of the detached prologue. It is this same change evidently which led Tacitus to vary the form of his prologue in the *Annals,* making it on the surface wholly action; only by implication introducing the elements of the rhetorical prologue; disclosing his own point of view by indirection; and finally making it even more inseparable from the rest of the work than had been the prologue of the *Histories*.

When we pass from the prologue to the narrative proper it must be remembered that Tacitus never abandoned the traditional annalistic framework handed down by his Roman predecessors. Year by year the consuls are announced and events are regularly recounted. Furthermore, the method is emphasized by such phrases as *eodem anno, iisdem consulibus, fine anni*. Most frequently these appear at the end of a given year to introduce scattered miscellaneous events of minor significance or lists of the men of importance who died during the year or (in the later books of the *Annals*) lists of prodigies and portents. Tacitus retained the annalistic framework, but within it he made changes and from it he made significant variations.

In the first place it is to be noted that there is comparative unity given to the account of each year either by the omission of minor irrelevant events or by the gathering of them together into the end-of-the-year summaries, where they do not distract attention from the central narrative but serve rather as an intermission or pause, tending to divide the main theme into significant chapters or acts. This tendency becomes evident in the instances in which Tacitus breaks his own rule and abandons the exact chronological method. The first time that he does this (*Ann.* 6. 38) he calls attention to what he is doing and gives as his reason a desire to relieve the monotony of the domestic misfortunes which he is forced to narrate. This is no doubt a large element in his purpose, but it must also be remembered that this very accumulation of cases under the *lex maiestatis* is one of his best devices for strengthening his indictment of Tiberius. He is willing to have them boring if he can create a cumulative impression of tyrannical pressure. If this were not the case he might well have retained the year-by-year method and thus had two breaks to furnish relief rather than one. As a matter of fact the cases of treason as presented by Tacitus are, as we shall see, presented in such a way as to make an increasingly strong impression. In the year 34, the account of which is concluded in chapter 30, there has been a sharp increase in the number of trials, convictions, and suicides recorded by Tacitus, and the account ends with Lentulus' successful defiance of Tiberius when charged with friendship for Sejanus. Seven chapters on eastern affairs furnish suspense before the rapid account in 38–51 of the culmination of the orgy of trials and the downfall of Tiberius.

In the books in which the life and reign of Nero are developed this practice becomes so frequent as to suggest the choral interludes in a tragedy dividing the action into significant episodes. In 11. 8, no longer specifically admitting the fact, Tacitus telescopes five years of the eastern history. The dramatic break comes at the culmination of Messalina's machinations with Suillius as her henchman. The digression on the east creates suspense which emphasizes the significance of the first incident in the Nero-Britannicus rivalry which immediately follows. After the death of Messalina and the marriage of Agrippina and Claudius comes the second significant event in Nero's youth, his betrothal to Octavia (12. 9). This is immediately followed by a digression on Parthian affairs. Between this and the next interlude (this time on German and British affairs) the significant incident is the adoption of Nero by Claudius. In chapter 40, at the end of his account of affairs in Britain, Tacitus says: *ad temporum ordinem redeo* and begins the record of the next year with the premature granting to Nero of the *toga virilis,* a further blow to Britannicus, and Agrippina's arrogant ascent of the capitol in the vehicle reserved for priests. A list of evil prodigies follows, and after the suspense of another eastern digression, the climax of this act is reached in the murder of Claudius and the succession of Nero. From this point on, the interludes of foreign war mark off the stages of Nero's reign: the conservative start under Seneca; the murder of Britannicus and the increased struggle between Seneca and Agrippina; the murder of Agrippina; rising opposition, with the fall of Seneca and death of Octavia; the Pisonian conspiracy.

Evidently it is chiefly in the reign of Nero that the chronological framework gives way in some degree. Small as this variation is, it is significant, for this very practice of putting in the interludes of foreign affairs at any point desired rather than forcing them into the chronological framework is what makes possible a secondary principle of arrangement. The position of the breaks is almost always significant.

In Livy among the things usually listed at the close of a year where the omens that had been reported during the year. There are three specific instances of omens in the *Histories* (1. 86, 2. 78, and 3. 56) but only one list which comes, like those in Livy, at the end of the year. It comes also, however, at a most critical turning point in Otho's career. Aside from this list there is none similar until we approach the story of Nero. A great number of prodigies are listed for A.D. 51, not at its close but nevertheless with the words *eo anno*. And during the account of Nero's reign, prodigies are listed four times and specific omens four other times (12. 43, 64; 14. 12, 22, 32; 15. 7, 47; 16. 13). This use of omens in the history of Nero must be considered more in detail.

The first list of omens in the *Annals* is in 12. 43, in the year 51 and in the reign of Claudius. It has the traditional introduction *eo anno*, but it does not come in the traditional place at the end of the account of the year. Instead, it follows directly the chapter which recounts Agrippina's significant assumption of the offensive in her attempt at the supreme power (in other words one of the first steps in Nero's preferment): *nondum tamen summa moliri Agrippina audebat, ni* etc. Released from fear of the praetorians by the appointment of Burrus to their command, Agrippina rides up the Capitoline in a carriage and protects in court her champion Vitellius. The first act is almost blasphemy as Tacitus presents it, for the honor was reserved for priests and the sacred objects; the second was an act of political interference, a show of power. The next chapter begins: *multa eo anno prodigia eveniere*. Only a few omens are cited, but these are followed by an account of a severe food shortage. This shortage is looked on as an omen and rouses popular complaints against Claudius, leading Tacitus to comment on the economic weakness of the Empire.

At this point, with the reader's excitement aroused in anticipation of some threatened stroke of fate, human or divine, about to fall on Claudius, the scene shifts to the affairs in the east and a long interlude of suspense follows.

In this same story of Claudius and Agrippina, Tacitus uses again the same device of the foreshadowing omens. In chapter 64 at the beginning of the year comes a list of omens, and Tacitus practically states his reason for listing them: "M. Asinio M'. Acilio consulibus mutationem rerum in deterius portendi cognitum est crebris prodigiis." Again affairs not really in the realm of prodigies are taken as such, this time the number of natural deaths among officials. But for Agrippina the chief omen is a chance, drunken word of Claudius which inspires her to hasten his death, the story of which fills the rest of the book.

Book 13, which covers the *quinquennium Neronis,* contains no omens until we come to the last chapter. This last sentence comes between a digression on Germany, ending with the great and disastrous peat fire among the Ubii, and the murder of Agrippina by Nero: "Eodem anno Ruminalem arborem in comitio, quae octingentos et triginta ante annos Remi Romulique infantiam texerat, mortuis ramalibus et arescente trunco deminutam prodigii loco habitum est, donec in novos fetus revivisceret." It should be noted that the next sentence (14. 1. 1) is "Gaio Vipstanto C. Fonteio consulibus diu meditatum scelus non ultra Nero distulit."

It can hardly be questioned that Tacitus has placed these two lists of omens where they are for dramatic reasons. The murder of Agrippina is followed by the insincere flatteries of the senate, accompanied by Paetus Thrasea's withdrawal from the chamber. The next sentence is: *prodigia quoque crebra et inrita intercessere,* with a list of the omens followed by the comment: "quae adeo sine cura deum eveniebant ut multos post annos Nero imperium et scelera continuaverit." The dramatist and the ironic skeptic at odds with each other.

At 14. 22, 14. 32, and 15. 7 special omens with special indications are instanced: the comet which, reinforced by a stroke of lightning, brought about the exile of Rubellius Plautus; the unmotivated crash of the statue of Victory at Camelodunum, presaging the great British revolt; the inexplicable burning of a soldier's pike, ignored to his sorrow by Paetus. Much the same is the collapse of the theater at Naples in 15. 34, which Nero takes as a good omen and plunges into further excesses in which *ne inter voluptates quidem a sceleribus cessabatur.* The strange trembling which overtook Nero (15. 36) in the temple of Vesta and kept him for a time from visiting Greece is a dramatic device with a Greek flavor.

In 15. 47 occurs the only list of omens actually at the end of a year's account, these also with a broad hint as to their purpose: "fine anni vulgantur prodigia imminentium malorum nuntia." The next year begins (15. 48. 1): "Ineunt deinde consulatum Silius Nerva et Atticus Vestinus, coepta simul et aucta coniuratione" etc., introducing the story of the great conspiracy of Piso.

In the text as we have it there are only two other suggestions of omens. In 15. 74 Nero avoids the "bad luck" of a temple proposed in his honor, and attention is called to the equally "bad luck" of dedicating Scaevinus' dagger to Jupiter Vindex. Finally, the storms and pestilence in 16. 13 are used to foreshadow evil fortune; and 15. 22 should be noted, although the events cited are not spoken of as *prodigia.* They come, however, at the end of the year with the formula *isdem consulibus.* They comprise the destruction of the gymnasium by a stroke of lightning, with the melting down of Nero's statue and the earthquake which destroyed Pompeii. These follow directly after the speech of Thrasea in 62—which was looked on as perhaps the boldest affront to Nero—and precede the account of the birth and death of Poppaea's child.

It is clear that Tacitus presents prodigies not as a regular

part of each year's procedure and not in the traditional position at the end of the chronicle of each year. He uses them or
not, as their use appeals to him and the motive seems to be
the dramatic foreshadowing of events to come.

While this is not the place to consider Tacitus' philosophic or
religious beliefs, or his attitude toward fate in general, it is
relevant to take note of several instances in which *Fortuna*
serves as a dramatic personification interfering in human affairs. Book 4. 1 marks the beginning of the reversal in the for-
tunes of Tiberius. It opens: "C. Asinio C. Antistio consulibus
nonus Tiberio annus erat compositae rei publicae, florentis
domus . . . cum repente turbare fortuna coepit, saevire ipse
aut saevientibus vires praebere. Initium et causa penes Aelium
Seianum." Somewhat parallel is the opening of Book 16, after
the Pisonian conspiracy has been crushed and Nero has been
lured into a false confidence: "Inlusit dehinc Neroni fortuna
per vanitatem ipsius et promissa Caeselli Bassi." The reversal
is less dramatic in this case, just as the incident related is insignificant in comparison with the rise of Sejanus. But the technique is identical, Fortuna entering on the scene to destroy an
overconfident character through human agencies. The similarity and the difference of the opening passage of *Histories* 2 is
interesting: "Struebat iam fortuna in diversa parte terrarum
initia causasque imperio, quod varia sorte laetum rei publicae
aut atrox, ipsis principibus prosperum vel exitio fuit." The
introductory wording is like that used later in the *Annals*. But
fortune here is neutral. There is no dramatic reversal suggested; Fortuna has no kinship with Nemesis but plays the
same role as that of the fates. Another chapter discusses the
religious and philosophic background of Tacitus, but the literary use of the supernatural is what is of importance here. In
the earlier work the predestination of the stoic faith gives tone
to the narrative, but in the later books Fortuna becomes more
closely identified with the Nemesis of tragedy. The gods of
Tacitus are not the individual gods of the Roman calendar
but the grim and jealous gods of the Greek drama, and his at-

titude toward omens and prophecies is not far removed from that of Sophocles.

If, in reality, Tacitus was influenced by the dramatic method of presentation, the result would necessarily appear in his narration of incident and in the way in which he brought his characters into action in such narration. A writer like Livy was sometimes induced by a particular event to become dramatic in his treatment for the moment. It has even been thought, for example, that in telling of the death of Servius Tullius he may have had before him a tragedy dealing with that dramatic situation. But he was in general a narrator of events; only occasionally did the clash of personal character and motive become a stronger influence with him than the march of history. His theme was the glorious achievement of Rome, not a tragic subject. Tacitus' theme, on the other hand, was a conflict. It was a conflict between individuals, not primarily the meeting of the Roman state with foreign enemies. Such foreign wars as he had to recount, if he could not relate them to the more personal struggle, he relegated to the rôle of interlude. Consciously and inevitably the real story of his histories was the series of personal tragedies involved in the great drama of the struggle between liberty and tyranny. His material as well as his predilection was inclined toward tragic drama. The reign of Tiberius furnished somewhat less of the dramatic element than that of Nero, but the treatment is much the same. It will be best to treat the two sections separately. The reigns of Gaius and Claudius must have been midway between the two in point of dramatic interest, but they are largely lost.

In order to avoid repetition, the dramatic procedure in the books that recount the reign of Nero will be considered by means of a study of Tacitus' methods of character drawing in the next chapter. It will then be clear that the technique is the same as that here presented for the age of Tiberius, except that it is more obvious. This obviousness is due in part to the more dramatic character of the struggle over Nero and the more vivid personalities engaged in that struggle. But also the dra-

matic skill of the writer has developed, and there seems to be a
more conscious intent on his part to give to his history the
character of the drama.

"Primum facinus novi principatus fuit Postumi Agrippae
caedes." The *Annals* proper begin with action and with action colored to produce the dramatic effect desired by Tacitus.
Facinus once meant any act, good or bad, but always the tendency was toward the more sinister meaning and it is hard to
find an instance after the Augustan Age in which it is used for
an unequivocally good act. There is perhaps a technical ambigu-
ity which no doubt determined in part at least the choice of
word, but the connotation is clear beyond the vestige of a
doubt. *Principatus* brings to the fore the contrast between the
old order and the new suggested in the prologue, and is con-
fronted with *consules, patres, eques* at the opening of the following chapter. This is the struggle which is to give the govern-
ing tone to the whole work. It is not that a great dramatist or a
great historian must have a thesis into relation with which he
brings each detail of his work. But the great creative artist does
usually have a very potent directing philosophy. What foreor-
dained fate had been to Sophocles—that, to the embittered
Tacitus, was the grim political fate of the Roman empire. It is
on the basis of this guiding theme that Tacitus largely makes
his selection of incidents to relate. For obviously no historian
can make use of all available incidents: on his selection depends in large part the significance of his work.

Tacitus selects for the swift opening act the death of the
banished prince Agrippa. From the account of Suetonius it is
clear that Augustus had been convinced that Agrippa's mind
was hopelessly deficient. Tacitus' account aside, we should find
it hard to believe that there was any great importance in this
intractable mad man. But he was introduced into the prologue
and the disposal of him serves as an ominous opening for Tiberius' reign. Tacitus is able by means of it to suggest the arbitrary power of the principate supported by the suggestions

of the diplomatic Crispus. And Agrippa does more than this; the helpless prince in exile is brought into contrast with the efficient Germanicus, another possible rival; the slight Agrippa incident serves as a foil for the great Germanicus scenes to follow. Twice again in the *Annals* Agrippa is mentioned (2. 39, 40; 3. 30), each time in conjunction with Crispus to assure the identification of the motif. And the first time is at the end of the year in which Germanicus earns his triumph, the account of which follows closely; the second is at the end of the year which winds up the tragedy of Germanicus with the trial and death of Piso.

Another striking example of selection for dramatic purposes is to be found in the stories of a group of men who begin to appear almost immediately after the opening of the *Annals*. Tacitus dwells at considerable length, in view of his concise habit, on the situation in Rome. The forces of *principatus* and of *res publica vetus* are presented from this angle and that. It is sound dramatic technique; the time required can be made up later, but the exposition must not be hurried. The leading character is also being created in these chapters and the audience induced to see him and accept him as the character which Tacitus will have him to be for the purposes of his drama. Toward the end of this presentation, and partly as characterization of Tiberius, Asinius Gallus appears in what would seem to be a rather unimportant tilt with the emperor; then L. Arruntius incurs the Claudian anger, and a remark of Augustus is quoted grouping these men with Cn. Piso and M'. Lepidus. Tacitus adds: "Omnes praeter Lepidum variis mox criminibus struente Tiberio circumventi sunt." In the very next sentence Q. Haterius and Mamercus Scaurus are mentioned in such a way as to associate them with the group. Historically, none of these men is of first rate importance with the exception of Cn. Piso. And yet they appear again and again and Tacitus carries each one through to his death. Later on, Ateius Capito and L. Piso are added to the group. For "group" it certainly remains; not that they are all mentioned together at any one time, but when any one appears, one or another of the rest is sure to be active within a paragraph, and all appear more frequently than their prominence would seem to justify.

In 1. 8 two unimportant motions are recorded, one by Gallus, one by Arruntius. On any conceivable historical grounds these motions are too insignificant altogether to be mentioned. It is a device not uncommon in tragedy—one of the simpler ways of preparing for the entrance of a character by having someone already on the stage mention him. The entrance in this case is made in chapters 12 and 13, where Gallus and Arruntius appear at greater length in another minor clash with Tiberius, and with them enters the rest of the group as already indicated. These men are not as yet, however, in open conflict with the principate or with Tiberius, but serious friction is already present and the remarks of Augustus with regard to the possible relation of three of them to the throne indicates that opposition is to be their rôle. The word *ferociam* is used in connection with Gallus, and the suggestion is made that he is planning *plus quam civilia* (a phrase taken directly from Lucan, thought not noticed by Courbaud). No more is heard of the group until 1. 74 ff., when Gallus, Arruntius, and Piso appear and the word *libertas* assumes prominence. Piso's outburst is prefaced by the significant statement: "Manebant etiam tum vestigia morientis libertatis." This is the real keynote, which gives the unity of a single character to the group, and it is further defined in the scene that follows. This is in connection with Tiberius' decision to sit on the bench to ensure justice. Tacitus admits that justice was furthered, but cannot approve because it is an infringement of the old liberty: "Dum veritati consulitur, libertas corrumpebatur."

It is not worth while to trace the group through its whole career. Throughout the first six books these men of no great importance are constantly reappearing, always representing a quasirepublican opposition to Tiberius. *Libertas* is used in referring to all of the original group except Scaurus, who is the least important of them and included apparently because he died in a fashion "worthy of the ancient Aemilii." A few lines at least are given to the deaths of each, usually with some sort of expressed or implied approval. The only one that can be really treated in any large dramatic way is Cn. Piso. As a leading character in the Germanicus affair, Piso has a significance independent of that of the rest of the group. Nevertheless at the close of that dramatic episode the group is marshaled in such a way as to leave the impression that they and the *libertas* for which they stand have been involved. In spite of Tacitus' intense admiration for Germanicus, which is not wholly due to his value as a dramatic figure and which deceives the historian into actually commending Agrippina for assuming a masculine role, he must, notwithstanding, present him as he was: the representative of *principatus* rather than *libertas*. Personally, dramatically, Germanicus is in conflict with Tiberius; politically they are very different representatives of the same conception. The side of the angels is played here by the less appealing Piso. To such an extent is the group identified with his cause by the time of his death that less care is taken by Tacitus in the following sections to emphasize the association of the individuals.[6] They appear with extraordinary frequency, singly or in pairs, and three of them are brought together to make more noteworthy the death of L. Piso. And as the tragedy of Tiberius draws to a close, the group is once more gathered and made prominent in its downfall. The three most important members (apart from Cn. Piso) meet their ends in fairly rapid succession: Gallus, 6. 23; Lepidus, 6. 27; Arruntius, 6. 47 f. This last member to survive was one of the two who were first introduced; and his dramatic death, with its characterization of the reign that was about to close and its prophecy of the tyranny of Gaius, is not merely the death of Arruntius. It is the exit of the composite character—liberty has received a death blow and Tacitus commends its last representative for refusing to live: "Documento sequentia erunt bene Arruntium morte usum." And scarcely surviving the republican opposition that has dogged him since the day he made his inaugural address to the senate, Tiberius himself follows his antagonists in the three

6. See 3. 22 f., 31, 35, 50, 57, 66, 68, 70, 75.

paragraphs that are left. The catastrophe is swift, as it should be. How the aftermath was handled cannot be known, for the next books are lost. The events to come have been foreshadowed to a certain extent. Even the Greek drama left always in the reading mind a suggestion of the future, for life is continuous and never consists of disconnected dramas. But Tacitus has given to the drama of Tiberius an essential unity, and in part accomplished this by the device of this group that formed a composite character, that made its entrance with the hero and did not outlive him.

While Gallus and Haterius and the other exemplars of liberty serve to personify the dramatic struggle throughout the reign of Tiberius, there are two major characters who are protagonists of dramas within the larger one or, to be perhaps more accurate, successively the chief characters in the Tiberius drama. They represent two very different types, the one standing for the opposition which Tacitus approved, the other embodying all that the historian hated: Germanicus and Sejanus.

Germanicus was one of the characters introduced in the prologue, where two things were suggested in connection with him: first, Augustus' favorable estimate and support; second, the possibility of difficulties between him and Tiberius. The latter phase is immediately emphasized by Tiberius' fear of Germanicus (chapter 7). The German wars, as later the affairs in Syria and the East, are used almost exclusively by Tacitus to further the tragedy of Germanicus. The Pannonian fracas, with its weak handling on the part of young Drusus, serves to enhance the glory of Germanicus' success with the revolt of the German armies. This is made all the more evident by the somewhat lengthy characterization of Germanicus (31, 33) and his association with the old regime. In his refusal to march on Rome, as his enthusiastic troops desire, there is further characterization in action. We are given a rather melodramatic incident in the departure of Agrippina and her children from the Roman camp, the speech of Germanicus is played up, as well as the feeling in Rome, and the hero finishes the first great stage in his career with complete success but with Tiberius decidedly ill satisfied. The second stage is his triumphant campaign against the Germans with his now loyal troops and the further dissatisfaction of Tiberius, who finds in the growing eastern troubles a chance to curb the popularity and greatness of Germanicus. Here is the turning point in his career. That it was so intended by Tacitus is indicated by the way in which he works up to the triumphant success—the dream of Germanicus, the speeches of the two generals, the dreadful difficulties in the way of the Roman commander, his complete mastery in spite of these—and by the abruptness of the change brought about by his recall.

During this second stage it should be noted how dramatically Sejanus is introduced in chapter 69. He had made an inconspicuous entry during the Pannonian prelude (chapter 24), but now his significance is more definitely hinted at as he feeds Tiberius' suspicions against Agrippina, the wife of Germanicus: "Accendebat haec onerabatque Seianus, peritia morum Tiberii odia in longum iaciens, quae reconderet auctaque promeret." Immediately after this comes the introduction of the *lex maiestatis,* to be the great weapon of Sejanus and Tiberius.

For there is real continuity in that the larger drama is neither that of Germanicus nor that of Sejanus but the tragedy of Tiberius. Up to the definite entry of Sejanus all is prosperous with the emperor and, to make the turning point dramatically clear, Tacitus is altogether explicit. Fortuna, who surely has no place in an objective chronicle, appears in 4. 1 as the real cause of the impending catastrophe, with Sejanus as her tool. This turning point is worth some further study. Book 3 ends on an ominous note with the death of Junia. She does not figure otherwise in the story, and historically she seems to have had no real importance. But she is a niece of Cato, the wife of Cassius, and the sister of Brutus. She ignores Tiberius in her will, but he does not forbid a public funeral with its *laudatio:* "Sed praefulgebant Cassius atque Brutus, eo ipso, quod effigies eorum non visebantur." The fourth book then opens with

the equally ominous sentence: "C. Asinio C. Antistio consulibus nonus Tiberio annus erat compositae rei publicae, florentis
domus (nam Germanici mortem inter prospera ducebat), cum
repente turbare fortuna coepit, saevire ipse aut saevientibus
vires praebere. Initium et causa penes Aelium Sejanum." There
follows a sketch of Sejanus' origin, indicating the importance
of his entry.

The Germanicus tragedy fulfills its next stage in the East.
Piso becomes the great character in opposition and is characterized at length with more than a suggestion that he was the
chosen tool of the emperor. There is much dramatic suspense
as the slow progress of Germanicus toward his post is contrasted with the activity of Drusus, and while the affairs in
Thrace are disposed of. Then once more the catastrophe comes
swiftly. The death of Germanicus is followed by the trial and
death of Piso the tool. Agrippina, left to represent the line of
Germanicus, remains to establish continuity between this and
the following drama of Sejanus.

With the Sejanus stage of the drama Tacitus has his most
congenial subject. He links the progress of oppressive legislation with the career of the Tuscan knight, till it too becomes
almost a *dramatis persona*. Much of the story of Sejanus is lost,
but it was most carefully prepared. His appearances up to the
moment when he became the protagonist are each significant
of his growing prestige. At the opening of Book 4 his earlier
life and personality are sketched, and his characteristic opposition to Drusus. In the midst of the tragic story of his circum-
vention of Drusus, the narrative pauses to review the state of
the Empire. Nothing could more effectively indicate the importance of this turning point in the career of Tiberius, whose
fatally evil genius is just coming to the fore. At one point as
the drama proceeds, Tacitus seems to feel the difficulty of the
material and apologizes for the dullness of case after case of
treason, warning his readers of the ultimate importance of
much that seems slight and uninteresting and showing his own
clear perception that he is not writing ordinary history. The
drama is reaching its climax when the manuscript fails at the

beginning of Book 5, not only leaving incomplete the Sejanus act but also damaging the larger tragedy, which winds up in Book 6 with the death of Tiberius. The familiar summary of Tiberius' life at the end of the sixth book confirms the general divisions which have been here assumed in the dramatic presentation. The first act would be amplified if Tacitus had written a history of Augustus. As it is, there are only the few swift touches in the prologue to Book 1 to cover the period which Tacitus calls his private life under Augustus and which he characterizes as *egregius;* then comes the period *occultum ac subdolum,* while Germanicus survived; third, a period of mixed good and bad till Livia's death; a stage during which vices were rampant but lusts restrained, so long as he loved and feared Sejanus; and finally the last days of utter degeneration under his own evil genius. The Tacitean theory of suppressed villainy is not one-half so effective as the Tacitean dramatic genius which makes these periods absolutely convincing entirely apart from the untenable hypothesis.

In this discussion of the Tiberius chapters it has been noted that the prosecutions for *lèse-majesté* almost form a composite character, like the group of reactionary oppositionists. A brief review of these prosecutions will make more obvious their dramatic character and value.

For, with some indication of a point of view which influenced Tacitus in organizing his material, it is now possible to consider how this point of view affected his narrative as a whole. It has or should have definite bearing on the inconsistencies noted by critics between some of the generalizations made by Tacitus and the facts as cited by him. A test instance is made by T. S. Jerome of these trials on charges under the *lex maiestatis*.[7] He finds, in all, 108 senatorial cases under Tiberius reported in Tacitus. Of these, fifty-eight were on charges of "revolutionary attempts, insubordination, slander of the prince and the like." Of these, twenty-two ended in condemnation, twenty-six in acquittal, ten in suicide before trial. If the pur-

7. *Aspects of the Study of Roman History* (New York and London, 1923), pp. 328 ff.

pose were simply to prove that under Tiberius there was no extreme misuse of the *lex maiestatis,* these figures would be at least impressive, but they have no bearing on whether Tacitus falsified or not, as Jerome believes they have. On the other hand they are most illuminating toward an understanding of the method of Tacitus. In the first place, these are all to him cases of importance, coming up as they do for trial before the senate itself. In the second place, Tacitus makes no claim whatever to report *all* cases. The necessity of selection makes more significant by far the cases shown as regards both their number and their characteristics.

The first mention of the matter is in the familiar 72d chapter of Book 1. Tiberius has just refused the title of *pater patriae.* "Non tamen," adds Tacitus, "ideo faciebat fidem civilis animi; nam legem maiestatis reduxerat." After noting that in the Republic this law had been applied only to treasonable acts and that Augustus had somewhat ambiguously approved of its invocation, the historian proceeds to recount a case which he himself admits was of slight importance except for its implications, that of two obscure *equites,* Falanius and Rubrius. Tacitus is surely not pretending to be a mere annalist, recording events. He states frankly that he wishes to show how this evil—the abuse of the *lex maiestatis*—crept in, retired, emerged all powerful, and did this as a result of the clever machinations of Tiberius. It is a part of the dramatic construction, for the law stands for the tyranny of empire, represented personally by Tiberius, in struggle with *Libertas* in the persons of M'. Lepidus and the rest of his group as well as in the composite character of the senate.

The case of the two knights is a new extension of the *lex maiestatis* so far as interpretation is concerned, because the charge is that of abusing the divinity of Augustus. In spite of the fact that the defendants are acquitted, the very existence of the charge is subtly dangerous and serves as the first step toward tragedy. Only one other case is reported for the year 15, that of Granius Marcellus (1. 74). This time the charge is one of speaking ill of the emperor, a further extension of the implications of the law. Again the defendant is acquitted with the consent of Tiberius. But dramatically, aside from the novelty of the charge, the case offers two elements of importance to the general action. It furnishes an opportunity for characteristic remarks by Cn. Piso and it depicts the first striking activity of the delators in this new field.

No case is recorded in A.D. 16, but in A.D. 17 Tacitus introduces the trial of Appuleia Varilla (2. 50) with the words "adolescebat interea lex maiestatis." This, according to Jerome, is disingenuous, because the historian does not give a great many examples. He cites only this case of Appuleia on the charge of disrespect, during casual conversation, toward Augustus, Tiberius, and Livia. Again, the emperor is inclined to quash the charges, divides the question, and accepts an acquittal. But again there is a slight extension of the law.

Until A.D. 21 there is no more heard of the *maiestatis* cases. Then Clutorius Priscus is charged (3. 49–51) with writing a poem in memory of Drusus before Drusus was dead. The charge seems rather frivolous but this very fact is significant, since the senate convicts Clutorius in the absence of the emperor and has him executed. That in itself is evidence of the changed conditions, which Tacitus has suggested by scattered cases and which Jerome doubts. Shortly after, Tacitus makes another comment: "Tiberius, fama moderationis parta quod ingruentis accusatores represserat, mittit litteras ad senatum quis potestatem tribuniciam Druso petebat" (3. 56).

In spite of a dramatic lull in the growing storm, the cases begin again, and the effect of increasing momentum is carefully produced. The year 22 sees two cases. One is that of C. Silanus (3. 66 ff.) on a charge of disrespect toward Augustus and Tiberius, coupled with a charge of definite maladministration. A new feature is the unfairness of Tiberius at the trial and the conviction of the defendant. An opportunity is given for Lentulus to make a characteristic motion. The second case of the year does not come to trial but illustrates the extreme to which flattery of the emperor had gone by means of the speech of Ateius Capito and the extremely frivolous charges that could be brought: L. Ennius was indicted for making practical use of the silver which he got from a statue of Tiberius that belonged to Ennius himself (3. 70).

The year 23 is occupied with more important affairs, but 24 produces five cases. Cassius Severus has his sentence for libeling prominent citizens made more severe (4. 21); Calpurnius Piso, charged with secret conversations against majesty, commits suicide when his trial is going entirely against him (4. 28); but the indictment against C. Cominius is for writing verses against the emperor, and he is acquitted by Tiberius (4. 31); Catus Firmius is accused of bringing false *maiestatis* charges against his sister and is expelled from the senate (4. 31). After his account of the last case Tacitus apologizes for introducing so many minor trials but insists on their importance in addition to the lack of more striking events to narrate. He then proceeds to the year 25 and presents the case of Cremutius Cordus (4. 34), who committed suicide when sure of conviction on the charge of having praised Brutus and Cassius in his history. Tacitus remarks the novelty of the charge and also notes that there were so many cases during that year that when the consuls were absent at the time of the Latin Festival and Drusus as Prefect of the City was about to take the auspices, he was approached by Calpurnius Salvianus seeking to prefer certain charges. Calpurnius was himself punished for his improper action but the significance of the story is such that, without imputing deliberate and extensive dishonesty to the first lawyer of Rome, one cannot deny that Tacitus is right in speaking of the great prevalence of prosecution at the time. And this is true even though, with the proper sense for his dramatic art, he presents only two other cases for the year, Votienus Montanus, convicted of slandering Tiberius, and Apidius Merula, expelled from the senate for not swearing to the acts of Augustus (4. 42).

After a year with no reported cases, Tacitus again resorts to pungent explanation. Tiberius had tried to gain some popularity by relief measures after the fire of 27. Tacitus' comment is: "Sed ut studia procerum et largitio principis adversum casus solacium tulerant, ita accusatorum acrior in dies et in-festior vis sine levamento grassabatur" (4. 66). One case only, and that on an unspecified charge, represents the year 27: Varus Quintilius (4. 66). The case was postponed. The next year has one condemnation—that of Titus Sabinus on the charge of loyalty to Germanicus. Then comes the lacuna in Book 5, and the last part of Tiberius' reign is complicated by the confusion after the fall of Sejanus.

Even such a rapid review as this can hardly fail to indicate the method and to justify it. The cases are selected cases. There are almost no two with the same charge, and the charges in-dicate a growing range and recklessness. There is also a fairly steady increase of momentum resulting from the increasing number of cases reported and suggested. It has been held that the small total number of trials and the large proportion of acquittals show that Tacitus had no evidence to support his picture of the working of the *lex maiestatis*. It appears how-ever that his purpose in selecting as he did was to show the extreme frivolity of many of the charges, and there is dramatic power in the increasing proportion of convictions that Tacitus records as the story unfolds, with Tiberius consenting ever more willingly. The loss of the fifth book is unfortunate, for it mars the dramatic continuity. But it does not destroy the ef-fect of Tacitus' technique.

For one great impression stands out in the reading of Book 6: the enormous number of convictions, speaking compara-tively with reference to the preceding books, is intended to come and does come as a climax to the dramatic development of this phase of the earlier story. They are not all of them logically in the same category, but the power of the emperor to cause the conviction of citizens that he wishes to remove seems not at all strange after the gradual but wide extension of the *lex maiestatis*. And the more the power is abused, the more the shadows gather about the old man at Capri.

Tacitus could hardly have included more trials and still have made his *Annals* readable. By proper selection, one of the first requisites of the dramatic historian, he has made convincing the tradition as he received it.

7. CHARACTER DELINEATION

OF THE Roman historians Tacitus is generally recognized as the one whose individual characters emerge most vividly and unforgettably. In part this is due to his brilliant, epigrammatic style. But it is also in great part the result of his tendency to regard history as a series of dramas in which the characters have a determining influence. Livy was primarily interested in the march of events, in the story of Rome. Many of his characters are lay figures important only as part of an interesting tale. As he approached his own day the individuals may well have emerged with greater definition, but in general they were of less account than the narrative. The essays of Sallust more nearly approach biography in this regard, and his characters are therefore more vital. It is more than probable that the same would have been true of his longer history. In the *Commentaries* of Caesar the objectivity is conscious and conspicuous; the character of Caesar, as the writer wished it to appear, does unfold throughout the account, but it is a result of the total work and not a means to the development of successive situations.

In his earliest production, the *Dialogus,* Tacitus gives no descriptive characterization of the speakers beyond a certain minimum identification. Maternus is the writer of a Cato, Aper and Secundus are leading lawyers of the day; for Messalla there is not so much as a word of description. Yet each of the four is clearly differentiated, and each is a living individual to the reader when the dialogue is over. This result comes about in part from what each has to say about the others and to a large extent by the remarks of each in the course of the conversation. Of Secundus, because of the lacuna in the manuscript, we have the least vivid impression. The method is that of the drama and more particularly of the dramatic dialogue as practiced by Plato.

The *Agricola,* the eulogistic biography of a contemporary,

uses all the means available in a direct characterization of the subject. Explicit physical as well as mental and moral description is reserved for the final summary. But every opportunity is taken to suggest by the account of his background, upbringing, and early training the sort of man Agricola was to be. In the account of his career the same emphasis on character is omnipresent. Sometimes the author comments on an action to make sure that its significance is clear, at other times the same result is obtained by noting the effect of an action on others, and again the action is left to speak for itself. Tacitus quotes the speech of Agricola before the battle in sufficiently characteristic style, especially in contrast with the speech of Calgacus, to make that, too, an element in characterization.

Of the minor characters in the biography only sufficient characterization is given to make them play their part adequately in the story of Agricola. Calgacus alone is given marked individuality, and the purpose of his prominence is clear: he it is who must be great enough for his defeat to be a climax to Agricola's career. So he is given the imposing speech before the battle, concentrating the fury and the hatred of the Britains in his fiery words. But even Calgacus is not a real character: he simply represents the collective character of the enemy, and it is noteworthy that he is not personally described nor are we given even a glimpse of his actions after the speech is concluded. Domitian is, it is true, described to a slight extent. His nature is *praeceps in iram et quo obscurior eo inrevocabilior,* but this is told merely to bring out the *moderatio* and *prudentia* of Agricola. Agricola's father and mother are identified, the one as a senator known for his eloquence and philosophy, the other for her *rara castitas.* In the same way, the various governors of Britain are identified, but not made more vivid than is necessary to play their part in the tale of Agricola. There are none of the brilliant vignettes for which Tacitus was to be famous.

It is clear that Tacitus came to the writing of his historical works with an understanding of the methods both of the dramatic presentation of character and of the eulogistic, of both indirect and direct characterization. His subject matter would seem to have kept him hitherto from developing the terse verbal description, illuminating a character with a sudden revealing flash.

After the personal prologue to the *Histories,* Tacitus gives a survey account of conditions in the Empire at the time he has chosen for the beginning of his narrative. The reason given is to make clear the logic and the causes of the events whose particular forms are a matter of chance. It is soon clear that among the causes the chief one is human character. The situation in the provinces, in the armies, and in Rome is brilliantly summarized and out of the summary emerges the first picture of Galba's character. He is not described, but in connection with the suppression of Nymphidius' plot, voices are heard criticizing his old age and his avarice, others resenting his reputation for old-fashioned discipline. The latter trait is brought out by a remark of Galba's that he drafted soldiers but did not buy them, with an insinuation on the part of Tacitus that he was not wholly consistent in this attitude. In connection with certain political murders, Galba's *mobilitas ingenii* is brought out and again and again his old age exposed to the mockery of those about him. Without specific description, the reader is vividly aware of Galba as a person. For the minor characters a word suffices: "Titus Vinius et Cornelius Laco, alter deterrimus mortalium, alter ignavissimus. Hordeonium Flaccum—senecta ac debilitate pedum invalidum, sine constantia, sine auctoritate. Cluvius Rufus, vir facundus et pacis artibus clarus, bellis inexpertus." A fuller account is given of Mucianus. This is suggestive, for he is immediately followed by Vespasian in the survey. Neither of them are to be of importance until the end of the first book. That their emphasized appearance here is a bit of dramatic foreshadowing is indicated by a sentence in each case. Of Mucianus, Tacitus says: "cui expeditius fuerit tradere imperium, quam obtinere." Of Vespasian: "Occulta fati et ostentis ac responsis destinatum Vespasiano liberisque eius imperium post fortunam credidimus."

The survey has just this touch of the dramatic, which is continued to some extent in what follows. Piso is introduced as "nobilis utrimque, voltu habituque moris antiqui et aestimatione recta severus, deterius interpretantibus tristior habebatur." And Otho enters as another Nero, luxurious, licentious, suave, the favorite of the court, throwing kisses to the crowd. The stage seems to be set, but the movement of history was too fast. In short order, Piso, Vinius, and Galba are gone, each with a summary at the close of his life, an *elogium* in good historical tradition. In the tradition, but very definitely with the epigrammatic and ironic touch of Tacitus. The comments on Piso conclude: "ad hoc tantum maiori fratri praelatus est ut prior occideretur." Of Vinius: "pravus aut industrius eadem vi." And of both: "Testamentum Titi Vini magnitudine opum inritum, Pisonis supremam voluntatem paupertas firmavit." And finally of Galba: "Omnium consensu capax imperii nisi imperasset." Otho's death is not reached until the middle of the second book, where we are reminded of his murder of Galba and his own heroic suicide: "Duobus facinoribus, altero flagitiosissimo altero egregio, tantundem apud posteros meruit bonae famae quantum malae."

The technique indicated is typical of the *Histories*. Death notices for characters of importance are usual and always with a moral evaluation. But these same characters are usually introduced with some characterization expressed tersely and often with a touch of irony. So of Vitellius: "Et Vitellius ut apud severos humilis, ita comitatem bonitatemque faventes vocabant quod sine modo, sine iudicio donaret sua, largiretur aliena." We have summaries at death of Valens, Sabinus, Vitellius, of Tigellinus and of Junius Blaesus. We have thumbnail sketches of Venutius and Cartimandua, of Calvia Crispinilla, Trebellius Maximus, and Hordeonius Flaccus. Flaccus is *segnis, pavidus et socordia innocens*. Tigellinus *infamem vitam foedavit etiam exitu sero et inhonesto*. The mordant phrase comes into its own in these short characterizations, and it is largely because of it that the characters of the *Histories* seem to be so sharply etched and so impressive, yet do not on the whole continue to live for us as do those of the *Annals,* especially those of Nero's reign.

It was suggested, in discussing the opening survey of conditions, that the introductions of Mucianus and Vespasian were somewhat different from the rest. The two reappear in 2. 5; again each is made more vivid by contrast with the other; in 2. 76 Mucianus is given a speech of considerable length addressed to Vespasian, and the effect on the latter is noted. Mucianus becomes a prominent actor throughout the rest of the *Histories;* although Vespasian remains in the background, and only occasionally is mentioned, his influence is always felt. This looks like more dramatic handling. We have not the end of either Mucianus or Vespasian; we can only say that there is some indication of dramatic technique in what we have. The same may be true also of Suetonius Paulinus and Antonius Primus. It may well be that the more leisurely pace of the later books, or rather of the history which they depict, led to a greater use of a dramatic characterization through action.

If this were true, it would be only natural that Tacitus' power in this direction should have increased rapidly with the telling of Domitian's reign. This was the period which impelled him to write history. Domitian was the man who represented to Tacitus the personified crime of tyranny. His was not, to be sure, the character of the true hero of Greek tragedy, but rather that of the Senecan Thyestes. Into the depiction of Domitian's villany must have gone the full power of Tacitus' hatred. Its fifteen years were not filled with great military actions but they were studded with political crimes, as the senate was gradually suppressed and the tyranny made absolute. It may well have been in his treatment of Domitian that Tacitus developed the dramatic technique characteristic of the *Annals.* It should be in a study of Annals 11–16 that we ought most easily to find out the method, if there is one, by which Tacitus presents his characters and makes them live.

In drama we expect to find leading characters who carry the brunt of the action, with one figure around whom the action centers and minor characters who contribute to it in greater or less degree. If Tacitus really thought to some extent as a dramatist, the same should be true of his historical characters as he presents them, and it is reasonable to consider the personalities of his pages in these two categories of major and minor characters. It is to be expected that the presentation of minor characters may be modified because of their use in building up the picture of major characters, but this should not alter the nature of the investigation. In investigating the presentation of a major character, certain others may be elements in the investigation, but that does not change the problem when they themselves take the center of the stage. As good an illustration of this as any is Seneca. It is difficult to say whether he should be considered a major or a minor character, but on the whole he plays the lesser role to Agrippina's and Nero's lead. He is introduced well in advance of his first important entry by the action of Agrippina in obtaining his recall from exile (12. 8. 3). By this act, which dramatically amounts to the mention of a character later to appear on the stage, she hopes to achieve some merit. This comment in itself is favorable to Seneca. Also she believes the move will be popular because of Seneca's fame for eloquence and because he would appear to be a proper tutor for a young prince. But there is also the hint of a certain weakness: he will owe her a debt of gratitude and his feelings toward Claudius will be unfriendly because of the injury involved in his exile. The comment is not wholly favorable, certainly not eulogistic, and the possibility of political complications is at least suggested.

The entry of Seneca onto the stage is made when Nero's reign begins: "Ibaturque in caedes nisi Afranius Burrus et Annaeus Seneca obviam issent" (13. 2). The two advisers are presented in opposition to the cruelty of Nero. There is a nice distinction made between them. Burrus, in addition to his military prestige, has *severitas morum,* while Seneca has *eloquentia* and *comitas honesta.* The philosopher is not called weak, but the implication is clear that Burrus is at least the stronger character. At once the dramatic situation is presented of their duty to control Nero in face of the *ferocia* of Agrippina. This

seems to mean unrestrained ambition that brooks no opposition. The implication of Seneca's weakness is strengthened in
the scene which follows, the funeral of Claudius. Nero delivers
the *laudatio* written by Seneca and Tacitus speaks of his *amoenum ingenium et temporis eius auribus adcommodatum* (13.
3. 2). This is definitely limited praise. His quick thinking saves
Nero from the disgrace of having Agrippina mount the throne
with him, a minor act pointing up the inevitable opposition of
the queen mother (13. 5. 3). More speeches follow, with the
implication that Seneca is perhaps showing off his wares. This
latter point is made by means of a familiar device of style
by which Tacitus often registers an item of characterization
without actually vouching for it. He gives alternative explanations for some action—the second, unconfirmed but undenied,
remaining in the reader's mind as the more effective. A slight
incident, the beginning of the love affair of Nero and Acte, is
made to color the character of Seneca by means of the phrase
ne senioribus quidem principis amicis adversantibus (13. 12.
2), and Acte as the rival of Octavia becomes a pawn in the
struggle of Nero, supported by Seneca against his mother.
This closes the exposition of the Seneca drama. Before the
opening of the next act there is only one reference to the
philosopher. The trial of Suillius is said to be *haud sine invidia Senecae,* for Suillius charges Seneca with hostility toward the friends of Claudius and, in his devotion to the less
virile rhetoric, toward men of a more vigorous legal tradition.
These insinuations are simply reminders of the qualities already suggested.

    With the fourteenth book, the great chapter of Agrippina's
fall brings Seneca into prominent action. First (14. 2. 2), he
supports Acte against Agrippina, a position already foreshadowed. Then, when the situation has become critical, he is
summoned by Nero and concurs in the death of the queen
mother (14. 7. 2 ff.). This is the culminating act of weakness
and the turning point in his career. It is made irrevocable when
he writes Nero's defense of the murder (14. 11. 4). With the
death of Burrus (14. 52 ff.) his position is weakened and

very soon complaints are heard of his great wealth inconsistent with his philosophical principles, a situation which culminates in the exchange of speeches between Nero and Seneca on the question of his position, his wealth, and his retirement. The space given to these by Tacitus is not only unusual but disproportionate to their importance, except as they are considered as the climax and turning point in the great drama of Nero and also in the lesser drama of Seneca. From this point the career of the prime minister descends rapidly to its tragic close. He partially withdraws from public life (14. 56. 6). Charged with friendship for Piso, he averts the accusation for the time being (14. 65. 2). Next he is associated unhappily with Paetus Thrasea by means of an ill-judged epigram (15. 23. 6). The fire and the persecution of the Christians warn him of trouble to come and he retires more effectively (15. 45. 5). It is hinted that Nero sought to poison him. At any rate the emperor determines on his death (15. 56. 2), and six chapters are devoted to his fall (15. 60 ff.). In this final act, Tacitus presents Seneca as the victim of Nero and, without withdrawing the impression of the weakness and indecision which were responsible for his position, he does depict his death as a dignified and tragic end to a stoic career.

Before discussing the technique of this presentation it will be well to glance at the way in which definitely less important characters are delineated. Antistius Sosianus is such a character. In the year 56 the tribune Antistius appears on the wrong side of a quarrel with the praetor Vibullius. His *licentia* is reprimanded by the senate. The incident is cited to show the traces of free senatorial action which still remained. It serves to introduce the name of Antistius. When, in the year 62, he is again noticed, the lapse of time has been such that Tacitus feels constrained to say: "quem in tribunatu plebis licentia egisse memoravi," emphasizing the *licentia*. On this occasion Antistius is tried by the senate for writing criminally libelous books in *patres et sacerdotes* (14. 48–9). The real reason for bringing him in is to present the speech of Thrasea mitigating the sentence, again illustrating the remaining shreds of *liber-*

tas. Antistius is exiled and years later, in 66, he returns from exile as an informer charging Anteius with astrological plots against Nero (16. 14). The character is slight but consistent, presented from one point of view and by a combination of characterizing word and typical action. Almost an exact parallel is the picture of Junia Silana (11. 12. 2). Mentioned in the account of the year 47 as forced by Messalina to divorce C. Silius, she is characterized only as *femina nobilis*. When she enters the action in 55 in rivalry with Agrippina, she is fully introduced as *insignis genere forma lascivia* (13. 19–22). Tacitus explicitly recalls the first reference to Silana, which might easily have been forgotten. She is really a person in the drama of Agrippina whom she unsuccessfully attacks, incidentally introducing another minor character, Plautus, and thereby suffers exile. Her death is cited when Agrippina is murdered and her victims restored. Each of these characters is used to further the story of another's more important role, but each is presented clearly and, from the important angle, consistently. Cornelius Sulla and Rubellius Plautus offer close parallels to this treatment which is used also in the case of even less important characters. Livineius Regulus (14. 17. 1) puts on games at Pompeii that end in a riot, giving the senate a chance to show its independence on a minor matter. Tacitus' only characterization of Regulus is the implication in his phrase *quem motum senatu rettuli,* a reference to one of the lost books where there may have been more specific information. Octavius Sagitta (13. 44), introduced merely to prepare dramatically for the entrance of Poppaea, is characterized only as *plebei tribunus* and by the phrase *nuptae amore vaecors* and the single action in which he figures, the murder of his mistress. These very minor characters are presented in one phase of their character only; they almost stand for a single quality, and the characterization consists of a pregnant phrase and a characteristic action.

The contrast is clear between the characters who make a single entrance and those who play a more continuing part. It is obvious now that there was no need of presenting Seneca all at once at his first appearance. His character is built up piece by piece by means of the descriptive phrases that perform the function of costume and make-up, by the things he says and does, and by the reaction of others to these acts and words.

In this treatment of Seneca it should be noted first that we almost certainly do not possess the beginning of the story. In all probability the banishment under Claudius was told in one of the lost books. This event took place in 41 or 42 and was therefore well in the past when in 49 Agrippina procures his recall. Nevertheless it explains why Seneca is not specifically introduced in 12. 8. Some knowledge of who and what he was is there assumed. So far, however, as his dramatic career is concerned, the tale begins with his recall: the use of his full name, the reference to his literary fame, the phrase *tali magistro* and the suggestion of his feelings toward Claudius, all serve to recall the character which must have been presented more fully in the earlier book. But also by means of that reminder they serve as a new introduction at the moment when his real career opens.

Several characteristics of the Seneca account are noteworthy. Tacitus departed from the annalistic technique in his accounts of the foreign affairs of Rome, bulking the events of several years together. He could therefore choose the point at which such a résumé should be inserted. It is significant in the present case that one section on the wars in the East comes at the point in Seneca's career at which he has reached the height of his power. He has joined Nero as against Agrippina and is undoubtedly among those rewarded richly by Nero after the removal of Pallas and Britannicus (13. 18). It is significant perhaps that Tacitus does not mention Seneca in connection with Britannicus' death. He *does* mention a very dubious rumor of Seneca's saving the political position of Burrus (13. 20) and—as often when the facts are doubtful—he makes considerable show of meticulous accuracy by the citation of authorities. It is of no great historical importance whether Seneca was powerful enough to save his stronger colleague, but the incident serves to indicate the peak of Seneca's political influence. The interposition of the eastern record furnishes suspense and emphasizes the implication of opposition when the Senecan story is resumed (13. 42). Incidentally, Tacitus marks the opening of a definite stage in Seneca's career by the reference to his attitude toward Claudius' friends which echoes the comment on the same point at his first introduction. The suspense is further maintained, after this one suggestion of threat to Seneca's prestige, by the account of affairs in Germany (13. 53–57). Immediately follows the murder of Agrippina, which proved to be the turning point in Seneca's career. The second long period of suspense precedes the final catastrophe and seems to be deliberate. For although Nero had not accepted his prime minister's proposal of retirement and he had only partially and unofficially withdrawn from politics, he is not mentioned even in local affairs except in two small but significant matters. One was a curiously unexplained charge of friendship or alliance of some sort with Piso. But Piso was still in good standing, and the whole thing seems to be a careless attempt to introduce a presentiment of evil on the horizon for both Nero and Seneca. It closes Book 14 as the withering Ruminal fig tree closed the thirteenth. The other matter is the incident, trivial from the historical point of view but ominous for Seneca, in which he was sufficiently off his guard to congratulate Nero rather than Burrus on the reconciliation between the two.

Similar in point of technique is the great space given to the two speeches of Seneca and Nero when, the climax of his success passed and a decline threatened, Seneca asks for the privilege of returning his wealth to the treasury and retiring. Aside from the importance of the exchange to serve its dramatic purpose, there is little excuse for the introduction of these long speeches. Similarly, the scene of Seneca's death, described at length and in detail, from a strictly historical point of view is inexcusable, but dramatically it is most effective.

An even more illuminating case is that of the younger Agrippina. She is first mentioned, long before she becomes a real part of the history, as the writer of memoirs (4. 53), the narrator of the misfortunes of her family, and the mother of the emperor Nero. And again, she is shown married to Domitius (4. 75), whose connection with the Julian family is stressed. Here, too, her royalty, as niece of Tiberius, is emphasized, and the fact that she is the daughter of Germanicus—all of which implies a certain kind of popularity. (How much this introductory build-up was added to in the lost books it is hard to guess. It is quite possible that she was not made prominent in order to make the introduction of Nero more dramatic. He is clearly *first* mentioned in 11. 11.) As the time for her great entry approaches (11. 12), she and her son are contrasted with Messalina and Britannicus, with the popular favor on her side, and the cruel hostility of Messalina inspires pity for Agrippina. The great part begins when the cabinet chooses a wife for Claudius (12. 1 ff.). She enters with the full regal title: *Julia Agrippina Germanico genita.* Her fecundity, her youth, and her noble lineage are all presented by her champion, Pallas. Then follows the exercise of her charms on Claudius himself, but no doubt is left that she uses them consciously and for a purpose: *struere maiora.* She is ambitious and ruthless for her very first step cannot be gained without crime: to get Octavia for Nero she has to eliminate Silanus. In true dramatic tradition she enters her reign with an ominous act of guilt. *Nihil arduum videbatur,* says Tacitus. A second omen occurs when the marriage is slightly delayed to remove the technicality of incest under the Roman law. In fact Tacitus lingers over this fantastic scene to give it dramatic significance, strengthened by the suicide of Silanus on the wedding day. Agrippina, to offset any odium from these omens, secures the recall of Seneca, a popular act but one also fraught with seeming advantage and ultimate tragedy for herself. Tacitus summarizes the situation: "versa ex eo civitas et cuncta feminae oboediebant, non per lasciviam ut Messalina rebus Romanis inludenti. Adductum et quasi virile servitium: palam severitas ac saepius superbia; nihil domi impudicum, nisi dominationi expediret. Cupido auri immensa obtentum habebat, quasi subsidium regno pararetur"

(12. 7). A Clytemnestra come back to earth. Up to this point the prologue has presented mainly the chief character, Agrippina, and has presented her in the prime of life and at the height of her power, a regal and determined figure, unscrupulous in her ambition for power which she has gained by her marriage and plans to enhance by making her son emperor. After a considerable break in the drama, while Tacitus recounts the current war in the East, the next act (12. 22) shows Agrippina, *atrox odii,* disposing of her former rival, Lollia, and going ahead with her plans by securing the adoption of Nero by Claudius, using her physical charms to make sure of the continued support of Pallas. She acquires the title Augusta (12. 26) and ostentatiously fosters a colony at her birthplace which is renamed in her honor. The same quality of ὕβρις is indicated by her presiding with Claudius at his audience for Caratacus (12. 37) and by her riding to the Capitol in a carriage (12. 42), a privilege reserved for priests and sacred images. After another interlude dealing with the eastern wars, the arrogance of Agrippina is further pictured by her presiding at the games in a *chlamys* wrought of gold thread. Murmurs of criticism begin to be heard: Narcissus complains of her *impotentia* and of her "too high hopes." The senators furnish an informer *contra ambitum Agrippinae* (12. 59). For a second time since her accession to power Tacitus enumerates the evil omens that were recorded year by year but not regularly included in the *Annals.* To Agrippina the worst omen is a casual word let drop by Claudius which indicated that he had had enough of her. She proceeds to sweep from her way her nearest rival (12. 64), Lepida, and then contrives the murder of Claudius (12. 65–9). The first move, against Lepida, gives Tacitus the chance, in a comparison of the two, to bring out a further characterization of Agrippina. The two are rivals in beauty, wealth, shamelessness, and violence. Both wish to control Nero. His mother, however, does not emulate the blandishments and bribes of Lepida: *trux ac minax,* she was ready to give the Empire to her son but not to brook his command. At last she accomplishes this by the aid of a poisoned mushroom

and Nero is proclaimed emperor. At Claudius' funeral she rivals, as Tacitus says, her ancestress Livia, but he adds the ominous touch that she dared not read her husband's will to the public for fear of calling their attention to the disregarded Britannicus.

With Nero on the throne (13. 1 ff.), Agrippina has reached her greatest height, and characteristically Tacitus begins the account of the new reign with an ominous note: "Prima novo principatu mors Junii Silani proconsulis Asiae ignaro Nerone per dolum Agrippinae paratur." Narcissus, her old enemy, is immediately disposed of and her thirst for vengeance rouses the opposition of Burrus and Seneca, the elder counsellors of Nero. Both, says Tacitus, sought to combat the *ferocia* of Agrippina, who was *cunctis malae dominationis cupidinibus flagrans*. She asserts herself by making the senate meet in the palace, where she can listen behind the arras (13. 5), and she is only thwarted by Seneca's quick wit when she tries to sit as a queen to receive the ambassadors from Armenia. The opposition begins to work subtly but effectively through its pawn, Acte. *Infracta paulatim potentia matris* (13. 12). Nero is estranged and turns to Seneca for help. The terms that Tacitus uses of Agrippina become more frankly derogatory: *severitas, atrox, superbia.* Pallas is eliminated by Nero. Agrippina loses something of her self-control and threatens to support Britannicus (13. 14), causing his murder. Fear and consternation drive Agrippina to collect money and supporters *quasi quaereret ducem et partes* (13. 18). Her flatterers begin to fall away. Tacitus marks the change by the significant sentence: "Nihil rerum mortalium tam instabile ac fluxum est quam fama potentiae non sua vi nixae." Junia Silana ventures to manipulate charges of treason against Agrippina, and Nero comes to the determination to do away with her. For a moment her old power returns, and Tacitus quotes the speech with which she refutes the charges. But the die is cast. There is a long interlude in which Tacitus catches up on local and foreign events before he returns to the last act in the tragedy of Agrippina, preceded by the omen of the Ruminal fig tree.

Poppaea is the instrument of fate in driving Nero to action. In one final desperate play Agrippina attempts to meet the issue by seducing her son, and when that fails she is finished. Only the details of the murder remain to be carried out. Because of the interrelation of Agrippina's story with Nero's, Tacitus does not make too much of the courage of Agrippina in the face of death but he does give her back some of her regal fortitude and pride and recalls her foreknowledge of the end by quoting her remark, *occidat dum imperet*.

Like the character of Seneca, that of Agrippina is consistently and dramatically drawn. The intermixture of admirable qualities and fatally weak or vicious ones prevents each from becoming wooden or unreal. Seneca is a weak character but an understandable one and by no means negligible. Agrippina is not the conventional villainess of melodrama but a human being of strong passions which are in the end her undoing. Both are convincing and both are progressively developed, largely through action but always with the significant comment—which in history, is forced to fulfil the function of make-up, expression, and gesture. How concise and potent this element could be is shown by the characterization of Poppaea, whose part, though important, is brief and who must be convincing even though her rôle gives no room for development. Of her Tacitus says: "Huic mulieri cuncta alia fuere praeter honestum animum" (13. 45. 2). In the case of more important characters the use of such mordant phrases is not frequent. Agrippina is rather presented by a series of great scenes which advance inevitably to the logical conclusion of her death at Nero's hand. But the character is also filled out by lesser incidents that illustrate particular characteristics. A good example is the attitude she shows when Nero presents her with the best of the royal jewelry. Her greed leads her to resent his failure to give her *all* instead of the best.

These two, Seneca and Agrippina, are the most prominent supporting characters in the drama of Books 11–16, of which Nero is the star. But there are a host of minor characters who appear only once or at most a few times to play their rôles.

These range all the way from the consuls of each year who are merely part of the machinery to keep the chronology reasonably clear and who require no characterization, to persons like Acte who play a vital but very minor part. Acte seems perhaps to be made too little of. From Suetonius (*Nero* 50) we learn that she was one of those few devoted women who remained faithful in their love for Nero and at the end buried his remains. Whether Tacitus, in the lost books, made more of Acte we cannot say, but, as we have the story, he wishes to make her a foil to Agrippina and Octavia, and he overlooks her claims to noble birth and her considerable wealth. She is to him an inconsiderable pawn and he makes this clear by his first characterization (13. 12. 1). Two words are sufficient. At her first appearance he identifies her as a freedwoman, *cui vocabulum Acte fuit,* and, shortly after, speaks of her as *muliercula.* Additional emphasis is given to this innuendo by quoting Poppaea's jealous characterization of Acte, *paelice ancilla* (13. 46. 4), and her scornful thrust at Nero, *nihil e contubernio servili nisi abiectum et sordidum traxisse.* Finally she appears once more in unfortunate contrast with Agrippina when Seneca, as a last resort, tries to use her (14. 2. 2).

Between these two extremes there is a group of characters who appear more than temporarily but not in really primary rôles: Burrus, Corbulo, Suetonius Paulinus, Tigellinus, Paetus Thrasea, Poppaea, Britannicus and Octavia, and the freedmen, Pallus, Narcissus, and even Callistus. Corbulo and Suetonius appear almost exclusively in the interludes that deal with foreign affairs. Their stories are incomplete in the text that has been preserved, but even so they show more of the technique of biography than of the drama. This may be due to the fact that both left memoirs which Tacitus presumably used, but the more probable reason seems to be that they are largely unconcerned with the drama that was played out at court.

In the case of Corbulo (11. 18–20), his introduction was presumably in one of the lost books. The Domitius Corbulo in 3. 31 must have been his father, as he was already mature in the year 21. When the great general first appears in Book 11, he is mentioned as Corbulo, not by his full name, and obviously as having already been appointed to the command in Germany. He is, however, just arriving in his province, and the tone is given by the phrase *magna cum cura et mox gloria*. Various items are cited of his quick and effective suppression of the activities of Gannasco and his Chauci and then immediately of his discipline of the demoralized troops, rigid but essential. The effect on both barbarians and legions is noted with approval. There is just a suggestion of personal ambition made by the indirect method of recounting the reaction of his activities on some of the observers and by the order of Claudius to curtail operations. To point his military correctness and at the same time his personal *libertas,* Tacitus quotes his comment on obeying the orders of the emperor, *beatos quondam duces Romanos.* Claudius gives him triumphal honors in spite of restraining him, in itself a great distinction. Corbulo was presumably recalled. He does not appear again until once more, just after Nero's accession, a strong general is particularly needed for the Parthian situation (13. 8). At this point the treatment is definitely eulogistic. Nero gains favor by the appointment of Domitius Corbulo—*videbaturque locus virtutibus patefactus.* The opportunity for comparison is given by the retention of Ummidius Quadratus as governor of Syria. The allied kings prefer Corbulo. All eyes are on him, *corpore ingens, verbis magnificis et super experientiam sapientiamque etiam specie inanium validus.* This impression is intensified by the following incidents, including Corbulo's unrefuted claim that it was his arrival that induced Vologeses to give hostages. There is a slight suggestion of dangerous pride and ambition, just as there was in the German presentation (13. 34–41). In the subsequent campaign in Armenia, Corbulo is always to the fore. His ambition to rival Lucullus is cited, as also his discipline of the troops, with incidents of its rigor, but at the same time his own example of hardihood and his sympathy when merited. Then follows the objective account of his campaigns, combining diplomacy with military vigor. Tiridates tries in vain to fool him; he dominates the situation. The campaign culminates in the capture and rather vainglorious destruction of Artaxata. Honors at the hands of the senate are extravagant enough to elicit an ironical remark from C. Cassius, one of the obstinate conservatives. The story is picked up at Artaxata in Book 14 (23–26). Corbulo again is presented as a great strategist, full of care and wisdom, economical of Roman blood, endowed with unique patience. He returns to Syria where his weak foil, Ummidius, has died, and assumes the governorship. When the tale is resumed (15. 1–17) after a dramatic pause, a new and even more effective foil is furnished for Corbulo in the person of Caesennius Paetus. But there is a suspicion of Corbulo's motives introduced (15. 6. 1). Tacitus cites the rumor that while making bold threats in public Corbulo had made a secret deal with Tigranes. The device of the second alternative gives this some emphasis, and reasons are given for thinking it probable. It is confirmed to some degree by the fact that Corbulo had asked for a separate leader for the Parthian war, retaining for himself the safer job of defending Syria. In the chapters that follow, recounting the inffective acts of Paetus and his defeat and disgrace, Corbulo is depicted as the hero, coming to the rescue: Paetus' mistakes and humiliations are given full emphasis. Corbulo shows some consideration for the miserable soldiers of Paetus but not much for the general himself. After another interval, the story is resumed (15. 24–31) with the appointment of Corbulo in Paetus' place and the latter's humiliating return to Rome. Corbulo, who, we are reminded, inspired no hate in the enemy, had immediate and easy success and added suavity and courtesy to his power. Corbulo's triumph is complete. This is the last that is heard of Corbulo in the surviving books of Tacitus. It can hardly be doubted that in the account of his death at Nero's order, Tacitus would have given him something of the eulogistic treatment that he gives to Paetus Thrasea. Corbulo is a general of the old type (cf. *admiratione prisci moris,* 15. 30. 1). The touches of pride and even vainglory do not seem to be defects to Tacitus but rather the proper attitude of a Roman general in the face of barbarian enemies. His acts of cruelty are stern Roman justice. Tacitus so far forgets himself in his admiration for Corbulo as to say: *apud* (*nos*) *vis imperii valet, inania tramittuntur,* a belief which he cherished for the old days but hardly for the reign of Nero. Except for his appointment Corbulo hardly figures (save perhaps in the lost books) in the court drama. His is a somewhat isolated eulogistic biography.

Very similar is the less extensive treatment of Suetonious Paulinus. Except for the mention of his name to fix the chronology (16. 14. 1), all that we have of him is in one section on Britain (14. 29 ff.). He is presented as the rival of Corbulo in the estimation of the people and eager to gain glory. The seriousness of the rebellion in Britain is stressed; the strange crossing to Mona and the picture of the Druids lends color to the narrative; Paulinus' *constantia,* his foresight, his care of the strategic situation, his stern discipline but just discrimination, his eloquence and the response of the troops—all of these build up the eulogistic picture of the great commander. His mistakes are nowhere mentioned. (This is not wholly true if we include the *Histories* in our discussion, but I am dealing with the *Annals* as a unit.)

In both of these sketches, the geographical background is vague but colorful. In both there are miraculous events introduced. In both the effect of the subjects on barbarian foes is emphasized. In each case characteristics are both named and fully illustrated. In neither do we have the death scene to tell whether there is a eulogistic climax.

Paetus Thrasea occupies a position of relative importance, if judged by the amount of space devoted to him in the *Annals,* about equal to that of Corbulo or Suetonius. He might well have been given a treatment similar to that of the two generals, for he, too, is a hero in the eyes of the historian, a hero who lost his life in the great struggle in which he was an important minor character. There was also biographical material at hand for Tacitus to use, a life of Thrasea by Arulenus Rusticus (*Agricola* 2). But there is a definite difference in the presentation of the Stoic "leader of the opposition."

Thrasea appears but five times in the *Annals* and each time at a crucial turning point in the career of Nero. This can hardly be the result of chance; his position of prominence in the senate must have led him to take part in their actions more often than would be indicated by these appearances, even though his silence was notorious and construed as opposition to the emperor. We know, for example, that Thrasea was active in the condemnation of Capito in 57 (cf. 16. 21), although his part is not mentioned at the time (13. 33). The fact is, he is brought in, at his first appearance (13. 49. 1) on a case of such small importance that Tacitus explains his account of it by noting the significance of the comment of Thrasea, who speaks on this minor matter to prove that the senate will take its part in *all* affairs and will be ready when greater events call. The occasion is directly after the appearance on the scene of Poppaea Sabina, with her baleful influence on the life of Nero. The opponents of Thrasea, who seem to have built up considerable hatred for him, sneer at *libertas senatoria,* which he seems to represent. This is really the key to his importance.

Thrasea's next appearance (14. 12. 2) is directly after the death of Agrippina, when he leaves the senate in disgust. Again the word *libertas* figures and again it is at a turn in the affairs of Nero. *Libertas* is stressed once more when Thrasea next speaks out in the senate (14. 48, 49). His speech is indirectly quoted in this instance, and it is made in the first case brought up under the revival of the *lex maiestatis,* to Tacitus the most vital instrument of tyrannical power. Immediately after the death of Octavia (15. 20, 21), Thrasea makes a speech which is quoted at some length. It is on the case of a provincial governor who has mismanaged his office. Thrasea recalls the former high principles of Roman government and attacks *ambitio* and *avaritia.* In growing disfavor with the emperor, he is excluded from the celebration at Antium when Poppaea's child is born. Finally comes the great account of his fall and death (16. 21–35). To this Tacitus devotes an unusual amount of space and introduces the narrative with a generalization that gives it significance: "Nero virtutem ipsam excindere concupivit interfecto Thrasea Paeto et Barea Sorano." Soranus serves largely as a foil to Thrasea's courage. The account brings in indirectly not only the *libertas* of Thrasea and his identification with the senate but emphatically his Stoic character, typified by his appearance, *venerabilis species, rigidus et tristis.* He is compared with Cato, Tubero, Favonius, Cassius, and the Bruti, all Stoic heroes of the past. His dying libation to Jupiter Liberator and his last remarks are noted.

It is obvious that Thrasea is presented from a definite point of view. His character is static and presents one facet only. He is always the symbol of Stoic integrity and independence and of senatorial prerogative, two things closely associated in the mind of Tacitus. He is presented through his speeches more than almost any other character. His is a personal opposition on moral grounds to an emperor who flouts the Stoic doctrines. The span of his activities is identical with that of Poppaea, who represents the opposite of his principles of living. He is not so much a living dramatic character as an animated symbol. The only time Thrasea seems to come to life as a vital personality is when the dramatic urge leads Tacitus to comment on his departure from the senate, when Nero is congratulated on his mother's death. Tacitus sounds the ominous note and at the same time comes close to adverse criticism of his hero: "sibi causam periculi fecit, libertatis initium non praebuit." This recalls the comment in the *Agricola* on those who "per abrupta sed in nullum rei publicae usum, ambitiosa morte inclaruerunt." Thrasea, however, is really a cause, not a character. He is himself a Stoic *exemplar,* and the material for his presentation, never remolded dramatically, may well have come from a Stoic encomium, very likely from that of Arulenus Rusticus. His dramatic value was not in his own tragedy but in that of Nero.

Of the remaining characters who are of comparatively major importance in the tragedy of Nero, Tigellinus might very likely prove to be more nearly in the class of Seneca and Agrippina if we had the books that dealt with the last days of Nero. He has the casual introduction of a major character (14. 48.

2), mentioned very incidentally shortly before his more formal entry with his full name (14. 51. 3), and some characterization by the naming of qualities, *impudicitia* and *infamia* and by contrast with his colleague, Rufus. His increase of power is noted (14. 57–60) (again with characterization: *malas artes quibus solis pollebat*) in his successful machinations against Sulla and Plautus and in his intrigues against Octavia on behalf of Poppaea. The same purpose—to show the freedman's growing ascendancy over the emperor—is to be seen in his promotion of Nero's banquets and revels (15. 37. 2 ff.), in his success in prejudicing Nero against Faenius Rufus (15. 50. 4), and in his association with Nero's cruelty (15. 58. 3). Even the suspicion of his connection with the spread of the great fire is another bond with Nero (15. 40. 3), until finally he and Poppaea are designated as Nero's chief counsellors (15. 61. 4). His triumphant advance is marked by the huge rewards granted him after the failure of Piso's conspiracy (15. 72. 2). There is little more of Tigellinus in the books that have survived. His eminence is emphasized by the fact that money is willed to him by Mela (16. 17), in the hope of protecting the rest of his property, and by the *libertas* of Petronius, who refuses to flatter either Nero or Tigellinus (16. 19). He is strong enough to eliminate even a merely personal enemy (16. 20). On the whole, in the parts of the *Annals* preserved to us Tigellinus is a static character out with dramatic traits and possibilities.

Of Poppaea we have all that there ever was. Her character is fixed once and for all at her first appearance (13. 45. 1 ff.), not only by the masterly delineation but by the picture of her itinerant loyalties. There is some slight comment at the time of her death (16. 6–7), and Thrasea's scorn of her is in the best dramatic technique. But for the most part she is a fixed quantity, made vivid only as a pawn in greater tragedies, that of Agrippina and Nero in particular (14. 1. 1 ff.). Even so, the appeals with which she impels Nero to the break with his mother, the reaction of the populace when she secures the divorce of Octavia (14. 59–61), the passing reference to her viewing the head of her victim—all this is in the dramatic tradition.

Almost the same may be said of Burrus. By necessity he becomes somewhat dramatic because of his part in other tragedies, but for himself, he is too fixed and static. He represents the good element in conflict with the bad, but he shares the weakness of Seneca at the crucial moment. His introduction by full name and with brief characterization (*egregiae militaris famae*—12. 42) is dramatic though not prepared for properly in advance. The weakness is hinted at in the insinuation that he knew whence his advancement came. Although he has *severitas morum* (13. 2. 1), he is, as Agrippina saw, a military hero at best, *debilis, trunca manu,* and he signed his death warrant when he condoned the murder of Agrippina. At his death, *incertum an veneno,* the public mourns his loss *per memoriam virtutis.* Like Thrasea he represents *virtus,* but not to the same degree and certainly without the same dramatic treatment.

Of the persons most deeply involved in the Nero saga, this leaves Britannicus and Octavia, closely akin in function and treatment, and the three freedmen, Callistus, Narcissus, and Pallas, also forming a logical group. Britannicus is more carefully introduced than his sister. He is casually mentioned twice before his real entry, which is not marked by striking incident or any concise characterization (11. 1. 1, 4. 6, 26. 3). He is a tool of Messalina (11. 32. 4). As such he is associated with Octavia who has not been previously mentioned and whose only characterization lies in the reported sympathy of the people for her unfortunate lot. Both the royal children are effective pawns, first of Messalina then of Agrippina; both are pathetic victims of Agrippina's ambition or Nero's passions; but neither is at any time a character with true individuality.

The same holds in general of the three freedmen. They appear together in a consultation over the affair of Messalina and Silius (11. 29. 1), although Tacitus says that he has mentioned Callistus in connection with the death of C. Caesar. The others, not having been mentioned apparently, are slightly identified,

Narcissus as *Appianae caedis molitor* and Pallas as *flagrantissima eo in tempore gratia*. All three appear shortly after with Narcissus in the position of prominence and scorning the other two. The occasion is that on which Narcissus stirs up Claudius to action against Messalina while Pallas shows cowardice and Callistus holds back through political caution. All three appear again together when a successor to Messalina is to be picked (12. 1–2). In this case Pallas' candidate wins. From this point on Callistus does not appear again, Narcissus' influence declines and through Agrippina's machinations he is forced to suicide (13. 1. 4), while Pallas has a somewhat more dramatic career. He hastens the adoption of Nero (12. 25. 1), fails to obtain the extravagant rewards proposed by a consul (12. 53. 2–3), is accused in court rumors of adultery with Agrippina (12. 65. 4), is characterized as *tristi adrogantia* (13. 2. 4), disliked as too forward for a freedman but used extensively by Agrippina, and finally deposed by Nero (13. 14. 1) on account of his position with the queen mother. His arrogance keeps him from popularity even when his innocence of conspiracy is proven (13. 23. 1–3) and his *superbia* is illustrated, and his death is attributed to his wealth, for which Nero was impatient (14. 65. 1).

The three men were almost a composite character representing the freedman power in the imperial set-up. Pallas comes closest to individual character, but all of them serve merely to personalize the incidents of the main story.

It remains to analyze the characterization of Nero and to note how the minor dramas are interwoven in the greater one, and the part played by the minor characters.

Nero, like the other great characters, is introduced by casual incidents long before his real entry on the scene, and always with some suggestion of the conflict of personalities that is destined to develop. The first reference to the future emperor is in connection with the secular games of Claudius in A.D. 47 (11. 11. 5–6). As a boy of eleven he takes part in the *ludus Troiae* along with Britannicus, and at once a contrast between the two is drawn. Britannicus is *imperatore genitus, Domitius, adop-*

tione mox in imperium et cognomentum Neronis adscitus.
Tacitus adds significantly: *favor plebis acrior in Domitium
loco praesagii acceptus est.* There follows a story of the serpent
or serpents attending his cradle when he was a baby and his
own insistence that there was but one, although he was *haud-
quaquam sui detractor.* The next year Agrippina, established as
wife of Claudius, begins her machinations by planning the engagement of young Domitius to Octavia (12. 3. 2). This is
accomplished, and again the rivalry with Britannicus is stressed
(12. 9. 2). In A.D. 50 Agrippina, with Pallas supporting her,
persuades Claudius to adopt Nero and favor him over Britannicus (12. 25–6). In 51 Nero is given the *toga virilis* and
many distinctive honors, again in sharp contrast with Britannicus and always with Agrippina managing everything (12.
41). In both of these last two moves it should be noted that
Britannicus is presented as sensing the situation clearly. In 53
Nero and Octavia are married (12. 58). Also, *ut studiis honestis et eloquentiae gloria enitesceret,* the young man pleads
the case of the Trojans, with much literary allusion. Tacitus
makes use of the case of Lepida, in the year 54 (12. 65), to
emphasize and even analyze the situation of Agrippina in relation to Britannicus and Nero, leading directly to the murder of
Claudius and the accession of Nero. The opening words of the
account of Nero's reign (13. 1) are ominous: *prima novo
principatu mors* but the first acts are not Nero's. The exposition is still to be completed, with a vivid sketch of the forces at
work: Agrippina's ambitious struggle for power through control of Nero, opposed by Seneca and Burrus, the less competent exponents of righteousness.

Such is the prologue to Nero drama. It is marked off from
the action that follows by an interlude occupied with eastern
affairs. Little characterization has been given to Nero. He is
only a boy of eighteen. His appeal to the populace has been
hinted at, as also his inheritance from the Domitius family and
his artificial training in rhetoric. But he is chiefly pictured as
the immature tool of stronger characters at war over the power
that rests in his hands.

The early events of Nero's reign (13. 11–24) all center around the growing antagonism of Agrippina to the control of Seneca over the young emperor, her gradual loss of influence, with the Acte affair as an incident, her threats, and finally the murder of Britannicus resulting from her attitude. It is after this tragic event that Nero's characterization begins to develop in the account of Tacitus, his irresponsible rowdyism in particular. The case of the growing arrogance of freedmen is told at considerable length with the arguments for and against legislation to restrain them, obviously to indicate a trend suggested by the trivial tale of rowdyism and pointed by the phrase *manebat nihilo minus quaedam imago rei publicae,* with instances to illustrate the statement. Eastern affairs again furnish an interlude.

With the reopening of the Nero story (13. 47–52), the significant item is the rise in influence of Poppaea. This is preceded by incidents like the attack on Suillius, *haud sine invidia Senecae.* Atmosphere is provided by the case of Octavius Sagitta. Poppaea is thoroughly characterized. Only by implication is the unjust exile of Sulla related to the influence of Poppaea, but it grows out of the increasing lawlessness of Nero's behavior. In opposition to the influence of Poppaea, the character of Paetus Thrasea is introduced. This short act is transitional but clearly indicates the trend of affairs and the decline of Agrippina.

After another interlude on foreign affairs, Book 13 ends with the omen of the withering Ruminal fig tree (13. 58) and 14 presents the climax of the Neronian tragedy, the murder of Agrippina, historically overextended but not so dramatically (14. 1–22). For not only is Agrippina eliminated but, by their tacit approval of the deed, Burrus and Seneca lose their strong grip on Nero. The implication is clear that he can now follow his own inclinations, and this is fortified by the new games and by the use of such terms, in connection with Nero, as *licentia* and *luxuriae cupido.* Finally, a comet gives the ominous touch.

Again foreign affairs mark a break in the tragedy. There is

a long period to cover between the climax of Agrippina's death and the catastrophe of the Pisonian conspiracy. This is treated in two scenes, with a foreign interlude separating them. The first (14. 40–65) presents the activities of the senate, alternating between a show of liberty and an exhibition of servility. These are marked by speeches of Cassius and Thrasea on the one hand, the death of Burrus and decline of Seneca on the other, the divorce of Octavia, and, finally and most important, the rise of Poppaea's determining influence. The significance of the period is made clear by the great space devoted to the matched speeches of Seneca and Nero. In the last chapter of Book 14 the Pisonian conspiracy, its seriousness and its failure, are specifically foreshadowed. But before that climactic event and after an interlude on the Parthian affairs, a further scene (15. 18–23) is devoted to the development of the struggle for control between the forces represented by Thrasea on the one hand and by Poppaea and her newly introduced supporter, Tigellinus, on the other.

After a final interlude on Parthia comes the result of this struggle (15. 32–16. 25). The scene is opened with Nero's play-acting, his more open tyranny, his public banquets instigated by Tigellinus, and finally his disgusting "marriage" with Pythagoras. Directly on the heels of this evidence of degeneracy comes the great fire, with more than an implication that Nero originated or helped it, certainly enjoyed it. The cruel punishment of the scapegoat Christians and the plundering of even the temples to get the wherewithal to rebuild Rome and his own palace are followed as if by a logical fate by the retirement of Seneca, the abortive revolt of gladiators, and the conspiracy of Piso. Tacitus makes his dramatic conception almost literally obvious when he opens Book 16 with the words, *inlusit dehinc Neroni fortuna per vanitatem ipsius,* and presently adds *gliscebat luxuria.* Illustrations of the trend are given, including the death of Poppaea, already outstripped in license by her pupil, and culminating in a long series of political murders which reach their climax with Paetus Thrasea and Barea Soranus, when Nero *virtutem ipsam excindere cupivit.*

The end of the Nero story is lost, but it has been dramatically prepared for. There was probably another digression on foreign affairs, presumably the revolt in Judaea. Then the trip of Nero to Greece, the climax of his insufferable arrogance, his insolent return to Rome, and the revolt of the armies on every side, culminating in the pitiable fiasco of his death.

Such is the tragedy of Nero if we concede that Tacitus viewed his history from a dramatic angle. The minor tragedies of Agrippina and Seneca—secondary plots if you will—blend successfully with the major plot and become integral parts of it, the lesser characters have found their places and in each case are sufficiently characterized to match the importance of their rôles. It must not be forgotten that while dramatic, the story is definitely not a drama but history. Except for the interludes, the annalistic method is faithfully followed, save for the use of ominous foreshadowing, which is a characteristic more suitable to drama than to history. Traits of biographical technique are constantly obvious. In the early Nero, attributes of *clementia, liberalitas,* and the like are noted and illustrated; in the later Nero these have become *luxuria, licentia, immanitas* and similar qualities. But they emerge in the course of action and not in catalogue form or descriptively. In special instances like those of Suetonius Paulinus and Corbulo, the biographical technique is more prominent, and it is significant that these cases are largely in the interlude sections. It is primarily the selection of the times for introducing these interludes, and the contrast between the orthodox historical technique employed in them with the methods in the rest of the work, that gives confirmation to the impression of dramatic tendencies in the bulk of the *Annals*.

8. TACITUS AS HISTORIAN OF MILITARY AFFAIRS

IF WE ACCEPT the general purpose of Tacitus to have
been, as he himself would have us believe, to present the
failure of liberty and its struggle against tyranny down to
a final compromise under the Ulpians, and his method of making this presentation vivid and convincing to be primarily dramatic in nature, we must face the question of whether or not
Tacitus is adequate in his treatment of the military history
which will be for him secondary in importance. Histories today
fall into the rough categories of political, social and economic,
cultural, and military. Ancient history will hardly be expected
to concern itself with the social and economic or the cultural
save incidentally and one might say unconsciously. These are
for the most part modern conceptions. Tacitus wrote primarily
a political history but military affairs are essentially part of any
political history and in ancient history they always loomed
large. To be sure, Tacitus regrets in the *Annals* the fact that
his choice of a period gives him no great conquests or triumphs
to record. But the great year of revolution, the year of the four
emperors, was largely occupied with war, and the political des-
tinies of the Empire depended on arms. The conquest of Britain
was also a conspicuous political event, and the wars in Armenia are inextricably involved in the political story of Nero's
reign. There are also military elements in the handling of the
German provinces under Tiberius that cannot be wholly disso-
ciated from the political history.

What then is to be required of the political historian in dealing with essential military material? Surely not what Henderson would like to have, an understanding analysis of strategic
policies and an expert criticism of campaigns.[1] That would be
the function of a purely military historian and the injection of

---

1. B. W. Henderson, *Civil War and Rebellion in the Roman Empire*, London, 1908.

such material would destroy the proportions of a political history. The demand for such technical information comes nearest to being justified when the campaigns involve the whole operation of state as they do in the year of civil war, when the candidates for the throne are concerned solely in the winning of it, when the normal action of the government is largely suspended, and when the outcome would seem likely to determine the future state of the Empire. We may therefore consider as two different problems Tacitus' treatment of the Civil Wars and his accounts of the other campaigns with which he deals.

It must be admitted that from the purely theoretical point of view the military strategy of the Civil Wars is not of prime political importance. It was their results that counted politically. But in undertaking to write the history of a year largely occupied with war it becomes *de facto* incumbent upon the historian to deal more fully with the details of warfare than would otherwise suit his purpose. At any rate Tacitus does in the *Histories* treat at length and with some pretense of military adequacy the campaigns of the four emperors and thereby invites the criticism of his account on military grounds. Such criticism has been on the whole unfavorable. Not all writers would go as far as Mommsen in calling Tacitus the most unmilitary of historians,[2] and few would endorse the tirades of Henderson, who states that "in matters military" Tacitus' information "represents the common gossip of the camp, the talk of the private or of the subordinate officer." But, except for E. G. Hardy,[3] almost all who have had anything to say about it assume that Tacitus is at least vague and on the whole unsatisfactory about the geography, strategy, and tactics of military campaigns. I suspect that in large part this assumption is the result of the difficulty of following his account of the Armenian Wars in the *Annals* but Henderson's vituperation is loosed against Tacitus when he is discussing the Civil Wars,

2. T. Mommsen, "Die Zwei Schlachten von Betriacum im Jahre 69 n. Chr.," *Hermes, 5* (1871), 161–73.

3. E. G. Hardy, *Studies in Roman History*, London, 1906; and "Tacitus as a Military Historian in the *Histories*," *Journal of Philology, 61* (1940), 21.

and Mommsen also condemns him in his paper on the two battles of Bedriacum.

One thing must always be borne in mind in any discussion of the present problem. The Romans had no maps for ready reference. Accustomed as we are to charts and maps of every sort to make clear the text of our history books, we are prone to overlook the enormous extent to which they simplify the work of the author. Tacitus could not refer the reader to a clarifying sketch map but had to depend on reference to towns, rivers, and highways which may or may not have retained their names and identities down to our day. Caesar, himself a general and the leader of the campaigns which he describes, often leaves the modern reader completely baffled by his geographical and military vagueness and confusion. "It is simply impossible" says T. Rice Holmes, Caesar's great editor and admirer, "to construct a complete map to illustrate the Gallic War which will not be misleading." [4] In spite of the scorn which Livy pours out upon historians who brought Hannibal by the wrong pass over the Alps, the location of his own "true way" is still a matter of controversy, as are the details of the great battle of Cannae. Geography and military strategy without maps and charts are complicated subjects of exposition.

No one so far as I know has criticized Tacitus' account up to the beginning of hostilities between Vitellius and Otho. His survey of the forces of the empire as well as that of the troops of Vitellius and Otho is clear and adequate. The military critics, however, do condemn Tacitus for not giving more consideration to the strategic plans of the two sides. He is, they say, too prone to pass judgment on the results rather than on the plan of campaign. It might be argued that such an analysis of strategic purpose would probably have been as hazardous and as fruitful of error for Tacitus as for modern theorists. But in this case the answer should be, I think, of a different sort. Tacitus makes it fairly clear that the two Vitellian armies were sent from Germany *without* specific plans for the campaign of the Po valley. He states that Caecina and his force of 30,000 were

4. *The Architect of the Roman Empire,* 2 vols. Oxford, 1928–31.

to proceed by the shorter route through Switzerland into Italy, while Valens with his 40,000 troops and a much longer distance to traverse was to go through Gaul and approach Italy from the west. Vitellius would follow with some 30,000 more men. The implication is clearly that there was no comprehensive plan for conquering the Othonian troops, or at least that none was evident. The three sections of the army were separated by considerable distances and moved with a large measure of independence. Their objectives were first the occupation of the territory between the Alps and the Po and then the invasion of Italy proper, but it is absurd to ask of Tacitus an outline of strategy that goes beyond this simple and obvious purpose. With regard to the strategy of defense on the part of Otho the explanation to be gleaned from Tacitus is quite the reverse of Henderson's explanation. With characteristic ordering of his material, Tacitus builds up a convincing picture of Otho's futility. The revolt at Ostia, spreading to the city and actually invading the palace where Otho was giving an elaborate mixed banquet, finds the emperor wholly incompetent to act. He saves himself and his guests by means of prayers, tears, and bribes. The speech which he later makes to the troops is carefully constructed by Tacitus to present the picture of a weak executive appealing for support by flattery and futile encouragement to the senate and army. His underestimate of the Vitellian strength indicates either weakness or ignorance. It fails of conviction and the situation in Rome approaches panic. Omens add to the confused terror. Under such conditions, brought on by his own weakness, Otho makes his dispositions for the campaign. The fleet, his most loyal branch of the service, is provided with landing troops to harry Narbonese Gaul. Its command is entrusted to two centurions and a tribune who had been demoted by Galba. To spy on their actions a freedman is added, as Tacitus bitterly says, to watch the fidelity of men more honorable than himself. In command of the army three excellent generals are appointed, but with them is designated a praetorian prefect who has the confidence of Otho and is sharply critical of his colleagues. Tacitus applies all his art to the final picture of this army departing for the front under an incompetent leader surrounded by those whom he feared to leave behind.

Henderson would have us believe that Otho had a masterly strategic plan for the defense of Italy and the defeat of the Vitellians. The fleet was to land troops in the rear of the enemy advancing from Gaul and cut their communications. The army from the Danube was to march from its rendezvous at Aquileia and, meeting the army from Rome which had already carried out a strategy of envelopment neutralizing the forces of Caecina, complete the annihilation of the Vitellians. The crux of his scheme is the battle of Bedriacum, so-called, which ended the war in favor of Vitellius. But it is first essential to follow the fleet in its raid on Narbonese Gaul. If this raid was to have been part of a larger strategy, it is hard to see why it was given a mere handful of soldiers, entrusted to incompetent commanders, and allowed to waste its time plundering the inhabitants of the northern coast of Italy. It did finally reach the Maritime Alps and continued its predatory course as far as Intimilium. At that point a detachment sent by Valens met the forces from the fleet and the resulting battle, while considered a victory for the "fleet," ended practically in a stalemate with the Vitellians holing in at Antipolis, the Othonians at Albingaunum. Tacitus' account is not wholly free from vagueness in detail, but the locations are definitely named and the over-all picture is clear.

The course of the war in the Po valley is clearly presented in the *Histories* by Tacitus and is satisfactory to Henderson in the early stages. The territory between the Alps and the Po is occupied with little difficulty by the advance forces of Caecina. He wins his first victory over a Pannonian cohort at Cremona and immediately crosses the Po to attack Placentia, held by Spurinna, who with Gallus had been sent ahead by Otho. The assault on Placentia fails and Caecina withdraws to Cremona. Gallus, summoned by letter to the aid of Spurinna, marches toward Cremona, stopping at Bedriacum when he learns of Caecina's defeat. The implication is clear that Gallus' legion was already in the neighborhood of the Po, probably near Verona, as Tacitus locates Bedriacum between Verona and Cremona. A minor engagement occurred at this point. Marcius Macer crossed the Po near Cremona with a detachment of gladiators and after scattering a group of auxiliary soldiers on the north bank returned without further action. Tacitus does not explain the presence of these gladiators, and we are left to assume that they form an outpost of Spurinna's force at Placentia. The only item of importance in Tacitus' account of this insignificant action is the grumbling on the part of the victorious soldiers which followed their withdrawal after the battle. This seems to have spread throughout the Othonian forces a feeling that they were being held back and not allowed to come to grips with the enemy. The distrust was played up by malcontents and used by Otho as a reason for summoning his brother Titianus from Rome to take charge of the campaign. This is highly significant in the sequel.

A more important engagement followed soon after at Locus Castorum, on the highway some twelve miles east of Cremona. According to Henderson, Tacitus' account of this battle is "a historical nightmare." Caecina, intent on bringing on a decisive action, planned an ambuscade on the road, a plan which was treacherously revealed to the Othonians. Suetonius Paulinus, in command of the infantry, and Celsus, of the cavalry, marched out from their camp (presumably at Bedriacum, but here Tacitus fails to give us the fact) and pretending to fall into the trap, themselves lured the Vitellians into a similar ambush. Tacitus names the forces involved and their march formation. Celsus with his cavalry advanced cautiously. The Vitellians sprang their trap. Celsus withdrew slowly, drawing his pursuers into his own trap. At this point Suetonius acted too slowly and cautiously and the enemy was given an opportunity to scatter in the woods and vineyards. But the infantry finally did advance and successfully. Furthermore, Caecina sent in his reserves piecemeal and they were successively defeated. Also, Caecina had to contend with a near revolt in his own camp because the whole force wished to join the battle at once.

The situation was critical for the Vitellians and would have been worse if Suetonius had not called a halt. For this he was commended by a few because of the risk of advance against unknown odds but generally criticized on the ground that the defeat of Caecina might have been made definitive. Undoubtedly the battle in the vineyards was confusing and Tacitus pictures the confusion well, but how the general lines of the action could be presented more clearly is hard to imagine. Certainly Henderson, in spite of his expansion on the nature of Roman roads and Italian vineyards, makes it no plainer. Tacitus could hardly be expected to explain for future generations the familiar landmarks of an Italian setting. In view of the fact that some 25,000 troops may have been finally involved in the action, a purely military historian might have given more tactical details but the result for· the general reader would hardly have been improved. On two points of judgment in particular, Henderson takes issue with Tacitus. He considers Caecina's strategical plan sound, to strike the Othonians before the Danube legions should join them. Tacitus ascribes the attack, made with more haste than wisdom, to Caecina's desire to retrieve his waning reputation and to win a victory before Valens arrived to share the glory. Both may well be right. The issue is not greatly important. Tacitus, interested in the characters of his history more than in the theoretical strategy that failed, has justification for his estimate of Caecina in his record both before and after this failure. The other judgment is on the wisdom of Suetonius. If I read Tacitus aright, he and Henderson are in agreement that Suetonius was justified in halting, but, more important, he points clearly to the popular belief that Suetonius was wrong, and it is this general belief which caused trouble presently and so was of more vital importance than any hypothetical decision on the rightness of the judgment itself.

This brings us at last to the main campaign. Valens and Caecina had united their forces at Cremona. Small parts of the Danube forces had joined at Bedriacum the Roman army of Otho. Actually Tacitus does not say, as Plutarch does, that the camp was at Bedriacum. He does say later that the first day's march was to a point four miles west of Bedriacum. This would suggest Bedriacum as the point of departure. At any rate a council of war was held (probably at Bedriacum), at which the three original generals led by Suetonius were in favor of delay, either a long delay while the enemy ran short of supplies and lost morale or at least a short delay until their own reinforcements from Dalmatia and Moesia should arrive. Otho, against this advice, decided on an aggressive policy— *decertare* and *pugnare* are the verbs used. On the advice of the staff, Celsus and Paulinus concurring, Gallus absent, Otho withdrew to Brixellum. Tacitus does not charge him with cowardice but does note the bad effect of this withdrawal on the morale of the troops. Meanwhile a minor action had been lost by Macer and his gladiators at the Po crossing near Cremona, leading to a revolt against Macer by his troops. Tacitus comments on the general mistrust of the Othonian armies toward their leaders. He is not quoting camp gossip—*invenio apud quosdam auctores,* he says. He digresses to show that ambition has often led men to seek power but that the followers have always been more ready than the leaders to prolong a struggle for the highest position. This digression is artistically a pause before the final action, but it definitely adds to Tacitus' testimony against the rumor that the leaders were treacherously holding back.

The first camp, as noted above, was pitched at a distance of four miles from Bedriacum. The place for the camp was badly chosen: there was no supply of water and this in the spring season produced in the army an unnecessary weariness. Again there was a discussion as to whether they ought to proceed to battle, but orders from Otho set them in motion. They marched out, not in battle array but in route march order, for the confluence of the Po and Adua, sixteen miles away. Paulinus and Celsus protested against exposing an army weary with a march with baggage to a fresh enemy only four miles away, who would certainly attack while the Othonians were pitching camp, but Titianus used his position to enforce the demand of Otho for haste toward the conflict.

All of this seems straightforward enough. To be sure, it is twenty-two miles rather than Tacitus' twenty-four from Cremona to the spot which most commentators have selected for Bedriacum. As Tacitus places this town on the road from Cremona to Verona (*Hist.* 2. 23) and also on the road from Hostilia to Cremona (*Hist.* 3. 15), it was presumably situated where the road from Verona joined the Via Postumia. But both roads have disappeared and therefore the location is now only approximate. The significance of the two miles disappears. Unfortunately there is a river Adda seven miles *west* of Cremona and, assuming this to be the Adua of Tacitus, Henderson has developed a theory that the march was to bypass Cremona, according to which he turns the four first miles into fourteen and saves his arithmetic. This is the basis for his whole "strategy of envelopment." But Tacitus' Adua was surely thought by him to be between Bedriacum and Cremona; the orders were to make for contact with the enemy at all speed, and the by-passing of Cremona at such close quarters would be almost too suicidal even for Otho's type of planning. If we take Tacitus' account as it stands, we have only to assume either that the name of the river is corrupt in the MS tradition or that we have not properly located it. There is a small river Adra (as close as Adda in derivation from Adua) at approximately the correct position.

As Suetonius had foretold, Caecina, on learning of their approach, proceeded to the assault. His first cavalry attack was repulsed, but the confusion in the Othonian ranks was immense and the battle, described by Tacitus in a somewhat sketchy fashion, went definitely against them. It developed into a rout headed for Bedriacum. The Vitellians stopped their pursuit five miles short of the town and waited in hope of surrender. This followed on the next day, and Otho at Brixellum committed suicide.

One element in the campaign has been neglected in this account: the march of the Vitellians from Germany to the Po valley. But little in that account has been criticized. The course of Valens through Gaul is precisely indicated by the names of tribes and towns. The march of Caecina through Switzerland is less precise but sufficiently clear. The only point of attack on the part of Henderson is that Tacitus does not realize that Caecina's hesitation between a route directly over the Alps and one by way of Noricum was due to the momentary consideration of a "strategy of penetration" by which he would march well to the east and come down to Aquileia and so intercept the eastern forces of Otho. What Tacitus says is that Caecina hesitated whether to first attack the governor of Noricum or to proceed directly to Italy to support his advance guards. In Noricum, Petronius Urbicus had collected auxiliary troops and destroyed the river bridges, determined to help Otho. Henderson says that Caecina was worrying only as to which pass into Italy he should use and was not concerned with the hostile governor, and that Tacitus "has no right to be so blind" as not to see this. But Henderson agrees that the change would have been a violation of his orders from Vitellius. To delay his march to wipe out a source of disaffection would hardly have been as much of a violation, and on the whole Tacitus' explanation of this minor point seems as good as Henderson's even if less subtle.

There would seem to be little to criticize in the over-all method used by Tacitus in the narrative of this, the first of the great campaigns of the Four-Emperor Year. A military expert might like to know more of the operations plans and also of the details of their execution, but in the first place such documents if they ever existed are not filed and such action reports are a modern invention, and in the second place their inclusion would have completely changed the character of Tacitus' history and would have dwarfed his main purpose of writing the memorial of the Empire. His account is somewhat condensed but it is not vague or obscure. If we have lost track of some locations named by Tacitus, that is not his fault. If we require of him the use of modern terminology and an understanding of

modern strategy, that is our own mistake. The charge of repeating only the gossip of the camp must be considered at
greater length.

The main lines of Tacitus' account agree with the much
shorter story told by Plutarch to such an extent as to suggest
the use by both of the same general history as a basic source.
The same is perhaps true of the still shorter account of Suetonius. But Plutarch mentions other sources of information, and
Seutonius says that his own father fought in the battle, which
suggests that he used information gleaned from him. Tacitus,
too, had acquaintances who were in action. Outstanding was
Verginius Rufus, whom he succeeded in the consulship and
whose eulogy he pronounced. On the other side was a leader
whom he would seem to have admired but on different grounds
and in different degree. Suetonius Paulinus had given to Agricola his first military training, using the young man as his personal aide in Britain. The memory of this tour of duty would
seem to have made the general something of a hero to the
young officer and so perhaps to his son-in-law. At any rate
Tacitus treats in kindly fashion the rashness of Suetonius in
the Mona campaign and the disaster this brought to Roman
prestige in Britain and stresses only the grim and brilliant recovery made by Suetonius. That Suetonius was later the best
general on Otho's staff leads Tacitus to speak in high terms of
his judgment, which was overridden by Otho. The end of Suetonius' career was inglorious. A fugitive from the rout of the
Othonians, he appeared before Vitellius claiming to have deliberately betrayed his own side by confusing the situation before Bedriacum. Vitellius believed the degrading defense and
Suetonius passes from sight. Tacitus cannot commend—but
curiously for him, excuses—the action of Suetonius: *neces-
sariis magis defensionibus quam honestis;* yet the discredited
general seems to have had no more recognition from the state.
Pliny cites the memoirs of Suetonius for facts associated with
his early life, and much of Tacitus' account suggests that these
memoirs covered the later years also and that the general occupied his compulsory leisure in composing the apology for

his own life. If Tacitus did, as seems probable, make use of Suetonius' memoirs or reminiscences, it explains far better than the theory of camp gossip his account of the divided opinion of the Othonian leaders and the stories of the mistrust of the soldiers toward their most competent officers. Tacitus' record undoubtedly here as elsewhere shows bias in the sense that he has made up his own mind on the evidence and presents his conclusions for the most part as facts, but that his conclusions were based on the gossip of the camp is a verdict for which the only evidence is his disagreement with Henderson.

With the second great campaign of the year of civil war, that between the Vitellians and the Flavians, the critics find less to complain of in Tacitus' account, and it will be unnecessary to follow his account in detail. Even Henderson accepts it almost *in toto*. There are a few points at which he complains of its inadequacy. The first concerns whether the Vitellian camp on the Tartaro was on the south or north side of the river. Hardy stoutly defends Tacitus, but history will never care greatly whether he was specific or not on this point: it has no significance in the event. Somewhat more serious is the charge that he is vague about Valens' march to the north from Rome to join Caecina. Tacitus is indeed vague, and the reason seems to lie in the complete futility of Valens' movement. In the first place he was not moving with any considerable forces. In fact there is no indication that he had anything but his entourage of entertainers. He was sent to furnish a leader, not reinforcements. On the way he hears of the revolt of the fleet at Ravenna and hesitates between a decision to avoid Ravenna and slip through to the Vitellian camp on the Po or to send to Rome for forces to enable him to break through Ravenna. He decides on the latter course but does not receive sufficient forces to carry it out. He therefore sends what troops do arrive on ahead to Rimini, with the cavalry as a rear guard. This rear guard is hard to explain unless the whole district around Ravenna was disaffected. At best, Tacitus' statement is unsatisfactory. Henderson thinks that Valens has passed Rimini and sends the troops back to that town. This would explain the rear guard, but Tacitus says distinctly *praemittit* and is therefore in error if this be the explanation. Valens himself goes into Umbria, then into Etruria, and so takes ship for Gaul. The only difficulty here is that according to Tacitus he would already be in Umbria, but *flexit in Umbriam* might easily mean "turned inland through Umbria." After his capture off the coast of Gaul, Valens is not mentioned again until his death, which occurs at Urbinum. Henderson is rhetorical in his comments on the failure of Tacitus to explain how and why he got to Urbinum, but surely Tacitus makes it clear. The main forces of the Flavians, marching toward Rome, came down through Umbria. Tacitus mentions Mevania and Carsulae and the events that occurred in those towns. Then he says: *iisdem diebus Fabius Valens Urbini in custodia interficitur.* He has been brought a prisoner, to be handed over to the commander. The reason is also made clear, for it is the sight of Valens' head, displayed to the army, which relieves them of the fear that he has escaped and is rousing Gaul and Germany in their rear. (Only by arbitrarily choosing the wrong Urbinum can Henderson create a minor difficulty.) The whole discussion (i.e. of Valens' movements as officer and prisoner) illustrates what Henderson calls "inexcusable vagueness" in Tacitus' military history. His interest in geography is obviously casual, but it is adequate, and as for inexcusable vagueness, the charge is groundless. Valens' movements and his relation to the whole campaign are adequately described. On the unessential points of whether Valens did or did not pass Rimini and by what route he was brought from Gaul to Urbinum, Tacitus is quite justifiably vague or silent.

A minor difficulty is made of the fact that the Moesian legions already at Aquileia are summoned in haste by Antonius, and presently Aquileia is taken over for him by Primus and Varus. There seems to me no inconsistency. To be sure, Tacitus does provide for the security of Moesia at this point, security made necessary, however, not by the immediate departure of the legions at this moment but by their prospective absence in Italy. And *Aquileia occupata* does not imply that the town had to be taken from enemies.

Finally there is criticism of the fact that "Tacitus has not the least interest in the march" of the Vitellians from their camp on the Tartaro to Hostilia and thence to Cremona. It would presumably be of interest to one primarily studying a single campaign to know by what route these troops made their way to the scene of battle, but it is not a fact significant in the whole picture. No element of the situation depends on it. They left Hostilia and they reached Cremona, and there they are found by Antonius weary but ready to fight. It may be Tacitus' delight in the melodramatic touch that leads him to telescope the tale of the march as he does, but he does not on that account weaken the historical value of his narrative. His "interest in the march" may not be that of his critic but interest he certainly had.

The second campaign of Bedriacum, then, appears to be treated by Tacitus with even less vagueness than the first. There is a third campaign forming a direct part of the historical narrative, the revolt of Civilis. This, however, is not quite of the same political importance as the other two, for it occurs after the end of the civil wars and therefore falls between the two categories of military narrative, coming closer to the second category, which includes not civil strife between aspirants for the throne but action of the Roman armies against foreign foes. Its origin in the final state of civil war does make a difference, however, and it must be discussed in the first category as a campaign of primary political importance.

In general there has been no complaint of the clarity of Tacitus' account of the Revolt of Civilis. It will be sufficient to consider the specific criticisms of that account which have been more or less generally accepted. One is that the judgments made by Tacitus are incorrect, the other that his geographical knowledge is vague and "incredibly unsatisfactory." They may best be considered in the reverse order.

It is largely in the opening scene that Tacitus' geographical

knowledge is questioned. The historian begins, as he so often
does, with a general statement, to be made more precise, if
necessary, later: "caesos exercitus, capta legionum hiberna,
descivisse Gallias, non ut mala loquebantur." He then explicitly states that he will explain the situation. He gives an adequate account of the Batavi and their leader, Julius Civilis.
He indicates clearly the immediate grievances of these people,
their appeal to their neighbors and their preparations for war.
What he does not do is specify where the first action took place
which cleared the "Island of the Batavians" of its few Roman
troops. The Island is sixty miles long by less than twelve wide.
The incident is used by Tacitus because it is vivid and indica-
tive of the treachery which was to color the whole campaign.
But its prime significance lies in the preliminary clearing of the
Island of its Roman occupation troops and the exact spot on
the sixty miles of river front is of comparatively small importance. Hordeonius sends troops from Roman Germany to make
good this defeat, but no sooner have they crossed the river into
the Island than they are met and defeated by Civilis and they
retreat to Castra Vetera or, as it is more commonly called,
Vetera. The place of this battle is also unnamed by Tacitus,
but this time there can be little criticism. The Roman forces
could enter only at the eastern end of the Island and that they
did so is confirmed by their quick retreat to Vetera. There is
no vagueness. The preliminaries are over and, with the Roman
forces entrenched in Vetera, the war is on. Obviously this is
an introductory chapter and except for a specialist on the particular campaign a satisfactory one. From this point on, there
is no further possibility of questioning the geographical clarity
of the account save for the disappearance of some towns or
camps familiar enough to the Romans but now less surely located after the lapse of centuries. And in this particular locality
the names have shown great persistence, so that practically
every location is certain. I should conclude that Tacitus' geographical knowledge in this part of his history was vague only
in the background sketch and unsatisfactory never.
    The second defect charged against Tacitus in his account of

the revolt of Civilis is his mistaken judgment of Vocula's motives. "This too" says Henderson, "must be added to the large rubbish-heap of Tacitus' military judgments." Tacitus' words are *corrupta totiens victoria non falso suspectus bellum malle* (*Hist.* 4. 34). It is a serious charge that Tacitus makes against a Roman general and it would seem that he recognizes this fact, for his whole picture of Vocula is developed as if to justify such a judgment. Vocula is first presented as winning the soldiers' support at Bonna with firm and vigorous action and so replacing his chief, Hordeonius Flaccus. He handles the soldiers roughly again when they attack his colleague Gallus, left in charge of the camp at Gelduba. Civilis makes a sudden and fierce attack on the camp, which is finally repelled, and Civilis is beaten. Tacitus criticizes both generals, Civilis for underestimating the force required and Vocula for not following up the victory and relieving Vetera at once. This is the first time that Vocula withheld a decisive blow. When the best moment has been lost, Vocula does advance to Vetera and does relieve the town, driving off Civilis, but again fails to follow up his victory. It is on this second occasion that Tacitus makes the comment quoted above. The use of *totiens* is open to valid criticism, but Tacitus has made it clear that in his opinion Vocula has twice failed to use his victories. The rest of the story to a certain extent justifies the conclusion. Vocula abandons Vetera but does not withdraw all of the garrison, merely strengthening it against further siege. The dissatisfaction is great. His own soldiers are unreasonably hostile on the return trip, and at Novaesium they revolt. Hordeonius is killed and Vocula escapes in disguise. Whom the soldiers had so recently demanded as their commander they now repudiate. Since he had been chosen for his aggressive vigor, the suspicion of the soldiery whether justified or not had certainly fastened on him. In default of another leader, however, they returned to him presently, but not with the old enthusiasm, and he led them to the relief of Novaesium, beseiged by the Germans. On the defeat and death of Vitellius the German revolt flared with new violence; the Gauls joined the revolution and there was much

disaffection in the old Vitellian legions. Vocula found himself
hopelessly outnumbered and surrounded. After a flamboyant
speech he failed at suicide and was assassinated. His last play
for glory was in character, but it is clear that he had no avenue
of escape. Tacitus gives him no eulogistic summary and obviously does not credit him with any real nobility or deep courage. It is difficult therefore to see why the historian should be
condemned for a judgment which he supports with evidence
and against which the modern critic can bring only hypotheses.
Like every other *ex post facto* judgment it may have been right
or wrong. It is still at the very least plausible.

We have covered the military sections of the *Histories*,
which form the main thread of narrative, broken at intervals
to give literary relief in the form of summaries of events, mostly
at Rome, outside the main stream of the story. As these books
are the basis for the characterization of Tacitus by Mommsen
and his condemnation by Henderson, it might seem unnecessary to study the military evidence of the other works. But I
believe that it is just this evidence which has led many to accept
unhesitatingly the judgment that Tacitus is the most unmilitary
of historians. Surely more students of Tacitus would have followed the example of E. G. Hardy in modifying if not refuting
the verdict of Mommsen if the *Histories* alone had been preserved.

In the *Annals* we have the story of two periods of history,
each of approximately twenty years, during which there is no
civil war. This, in contrast with a year and a half presented
in the *Histories*, at about the same length as each of the longer
periods in the *Annals* and during which there was constant
civil war, on which was concentrated not only the interest of
the Empire but that of the historian. During the two periods
covered by what we have of the *Annals* there were mutinies
in the Roman armies on the Rhine and a minor revolt in Gaul
which involve some military history, and wars in Britain and
Armenia calling for definitely military narrative. But these
wars are at a great distance from Rome, causing only incidental interest in the minds of the citizens there and serving

the historian as breaks in his main line of narrative rather than comprising that major stream.

The mutiny of the German armies began in Pannonia. The three legions there were in a common summer camp. The location is not named and is even now uncertain. During the account of this Pannonian affair only one town, Nauportus, is named. The setting seems almost deliberately vague in contrast with the vivid picture of Blaesus, the commander of the camp, of Rufus the prefect, and finally of the young prince, Drusus, and their handling of the mutiny. The whole story is a dramatic scene leading up to the more important revolt of the legions in Germany. Here Germanicus held the proconsular power, and the possibility that he might, as inheritor of his father's ambitions and popularity, lead a movement for the restoration of the Republic, lends dramatic interest to the situation. Once more there is no geographical precision given to the setting. The armies of Upper and Lower Germany are identified by their commanders, and Germanicus is described as busy with the census in Gaul. The camp of the army of Lower Germany to which Germanicus proceeds is not located; the resulting scenes are vividly presented. The winter quarters of the army of Lower Germany at Ara Ubiorum and Vetera are specifically named but late in the account. The campaign against the Marsi, used by Germanicus to revive the loyalty of his troops, cannot be followed in any detail. This is partly because the *Silva Caesia* and the *limes Tiberii* are impossible of identification but largely because of the complete vagueness of the account, which is introduced not for its own sake but only as the concluding scene of the tale of mutiny. It also serves as the background of the march into Germany which opens the account of the following year. From the military point of view the story of this campaign to revitalize the troops, avenge Varus, and if possible crush Arminius becomes, the moment it has told of the passage of the Amisia, a model of confusion. The reader who tries to follow details is almost as lost as the soldiers of Caecina in the forest-encircled swamps. Impressionistically the effect is superb. The horror of the situation as the army moves into the unknown country, surrounded by an enemy at home in the frightful terrain, coming upon the relics of Varus' lost legions, and almost annihilated on the march back—all this is enhanced by the topographical vagueness, made doubly effective by the picture of Agrippina's firm decision to save the bridge by which the shattered troops emerge once more from the shadowy land of horror to the familiar realities of the Roman province. The whole account is a brilliant incident, significant in the major story of Tiberius and Germanicus but not in itself a part of the main stream of political history.

Like the history of the revolt of Civilis, that of the great rebellion in Britain in the year 60 begins with a general statement, *gravis clades in Brittania accepta,* followed by a more detailed account. But in a previous book the prologue to the rebellion has already appeared. In 12. 31–40 Tacitus departed temporarily from his annalistic framework and summarized the events of four years in Britain. Camulodunum is the only place name specifically used. For the rest, the names of tribes indicate roughly the place of various actions, and leaders are more stressed than tactics. The general course of events is indicated, arriving finally at a lull in activity under the governorship of the elderly Aulus Didius. The tale is resumed in 14. 29 with an introduction of Suetonius Paulinus filled with ambition for glory to match that of his rival Corbulo. To gain this he attacks the island of Mona, the seat of Druid leadership. From the conquest of this island he is recalled by the rising of the Britains in his rear. They had already sacked Camulodunum and wiped out the ninth legion coming to its relief. Tacitus does not bother to state the point from which the legion started or the place of the disastrous battle, nor does he follow Suetonius from Mona; he is content to describe his arrival at Londinium. Suetonius determines to abandon London and Verulam to the foe and marches off. Tacitus does not say in which direction, nor does he state the location of the spot he chose to make his stand. The wisdom of Suetonius in its selection is made clear; his forces and their disposition are made reasonably so. The importance of the struggle is stressed by indirect quotation of speeches by Boudicca and Suetonius. The battle is briefly but adequately described. We are not informed of the location of Suetonius' new camp after the battle, and the incident is rounded out by the inspection visit of Polycleitus and the recall of Suetonius. With his replacement by Petronius Turpilianus, Britain subsides into uneventful peace.

Here is another incident of foreign warfare introduced almost as a digression from the main current of political affairs and treated in an impressionistic fashion that may justly be called vague. In this case we may be sure that had he desired to do so, Tacitus could have written a detailed military account of the whole affair. His father-in-law, Agricola, was an aide to Suetonius Paulinus and could have furnished all the necessary facts. Obviously, the historian preferred his own method of narrating the disaster and recovery.

Most extensive of all the military undertakings described in the *Annals* was the war with Parthia. The situation in the East is referred to not infrequently in Books 11 and 12, but these notes on the affairs of Parthia and Armenia are really preparatory to the account of the war conducted by Corbulo, contained in Books 13–15. This appears in sections serving as interludes to the domestic history and therefore violates the rule of annalistic narrative generally followed by Tacitus. Whether it is partly on this account or wholly for other reasons, it is true that the general verdict on this narrative has been, with entire justice, that it is completely vague in matters of chronology, geography, strategy, and even, to a lesser extent, political significance. The events of the different years are not kept distinct except for their over-all context. Few place names are given, and the important geographical characteristics of the difficult country are largely ignored. Everything is made subordinate to the presentation of Corbulo as a military hero. Here again Tacitus could have been precise and complete in his narrative if he had so desired. He had the memoirs of Corbulo at his command and even used them. From Pliny we know that Corbulo added much to the already considerable

geographical knowledge of Armenia, and no matter how much
he devoted himself to his own aggrandizement, he must have
given far more information on the strategy and tactics of the
war than appears in the dramatic but picturesque account of
Tacitus. The historian clearly chose deliberately the method
which he follows. To have given a fuller analysis of the campaigns would have thrown the account out of proportion with
the rest of the narrative. He uses what to him is an incidental
situation to create dramatic interludes for his main plot and to
develop one or two of the characters important in that plot.

The question of Tacitus' competence as a military historian
takes on a different color with a recognition of his two different
approaches to military situations. To the sensitive literary artist
the question was not so simple as it has appeared to some of
his critics. If, however, Tacitus had not followed two distinctly
different methods under distinctly different circumstances,
these critics would not have found scholars so complacently
accepting the verdict that Tacitus was the most unmilitary of
historians. The statement, of course, was itself a rhetorical
exaggeration and could never have been intended for literal
acceptance. To the long line of German investigators who have
sought to unravel the mysteries of the Teutoburg Forest the
account of Tacitus is of course infuriating, but to the student
of Roman imperial policy on the Rhine frontier it is adequate.
To the average reader of history it may be a passage of stun-
ning brilliance.

It is easy to forget that Tacitus himself felt a marked difference between the two sorts of history writing. When he began
his history he wrote enthusiastically and confidently that he
was going to unfold a tale rich in catastrophic events, full of
battles and revolts, civil wars and foreign wars and wars that
were both civil and foreign. His purpose then was in part at
least a moral purpose, to hold up examples of heroism and to
prove that the mills of the gods *do* grind exceeding fine. His
first work required no great dramatic construction to carry
the interest of the reader, at least not in its early stages. What
was his method in the later books we cannot tell. But events

carried the tale in that crowded first year and a half. In the *Annals* he sighs for the wars and conquests which the historians of the Republic had as their material, but he makes the losing struggle of liberty against tyranny the dramatic substitute. Such wars as he has to relate must therefore take their proper place in this larger drama. They can still serve to illustrate the ideal Roman heroism or the degeneration that goes with unrestricted power, but they can no longer claim to be the central theme. And so the military sections of the *Annals* make no pretense of strategic knowledge or tactical detail.

Perhaps the best illustration of this use of the military element may be had from one of the least important minor wars of the *Annals*. From the opening of the account in 2. 52 the reader is almost deceived into expecting a great war: "eodem anno coeptum in Africa bellum, duce hostium Tacfarinate." The only warning against this expectation is the *eodem anno*, which is not necessarily but usually the formula for introducing minor events. The paragraph presents vividly the leaders, Tacfarinas and Mazippa on the one hand, Camillus on the other, and the various types of warfare, the battle, and the triumph of Camillus. No mention is made of any location; the setting is left as wide open as the African desert. The incident is pointed by the ironic comment with which Tacitus brings it to a close: *quod Camillo ob modestiam vitae impune fuit*. In the next book however (3. 73) we find that the African incident was no casual insert. Blaesus, the uncle of Sejanus, gets triumphal insignia as an honor to Sejanus, although to be sure, Tacitus says, his deeds were quite worthy of the honor. He thus introduces the second chapter in the African War. Again there is no geographical precision, no locations are named, the impression is deliberately given of a roving, scattered warfare, from which Tacfarinas escapes to fight another day. The two paragraphs end as they began, with the honors paid to Blaesus, the last general not in the imperial family to receive the title of imperator. Finally, in 4. 23 we are reminded of the phrase that introduced Tacfarinas when the paragraph opens: "Is demum annus populum Romanum longo adversum Numidam

Tacfarinatem bello absolvit." As the contest is being wound up, there is slightly more precision. Two places are named, Thubuscum and Auzea; otherwise the vagueness of the picture is not disturbed. Dolabella is the hero, but now the irony of the conclusion is more bitter. Camillus had been honored because he was harmless, Blaesus because he was the uncle of Sejanus. Dolabella is refused the honor that glory may not be withdrawn from Sejanus' uncle. Such reward as was made went to Ptolemaeus, son of Juba, for slight and questionable aid given to Dolabella. This war in Africa may have been a minor affair, yet there were three statues with laurel wreathes that stood in Rome to commemorate its leaders; two generals had been given triumphal insignia during its course and one earned but did not receive them by its successful conclusion. It could hardly be overlooked by Tacitus; so he weaves it into his narrative and seizes upon its political aspects to integrate it with his dramatic tale of Tiberius.

We may conclude that Tacitus was indeed not a military historian but he was what he was from choice and not from incompetence. When the nature of the history that he was writing made it essential, he could and did write military history and wrote it adequately. When it was not required, he made the military events serve his general plan with a perfectly deliberate purpose not to permit any detail to ruin the proportions of the whole.

9. DIGRESSIONS IN THE HISTORICAL WORKS

I N HIS DIGRESSIONS an historian tends to disclose the trend of his personal beliefs and interests, the qualities of mind that may have had their influence on the narrative itself. At the same time, indulgence in digressive habit or avoidance of digression may throw light on an historian's relation to the traditions of his craft. Strict definition might consider anything that goes beyond the mere listing of events as a digression and endless as well as fruitless argument might well result. For the insertion of a *credo* or an *ita dis visum* may well be a more significant digression than the introduction of a geographical excursus on Africa.

If then it seems of some importance (as it does) to consider what use Tacitus made of the digression and what light this usage throws on his methods and his interests, it is essential to define the limits within which digressions shall be considered. Fundamentally, we may assume that a digression is essentially marked by a break in time sequence. Either the reader is carried forward to the time of composition to listen to a comment by the writer or else the writer carries the attention back to some antecedent situation which he considers of importance or interest in connection with the event which he is at the time narrating. The first type of time break is most naturally accompanied by a shift from the narrative third person to the first, the second type is not. Even such general and fundamental characterization of digressions requires a word of caution. The second or informational type may not at first glance appear to refer to a time antecedent to the event under consideration. When Caesar undertakes to describe the customs of the Gauls and Germans or Sallust the geography and peoples of Africa, it may be said with some justice that they are speaking of conditions existing at the time of writing and that the time break, if any, is from past to present. But the excuse for introducing such material is to clarify the narrative at a given point, and the digression therefore presents material logically antecedent to that point. The writer may be taking advantage of a familiar device to introduce contemporary information, but this only serves to throw light on the writer and does not change the fundamental assumption.

Certain general types of digression had already in Tacitus' day become familiar in the writing of history. Of such perhaps the most familiar, certainly the most obvious, is the discussion of the geography and people of a district under discussion. Such are the eighteen chapters in the sixth book of Caesar's *Gallic War,* introduced in chapter 11 by the words "Quoniam ad hunc locum perventum est, non alienum esse videtur de Galliae Germaniaeque moribus et quo differant hae nationes inter sese proponere." Such is Sallust's discussion of Africa in *Jugurtha* 17 ff.: "Res postulare videtur Africae situm paucis exponere et eas gentes quibusnam nobis aut bellum aut amicitia fuit attingere." Caesar, in his character of *commentarius* does not remark on the close of his digression; it is indicated simply by the resumption of the narrative exactly as if there had been no break whatsoever. The digression is, however, completely detachable. Sallust winds up his comments on Africa: "De Africa et eius incolis ad necessitudinem rei satis dictum." Tacitus' most notable digression is in *Histories* 5. 2 ff. It begins: "Sed quoniam famosae urbis supremum diem tradituri sumus, congruens videtur primordia eius aperire." The conclusion of the digression is an artistic compromise between the methods of Caesar and Sallust. Its final chapter recounts civil war within Jerusalem itself, concluding with the sentence: "Ita in duas factiones civitas discessit donec propinquantibus Romanis bellum externum concordiam pararet." The narrative is resumed with *Evenerant prodigia,* which might follow directly the last sentence before the digression: "haud procul Hierosolymis castra fecit."

This type of digression is scarcely traceable in Livy. Only on the occasions of military action at Croton (24. 3) and New Carthage (26. 42) does he digress to give any account of the place, and then only the military aspect interests him; there is no systematic account with geographical or ethnographical appeal. Sallust is apparently the model for Tacitus insofar as he had a model. That he was familiar with Sallust's account of Africa is clear from the echoes of its phraseology to be found in the *Germania* and *Agricola*. These two essays furnish information about foreign peoples on a somewhat larger scale than the familiar digression but in much the same manner, and raise the question of why Tacitus did not introduce geographical excursuses on Britain, Germany, and Parthia into the *Annals*. At present it can only be suggested that although he had the material on hand—certainly for two of them if not for all—he was restrained from using it by his dramatic sense in the *Annals,* a pressure which in the *Histories* was not sufficient to deter him from following the earlier pattern.

In connection with one digression which might seem irrelevant to the reader, Livy makes a first-person statement of his reasons for halting the narrative (9. 17): "Nihil minus quaesitum a principio huius operis videri potest quam ut plus iusto ab rerum ordine declinarem varietatibusque distinguendo opera et legentibus velut deverticula amoena et requiem animo meo quaererem; tamen tanti regis ac ducis mentio, quibus saepe tacitis cogitationibus volutavi animum eos evocat in medium ut quaerere libeat quinam eventus Romanis rebus si cum Alexandro foret bellatum futurus fuerit." In spite of his protest it is hard to see any reasons other than those which he disclaims for the digression which follows. In the same manner, in *Hist.* 2. 50, Tacitus makes his apology for an incident included for its inherent interest: "Ut conquirere fabulosa et fictis oblectare legentium animos procul gravitate coepti operis crediderim, ita volgatis traditisque demere fidem non ausim." Both Livy's and Tacitus' statements are explanations of their theory of writing history and they are approximately the same. Tacitus goes further in *Annals* 4. 32. 33.

This statement of his literary credo is well worth considerable analysis. A personal explanation introduced at length into the narrative may well raise a doubt as to the theory that the *Annals* are the more dramatic of Tacitus' major productions.

"Pleraque eorum quae rettuli quaeque referam parva forsitan et levia memoratu videri non nescius sum." The duty of the historian to interest the reader, or at least the desirability of having interesting material to present, is clearly recognized: "Sed nemo annales nostros cum scriptura eorum contenderit, qui veteres populi Romani res composuere." This is equivalent to a comparison of his own subject matter with that of Livy's and by way of making a vivid point he applies to his own work the half-apologetic term "annals." He then illustrates in detail the two types of subject matter, defending his own account as follows: "Non tamen sine usu fuerit introspicere illa primo aspectu levia, ex quis magnarum saepe rerum oriuntur." He elaborates this generalization by a detailed statement of the types and changes of Roman government and suggests the lessons to be learned from a study of the details of government: "Ceterum ut profutura, ita minimum oblectationis adferunt." This brings up the motive which Livy suggested, the entertainment of the reader. But Tacitus insists that in addition to being dull his subject matter is also dangerous, because of the tense state of personal feelings involved. He winds up: *sed ad inceptum redeo,* indicating that the digression was deliberate. The next chapter begins a new year with the consular formula. It takes very little consideration to see that Tacitus, in the presentation of the *maiestatis* cases desires to create not only a cumulative impression but a crescendo effect. He sees the dramatic necessity for some break in the tense narrative but does not wish to create too much distraction by an end-of-the-year summary of minor events in the Empire at large. The discussion of purpose serves as a break in the monotonous line of trials while keeping the attention riveted on the cases, and creates an ominous conviction that they are not casual, unconnected incidents but that they are gradually leading to a tragic climax. In other words, Tacitus has, in this instance, used the particular type of digression already employed by himself and by Livy in a special way to furnish the relief and commentary that it is sometimes the function of the dramatic chorus to give. Incidentally, in this digres-

sion, Tacitus registers once more his serious motive in writing
history. His purpose is not merely to entertain and not merely
to exhibit his ability for the sake of glory: *Profutura* implies the
didactic motive in history, the desire to improve the world in
some degree. This motive was shared by history and drama.
With Tacitus the serious aim is primarily political. In Livy and
Sallust it had been moral. In the *Histories* (3. 51) Tacitus recounts a rather improbable incident and recalls a similar happening from the days of Cinna and Pompey to point a moral:
"Tanto acrior apud maiores sicut virtutibus gloria, ita flagitiis
paenitentia fuit." He adds his excuse for the digression: "sed
haec aliaque ex vetere memoria petita, quotiens res locusque
exempla recti aut solatia mali poscet, haud absurde memora-
bimus." The particular incident has mainly the interest of the
melodramatic, but the effort to give it moral significance brings
it close to another type of digression familiar in the earlier
authors.

Consistently with the Stoic origin and trend of literary history at Rome, Sallust presents a long diatribe on luxury in
Jugurtha 41. 42, returning to his narrative with the words *ad
inceptum redeo*. In *Hist.* 2. 38 Tacitus does the same thing with
regard to *ambitio* and resumes the narrative with *nunc ad
rerum ordinem redeo*. The only similar digression in the *Annals* is not a true parallel. In 3. 55, after the quotation of a
letter from Tiberius to the senate dealing with the question of
table luxury, Tacitus digresses to indicate the trend of that
luxury from the beginning of the Empire to his own day and
for once commends the current attitude. The purpose is to
bring out the crafty intentions of Tiberius. In general, his
Stoic moralizing is confined to sententious phrases or ironical
insinuations rather than presented *en bloc* in digressions.

But I have myself digressed from the discussion in hand.
There is one other case in which Tacitus digresses to discuss
his methods. In *Ann.* 16. 16 he apologizes for the monotony of
the trials and executions following the conspiracy of Piso:
"Etiam si bella externa et obitas pro republica mortes tanta
casuum similitudine memorarem, meque ipsum satias cepis-

set aliorumque taedium exspectarem." His excuse at this point
is that these men who died as it seemed so tamely were
deserving of more recognition than they would otherwise
have received. Once more he is relying on cumulative force
and on his crescendo technique to reach an effective climax.
The digressive comment is in this case brief, and the fatalistic
progress of doom is indicated by referring the wholesale slaugh-
ter to the wrath of the gods.

A third traditional type of digression which Tacitus uses is
that which deals with sources. Comparison here must be with
Livy, for Sallust and Caesar were writing of events contemporary or nearly so and with other than purely historical purposes.
Livy does not disclose his method of using sources in any
general statement. In 38. 55 he states that certain figures are
taken by him from the account by Valerius Antias. He considers these figures unreasonable and so questions the accuracy
of his source. In the two following chapters he completes his
summary of the life and character of Scipio, noting that the
authorities are in disagreement on many points. He does not
give names: they are *scriptores* or *auctores* or simply "they."
Livy cites their disagreement under the formula *alii, alii.* He
seems to use nothing but his own judgment of probability to
decide between them, although he does cite documents and
monuments, equally indecisive. This method is in general followed by Tacitus in his *Histories.* He uses the terms *scriptores*
and *auctores* and occasionally notes divergent opinions. For
two incidents of little importance but of perhaps questionable
probability he cites authorities, Vipstanus Messala and the
Elder Pliny. The extent to which his source references constitute a digression is less than, but comparable with, that of
Livy. In the *Annals* he goes further, not to any great extent in
the first six books, but definitely in 11–16. In 13. 20 he pauses
to discuss sources, compares Fabius and Cluvius, and states as
a principle: "nos consensum auctorum secuturi, si qui diversa prodiderint, sub nominibus ipsorum trademus." In almost all of the instances in which authorities are cited or discussed the events or motives under consideration are histori-

cally of minor importance but dramatically significant. Hence perhaps one reason for their increased frequency in the later books and the divergence on Tacitus' part from historical tradition.

A similar development in Tacitus' method may be noted in the digressions which summarize the life or character of an individual. This type of digression is frequent in Livy and in Sallust. One of the most extensive and deliberate instances is Sallust, *Jugurtha* 95. After a casual mention of L. Sulla, the author continues: "Sed quoniam nos tanti viri res admonuit, idoneum visum est de natura cultuque eius paucis dicere." His excuse for the account which follows is that he is not going to treat Sulla elsewhere and previous writers have been unjust to him. He resumes his narrative with *igitur*. Livy, in 39. 40, is describing the election of a censor. One of the candidates was M. Porcius Cato. "In hoc viro," he says, "tanta vis animi fuit" etc., describing him at length and discussing his speeches and writings as well as his character, winding up: "Hunc, sicut omni vita, tum pententem premebat nobilitas." In *Hist.* 4. 5 a long account of Helvidius Priscus begins with the words, "Res poscere videtur, quia iterum in mentionem incidimus viri saepius memorandi, ut vitam studiaque eius, et quali fortuna sit usus paucis repetam." The resumption of the narrative is somewhat more abrupt than in the case from Sallust but of the same type: "Tum invectus est Musonius Rufus in Publium Celerem."

It was traditionally more usual to insert the account of the life and character of an individual at the time of his death. Tacitus follows this tradition frequently in the *Histories* although there are about the same number of summary descriptions of characters at other points in their careers. In the *Annals* Tacitus followed the death notice tradition in the cases of C. Petronius and Ateius Capito, but much more commonly the characterization was made at the time of the first or most important entrance. So Sejanus is presented in 4. 1: "Nunc originem, mores, et quo facinore dominationem raptum ierit expediam." So Poppaea in 13. 45: "Erat in civitate Sabina Poppaea. . . . Huic mulieri cuncta alia fuere praeter honestum animum," with details of her personality and origin following. In the same way the origin and character of Piso is outlined in 15. 48 at the beginning of the Pisonian conspiracy. A striking case is that of Nymphidius, a minor character, in 15. 72, with reasons given for the insertion: "Nymphidio . . . quia nunc primum oblatus est pauca repetam: nam et ipse pars Romanarum cladium erit."

Such biographical summaries were considered traditionally suitable to historical narrative and are less definitely digressions than the geographical discussions, for example. They are not, however, strictly a part of the narrative, and the tendency on the part of Tacitus to transfer them to the first rather than the last appearance of a given character in the more dramatic *Annals* has some significance.

Finally, tradition sanctioned the introduction of somewhat irrelevant items merely for the sake of their inherent interest, what might be called decorative digressions. In chapter 79 of the *Jugurtha,* Sallust writes: "sed quoniam in eas regiones per Leptitanorum negotia venimus, non indignum videtur egregium atque mirabile facinus duorum Carthaginiensium memorare: eam rem nos locus admonuit." At the close of the anecdote he returns to his narrative with the formula *nunc ad rem redeo,* indicating that he recognized the fact that he had digressed. So Tacitus in the *Agricola* told of the *magnum atque memorabile facinus* of the crews that sailed off on a wild and futile venture. And such also is the digression in *Hist.* 4. 83, 84 on the cult of Serapis, beginning "Origo dei nondum nostris auctoribus celebrata." The narrative is resumed with *At Domitianus.* It is in these decorative digressions that the individual interests of the author tend to emerge, and although the type is traditional, the content may best be considered when we try to estimate Tacitus' specific digressions as evidence of his personal interest.

It is clear that Tacitus makes no sharp break with historical tradition in the matter of digressions. He gives a summary of the status quo of the Empire at the beginning of both of his major works. The quality of the summary is in each case thoroughly individual, but the fact of its presentation is in line with tradition. The same is true of his discussions of his own methods and of his criticisms of sources, of his digressions on luxury and ambition, of his summaries of character and personality, and also of his introduction of extraneous matter for the sake of making his history more interesting.

But, if Tacitus accepted in general the tradition of historiography, it is equally true that throughout he left his personal stamp, and this is nowhere more evident than in the use of the digression in its broadest sense. The Roman historian did not employ footnotes. Much, therefore, which today would be found in the footnote is incorporated in the Latin text. Editorial comment and explanatory material are both a part of the narrative in Roman histories. *Ut supra memoravimus* or *suo loco reddemus* is for Tacitus the equivalent of a footnote reference. Such phrases as *ipsa verba referam, credo, nec sciri potest, parum compertum, non ausim adseverare,* indicate an author more meticulous in his attempt at accuracy than we should judge his predecessors to have been. Tacitus also uses the first person frequently in introducing an historical explanation of some act or in sketching its background: *quam altiore initio repetam* (*Hist.* 2. 27); *id bellum quibus causis ortum . . . altius expediam* (*Hist.* 4. 12). But he also introduced historical explanations with a general statement, such as his account of Cremona in *Hist.* 3. 34: "Hic exitus Cremonae anno ducentesimo octogesimo sexto a primordio sui. Condita erat" etc. Such digressions are not sharply distinguished from brief explanations of a single fact, which in the more extreme cases are merely indicated by the use of the pluperfect tense with or without a reinforcing adverb such as *quippe, nam, enim,* or *sane.* The digression tends in these instances to become a mere parenthesis particularly when the imperfect, pluperfect, or present tense is used or when the verb is omitted in such phrases as *ita illis mos* or *etenim modicae municipio vires.* Definitions are similarly introduced, as in *Hist.* 2. 20, *bracas, barbarum tegumen.* These explanatory phrases and such sententious parentheses as *rarum in societate potentiae* (*Ann.* 13. 2) or *adeo invisa scelera sunt* (*Hist.* 3. 31) can only loosely be classed as digressions, but they have one thing in common with these: they indicate the lines of interest of the writer.

The editorial comment and the explanatory note are about equally common in the *Histories* and the *Annals* and are definitely more frequent in Tacitus than in his predecessors. The former contribute largely toward the ironical tone of Tacitus' product; the latter make clear his keen interest in historical background, in the causes for events, and in antiquarian lore in general. In the larger digressions there is a differentiation between the two major works. The geographical excursus does not appear in the *Annals*. The death notice type of biographical summary is much more frequent in the *Histories* than in the *Annals,* where character summary is reserved largely for minor characters who make only one or few entries. Digressions on sources appear in both works, but those in the *Annals* are regularly motivated by a desire to introduce a dubious fact which has dramatic value. Finally, the considerable group of digressions which deal in general with the historical or archaeological background show also a different trend in the two works. In the *Histories* they are more conventional. They deal with history proper: the story of Cremona, the history of the Capitol, of the Batavi, of the Jews, of Africa. In two cases they give an account of a foreign cult of particular interest at Rome: Serapis, and the Paphian Venus. In two other instances they follow the Stoic tradition by developing the evil influence of luxury and ambition. In the *Annals,* on the other hand, with a few exceptions, they deal with matters of legal or political import, sketching the history of such institutions as the pomerium, the management of the treasury, the legislation on usury, the quaestorship, Roman law, the alphabet. Such extraneous matters as the customs of Egypt and the history of the phoenix are introduced for the dramatic value of suspense. The digressions become progressively fewer as the dramatic character of the history becomes more conscious.

10. SOURCES

TACITUS was no exception to the body of Roman historians insofar as his chief purposes in writing are concerned. Presumably, as an anti-imperialist under Domitian, his feelings were more involved than were those of Livy, writing under Augustus. The urge to write came nevertheless from the desire to present what was known in better form than it had been presented, and to add new material from new sources. History, as a branch of oratory, had laid stress on the form of presentation since the days before Cicero. It was this which differentiated history from annals. But the honest historian always tried to add to the sum of historical knowledge, and it was rather this desire than a purely moral one that inspired even those who gave as their purpose the presentation of good and bad examples.

The requirements of exactness and novelty were not just those of today. Of this there can be no question. But they were, on the other hand, fairly severe. Pliny's letter to Titinius Capito (5. 8) is a naive presentation of the situation of an historian in the time of Tacitus. He warns his friend against thinking that the writing of history is easy. But, easy or hard, he would like to write history to win immortality for those he wrote about and for himself. Oratory and poetry require pre-eminence to win fame, "historia quoquo modo scripta delectat. Sunt enim homines natura curiosi et quamlibet nuda rerum cognitione capiuntur, ut qui sermunculis etiam fabellisque ducantur." In spite of this flippant remark, Pliny proceeds to define the task of the historian, differentiating it from that of the orator and finally coming down to a sharp distinction between contemporary history and history of the more distant past. Of the latter he says: "Vetera et scripta aliis? parata inquisitio sed onerosa collatio." Of the former, "intacta et nova? gravis offensae, levis gratia."

It seems safe to assume that the fundamental attitude of

199

Tacitus was not unlike that of Pliny. He had been estopped from political activity under Domitian and had turned to literary work. His concern for the fame of Agricola indicates his own desire for reputation, less naive and perhaps less consuming than that of Pliny but no less real. His infinite care as a stylist needs no comment. His respect for the truth has already been discussed. The question at present is this matter of *vetera et scripta aliis* as against *intacta et nova* and the use of source material in each case. When Tacitus praised Livy as *eloquentiae ac fidei praeclarus in primis,* he included his whole code for an historian, for *fides* must sum up his conception of the historian's responsibility.

It must first of all be borne in mind that Livy was writing a history of long ago and that in much of it there was no chance to investigate the evidence afresh. Cicero and Lucian, in their comments on history, are in the main thinking of *intacta et nova.* In the case of *vetera et scripta aliis,* Pliny and Tacitus would require *collatio,* not the reinvestigation of evidence but careful comparison of the previous writers, implying intelligent selection. While Livy, dealing with semimythical periods, might follow a single annalist—merely giving his bald narrative a literary embellishment—the intermediate history such as that of Augustus or Tiberius, from Tacitus' point of view, required more than this. *Collatio* certainly implies much more than this. There is no expectation of argument in Pliny's mind when he assumes that of course the historian will compare previous accounts and decide between conflicting ones. Where there is no conflict, the assumption would be that the facts are as they have come down. There was no demand on the historian to check the evidence where there was no disagreement between authorities.

When, therefore, Tacitus began to write history he had before him a project which involved both types of treatment. His program as announced in the *Agricola* was to write a memorial of the former enslavement under the tyrants and a testimonial of contemporary blessings under Nerva and Trajan. In practice this program expanded somewhat, and the revision appears in the opening of the *Histories*. He is going to write first the history of Rome from the year of revolution down to the death of Domitian; afterwards he hopes to write of the reigns of Nerva and Trajan. Tacitus was about fourteen years old in the year of revolution. The events covered in the *Histories* may not be *intacta aliis,* but they certainly come under the category of *nova* and a man of Tacitus' intellectual acumen could scarcely have been content to accept unquestioningly another's account of the events of his own lifetime. He was himself actively interested in politics. He had about him a circle of friends many of whom had been participants in the events which he records. It is a safer presumption that Tacitus did not blindly follow in the *Histories* even so dependable a source as Pliny the Elder but that he followed the principle enunciated many years later by Lucian that the historian should see for himself as far as possible and, failing this opportunity, should prefer the most disinterested account. Tacitus sought first-hand information from Pliny, and even more convincing is the information which Pliny volunteers: "Demonstro ergo quamquam diligentiam tuam fugere non possit, cum sit in publicis actis, demonstro tamen," etc. (7. 33).

In the *Histories* there are sixty-eight instances in which Tacitus indicates either a recorded statement or a belief on someone's part with regard to something which he himself is unwilling to assert as a fact; in other words, he cites divergent authority for some fact or motive. Two-thirds of the instances consist simply in such phrases as *ut quidam crediderunt* or *ferunt, creditum est* or *incertum an.* Usually they refer to some assigned motive or attitude which could not ordinarily be known with assurance. They suggest a cautious writer and give the impression that Tacitus is recording beliefs with which he has been personally acquainted, not necessarily in print but more probably in the talk of his friends or acquaintances. Of the remaining instances some form of *trado* is the commonest. This of course does not of necessity refer to written tradition, but *multi tradidere, ut alii tradidere* certainly implies recorded opinion. The following examples indicate more than one written authority in a given instance. *Extremam vocem ut cuique odium aut admiratio fuit varie prodidere. Alii . . . ; plures . . .* (1. 41). This could, of course, refer to oral tradition, as might also what follows immediately: *De percussore non satis constat: quidam Terentium evocatum, alii Laecanium, crebrior fama tradidit Camurium . . . iugulum eius hausisse.* Only written authorities can be referred to in 2. 37: *Invenio apud quosdam auctores.* This has reference to a theory that the army hesitated about giving up the fighting and going into conference. Tacitus cites the tradition only to argue against it on the grounds of probability. Even more striking is 2. 101: *Scriptores temporum qui potiente rerum Flavia domo, monumenta belli huiusce composuerunt . . . tradidere.* Such writers, says Tacitus, to curry favor imputed fair motives to Caecina and the others who abandoned Vitellius for Vespasian. He himself cannot agree with them. Again in 3. 51, to substantiate the story that a common soldier killed his own brother and claimed the reward he says: *celeberrimos auctores habeo.* In 3. 25, again to substantiate a rather unbelievable story, he states explicitly: *rem nominaque auctore Vipstano Messalla tradam.* Three paragraphs further on he admits that he cannot decide between the evidence of Messalla and C. Plinius. These are the only authorities cited by name in the *Histories*.

Especial interest attaches to narratives in the latter part of Book 4 and in Book 5. With regard to miracles supposed to have been wrought by Vespasian in Egypt (4. 81) Tacitus says, *utrumque qui interfuere nunc quoque memorant.* In 83 he discusses the god Serapis, beginning: *Origo dei nondum nostris auctoribus celebrata: Aegyptiorum antistites sic memorant.* Many varying theories are cited. He begins his long digression on the Jews (5. 2) with *memorant,* continues in chapter 2 with *plurimi auctores consentiunt,* uses *ferunt, accepimus, quidam arbitrati sunt,* and finally: *sic veteres auctores, sed gnari locorum tradunt.*

All of this would seem to indicate a writer who had not only read what was written by historians, as well as books on other lands, but had also talked with eye witnesses and considered with some care the probable truth where doubt or uncertainty existed. It seems to confirm the picture of Tacitus at work presented by Pliny, who adds to the possible sources the public records.

Of the points for which Tacitus feels compelled to give authority, a dozen are matters of antiquarian interest or questions of foreign customs and practices. The rest are about evenly divided between questions of motive and intent and facts which could never be actually known, such as whether a man's suicide was voluntary or not, whether there was a secret agreement between two men, how much money Vitellius spent. Much of this is on the borderline between fact and intent or motive. The facts are never the main facts of the narrative. It would seem that on these Tacitus felt the obligation to determine what he believed to be the truth and then to assume responsibility. It should be noted that in many cases the minor facts for which he does not care to take full responsibility are such as to lend color to the character of some person or action. In the case of the son who killed his own father (3. 25) it is the horror of civil war which he wishes to enhance. When he raises the question of Paulinus' implication in a defeatist movement in the army (2. 37), only to refute it, it is the character of his hero, Paulinus, which he would magnify. His unfavorable picture of Antonius Primus (2. 86) is in part produced by citation of a rumor which he does not confirm. There is another category which is made up of instances in which rather incredible items are introduced largely for their inherent interest, the strange bird that was an omen of Otho's death (2. 50), the miracles effected by Vespasian in Egypt (4. 81), the origin of Serapis (4. 83).

The sum total of the picture is clear. For the main narrative, Tacitus assumed the responsibility of the historian to get at the truth and present it. His guarantee was his own reputation. To make this narrative colorful and dramatic, he felt justified in introducing facts and motives which he might refute on logical

grounds or leave uncontested but for which he did not personally vouch. There is no indication that he followed blindly the
account of any predecessor.

When he came to write the *Annals,* Tacitus was definitely
dealing with *vetera et scripta aliis.* This is especially the case in
the early books, and as the text has come down to us in two
sections it will be convenient to consider Books 1–6 first and
then Books 11–16.

At the very outset Tacitus discusses, by way of introduction,
the writers that have preceded him, indicating his knowledge
of historians of the Republic, of the early Augustan age, and
of the later Augustan period, as well as those of the Empire
from Tiberius through Nero. He implies that these latter must
be discounted because of distortion due to fear or hatred. Of
possible writers to whom he may refer he mentions, in the first
six books, only Pliny, citing his history of the German wars
(1. 69). Otherwise his references in these books are to *auctores
rerum* (3. 13), *plurimis maximaeque fidei auctoribus* (4. 10),
temporis eius auctores (5. 9), *scriptores annalium* (4. 53),
scriptores senatoresque eorundum temporum (2. 88), and so
on. The *commentarii ad senatum* are mentioned (6. 47) and in
connection with them he states that there were *nullae imperatoris litterae* bearing on the matter under discussion. He mentions *Attii centurionis et Didymi liberti epistulae* (6. 24) as
presenting names in a given case. In 3. 3 he states that he fails
to find something in *diurna actorum scriptura,* while in speaking of Tiberius (2. 63) he states flatly, *extat oratio.* Speeches
of the emperor are discussed also in 1. 81, obviously as accessible. Of letters sent to Tiberius and of others attacking Nero
and Agrippina he speaks (5. 16 and 5. 3) as though they might
still be consulted. This is certainly true of the one to Tiberius.
The *commentarii Agrippinae* are specifically mentioned in 4.
53. Finally, in 3. 16, he uses the phrase *audire me memini ex
senioribus.* This is with reference to the trial of Piso, a long
span of memory even for *seniores* but not impossible, or even
improbable.

In addition to these specific citations Tacitus makes the following definite statement in 6. 7: *nobis pleraque digna cognitu obvenere quamquam ab aliis incelebrata*, and he uses the words *comperimus, comperior*, and *repperi* (5. 10, 4. 20, 6. 7), indicating something in the nature of research. There are also over thirty instances in which he makes use of general phrases like *ferunt, constitit, memoriae traditur*, to substantiate a statement or to present a statement which he refutes or for which he does not care to vouch. As in the *Histories*, these instances do not have to do with the main thread of the story but deal rather with minor phases which are usually beyond the range of proof. Some have to do with facts: whether Augustus was still alive or not when Tiberius arrived at Nola (1. 5), whether there were signs of poison on the body of Germanicus (2. 73), whether the daughter of Sejanus was violated by the executioner (5. 9). Others deal with motive or intent: why Tiberius stayed away from the games over which Drusus presided (1. 76), reasons for Tiberius' withdrawal from Rome (4. 57), the thoughts of Nerva (6. 26). Also there is confirmation of interesting but unimportant or irrelevant events for the sake of color: the history of the consular elections (1. 81), speech of Tiberius on Maroboduus (2. 63), omens in Asia (2. 47). A few cases deserve special consideration.

In 6. 7 and 8 two cases are brought together by an important transitional sentence. The first case is that of Q. Servaeus and Minucius Thermus, charged with friendship with Sejanus. They had not profited by the friendship and there was some sympathy for them, so that the cruelty of Tiberius is emphasized especially when he orders a respectable senator to prosecute. Otherwise the case is unimportant. The victims turned state's evidence. Two provincials are named on the same charge, and then Tacitus explains that he does not know the origin of one of them, implying that it is because many writers about the period omitted names to save themselves and their readers from being bored. He has himself found out some facts of importance hitherto unrecorded. This at first seems to be in explanation of part at least of what has preceded. But its chief importance appears to be anticipatory. For the next paragraph

begins with *nam* and introduces a new case, even more important to the general picture that Tacitus is creating. It is that
of M. Terentius, who dared to admit his friendship with Sejanus. The substance of his speech in his own defense is given at
length. The genuineness of this speech has been called in question because of the close parallel between it and a speech of
Amyntas in Curtius Rufus. In reality it is the two situations
which are parallel, and Tacitus has borrowed here as elsewhere
from the language of Curtius Rufus, making it his own by characteristic changes. He does not pretend to give the exact speech
but introduces it with the formula *ad hunc modum*. The speech
is important to him because it is one of those outbursts of the
opposition, like others by Paetus Thrasea, for example, later
on, which thrilled him in spite of his intellectual disapproval.
In this case it was successful and, like many of the last epigrammatic words which were the dying gestures of political
martyrs, it was probably cherished among the members of the
opposition, who were in many cases friends of Tacitus. Seneca
dictated his last remarks and they were generally circulated;
Subrius Flavus' words were not widely circulated but they were
preserved and Tacitus knew where to find them (15. 63, 67).
It is largely for its dramatic effect that Tacitus preserves this
piece of new information.

The story of Agrippina standing at the bridgehead to receive
the soldiers returning from Germany (1. 69) is one that has no
great historical significance and which might be thought to be
merely envious gossip. To Tacitus it is important as a dramatic
presentation of the character of Agrippina. He therefore includes it and cites his authority, Pliny, in order to maintain
his own integrity. In much the same way he introduces the discussion of whether Vibulenus and Percennius were buried in
the general's tent or exposed in public (1. 29). He does not
vouch for either version but gets what he aimed to get, the impression of Drusus' ferocity. At the time of Drusus' death (4.
10, 11) he uses the same method to enhance the horror of the
situation and blacken the characters of Livia, Sejanus, and
Tiberius. He tells a fantastic story based only on persistent

rumor, which he refutes by the application of logic. The effect which he wished to create remains in spite of the refutation. Indirect characterization of Sejanus and Agrippina is similarly accomplished when Tiberius' withdrawal from Rome and its motives are discussed (4. 57).

In Books 11–16 of the *Annals* Tacitus concerns himself with the evidence and source reference to a greater extent than in the earlier books. The types of source are much the same: Cluvius Rufus, Fabius Rusticus, and Pliny are the historians cited (13. 20, 14. 2, 15. 53, 15. 61); the *commentarii senatus* furnish the motion made by Cerialis (15. 74); the *acta publica* contain the record of Claudius' treatment of the *pomerium* (12. 24); and an inscription on bronze is cited for evidence of Claudius' additions to the Roman alphabet (11. 14); Corbulo's reports or memoirs furnish evidence against Paetus (15. 16); the personal testimony of returning exiles is used to prove the fact of the Conspiracy of Piso (15. 73); the physical evidence of abandoned workings is invoked to prove Nero's folly in attempting a canal from Lake Avernus (15. 42). *Audita scriptaque senioribus* (11. 27) and *ut . . . seniores meminerint* (15. 41) indicate a personal search for first-hand evidence, and *temporum illorum scriptores* (12. 67, 13. 17) a similar search for written evidence, more generally referred to by the words *auctores* (15. 38) and *scriptores* (16. 6). Tacitus definitely mentions the publication of Seneca's last words dictated on his death bed (15. 63) and the historian had access to the similar record of Subrius Flavus' (15. 65) which had not been as thoroughly circulated. A gossip book by Fabricius Veiento is a possible source of material, although Tacitus speaks only of the circulation of the book and not of his own use of it (14. 50). In the same way he speaks of the *acta diurna* (16. 22). In addition to all of these specific citations of source these last books have more than fifty general references to source: *tradidere quidam, fama fuit, credebatur, constitit, ferebant, ferunt*, etc.

Aside from the amount of "documentation," Tacitus' discussion of his own use of sources becomes prominent in these later books. As he reaches the period which is within the memory of some still living and develops his indictments of Nero and his entourage, he would seem to have taken more pains to substantiate his statements, especially those which by their strangeness invited skepticism. For example, the fantastic wedding of Messalina and Silius draws from him the protest: *sed nihil compositum miraculi causa, verum audita scriptaque senioribus trado* (11. 27). In 13. 20 the story is told of how Paris went to Nero by night and so terrified him that he proceeded to plan the deaths of Plautus and Agrippina and even Burrus. It is a difficult story to prove, but it is important in the development of the Agrippina drama. Tacitus, therefore, pauses and cites Fabius Rusticus, Pliny, and Cluvius with their divergent opinions, shows how partiality for Seneca vitiates Fabius' evidence, and then states this principle: *nos consensum auctorum secuturi, si qui diversa prodiderint, sub nominibus ipsorum trademus.* It is a rash promise and certainly Tacitus makes no systematic effort to carry it out. It is important as representing his general procedure, for he does carry it out to that extent—only the *sub nominibus* is later ignored. But he does actually keep his promise in 14. 2. Cluvius ascribes to Agrippina the initiative in the incest episode with Nero. *Ceteri auctores* agree with Cluvius as does *fama* or general rumor. Fabius Rusticus assigned the initiative to Nero, and Tacitus cites the fact but follows the consensus of opinion, which he also supports with argument. The point seems hardly of sufficient historical importance to receive so much attention, but to Tacitus it was surely most important. The story of Agrippina's relations with Nero had become a drama: if Agrippina did make the proposal of incest, then the matricide is properly motivated and understandable. Historically the point is a minor one, but not dramatically. As a matter of technique there is some importance in this treatment of the evidence. Just as in the matter of Agrippina's behavior with the army in Germany (1. 69) Tacitus called in the authority of Pliny in order to make convincing a minor historical fact which contributed much to his character drawing, so here his motive is obvious.

And so, too, in the instance cited above (13. 20), the fact of whether Nero considered appointing Caecina to the position held by Burrus or not is of no great historical significance. In fact, Tacitus discards the suggestion on the basis of the evidence. But it has been introduced to the reader's attention, and the dubious position of Burrus and Seneca is dramatically suggested without commitment to the discarded detail. A somewhat similar result is obtained in 15. 53 by quoting a statement of Pliny's which is refuted by Tacitus but which leaves its unpleasant suggestion, confirmed at the end of the paragraph by the insinuation *nisi si cupido dominandi cunctis affectibus flagrantior est.* Similarly, in 15. 61 Fabius Rusticus is cited as authority for a somewhat minor point which has importance only as it confirms the general impression that Tacitus is trying to establish.

Probably the most conspicuous instance of acknowledgment of his sources by Tacitus is the account of the conspiracy of Piso in the fifteenth book. At the outset (49) he calls attention to the difficulty of accurate knowledge of such a conspiracy: *nec tamen facile memoraverim, quis primus auctor cuius instinctu concitum sit quod tam multi sumpserunt.* Because of their constancy in the face of death, he selects two men that he thinks must have been leaders—*constantia exitus docuit.* He indicates by the use of *ferebantur* the uncertainty of his knowledge about the place where they planned to kill Nero. With regard to minor facts he uses the word *crediderunt* and the phrase *ut alii tradidere.* This would indicate the existence of narrative accounts even without the *quod C. Plinius memorat* (53) following. Pliny is not quoted as positive evidence because Tacitus states definitely that he considers Pliny's statement which he quotes wholly absurd. Except for one *ut plerique tradidere* the detailed procedure of the plot is unsupported by source citation until paragraph 61, where a divergent account is credited to Fabius Rusticus. Seneca's dying words are not recorded because, says Tacitus, he dictated them to scribes and they have been widely published. A rumor about Subrius Flavus is given with the introduction *fama fuit,* and a comment of his is quoted as evidence of its probable correctness. The last words of Subrius are quoted *quia non ut Senecae volgata erant*. It is clear, I think, that there is a rather large amount of reference to authority in this matter of the conspiracy. At the end Nero summoned the senate, made a speech, and added it to the collection of informers' statements and confessions. And, says Tacitus, he was abused in the public gossip for having attacked innocent men. But, he adds, those who investigate such things admit that there was a real conspiracy, and the exiles who returned after Nero's death confess the same thing. Finally he cites the records of the senate (*reperio in commentariis senatus*) with regard to a motion by Anicius Cerialis. This long account of one of the greatest internal affairs in the days of Tacitus' own boyhood derives its authority from published histories, from senate records, from general rumor, and from oral evidence, with logic applied to test each.

In general the same principle seems to rule throughout the *Histories* and *Annals:* the main thread of the story Tacitus has determined in his own mind on the basis of the consensus of evidence. Minor historical points, important for their bearing on the depiction of character or dramatic action, are substantiated or suggested by means of cited evidence. The fact that some form of *tradere* is used twenty-four times in the *Annals* as against six in the *Histories* would indicate an increased use of written authority in dealing with the earlier periods. But whether he was dealing with *vetera et scripta aliis* or with *intacta et nova,* Tacitus made careful and thorough investigation of the available evidence, and his request made to Pliny for information about the eruption of Vesuvius (Pliny, *Ep.* 6. 16, 20) was not an isolated incident but typical of his procedure.

There were some twenty years between Tacitus' announcement of his purpose to write Roman history and the publication of the *Annals.* Before his published announcement he had spent fifteen years in semiretirement under Domitian, during which it seems reasonable to assume that he was preparing the material for his historical works. Even if this earlier period of research is not included, he had ample time to consult the possible sources of information indicated above. Philippe Fabia in an exhaustive essay on the subject, would have us believe that Tacitus always followed a main source.[1] He finds Pliny the Elder to have been this main source for the *Histories,* Cluvius Rufus for the reigns of Claudius and Nero, and Aufidius Bassus for Tiberius, in the *Annals.* His secondary sources, according to Fabia, were used only sporadically and not, as Tacitus himself would indicate, systematically. Primary sources, documents, records, inscriptions, and the like, Fabia thinks, were rarely consulted. Fabia's book is elaborate and detailed in its treatment of the question and has always enjoyed great prestige. In spite of its demonstration of industry and its appearance of logical cogency, however, the conclusions drawn are inconsistent with the reputation of Tacitus as evidenced by the letters of Pliny and with the impression given by Tacitus himself. For, as we have seen, Tacitus not only states that he intends to compare various accounts, but constantly cites sources of information, even though he less frequently names the authority. There are forty-nine instances of specific acknowledgment and no less than one hundred and fifty more general references to sources. F. B. Marsh, "Tacitus and Aristocratic Tradition," [2] well expresses the position of those who distrust Fabia's conclusions, and in appendix I to *The Reign of Tiberius* [3] he discusses at length the whole problem.

It should be recognized that the method of writing history was not the same in Tacitus' day as it is (theoretically at least) in modern times. But the standards of research were by no means low, and Tacitus was a sincere and diligent research worker with standards certainly no lower than those prevailing in his own time. It is impossible to believe that for the bulk of his work he followed a "main source" more blindly than the average historian of today. The known source material at his command, all of which there is some evidence that he consulted, is the following.

1. *Les Sources de Tacite,* Paris, 1893.
2. *Classical Philology,* 21 (1926), 289–310.
3. Oxford, 1931.

PRIMARY SOURCES

Acta Senatus. These records, which are called by Tacitus *commentarii senatus* and *acta patrum* would probably be accessible to him as a member of the senate. He cites them twice (*Ann.* 5. 4 and 15. 74), and much more extended use is implied by his detailed reports of proceedings in the senate.

Acta Diurna. The daily public gazette is cited as *diurna populi* (*Ann.* 16. 22), *acta diurna urbis* (13. 31), *acta publica* (12. 24), and *diurna actorum scriptura* (3. 3).

Speeches of the Emperors. In *Ann.* 2. 63 Tacitus says of a speech of Tiberius, *extat oratio.* In what form this was preserved is not stated. A speech of Claudius was preserved on an altar at Lyons,[4] and it is not impossible that the *Commentarii Principum* or journals of the emperors may have contained speeches. These latter, however, were probably not available to Tacitus. Parts of speeches may well have been included in the *Acta Diurna.* It seems altogether probable that collections of letters and speeches of the emperor may have been published. Fabia (pp. 326 ff.) presents convincing evidence for such a collection of Tiberius' communications.

Inscriptions. Tacitus cites an inscription in *Ann.* 11. 14 and elsewhere mentions the recording of certain acts in inscriptions.

Private Journals. Tacitus cites the *Commentarii Agrippinae filiae* (*Ann.* 4. 53) and probably refers to the *Commentarii Corbulonis* (*Ann.* 15. 16). Pliny (*NH* 5. 1. 14) refers to the memoirs of Suetonius Paulinus, which it would seem highly probable that Tacitus used. Presumably such journals were preserved in large numbers, especially in the older aristocratic families.[5] Probably in this group of memoirs should be included Tiberius' memoirs of his own life and Claudius' autobiography in eight books (*Suet. Tib.* 61, *Claud.* 41).

Fugitive Literature. In *Ann.* 1. 72 Tacitus mentions the scurrilous pamphlets of Cassius Severus and in 14. 48, 50, publications of the same sort by Antistius and Veiento. The

4. *CIL, 13,* Pt. I, 232–3.
5. See Marsh, "Tacitus and Aristocratic Tradition."

satire on the death of Claudius ascribed to Seneca represents a similar type of production and tendentious pamphlets both satirical and eulogistic may well have been numerous and cannot have been totally suppressed. Perhaps the books entitled *Exitus Clarorum Virorum,* such as that of C. Fannius mentioned by Pliny (*Ep.* 5. 5. 3) and that of Titinius Capito (Pliny, *Ep.* 8. 12. 4) should be included here.[6]

Archaeological Remains. Tacitus cites the remains of Nero's attempted canal near Misenum (*Ann.* 15. 42), and this type of evidence cannot be wholly ignored.

Eye-witness Evidence. Verbal evidence was available to Tacitus for a great part of the period which he covered, and he gives ample evidence of having used it. This ranged from the specific references, such as *audire me memini ex senioribus* (*Ann.* 3. 16) to such general statements as *ferebant* (*Ann.* 6. 47 and passim). At its lowest stage it represents mere gossip, which may be used to give color to a situation but which Tacitus in general discards as evidence.

SECONDARY SOURCES

General Histories. Tacitus specifically cites C. Plinius, who wrote both a history of the German wars (cited in *Ann.* 1. 69) and a history of Rome which covered his own times (cited in *Ann.* 13. 20, 15. 53, and in *Hist.* 3. 28). Cluvius Rufus is cited twice by Tacitus as an authority (*Ann.* 13. 20, 14. 2). Cluvius' history probably extended from the reign of Gaius through that of Vitellius. Fabius Rusticus probably covered the period from Claudius through Nero and possibly beyond, as he was living in Trajan's reign. He is cited three times by Tacitus (*Ann.* 13. 20, 14. 2, 15. 61). Vipstanus Messalla is cited in *Hist.* 3. 25, 28, but it is not known whether he wrote a general history—probably not. Aside from these historians specifically cited by Tacitus, there are two whom he mentions in *Dial.* 23 who wrote general histories. It is not known how much of the period was covered by M. Servilius Nonianus.

6. See F. A. Marx, "Tacitus und die Literatur der exitus illustrium virorum," *Philologus,* 92 (1937–38), 83 ff.

Aufidius Bassus wrote both a general history from republican times down to the days of Claudius and a history of the German wars.

Special Histories. The following special treatises may be mentioned as an indication of the wealth of material available to an historian of the early Empire. It is safe to assume that they represent only a fraction of the total. Velleius Paterculus wrote a still extant history of the early part of Tiberius' reign. Pompeius Planta published in 98 a history of the Civil War of 69. (*Schol. ad Juv.* 2. 99; Pliny, *Epp. ad Traj.* 7. 1). Antonius Julianus wrote a monograph on the Jews, including the fall of Jerusalem. P. Anteius Rufus wrote a biography of M. Ostorius Scapula, of which Tacitus speaks in *Ann.* 16. 14. Tacitus also tells in *Agric.* 2 of the biographies of Paetus Thrasea and Helvidius Priscus by Arulenus Rusticus and Herennius Senecio. Pliny (*Ep.* 7. 31. 5) speaks of a biography of L. Annius Bassus by Ti. Claudius Pollio and (*Ep.* 1. 5. 2) of a Vituperatio of Arulenus Rusticus by M. Aquilius Regulus. With the information we have about the custom of semipublic literary reading in the first century, we can have little doubt that the number of minor treatises was legion.

THE AGRICOLA

The sources for the Minor Works furnish separate problems for each. The *Agricola,* insofar as it is considered merely as a biography of Tacitus' father-in-law, was presumably the product of first-hand knowledge. For the survey of the geography and ethnology and history of Britain further investigation was necessary. That the author was meticulous in checking his information is suggested by the fact that in chapter 2 he cites written authority (*legimus,* presumably in the *acta senatus*) for details that were of comparatively recent date and thoroughly familiar. At the opening of his account of Britain (10) he refers to the previous writers on the geography and people of Britain who have adorned with eloquence what was not yet actually known and states his purpose of now giving the authentic account because Britain was at last conquered and for the first time circumnavigated. This statement has two important implications. It indicates first-hand knowledge acquired by the author from those who had been on the campaigns. It also rather definitely suggests his familiarity with Livy who (according to Jornandes, *Get.* 20) definitely stated that Britain had not been circumnavigated and who gave the current conjecture as to its character. This reliance on Livy is explicitly confirmed by Tacitus, for he cites Livy and Fabius Rusticus as *eloquentissimi auctorum* and corrects their impression of the shape of the island, making no reference to the more standard description of the island as triangular which appears in Caesar, Diodorus, Strabo, and Mela. Pliny and Mela also mention the Orkneys, which according to Tacitus were first discovered by Agricola. Livy described Britain in Book 105, and by his day Caesar's comparatively meager information must have been largely supplemented by traders and travelers. Tacitus makes one addition to the common fund of information about the tides of Britain, which he says *multi rettulere.* In regard to the length of days and nights he is apparently unconscious of the difference between summer and winter which was clear to Pliny and Mela and is implied by Caesar.

All this does not amount to a great deal. Tacitus shows by literary borrowings that he had read both Livy and Caesar, but it would seem to be Caesar that he followed most trustfully in his researches on the geography and ethnology of the country. On the rhetorical side he uses, in chapter 13, the phrase *satis constat,* familiar in his historical works as indicating an agreement between nearly all sources. The revolt under Boudicca and its suppression under Suetonius Paulinus is given more space and importance than it would perhaps have merited, from a purely historical point of view, in so brief a summary. Little emphasis is given to the governor's responsibility for the critical situation, stress being laid on his brilliant recovery. It does not seem too rash to assume that Tacitus had access to the memoirs of Suetonius Paulinus mentioned by Pliny (*NH* 5. 1. 14), and it should be remembered that it was this general under whom Agricola served his military ap-

prenticeship and who reappears with favorable prominence
in *Ann.* 14. 29–39 and *Hist.* 1. 87 etc., with similar indications
that the writer was using the memoirs.

The specific point on which Tacitus seems to have used
Caesar, the reference to the Gauls and their degeneracy from
early greatness (*Agric.* 11) would have come from some part
of Caesar other than his account of Britain. Caesar in all probability had much less to say on the subject of Britain than Livy.

THE GERMANIA

In the Germania Tacitus cites explicitly only one authority,
Caesar, but he definitely disclaims any first-hand knowledge
by his statement in chapter 27 at the close of the general account of Germany: *haec . . . accepimus* (cf. *Hist.* 3. 38, 75;
5. 4. 13, as well as numerous cases in the *Annals;* also *Agric.*
11 and *Dial.* 12, etc.). Caesar was quite possibly the chief and
perhaps the best available source of knowledge about Germany, but it is equally possible that Tacitus drew freely from
Livy. He cites Livy as one of the authorities on Britain, and
the epitome of Livy 104 states: *prima pars libri situm Germaniae moresque continet.* Editors have found indications of
the use of Mela and Pliny's *Natural History,* and in view of
Tacitus' practice in general it is to be assumed that in an essay of this type, for which he is not known to have had access
to any unique source of information, he consulted all possible
authorities, including returning merchants and possibly Germans in Rome. Officials and army men from the Rhine provinces should be included among possible sources.

THE DIALOGUS

The literary sources of the *Dialogus* are of definite interest
and importance. But from the point of view of historical source
material there is not much to be said. Only Tacitus' information about the Roman orators of earlier days comes under
consideration here. If, as seems not impossible, Tacitus studied
under Quintilian, the *Dialogus* may represent largely the result
of his schooling. Certainly Tacitus knew the works of the ora-

tors discussed in the *Dialogus,* and it is unnecessary to look for the origin of his criticisms and judgments outside his own mind. For facts with regard to the orators and their careers such search would be useless.

A few general remarks may be made about Tacitus' geographical knowledge and interest. He cites no authorities on these subjects aside from the historians who treat them incidentally, nor do his literary borrowings indicate any use of Mela or Strabo or the other geographers. His geography is usually sketchy and vague. This is really as true of Britain as it is of Parthia and Armenia, the apparent difference being due to the greater extent of the latter and our better knowledge of the former. The fact seems to be that he was not interested either from personal curiosity or traditional method in giving precise geographical background to his historical accounts. The same is in general true of his military tactics. His interests were political, personal, and literary. The unusual appealed to him because of the color that it lent to his narration. For this reason he accumulated as much knowledge of Britain and Germany as would serve his purpose. He does not seem to have anticipated the same need for Parthia. He could well have used some further information about the strange country and picturesque people of Armenia, for example, but without it he makes the most of the personal drama of Corbulo to give life to the Parthian interludes. For Judaea, on the other hand, he not only collected a considerable amount of information but injected it into the narrative in a wholly exceptional manner. This information is entirely non-Jewish in its source, which is about all that can be said without the free use of imagination. Tacitus clearly knew nothing of either the Septuagint or Josephus. His sources are Roman or Greek. In view of his interest in Egyptian lore it has been guessed that Manetho may have been one of his sources, but this is pure guesswork. Agrippina in her memoirs may have passed on information received from *Germanicus,* but this hypothesis too is based on no evidence. We do not even know what caused Tacitus' particular

interest in Palestine and Egypt, and where he gathered his
curious information cannot be said. But here, too, the same
general characteristic stands out. Tacitus is interested not in
accurate geographical facts but only in that which is different
from the familiar and strange enough to give color to his treatment of affairs away from home. It is less like the scholarly interest of a Caesar than akin to the dramatic curiosity of
Aeschylus.

11. CREDIBILITY OF TACITUS' HISTORY

PRECEDING chapters have presented various aspects of Tacitus' background and method, with some suggestion of his attitude toward the writing of his essays and histories. A knowledge of these should make easier an understanding of his work, an understanding which can appreciate and make allowance for bias of one sort and another without assuming dishonesty or incompetence.

Since 1875 there have been at least five major attempts to discredit the works of Tacitus as either forgeries or fiction. Voltaire had perhaps been the first in modern day seriously to revive Tertullian's charge of mendacity, and his claims were elaborated by a lawyer named Linguet. Only with Napoleon, however, was this position given serious consideration. The leaders of the revolution had found tremendous comfort in Tacitus' anti-imperialism. For the modern successor to the Caesars it was important politically to discredit the historian and discount his popularity, but any effect which Napoleon's attacks may have had largely disappeared with the collapse of the emperor.

Two curious attempts were made toward the end of the nineteenth century to prove not that Tacitus was a liar but that what purported to be his writings were fifteenth-century forgeries. W. R. Ross published anonymously in 1878 a book entitled *Tacitus and Bracciolini,* intended to prove that Poggio Bracciolini was the author of what had come down from antiquity under the name of Tacitus. Twelve years later P. Hochart (*De l'Authenticité des Annales et des Histoires de Tacite*) maintained the same thesis with a much greater show of learning, following up by a supplementary volume. These two attempts gave ample assurance that the attack on these lines was futile, and only one further attempt of this sort has been made. That was in 1920 when Leo Wiener (*Tacitus' Germania and Other Forgeries*) sought in vain to prove by a bewildering display of linguistic fireworks that the *Germania* and, by implication, other works of Tacitus were forgeries made after Arabic influence had extended into Europe.

After Gaston Boissier's brilliant book (*Tacite*, 1903) had roused new enthusiasm for the historian, Eugene Bacha (*Le Genie de Tacite*, 1906) attempted to prove that Tacitus was the master of romantic fiction, and somewhat later T. S. Jerome (*Aspects of the Study of History*, 1923) presented him as a consistent liar both by nature and by deliberate choice. Bacha's book has some value for its comments on stylistic matters, Jerome's none because of its over-all inaccuracy, its complete confusion of *narratio* in a legal speech and *narratio* in history, and its wholly unconvincing method. Neither writer won any general acceptance of his estimate of Tacitus' integrity.

More recent critics have abandoned the extreme positions which marked these earlier arguments over the dependability of Tacitus as an historian. Scholars like Sievers, Freytag, and Stahr have done much to correct the total picture of Tiberius, and Marsh has had the last word in this area. In general, modern criticism has modified to a considerable degree the impression given by Tacitus of the Julio-Claudian emperors and of Domitian. Nevertheless, Tacitus' own emotional tension has too often aroused in his readers a corresponding amount of heat in the form either of violent adoration or more violent denunciation. But the general verdict of time has largely removed the suspicion of deliberate falsehood. Tacitus' standing in the Rome of his day, his reputation for high integrity, makes such a charge almost absurd, and infinite effort has failed to produce evidence of false statements beyond those occasional mistakes which no mere human can hope to escape.

This is not, however, to say that the total result of Tacitus' presentation can be accepted with confidence as the final and just interpretation of first-century Roman history. The foregoing chapters have attempted to indicate various characteristics of Tacitus which have to be considered if we are to appreciate his interpretation and properly evaluate it.

It is well to realize that every historian must be so appreciated and so evaluated. There can be no totally unbiased history except a mere list of events and dates, and even in such a list, which could never be complete, the personal element would necessarily enter by way of selection. The greater the literary ability of the historian, the greater the chance of his imposing upon his reader his own conviction of how to interpret the facts of history. What should be the concern of the critic is not the praise or scorn of the historian but the clarification of his approach to history, the evaluation of his various sorts of bias. The enormous influence of Tacitus' writings on the thought of succeeding ages is sufficient evidence of his greatness as a writer. The depth of his convictions, his burning indignation, gave unusual power to all that he wrote. If we would understand the world which he depicts, it is essential to understand the motives and interests which determined his own interpretation and as far as possible the means which he employed to make those motives convincing to his readers. If his presentation gives a biased impression of first-century history, as it undoubtedly does, it is not by falsification of the facts nor because of a failure to apply the best standards of scholarship known to his day. In general he follows an historical tradition already well established, applying to it a considerable critical ability. He interprets the facts in the light of his own convictions and by means of his own artistic methods.

He interprets them also under the influence of his own personal interests. From our study of Tacitus we would seem to be justified in the following conclusions. He was not greatly concerned with philosophy or religion; he was interested in the historical development of political forms and procedures. Economic conditions and social welfare were wholly outside his field of special interest, as were also the intricacies of military procedure. He was cold to any sympathetic treatment of the "common man"; he was vitally interested in the drama of court life, especially its crimes and tragedies, the opposition it aroused, and the resulting struggles in which by family tradition and by conviction his sympathy was with the losing side.

The modern historian must reinterpret the facts as he finds them in Tacitus in the light of accumulated understanding of these convictions and methods and interests but with confidence in the integrity of this brilliant partisan.

PART II

12. FROM PUBLICATION TO DISCOVERY

THE *Annals* were probably "published" in 116, the last of the works of Tacitus to appear. Only Pliny of Tacitus' contemporaries mentions him, and his writings and the evidence of subsequent use up to the time of Boccaccio is slight. It is not true, however, that Tacitus and his writings were practically unknown. They were neglected—possibly, in part at least, because of his strong republican bias on the one hand and because, on the other, the church fathers felt him to be unfair to Christianity. Vopiscus in his life of the emperor Tacitus (chapter 10) indicates the state of affairs in the third century: "Cornelium Tacitum, scriptorem historiae Augustae, quod parentem suum eundem diceret, in omnibus bibliothecis conlocari iussit neve lectorum incuria deperiret, librum per annos singulos decies scribi publicitus evicos archiis iussit et in bibliothecis poni" (the text is obviously corrupt in the reading *evicos archiis*).

Nevertheless, Tacitus is mentioned or quoted in each century down to and including the sixth. In fact, the seventh and eighth are the only centuries that have as yet furnished no evidence of knowing him. The following are the known references to Tacitus or use of Tacitean material after the day of Tacitus and Pliny until the time of Boccaccio. The material was well collected in 1888 and published at Wetzler by Emmerich Cornelius, but a considerable amount of new material has turned up from time to time since.

About the middle of the second century Ptolemy published his Γεωγραφικὴ Ὑφήγησις. In 2. 11. 12 (ed. C. Muller, Paris, 1883) he lists in succession along the northern shore of Germany the towns of Φληούμ and Σιατουτάνδα. The latter name occurs nowhere else and has a dubious sound. The explanation is to be found in Tacitus, *Ann.* 4. 72, 73: "Rapti qui tributo aderant milites et patibulo adfixi; Olennius infensos fuga praevenit, receptus castello, cui nomen Flevum; et haud spernenda

225

illic civium sociorumque manus litora Oceani praesidebat."
The governor of lower Germany takes prompt action, the
account of which winds up: "utrumque exercitum Rheno de-
vectum Frisiis intulit, soluto iam castelli obsidio et ad sua tu-
tanda degressis rebellibus." The source of Ptolemy's mistake is
obvious.

It is hard to believe that Cassius Dio (who published shortly
after A.D. 200) did not know at least the *Agricola*. In 38. 50
and 66. 20 he mentions Gnaeus Julius Agricola as having
proved Britain to be an island and in the later instance tells the
story of the fugitive Usipi. If we make allowance for the
method of Tacitus, which leaves his account far from clear,
and for the use of a different language by Dio, there can be
little if any doubt that Tacitus is the source for Dio. We know
also of no other possible source today. The last part of the section, dealing with Agricola's return and death, confirms the
conclusion that Dio drew from Tacitus, and it sounds as
though Tacitus had left the impression he desired.

In the third century Tertullian cites Tacitus with a hostile
tone. He had spoken without respect of the Jews and had implied that the Christians were an undesirable sect of the Jews.
It is not a surprise, therefore, to have Tertullian (early third
century) refer to him as *ille mendaciorum loquacissimus*. The
Apologist is defending the Christians against the charge that
they worshiped an ass. The origin of this scandal he ascribes
to Tacitus, *Hist*. 5. 3, 9. *Apologeticus* 16:

Nam et, ut quidam, somniastis caput asininum esse deum nostrum.
Hanc Cornelius Tacitus suspicionem eiusmodi dei inseruit. Is enim
in quinta historiarum suarum bellum Iudaicum exorsus ab origine
gentis etiam de ipsa tam origine quam de nomine et religione gentis
quae voluit argumentatus Iudaeos refert Aegypto expeditos sive, ut
putavit, extorres vastis Arabiae in locis aquarum egentissimis, cum
siti macerarentur, onagris qui forte de pastu potum petituri aestima-
bantur, indicibus fontis usos ob eam gratiam consimilis bestiae
superficiem consecrasse. Atque ita praesumptum opinor nos quoque
ut Iudaicae religionis propinquos eidem simulacro initiari. At enim
idem Cornelius Tacitus, sane ille mendaciorum loquacissimus, in

eadem historia refert Gneum Pompeium, cum Hierusalem cepisset
proptereaque templum adisset speculandis Iudaicae religionis ar-
canis, nullum illic reperisse simulacrum.

The same matter is covered by Tertullian in *Ad. nat.* 1. 11,
but in this instance he quotes it as *in quarta historiarum* and
omits *in eadem historia* in the last part. The quotation from
Tacitus, while free, is obviously genuine. The *Histories* (5. 2)
are referred to again by Tertullian in *Ad. nat.* 2. 12: "Extat
apud litteras vestras usquequaque Saturni census. Legimus
apud Graecos quoque Diodorum, quive alii antiquitatum arca-
nos collegerunt."

Lactantius, in the time of Diocletian, is at least once (*Div.
inst.* 1. 18. 8) somewhat reminiscent of Tacitean style but that
is as far as it is safe to go in claiming him as a reader of Tacitus, in spite of something of a resemblance between Lactantius
1. 11, 12 and *Germ.* 40.

At about the same date, Eumenius of Autun, in his *Pane-
gyricus ad Constantinum* 9, quite clearly has *Agric.* 12 before
him. He follows Tacitus in the error of thinking that the nights
are always short, and he assigns as reasons the same that the
Roman had: "nullae sine aliqua luce noctes, dum quod illa
litorum extrema planities non attolit umbras, noctisque metam
coeli et siderum transit aspectus; ut sol ipse qui nobis videtur
occidere ibi appareat praeterire." Not only the actual quotation
from Tacitus is of interest but the careful substitution of synonyms.

Vopiscus, still in the fourth century, cites Tacitus with Livy,
Sallust, and Trogus as the greatest of Roman historians. The
two references are worth quoting in full because of the comments which they contain on the technique of Tacitus as an
historian. In his *Aurelian* (2) Vopiscus is recounting a conversation with Junius Tiberianus about writing the life of Aurelian. He says: "Me contradicente neminem scriptorem, quantum ad historiam pertinet, non aliquid esse mentitum, prodente
quin etiam, in quo Livius, in quo Sallustius, in quo Cornelius
Tacitus, in quo denique Trogus manifestis testibus convince-
rentur, pedibus in sententiam transitum faciens ac manum

porrigens iocando: 'Propterea scribe' inquit 'ut libet. Securus, quod velis, dices, habiturus mendaciorum comites, quos historicae eloquentiae miramur auctores.' " The second comment is in *Probus* 2: "Et mihi quidem id animi fuit ut non Sallustios, Livios, Tacitos, Trogos atque omnes disertissimos imitarer viros in vita principum et temporibus disserendis, sed Marium Maximum, Suetonium Tranquillum, Fabium Marcellinum, Gargilinam Martialem ceterosque qui haec et talia non tam diserte quam vere memoriae tradiderunt." Surely Vopiscus had a text before him.

Ammianus Marcellinus, about 400, published his history, which began where Tacitus left off, indicating a knowledge at least of what Tacitus had written.[1]

At about the same time Sulpicius Severus of Aquitaine wrote his *Chronicorum libri* and, in 2. 28. 2 and 2. 29. 2, used Tacitus, *Ann.* 15. 37 and 44 as his source. On the detailed matter of Nero's marriage with Pythagoras and the punishment of the Christians the verbal resemblances make it impossible to think that he was drawing on any other source. *Chronicorum libri* 2. 28. 2: "Id tantum annotasse contentus sum, hunc per omnia foedissima et crudelissima eo processisse, ut matrem interficeret, post etiam Pythagorae cuidam in modum sollemnium coniugiorum denuberet; Inditumque imperatori flammeum; dos et genialis torus et faces nuptiales, cuncta denique, quae vel in feminis non sine verecundia conspiciuntur, spectata" (cf. *Ann.* 15. 37). *Chronicorum libri,* 2. 29. 2: "quin et novae mortes excogitatae, ut ferarum tergis contecti laniatu canum interirent, multi crucibus affixi aut flamma usti, plerique in id reservati ut cum defecisset dies, in usum nocturni luminis urerentur" (cf. *Ann.* 15. 44).

Jerome in his commentary on Zacchariah 14. 1, 2 (3, p. 914) cites Tacitus: "Cornelius quoque [i.e. as well as Josephus] Tacitus, qui post Augustum usque ad mortem Domitiani vitas Caesarum triginta voluminibus exaravit." He gives no proof

---

1. E. Wölfflin, in *Philologus, 29* (1870), 723 ff., points out what seem to be echoes of Tacitus in Ammianus 27. 9. 2, 27. 10. 14, 29. 2. 23, 31. 15. 6, 31. 15. 15, and possibly 14. 2. 9.

of having read Tacitus—he may not even have seen his works at all—but he did know of a tradition in which the thirty books were numbered consecutively.

Claudian cannot be safely claimed as a reader of Tacitus in spite of his suggestive references to Tiberius and Nero. 8, Fourth Consulship of Honorius, 311:

> Annales veterum delicta loquuntur.
> Haerebunt maculae. Quis non per saecula damnat
> Caesareae portenta domus? Quem dira Neronis
> Funera, quem rupes Caprearum taetra latebit,
> Incesto possessa seni?

20, *In Eutropium* 2. 58:

> Exquirite retro
> Crimina continui lectis annalibus aevi
> Prisca recensitis evolvite saecula factis:
> Quid senie infandi Capreae, quid scaena Neronis
> Tale ferunt?

Servius, on the other hand, at the end of the fourth century, while his reference is to a lost part of Tacitus, evidently had read the text. In his comment on *Aen.* 3. 399 he writes: "Hi vero [i.e. Locri], qui iuxta Delphos colunt, Ozolae nuncupantur . . . qui autem Libyam delati sunt Nasamones appellantur ut Cornelius Tacitus refert, oriundi a Naryeiis, quod ibi invenias ubi ait Libycone habitantes litore Locros."

Hegesippus made a free Latin version of Josephus' *Jewish War* with independent additions, many of which seem to come from Tacitus' *Histories*. An example is 4. 8: "denique neque pisces neque adsuetas aquis et laetas mergendi usu aves." Compare *Hist.* 5. 6: "neque vento impellitur neque pisces aut suetas aquis volucres patitur." There is a certain studied attempt at variation of wording without concealment of the source.

Of the fifth-century writers, two, Sidonius Apollinaris and Orosius, have left evidence of considerable familiarity with Tacitus as well as respect for him as a writer. In *Ep.* 4. 22. 2 Sidonius makes a pun on the name Tacitus. After comparing himself and Leo to Pliny and Tacitus he says that should the

latter return to life and see how eloquent Leo was in the field
of narrative, he would become wholly *Tacitus*. The name as
he gives it is Gaius Cornelius Tacitus. Again in *Ep.* 4. 14.
1 he quotes Gaius Tacitus as an ancestor of his friend Polemius.
He was, says Sidonius, a consular in the time of the Ulpians: "Sub
verbis cuiuspiam Germanici ducis in historia sua rettulit di-
cens: cum Vespasiano mihi vetus amicitia" etc. The quotation
is a careless one from *Hist.* 5. 26. The quality of Tacitus' style
as conceived by Sidonius is indicated in *Carm.* 2. 190 ff.:

> Qua Crispus brevitate placet, qua pondere Varro,
> Quo genio Plautus, quo fulmine Quintilianus,
> Qua pompa Tacitus numquam sine laude loquendus.

And again in *Carm.* 23. 153:

> Et qui pro ingenio fluente nulli
> Corneli Tacite, es tacendus ori.

In this case Tacitus figures in a list comprising Cicero, Livy,
Vergil, Terence, Plautus, Varro, Sallust, Tacitus, Petronius,
Ovid, the Senecas, Lucan, and Statius—all of whom would
pale before Consentius, who is being addressed.

The citations in Orosius are naturally quite different from
these casual references and general estimates. Orosius is always
after material for argument, and it is the content rather than
the style that interests him. He refers to Tacitus explicitly and
at length. He compares critically the statements of Cornelius
Tacitus and Pompeius Trogus and again of Tacitus, Suetonius,
and Josephus. The quotations and citations from Tacitus are
all in the *Adversus paganos* and all from the *Histories*. In 1.
5. 1 Orosius says: "Ante annos urbis conditae MCLX confi-
nem Arabiae regionem quae tunc Pentapolis vocabatur arsisse
penitus igne caeleste inter alios etiam Cornelius Tacitus refert,
qui sic ait: Haud procul inde campi . . . vim frugiferam per-
didisse. Et cum hoc loco nihil de incensis propter peccata hominum civitatibus quasi ignarus expresserit, paulo post velut
oblitus consilii subicit et dicit: Ego sicut inclitas . . . corrumpi reor." The quotation is from *Hist.* 5. 7 and, in spite of
some interesting variants, it is reasonably exact. The same is

true of his quotation of *Hist.* 5. 3 in *Adv. pag.* 1. 10. 1: "Anno autem ante urbem conditam DCCCV infanda Aegyptiis mala atque intolerabiles plagas incubuisse Pompeius Corneliusque testantur." According to Orosius, however, the testimony varies. He gives the evidence of Pompeius and Justinus and then proceeds: "At vero Cornelius de eadem re ait: Plurimi auctores consentiunt . . . praesentes miserias pepulissent. Itaque Cornelius dicit, quod ipsis Aegyptiis cogentibus Iudaei in deserta propulsi sint, et postea subiungit incaute, quia ope Moysi ducis in Aegypto miserias propulissent." Orosius refers to this passage later in 7. 27. 1.

The remaining citations in Orosius are to lost parts of Tacitus. They are as follows.

7. 3. 7: "Deinde, ut verbis Corneli Taciti loquar, sene Augusto Ianus patefactus, dum apud extremos terrarum terminos novae gentes saepe ex usu et aliquando cum damno quaeruntur, usque ad Vespasiani duravit imperium. Hucusque Cornelius."

7. 9. 7: "Sexcenta milia Iudaeorum eo bello (i.e. Titus' capture of Jerusalem) interfecta Cornelius et Suetonius referunt; Iosephus vero Iudaeus, qui ei tunc bello praefuit . . . scribit undecies centena milia gladio et fame perisse."

7. 10. 3: "Nam quanta fuerint Diurpanei Dacorum regis cum Fusco duce proelia quantaeque Romanorum clades, longo textu evolverem, nisi Cornelius Tacitus, qui hanc historiam diligentissime contexuit, de reticendo interfectorum numero et Sallustium Crispum elegisse dixisset."

7. 19. 4: "Gordianus . . . Iani portas aperuit: quas utrum post Vespasianum et Titum aliquis clauserit neminem scripsisse memini, cum tamen eas ab ipso Vespasiano post annum apertas Cornelius Tacitus prodat."

7. 34. 5: "Itaque Theodosius adflictam rempublicam ira Dei reparandam credidit misericordia Dei; omnem fiduciam sui ad opem Christi conferens maximas illas Scythicas gentes formidatasque cunctis maioribus, Alexandro quoque illi Magno sicut Pompeius Corneliusque testati sunt, evitatas, nunc autem extincto Romano exercitu Romanis equis armisque instructissi-

mas, hoc est Alanos, Hunos, et Gothos, incunctanter adgressus magnis multisque proeliis vicit."

Orosius not only used Tacitus, he became a source from which Tacitean quotations could be drawn. For instance, Landolfus Sagax, about A.D. 1,000, cites Tacitus four times, but all four extracts are to be found in Orosius, and there is no indication that Landolfus knew Tacitus directly.

Cassiodorus is a sixth-century writer who seems to have used Tacitus as source material. He does not, however, seem to know much about his source, for he speaks of "a certain Cornelius"; but he draws on *Germania* 45: "Hoc quodam Cornelio scribente legitur in interioribus insulis Oceani ex arboribus succo defluens, unde et succinum dicitur, paulatim solis ardore coalescere. Fit enim sudatile metallum teneritudo perspicua: modo croceo colore rubens, modo flammea claritate pinguescens: ut cum in maris fuerit delapsa confinio, aestu alternante purgata, vestris litoribus tradatur exposita" (*Var. lib.* 5. epist. 2. 2).

With this citation from Tacitus as evidence, it seems not unlikely that *Var.* 11. 31, *scuto impositus more gentis,* is an echo of *Hist.* 4. 15, *impositus scuto more gentis.*

Perhaps a hundred years or less after Cassiodorus, Jordanes wrote his *De origine actibusque getarum* which he took largely from Cassiodorus' history of the Goths. That one or the other of these two must have known *Agric.* 10 is shown by the following passage in Jordanes (2. 12, 13): "Mari tardo circumfluam quod nec remis facile impellentibus cedat, nec ventorum flatibus intumescat, credo quia remotae longius terrae causas motibus negant. Quippe illic latius quam usquam aequor extenditur . . . Noctem quoque clariorem in extrema eius parte memma quam Cornelius etiam annalium scriptor enarrat. . . Labi vero per eam multa quam maxima relabique flumina gemmas margaritasque volventia." The textual confusion *memma quam* is usually taken to come from *minimamque* but we should expect *brevemque.* The very last item is probably from Mela.

The Scholiast to Juvenal 2. 99 and 14. 102 refers to the

Histories, ascribing them in the one case to Cornelius, in the other to Cornelius Tacitus. The first note is as follows: "Hunc incomparabilis vitae bello civili Vitellius vicit apud Bebriacum campum. Horum bellum scripsit Cornelius, scripsit et Pompeius Planta, qui sit Bebriacum vicum a Cremona vicesimo lapide." The second is a twofold description of Moses: (a) "sacerdos vel rex eius gentis"; (b) "aut ipsius quidem religionis inventor, cuius Cornelius etiam Tacitus meminit" (cf. *Hist.* 5. 3).

Two very problematical pieces of Latin literature raise the question of Tacitean tradition. Meister, in his introduction to Dictys of Crete (Leipzig, 1872) includes Tacitus among the recognizable sources of phrase. He is not, however, any more specific than that and, being primarily interested in showing the influence of Sallust, he gives considerable evidence of the author's use of Sallust which in reality indicates rather a borrowing from Tacitus. For example, Dictys 4. 22: *neque sacro neque profano abstinuisse.* Meister compares this with Sallust, *Cat.* 11, *sacra profanaque omnia polluere.* Tacitus, *Hist.* 2. 56, reads *non sacro non profano abstinebant.* Now Tacitus presumably echoed Sallust. This is particularly likely in this case because he uses *polluere* in the preceding line. But Dictys, with *abstinuisse* would seem to have been following Tacitus, especially as the earlier part of the same sentence is also Tacitean. Compare Dictys, *parcum in suo atque appetentem alieni,* with Tacitus, *Hist.* 1. 49, *pecuniae alienae non appetens, suae parcus.* Dictys 1. 16, *magnus atque clarus habebatur,* might come equally well from Sallust, *Cat.* 53, *clarus atque magnus habetur,* or from Tacitus, *Agric.* 18, *clarus ac magnus haberi.* On the other hand, Dictys 2. 12, *ancipiti malo territos,* also cited by Meister as a parallel to Sallust, seems to be nearer to Tacitus, *Agric.* 26, *ita ancipiti malo territi Britanni,* than to Sallust, *Cat.* 29, *ancipiti malo permotus.* It is probable that Dictys used both Sallust and Tacitus.

It is less likely that the author of the correspondence between Seneca and St. Paul knew Tacitus. Barlow points out in his edition (Rome, 1938) that epistle 11, dealing with the fire, uses two phrases that suggest Tacitus. One is *mendacium vela-*

mentum, which he compares with *sceleribus velamenta* in *Ann.*
13. 47, and *grassator,* which is compared with *Ann.* 15. 40, in
which Tacitus uses *grassatus* of this very fire which is under
discussion. Barlow also suggests that the reference here in the
description of the fire to the gardens of Sallust may have suggested a similar reference in Epistle 1. The suggestions are not
compelling, but also they are not merely fanciful.

The period following Cassiodorus (or Jordanes) and lasting
over two hundred years has so far yielded no evidence of any
knowledge of Tacitus. Certainly not later than 840, Einhard
of Fulda, in his *Translatio S. Alexandri* [2] quotes extensively
and obviously, though without credit, from *Germ.* 4. For example: "nec facile ullis aliarum gentium vel sibi inferiorum
conubiis infecti, propriam et sinceram et tantum sui similem
gentem facere conati sunt. Unde habitus quoque ac magnitudo
corporum comarumque color tamquam in tanto hominum numero idem fere omnibus." There is much more of this direct
borrowing in this work of Einhard's. Manitius has undertaken
to show that his other publications also reveal the knowledge
of Tacitus.[3] In *Vita Caroli* 12, Einhard says: *Sueones quos
Nortmannos vocamus.* Sueones is therefore a strange name—
this is its first appearance since Tacitus, *Germ.* 44. Tacitus uses
misceri of rivers, to empty into, an unusual use which Einhard
also affects: *Vita Caroli* 15; *Ann. Ein.* 791, 793; *Translat. S.
Alex.,* 20. There is also evidence that Einhard knew the first
book of the *Annals.* In his own annals, 778, he wrote: "pari
modo sacra profanaque pessumdata; nullum aetatis aut sexus"
etc. Cf. Tac. *Ann.* 1. 51: "non sexus non aetas miserationem
attulit: profana simul et sacra . . . solo aequantur."

A little more than a quarter of a century later Ruodolfus, a
monk of Fulda, made fairly extensive use of the *Germania* in
writing the annals of the monastery.[4] In addition to this, he
has a specific reference to Tacitus, *Ann.* 2, in another entry in

2. *Monumenta Germaniae Historica,* L.L.I., 675.
3. Max Manitius, "Einharts Werke und ihr Stil," *Neues Archiv der
Gesellschaft für ältere deutsche Geschichtskunde,* 7 (1882), 519 ff.
4. *Mon. Germ. Hist.,* Script. 2, 675.

the records of Fulda.[5] The entry is: "Super amnem quem Cornelius Tacitus, scriptor rerum a Romanis in ea gente gestarum, Visurgim, moderni vero Wisahara vocant." It may refer to any one of four chapters of *Annals*—2. 9, 11, 16, or 17—but it must be to one of them and is the first specific reference cited with the name of Tacitus to the early books of the *Annals*.

This brings the tradition down to the time when our existing MSS begin to enter into the problem. The first Medicean, presumably of the ninth century and probably coming originally from Fulda or Hersfeld, would seem quite possibly to have been the source of information for Einhard and Ruodolfus. Presumably there was also a *Germania* MS available at Fulda from which they drew. Our earliest text of the Minor Works, in a hand quite suitable for Fulda, is a presumably ninth century fragment of the *Agricola*. But Poggio and the other fifteenth-century hunters had rumors of Tacitus at Hersfeld, near Fulda and closely associated. It is altogether probable that there was an *Agricola* as well as a *Germania* in the neighborhood. Adam of Bremen, about 1075, wrote the annals of the Church of Hamburg (see Migne, *PL, 146, 457* ff.). The introduction discusses the purpose of biographical history. Since, he says, there is no history of the monks of Hamburg, "fortasse dixerit aliquis aut nihil eos dignum memoria fecisse in diebus suis aut si fecerant quippiam scriptorum qui hoc posteris traderent diligentia carerent." Following the introduction, Adam begins: "Historiam Hammaburgensis ecclesiae scripturi, quoniam Hammaburg nobilissima quondam Saxonum civitas erat, non indecens aut vacuum fore putamus si prius de gente Saxonum et natura eiusdem provinciae ponemus ea quae doctissimus vir Einhardus aliique non obscuri auctores reliquerunt in scriptis suis." In chapter 6 and following, Adam quotes from Einhard and much of Einhard is Tacitus, taken from the *Germania*. But before reaching this material which he acknowledges to be from Einhard, he says in chapter 3: "Quaerentibus autem qui mortales ab initio Saxoniam coluerint vel a quibus haec gens primo finibus egressa sit, compertum est nobis ex

5. Ibid., *1*, 368.

multa lectione veterum, istam gentem sicut omnes fere populos qui in orbe sunt occulto Dei judicio non semel de regno ad populum alterum fuisse translatos; et ex nomine victorum provincias quoque vocabula sortitas." The notes in the *Patrologia Latina* call attention to Sallust, *Jugurtha* 17, "sed qui mortales initio Africam habuerint." But this is to overlook *Agric.* 11: "Ceterum Britanniam qui mortales initio coluerint, indigenae an advecti, ut inter barbaros, parum compertum." The last part of the paragraph also recalls definitely *Germ.* 2: "ita nationis nomen, non gentis evaluisse paulatim, ut omnes primum a victore ob metum, mox etiam a se ipsis invento nomine Germani vocarentur." It is not possible to say dogmatically whether Adam drew the *Agricola* hints from Einhard or from Tacitus directly but *multa lectione veterum* and the general arrangement of those paragraphs suggests the latter. At any rate, we have here evidence of an *Agricola* as well as a *Germania* and an *Annals* at Fulda or thereabouts.

By 1100 there is evidence that the last half of the *Annals* and the *Histories* were known at Monte Cassino. The Second Medicean MS was written there not far from that date. Only recently has it been discovered that the *Agricola,* too, was known there. In about 1135 Peter the Deacon made fairly extensive use of the first two chapters of the *Agricola.*[6] The Lombard MS lay in the monastery without attracting apparently much attention. It is Paulinus Venetus who first shows knowledge of it. He was made Bishop of Pozzuoli in June 1324 and in his *Mappa Mundi* he cites Cornelius Tacitus and quotes without acknowledgment from Books 13–15. These passages are frequently marked in the margin of Medicean II. Paulinus died about 1340.[7]

The twelfth century, which saw the writing of the Monte Cassino MS, also produced faint echoes of Tacitus outside Italy. Guibert de Nogent, who died in 1124, is quoted in Migne

6. See Herbert Bloch, "A Manuscript of Tacitus' *Agricola* in Monte Cassino about A.D. 1135," *Classical Philology, 36* (1941), 185.

7. For this Paulinus matter cf. K. J. Heilig, "Ein Beitrag zur Geschichte des Mediceus II des Tacitus," *Wiener Studien, 53* (1935), 95 ff.

(*PL, 156*, 858) as saying *modernum hoc saeculum corrumpi-tur et corrumpit*, recalling *corrumpere et corrumpi saeculum vocatur*, from *Germ.* 19. William of Malmesbury (*Gesta Regum Angl.* 68) recalls *Hist.* 2. 73 (*vix credibile quantum brevi adoleverit*) with his *incredibile quantum brevi adoleverit*. John of Salisbury names Tacitus (*Policraticus* 8. 18) among a group of historians but does not quote. The same is true of Peter of Blois (*Epist.* 101).

In Italy, a curious reference by Guglielmo da Pastrengo, a friend of Petrarch, indicates that the name of Tacitus was not wholly forgotten even though the writer may have known no more than the name. In his *De origine rerum*, fol. 18, he writes: "Cornelius Tacitus, quem Titus imperator suae praefecit bibliothecae, Augusti gesta descripsit atque Domitiani." It would be tempting to think that Petrarch, when he wrote *et cuncta vastantibus certa sunt pretia* (*De remediis utriusque fortunae*, Lib. I, dial. 43, p. 42), had in mind *Agric.* 30. 6, *postquam cuncta vastantibus defuere terrae*, but there is no supporting evidence.

Boccaccio "discovered" Tacitus in 1360, probably personally finding the Medicean MS and "rescuing" it from Monte Cassino. The material in it became at once known to others— Poggio, Niccoli, Rambaldi, Bruni, Domenico di Bandino— and even Jean de Montreuil by the turn of the century was quoting Cornelius Tacitus on the plagues of Egypt (*Epist. Ined. Cod. Vat.* 332, fol. 57ʳ). Secco Polento (MS Riccardiano 121, fol. 65) describes a MS of Tacitus which he has seen (*vidi*), this before 1426. By 1425 the frantic hunt is under way for MSS of Tacitus other than that of Books 11–16. Boccaccio's MS finally settled into possession of Niccoli Niccola, spurned by Poggio and appreciated by Bessarion.

It is evident from this survey that while Tacitus was not one of the frequently used writers of the Roman era, he was by no means completely lost or forgotten. Between the time when Boccaccio discovered and removed the Monte Cassino MS, which we know as the second Medicean, and the recovery of the first Medicean from Cörwey in 1509 by Leo X, all of the existing works of Tacitus were made generally available. Up to that period there had never been any mention or use of the *Dialogus* so far as our present evidence goes. Between Ptolemy in the second century and Ruodolfus of Fulda in the ninth, the same is true of the early books of the *Annals*. The later historical books were known in Gaul and Rome down to the sixth century and copied at Monte Cassino in the twelfth. The *Germania* and *Agricola* were known in Germany and Italy (possibly in Gaul) well into the sixth century and in the ninth. The question of the provenance of their archetype or archetypes will require further discussion.

13. DISCOVERY OF THE WORKS

THE MAJOR WORKS

THE DISCOVERY of the two sections of the major works of Tacitus, Books 1–6 and 11–21, raises no very difficult problems. The manuscript known as Medicean I (Laurentian Library, No. 68. 1) contains what we have of the first six books and is the sole authority for them. It was first used for publication in the edition of Tacitus made for Leo X by Beroaldus in 1515. In his introductory letters (to the Pope and to the reader) Beroaldus says that the MS was recently found in Germany and acquired at great price by Leo. A letter of Cardinal Soderini [1] indicates that the MS came to Rome in 1509, and a letter of Leo X of December 1, 1517, cites the papal generosity in the case of this MS as an incentive to other foundations to yield up their treasures. This letter adds the information that Laur. 68. 1 was originally stolen from the monastery of Cörwey. There has been considerable controversy over the matter, but the essential facts are clear. The MS, in ninth-century Carolingian minuscules, came from northwestern Germany, where the subject matter was known to Ruodolfus of Fulda in the ninth century. Dom Henri Quentin has made the notable observation that the page inversions of Med. II correspond almost exactly in the number of letters to a page with Med. I.[2] This obviously suggests that this first Medicean once contained all the books of the *Annals* and *Histories* and is the archetype of Med. II as well as of all of our MSS of the historical works. The volumes were apparently separated and Laur. 68. 1 was rebound with a copy of Pliny (now Laur. 47. 36) uniform with it in format and indicating by the quaternion numberings that the two were once bound together. The volume containing Books 11–21 presumably traveled from Fulda to Monte Cassino, where it was copied in

1. Quoted by Urlichs, in *Eos, 1*, 244.
2. *Essais de critique textuelle* (Paris, 1926), p. 176.

the eleventh century. This copy is preserved in the Laurentian Library (68. 2) and has been identified by the handwriting [3] and by the name *Abbas Raynaldus* in the otherwise empty column of 103^v. The manuscript was used at Monte Cassino by Paulus Venetus, Bishop of Pozzuoli before 1340.[4]

Boccaccio visited Monte Cassino and found the library in a distressing state of collapse.[5] The date of this visit is unknown but it is certain that between 1357 and 1362 Boccaccio gained access to a manuscript of Tacitus.[6] In 1371 he had loaned a "quaternion of this manuscript to Niccolo da Montefalcone, for he writes to him: "Quaternum quem asportanti Cornelii Taciti queso saltem mietas ne laborem meum frustraveris et Libro deformitatem ampliorem addideris.[7] Boccaccio's citations from Tacitus indicate that his manuscript was one containing the latter part of the *Annals* and the *Histories,* for he cites Tacitus as his authority on the Paphian Venus (*Genealogiae deorum,* 1. 3. 23) and uses Tacitus as a source in his *De claris mulieribus* in accounts of Agrippina, Epicharis, Pompeia, Poppaea Sabina, and Triaria.[8] In his *Comento sopra la comedia* [9] he says, *secondoche scrive Cornelio Tacito nel XV° libro delle sue storie,* confirming this fact. It is obvious from the letter to Montefalcone that his manuscript was a mutilated one, apart from the loss which resulted from his generosity, and that he had not as yet made a copy of it.

In Vespasiano's Life of Niccolo Niccoli, we learn that Boccaccio's books were left to the convent of S. Spirito [10] and that

3. E. A. Lowe, *The Unique Manuscript of Tacitus' Histories,* Casinensia, 1929.

4. Heilig, "Ein Beitrag."

5. Rambaldi, *Comentum super Dantis Aldigheri Comoediam* (ed. Lacaita, 1887), 5. 301. 2. The story is unconvincingly questioned by Luigi Tosti, *Storia della badia di Montecassino* (Rome, 1888), *3,* 99.

6. Pierre de Nolhac, "Boccace et Tacite," *Mélanges d'archéologie et d'histoire, 12* (1892), 8.

7. Francesco Corazzini, *Lettere edite e inedite di Messer Giovanni Boccaccio* (Florence, 1877), p. 59.

8. Cf. Attilio Hortis, *Studi sulle opere latine da Boccaccio* (Trieste, 1879), pp. 424 f.

9. Cf. de Nolhac, p. 10.

10. The will is given by D. M. Manni, *Istoria del Decamerone* (Florence, 1742), *1,* 117.

they were in danger of perishing until Niccoli, at his own expense, furnished strong wooden cases for them. The catalogue of S. Spirito [11] reads: "Item in eodem banco V liber 7. Id quod de Cornelio Tacito reperitur copertus corio rubro cuius principium est. Nam Valerium Asiaticum. Finis vero in penultima charta: machina accessura erat." This ending is Vitruvius 10. 16. 7, indicating that the Tacitus was then bound with Vitruvius.

In view of Niccoli's connection with the books of Boccaccio, his loan of a Tacitus manuscript to Poggio in 1427 assumes added significance. It was in a difficult Lombard hand and had lost some pages (*deficiunt plures chartae variis in locis*) so that Poggio found it impossible to use and returned it. But in the meantime he had written a significant letter to Niccoli on September 27, 1427: "Cornelium Tacitum cum venerit observabo penes me occulte. Scio enim omnem illam cantilenam et unde exierit et per quem et quis eum sibi vindicet; sed nil dubites: non exibit a me ne verbo quidem." [12] Niccoli must have cautioned him not to let the manuscript be seen. We know that it was returned to Niccoli in 1428 (Letter III, 17) and bequeathed by him to San Marco, whence it was transferred before the middle of the sixteenth century to the Laurentian Library. There is no further trace of a Santo Spirito Tacitus. It should be noted that Laur. 68. 2 is today bound not with Vitruvius but with Apuleius. This may be due to Niccoli's irregular procedure in sending the MS to Poggio. There is evidence of trimming (fol. 61^v) presumably for the purpose of rebinding.

THE MINOR WORKS

The assumption is generally made that one MS of the Minor Works was discovered in Germany and brought to Rome in the middle of the fifteenth century possibly by Enoch of Ascoli, and that from this archetype came all of the MSS which we possess today. One exception is made: the eight leaves of the

11. Cf. A. Goldmann, *Centralblatt für Bibliothekswesen*, 4 (1887), 137 ff. The catalogue of 1451 is given in Cod. Laur. Ashburnh. n. 1897.
12. Cf. *Poggii Epistolae*, ed. T. de Tonellis as an appendix to P. Hochart, *De l'Authenticité des Annales et des Histoires de Tacite* (Paris, 1890), Letters III, 14, 15, 17.

codex Aesinas which date from some centuries before 1450 and which contain part of the *Agricola* are held to be an actual part of Enoch's manuscript. Some scholars are skeptical of the part played by Enoch but still hold to the theory of a single "Hersfeld" original which came from Germany in the fifteenth century and which survives in part in the Jesi MS. A review of the known facts makes this view practically untenable, and indicates almost beyond doubt that at least two MSS came from Germany and that the Aesinas preserves no part of either of them.

The enthusiasm for manuscript hunting reached fever pitch in the early fifteenth century, if we may judge from the correspondence between scholars which has survived from that period. The church councils offered many opportunities to investigate new hiding places, and independent trips in search of treasures were not infrequent. There was the keenest rivalry, which no doubt often created or served to keep alive the many violent literary feuds of the day. Poggio Bracciolini, for example, was notoriously unrestrained in his epistolary vituperation of fellow scholars. He was distinctly of the Medici party, which was unfriendly toward Beccadelli, Il Panormita. At the same time Poggio and Panormita were competitors in the search for MSS from the monasteries of Germany. Guarino and Aurispa were estranged from Florence by the enmity of Niccoli, the friend and patron of Poggio, and there developed at Naples a definitely anti-Florentine group which included not only Beccadelli but also Bartolomeo Fazio and Jovianus Pontanus.

The keenness of competition led to many shady transactions as well as to the exchange of scurrilities. Everyone is familiar with the acquisition of the first Medicean MS, which came to Leo X admittedly as a result of theft, and this transaction is more respectable than many similar ones during the preceding century. The letters which Enoch of Ascoli carried with him for public display, containing instructions not to steal manuscripts, were quite probably the ancient counterpart of false receipts for use in the evasion of customs duties: at any rate, they are telling evidence of the prevalent practice in clerical circles. Poggio expounds unblushingly to Traversari [13] (Symonds 2. 100 citing Voigt) a plan to steal from Hersfeld in collusion with a pious monk a MS of Ammianus. The passion which in Boccaccio had begun the revival of learning had produced in half a century a vigorous cut-throat trade in MSS.

It is therefore no great surprise to come upon evidence from the years following 1422 of a considerable furore over some rumored Tacitus material new to the world of scholars. The first vague hint is given in a letter from Poggio to Niccoli (Letter I, 21. Voigt, *1, 254*). Bertolomeo Capra, he says, is reported to have found some new historians in Germany. Poggio hardly credits the rumor: "est enim res digne triumpho inventio tam singularium auctorum: sed mihi non fit verisimile. . . . Si tales historicos reperisset, personuisset ipsemet buccina nihil occultans." There is no compelling reason to think that the new historians included Tacitus, but the rumor may have incited Poggio to new efforts. At any rate he wrote to Niccoli on November 3, 1425, about a monk from Hersfeld who knew of some worth-while MSS in Germany: "Inter ea volumina est Iulius Frontinus et aliqua opera Cornelii Taciti nobis ignota." [14] The natural interpretation of the last phrase is that there were works of Tacitus other than the historical works of which those parts of the *Annals* and *Histories* contained in the second Medicean MS were already in the possession of Niccoli and had been known even to Boccaccio.

In April 1426 Panormita wrote to Guarino from Bononia.[15] The letter deals largely with his difficulties over a Celsus manuscript, but at the end he submits another piece of news:

Compertus est Cor. Tacitus de origine et situ Germanorum. Item eiusdem liber de vita Iulii Agricolae isque incipit: "Clarorum virorum facta" caeterave. Quinetiam Sex. Iulii Frontonis liber de

13. J. A. Symonds, *Renaissance in Italy* (New York, 1935).

14. This correspondence is published in the collected Letters of Poggio (Tonelli, Florence, 1832), and may also be found conveniently in Hochart and elsewhere.

15. MS Marcianus Latinus 14. 221, fol. 95. Cf. Sabbadini: *St. e Cr.*, p. 267.

aquaeductibus qui in urbem Romam inducuntur; et est litteris aureis transcriptus. Item eiusdem Frontonis liber alter qui in hunc modum iniciatur: "Cum omnis res ab imperatore delegata mentionem exigat" et caetera. Et inventus est quidam dyalogus de oratore, et est, ut coniectamus, Cor. Taciti, atque is ita incipit: "Saepe ex me requirunt" et caetera. Inter quos et liber Suetonii Tranquilli repertus de grammaticis et rhetoribus: huic inicium est: "Grammatica Romae." Hi et innumerabiles alii qui in manibus versantur, et praeterea alii fortasse qui in usu non sunt, uno in loco simul sunt; ii vero omnes, qui ob hominum ignaviam in desuetudinem abierant ibique sunt, cuidam mihi coniunctissimo dimittantur propediem, ab illo autem ad me proxime et de repente: tu secundo proximus eris qui renatos sane illustrissimos habiturus sis.

It should be noted that Sextus Iulius Fronto can only be Frontinus, as is shown by the *de aquaeductibus* and the *cum omnis res*. At the same time it is a striking fact that these "two works" of Frontinus are the two books of the *De aquaeductibus* in reverse order. The word *mentionem* is a misquotation for *intentiorem* and *requirunt* for *requiris*. The words *uno in loco simul sunt* may of course refer to the ultimate source, but it should be noted that Poggio, in the letter to Niccoli already cited, specified a rendezvous where the deal was to be completed: "Libri ponentur in Nurimberga, quo et deferri debent Speculum et Additiones [books to be exchanged], et exinde magna est facultas libros advehendi."

Johannes Lamola had introduced Panormita to Guarino, who had acknowledged the introduction from Verona on January 26 and who acknowledged the receipt of the letter quoted above under date of May 1, 1426. Now, Guarino was not on friendly terms with Poggio. Neither was Alfonso of Naples, the patron of Panormita. Furthermore, Poggio was trying to get this group of MSS for Niccoli, who had made Florence unbearable for Guarino. It is quite impossible to think that Panormita and Poggio were working together. Also, the action of the Hersfeld monk was suspicious. He brought an inventory only and not a single MS. Poggio became irritated and then discouraged. In May, 1427 he wrote to Niccoli that the monk had brought "inventarium plenum verbis, re vacuum." He adds later in the same letter: "Mitto autem ad te nunc partem inventarii sui, in quo describitur volumen illud Cornelii Taciti et aliorum, quibus caremus, qui cum sint res quaedam parvulae, non satis magno sunt aestimandae. Decidi ex maxima spe quam conceperam ex verbis suis."

One remark in this letter, following what has just been cited, is of particular interest: *Hic monachus eget pecunia.* Perhaps this is the key to the situation. Certainly it is by no means impossible that the monk was bargaining at the same time with Poggio and with the patrons of Panormita.

Niccoli did not give up the quest merely because Poggio, who had evidently hoped for at least a manuscript of the early books of the *Annals,* was disappointed on learning that there were only trifles to be had. He drew up a *commentarium* in 1431,[16] with a list of MSS which he knew to be in foreign monasteries and sent it to two cardinals, Giuliano Cesarini and Niccolo Albergati, who were on their way to Germany and France. It is obviously based on the information obtained from Poggio, and one part is worth quoting at length because of its close resemblance to the letter of Panormita, indicating that both men were really after the same MSS:

In monasterio hispildensi haud procul ab Alpubus continentur hec opuscula, videlicet: Iulii Frontini de aqueductis que in urbem inducunt liber I. Incipit sic: "Persecutus ea que de modulis dici fuit necessarium nunc ponam quemadmodum queque aqua ut principium commentariis comprehensum est usque ad nostram curam habere visa sit etc." Continet hic liber XIII (sc. folia). Item eiusdem Frontini liber. Incipit sic: "Cum omnis res ab imperatore delegata interiorem exigat et curam et me seu naturalis solicitudo seu fides sedula non ad diligentiam modo verum ad morem commisse rei instingent, sitque mihi nunc ab Nerva Augusto nescio diligentiore an amantiore rei p. imperatore aquarum iniunctum officium et ad usum etc." Continet XI folia. Cornelii Taciti de origine et situ Germanorum liber. Incipit sic: "Germania omnis a

16. See Sabbadini, *Storia e Critica,* pp. 1 ff.

Gallis Rhetiisque et Pannoniis Rheno et Danubio fluminibus a Sarmatis Datisque et mutuo metu a montibus separatur etc." Continet autem XII folia. Item in eodem codice: Cornelii Taciti de vita Iulii Agricolae. Incipit sic: "Clarorum virorum facta moresque posteris tradere antiquitus usitatum ne nostris quidem temporibus quanquam incuriosa suorum etas obmisit." Qui liber continet XIIII folia. Item in eodem codice: Dialogus de oratoribus, qui incipit sic: "Sepe ex me requiris Iuste Fabi cum priora secula tot eminentium oratorum ingeniis gloria floruerint nostra potissimum etas deserta et laude eloquentie orbata"; qui liber continet XVIII folia. Item in eodem incipit sic: "Grammatica Rome ne in usum quidem olim nedum in onore ullo etc." Continet hic liber folia VII. Ammiani Marcellini rerum gestarum libri XVIII qui pervenerunt, usque ad obitum Valentis imperatoris: qui est finis hystorie.

It would look as though Panormita had had a less complete memorandum. Neither he nor Niccoli, of course, had seen the MSS. Poggio had written on September 11, 1428: "Cornelius Tacitus silet inter Germanos." The monk had returned to Rome in February 1429 but without his treasure. The two cardinals were evidently too busy to attempt the commission or unable to carry it out. At any rate, we hear no more of them, but the *Commentarium* has a note in the margin indicating that the volume was actually found.[17]

There is however one further bit of light before the darkness settles down. It seems to indicate still another group that was striving for the same prize. Sabbadini[18] publishes a letter from Francesco Pizzolpasso, archbishop of Milan, to Nicolao Cusano of Gaul dated from Basle, December 17, 1432. It contains the following sentence: "Tu quoque memorie habeto ut habeamus codices illos Suetonii Tranquilli ceterosque alios de viris illustribus ducibusque iuxta firmata dudum; item et Frontinum de termis urbis." It seems pretty clear that rumor of the same group of new works had reached the archbishop and from the Council at Basle information of this rival search made its way

17. Rodney Robinson, "The Inventory of Niccoló Niccoli," *Classical Philology, 16* (1921), 251.
18. *Le Scoperte dei Codici Latini e Greci ne' Secoli XIV e XV,* 2 vols. Florence, 1905–14.

to Niccoli through the agency of Joannes Ceparelli Pratensis. So on the nineteenth of January, Niccoli's friend Ambrosio Traversari wrote from Florence to Iuliano Cesarini that they knew that Nicolao Cusano had shown certain important MSS to the Archbishop of Milan and that they begged him, Cesarini, to send them detailed information of the contents at once.

And then there is no more heard of this particular hoard until 1455. Under that date in his scrapbook or *zibaldone* [19] Pier Candido Decembrio makes the surprising entry that he has seen at Rome what cannot be other than this very MS group, or a copy of it. Again it is worth while to quote at length, not only to show that Decembrio is evidently referring to the same MS but also to show that he has further information to offer and that he did actually see the MS as he claims to have done.

Cornelii Taciti liber reperitur Rome visus 1455 de Origine et situ Germanie. Incipit: "Germania omnis a Gallis retiisque et panoniis Rheno et danubio fluminibus a Sarmatis dacisque mutuo metu aut montibus separatur cetera occeanus ambit." Opus est foliorum XII in columnellis. Finit: "cetera iam fabulosa helusios et oxionas ora hominum vultusque corpora atque artus ferarum gerere, quod ego ut incompertum in medium relinquam." Utitur autem cornelius hoc vocabulo "inscientia" non "Inscitia."

Est alius liber eiusdem de Vita Iulii agricole soceri sui in quo continetur descriptio Britanie Insule nec non populorum mores et ritus. Incipit: "Clarorum virorum facta moresque posteris tradere antiquitus usitatum, ne nostris quidem temporibus quamquam incuriosa suorum etas omisit." Opus foliorum decem et quattuor in columnellis. Finit: "Nam multos veluti inglorios et ignobilis oblivio obruet. Agricola posteritati narratus et traditus superstes erit."

Cornelii Taciti dialogus de oratoribus. Incipit: "Sepe ex me requiris iuste fabi cur cum priora secula tot eminentium oratorum ingeniis gloriaque floruerint, nostra potissimum etas deserta et laude eloquentie orbata vix nomen ipsum oratoris retineat." Opus foliorum XIIII in columnellis. Post hec deficiunt sex folia. Nam finit: "quam ingentibus verbis prosequuntur. Cum ad veros iudices ventum." Deinde sequitur: "rem cogitare nihil abiectum nihil

19. Ambros. R. 88, sup. fol. 112. Cf. Sabbadini, *St. e Cr.*, p. 279.

humile." Post hec sequuntur folia due cum dimidio. Et finit: "Cum adrisissent discessimus."

Suetonii tranquilli de grammaticis et rhetoribus liber. Incipit: "Grammatica rome nec in usu quidem olim nedum in honore ullo erat, rudis scilicet ac bellicosa etiam tum civitate necdum magnopere liberalibus disciplinis vacante." Opus foliorum septem in columnellis. Finit perprius: "Et rursus in cognitione cedis mediolani apud lucium pisonem proconsolem defendens reum. Cum cohiberent lictores nimias laudantium voces ita excanduisset, ut deplorato Italie statu quasi iterum in formam provincie redigeretur. M. insuper brutum cuius statua in conspectu erat invocaret Regum ac libertatis auctorem ac vindicem." Ultimo imperfecto columnello finit: "diu ac more concionantis redditis abstinuit cibo." Videtur in illo opere Suetonius innuere omnes fere rhetores et Grammatice professores desperatis fortunis finivisse vitam.

The evidence, then, of the various references down to this date of 1455 to the new parts of Tacitus discovered in Germany indicates a manuscript, in columns, which included the *Germania,* the *Agricola,* the *Dialogus,* and Suetonius, *de grammaticis et rhetoribus*. It seems to have had as a near neighbor, or perhaps as part of the same volume, Frontinus, *De aquaeductibus,* the two books of that treatise being reversed in order. After all the mystery connected with its removal from Germany, it seems actually to have reached Rome and to have been available at least to Decembrio by the year 1455. At this point a new complication enters into the problem.

In the archives of Königsberg there is a letter [20] from the pope, Nicholas V, introducing Enoch of Ascoli, who was sent out by him in 1451 to France, Germany, and Denmark to get copies of MSS. A letter from Gregorius Corrarius to Joannes Arretinus of October 28, 1451,[21] shows Enoch on his way as far as Verona. Another letter shows him in Denmark. Poggio felt that Enoch had neither the temperament nor the ability to be successful in this quest (Letter X, 17) but Poggio had had unpleasant words with Enoch already (Letter VIII, 41) and they were rivals in the search for manuscripts. It comes,

20. See Voigt, *2,* 200.
21. Cod. Vat. 3908, fol. 118. Cf. Sabbadini, *St. e. Cr.,* p. 276.

therefore, as no surprise when Poggio, at the time of Enoch's first return to Rome, expresses the self-satisfied opinion that Enoch's success had been as slight as he had prophesied (Letter IX, 12, presumably in 1453). Enoch evidently made a second trip with greater success. There is evidence of his visit to Augsburg on this trip and, under date of March 13, 1456, Carlo de' Medici wrote to his half-brother Giovanni about the finds that Enoch had made.[22] He states that four only are worth while and that, Enoch's patron Pope Nicholas V being dead (his death occurred March 24, 1455), Enoch is holding out for a big price and allowing no copies to be made. Aurispa also knew about the finds, had actually seen some of them, and had more definite information about Enoch's plans for making money out of them. It will be worth while to follow up Aurispa's information before considering the further evidence of Carlo de' Medici.

Aurispa, after the death of Nicholas V, gave to Teodoro Gaza a letter of introduction to Panormita, which he presented to the latter at Naples. Teodoro evidently spoke of some new MSS, for Panormita wrote to Aurispa at Rome: "Veniens vero fac tecum deferas Apicium coquinarium et Caesaris Iter, ut refert Theodorus tuus, nunc iam meus, inventos Romamque perductos. . . . Quae de Caesaris Itinere scripsimus, ita accipe ut nisi versibus compositum sit, Iulli Iter non sit, sed Antonini: hic enim prosa oratione Iter edidit, Iulius carmine; Antonini vero Iter iampridem et nos habemus." [23]

The answer of Aurispa is dated *idibus decembris,* the original letter to him being without date. "Apitium pauperem coquinarium quem petis vidi et legi; dictiones habet aliquas quae tibi forte placebunt. . . . Caesaris Iter prosa oratione est, non versu. Porphirionem quendam in Oratium hic idem, qui Apitium ad nos perduxit, attulit, qui mihi magis aestimandus videtur quam quicquam aliud ab ipso adlatum. Sed eum qui

22. For the whole correspondence, see M. Lehnerdt, "Enoche von Ascoli und die *Germania des Tacitus,*" *Hermes,* 33 (1898), 499 ff. First published by Victor Rossi, *Rendiconti della r. academia dei Lincei,* 1893.

23. Codex Ottob. 1153, fol. 25ᵛ. See Sabbadini, *St. e Cr.,* p. 283.

codices hos invenit et Romam perduxit ad vos mittam cum omnibus musis suis. Putat enim si hos libros regi donaverit aliquid praemii ab isto principe se habiturum, ad quod ego maxime illum exhortatus sum."

It is true that in this letter Aurispa does not name either Enoch or a MS of Tacitus. But on August 28, of a year not stated, he writes again to Panormita: "Hisce diebus fuit hic Enochus. Quum eum rogarem ut eorum codicum quos e longinquis partibus attulit mihi copiam faceret, et praecipue Porphirionem super operibus Oratii petebam, respondit se velle omnia prius Alphonso regi tradere; cui opinioni ego hominem maxime sum exhortatus."

To return now to the Medici correspondence, Carlo wrote to Giovanni on December 10, 1457, saying that Enoch was dead and that he had left his MSS with Stefano de Nardini of Ancona. The four good finds of which he had spoken in his first letter he now names specifically. They are Apicius, Porphyrio, Suetonius de viris illustribus, and the Itinerarium Augusti. There can of course be no doubt that Aurispa and Carlo were referring to the same discoveries.

The dating of the letters of Aurispa is not wholly satisfactory. They fall between March 24, 1455, when Nicholas V died, and November 1457, the latest possible date for the death of Enoch. It is customary to date the last letter August 28, 1457. This is based on a casual mention in it of a quarrel between Aurispa and Testa and would seem to be reasonably sure. Sabbadini (*St. e Cr.*, p. 285) places the first letter in 1455, on the ground that he speaks of *novus pontifex* and that Calixtus II became pope in April 1455. It must remain an open question whether the date should be 1455 or 1456. To Aurispa, Calixtus would always be the new pope.

Shortly after Enoch's death, according to the letter of Carlo de' Medici to Giovanni of December 10, 1457, Aeneas Silvius Picolomini came to Carlo and asked him how he could possibly see the MSS of Enoch. Carlo told him where they were, in the custody of Stefano de' Nardini. In the treatise on Germany which Picolomini sent to the Archbishop of Mainz on

February 1, 1458, he cited Tacitus as giving similar information about Germany. Finally, in a letter of January 13, 1458, Carlo shows that the MSS of Enoch were not as yet publicly known.

The final piece of evidence with regard to the Enoch discovery is found in a MS of the Minor Works of Tacitus now in Leiden and known as Leidensis 18 or Perizonianus 21. In this codex a note reads as follows:

C. Suetonius scripsit de viris illustribus cuius exemplum secutus hieronymus ipse quoque libellum de scriptoribus christianis edidit. Nuper etiam Bartholomeus facius familiaris noster de viris illustribus temporis sui libros composuit. Qui ne hos Suetonii illustres viros videre posset mors immatura effecit. Paulo enim post eius mortem in lucem redierunt cum multos annos desiderati a doctis hominibus essent. Temporibus enim Nicol, quinti pontificis maximi Enoc Asculanus in Galliam et inde in Germaniam profectus conquirendorum librorum gratia hos quamquam mendosos et imperfectos ad nos retulit. . . . Iov. Pontanus Umber excripsit.

It might be argued that the reference to Enoch indicates the discovery by him of the Suetonius material only. But on fol. 1^v of the manuscript is this note: "Hos libellos Iovianus Pontanus excripsit nuper adinventos et in lucem relatos ab Enoc Asculano quamquam satis mendosos. MCCCCLX martio mense."

The Leiden MS is known not to be in the hand of Pontanus but is a copy of his MS, and the notes are copied as well by the scribe of the MS. Bartolomeo Fazio, mentioned in the long note, died in November 1457. The Pontanus note therefore adds confirmation to the evidence that Enoch's finds were not made generally known until the end of 1457. It should be noted further that Pontanus found in his Enoch MS the *Dialogus* and *Germania* of Tacitus and the *De grammaticis et rhetoribus* of Suetonius, the last of which he calls *De viris illustribus*. It is almost impossible to believe that he found in his archetype an *Agricola* of Tacitus which he did not use.

It is obvious, I think, that the MS which Decembrio saw and examined in 1455 can hardly have been the one so carefully guarded by Enoch of Ascoli down to the time of his death in 1457. It becomes, therefore, of much more interest to compare the list of writings given by Decembrio with that ascribed to Enoch. In the former there was the *Agricola* as well as the *Germania,* the *Dialogus,* and the Suetonius fragment. The *Agricola* came after the *Germania* and before the *Dialogus.* Also, if we add the evidence of Panormita and Niccoli, there were "two works" of Frontinus, either in the same MS or with it. These two works were, of course, the two books of the *De aquaeductibus* in reverse order. The list of Enoch's finds never mentions an *Agricola,* nor does Pontanus include the *Agricola* with the Enoch discoveries which he copied. On the other hand the list did include *Porphyrio, Apicius,* the Suetonius fragment (but differently named), the *Itinerary* of Antoninus, *Elegies* to Maecenas, and an *Orestes,* none of which, with the exception of Suetonius, is ever associated with the earlier tradition. Combining the evidence of Pontanus with the rest of what is known about Enoch's discovery, it is generally and probably correctly assumed that the Suetonius fragment was the first item in a MS that contained as well the *Germania* and the *Dialogus,* which were at first overlooked because they followed the Suetonius, itself not considered of much importance inasmuch as it was assumed from its title to be the *Lives of the Caesars* of which other copies were already current.

It seems reasonably clear that two MSS came from abroad to Italy, one before 1455 and one with Enoch. The fact that they became known at so nearly the same time has caused the assumption that they were one and the same. But the first contained an *Agricola,* the second did not. For it is impossible not to believe that, if Decembrio's MS were the one brought by Enoch and if it contained, as accurately recorded by Decembrio, the *Agricola* of Tacitus, that essay could have been separated from it after he and others had seen it and concealed so that the copy from which the *editio princeps* was made less than twenty years later did not contain it or the printer de Spira know of it. For Enoch's MS, while not at once made available, was not kept secret; and if it had been identical with

Decembrio's, the *Agricola* would have been between the *Germania* and the *Dialogus* and very difficult to lose or remove. If, on the other hand, there were two MSS, the printer might easily have taken the more notorious one of Enoch and assumed that it had all that was known of Tacitus aside from the contents of Medicean II. Leidensis and Vat. Lat. 1862 alone call the Suetonius fragment *De viris illustribus* and alone have readings at variance with Decembrio.

It should be noted finally that in the only one of our miscellaneous MSS that includes the *Agricola* (codex Vat. Lat. 4498), there is also Frontinus, *De aquaeductibus,* while in at least one of the other miscellaneous MSS (Vat. 1518) not containing the *Agricola,* appears the commentary of Porphyrio on Horace, and in two others (Venetus and Laurent. 73. 20) Apicius.

All that remains today of any early MSS of the Minor Works of Tacitus are the eight leaves of the Jesi *Agricola,* in a ninth-century hand, generally ascribed to the district of Fulda. This MS was discovered in 1902 by Cesare Annibaldi in the library of Count Balleani. Inasmuch as the handwriting of the fifteenth-century part of the MS is that of Guarnieri, it seems probable that the whole was assembled for the library at Jesi by him. It has been held by most Tacitean scholars that these eight leaves are what is left of the Hersfeld archetype of all our MSS. Whether this came to Italy through the successful efforts of Enoch or of someone else has been the subject of much scholarly argument. There is, however, very definitely another possible provenance.

While the fifteenth-century Italian scholars were competing in the scramble for MSS and fighting over its results, the *Agricola* had been known at Monte Cassino for over three hundred years. Peter the Deacon quoted from it in his annals of the foundation. There is no evidence that this MS was ever known to the eager scholars who were on the hunt for new Tacitus material. But if Medicean II of the major works could be removed by Boccaccio from the dilapidated library, there is no inherent improbability that someone may have in the same way obtained the *Agricola*. If the Aesinas MS represents this copy rather than that which Decembrio saw, there is no necessity for the elaborate conjectures of Wissowa which reconstruct a codex corresponding to Decembrio's memorandum out of our present Aesinas. Wissowa is most ingenious, but his reconstruction leaves unanswered some of the most fundamental questions. Whence the Dictys material, identical in format and handwriting with the ninth century *Agricola* leaves? Why did Guarnieri discard the *Germania, Dialogus,* and Suetonius? Why was the rest of the *Agricola,* presumably in the middle of a volume, so injured as to be unusable? In general, the disappearance of Decembrio's *Agricola,* a difficult enough problem in itself, is rendered all the more difficult if it was not only available to Guarnieri but the best preserved part of the MS. There seems to be good ground for crediting Annibaldi with both the discovery of the oldest MS of any of the Minor Works and the recovery of a MS representing a separate line of descent from that producing the rest.

NOTE

An interesting sidelight on the trip of Enoch and on the possible source of his Porphyrio MS (with the added possibility of its leading to the source of his Tacitus) is reported by F. Joachimsen.[24] At Augsburg in 1454 Sigismund Meisterlin wrote an Augsburg chronicle. He was a Benedictine monk in the Abbey of St. Ulrich and Afra. He was writing about the origin of the Suevi and of Augusta Vindelicorum. He used with some hesitation information gleaned from a commentary on Horace's Odes. He wrote:

Da ich nun noch zweifel hett, was ich forschen ain vast gelehrten man, genant Eneas Asculanus, den unser hailiger Vater, babst Nicolaus quintus, hett ausgesant zesuchen etliche pücher, ob ich dem sollt glauben, der also het geschrieben. Er antwort mir also: Ist das Porphirius, der alt ausleger Oracii, geleich sagt, so wär es aun zweifel zu glauben. Dar nach an dem nachsten tag, da funden wir das puch Porphirionis in unser lieben frawen zu dem Thom

24. Neue Jahrbücher für das Class. Altertum, *27* (1911).

kirchen lieberey und zu hand sucht ich das und fand daz er auch sagt, wie die Vindelici die agst von den Amazonen hetten in gewonhayt genommen und darnach uber vil iar die Römer da mit uberwunden.

14. MANUSCRIPTS OF THE MINOR WORKS

Vat. Lat. 4498	All three essays
Aes. Lat. 8	*Agricola* and *Germania*
Tolet. 49. 2	" " "
Leid. XVIII. Periz. Q. 21	*Germania* and *Dialogus*
Neap. IV. C. 21	" " "
Ottob. Lat. 1434	" " "
Vat. Lat. 1518	" " "
Vat. Lat. 1862	" " "
Vat. Lat. 2964	" " "
Ven. Marc. Class. XIV. 1	" " "
Vind. Lat. 49	" " "
Vind. 711	" " "
Walters Gallery. 466	" " "
Vat. Lat. 3429	*Agricola*
Ambros. Lat. H. 29. sap.	*Dialogus*
Brux. 9145	"
Harl. 2639	"
Neap. Lat. IV. B. 4 bis	"
Ottob. Lat. 1455	"
Paris. 7773	"
*Syon. A. 55	"
Urb. Lat. 1194	"
Arim. IV. D. 112	*Germania*
Arund. 277	"
Bamb. S. 4	"
Cesena XVII. 2. 2	"
Harl. 1895	"
Harvard. L. 25	"
*Hummelianus	"
Laurent. 73. 20	"
Madrid. Bib. Nac. 10037	"
Monac. Lat. 5307	"
Ottob. Lat. 1209	"
Ottob. Lat. 1795	"
Paris. 1180	"
*Pesara	"
Riccard. 158	"
Rom. Aug. Fond. Ant. 1172. 6. 4. 42	"
Stuttg. Hist. Q. 152	"
Turic. C. 56	"
Urb. Lat. 412	"

* Lost MSS.

I. MANUSCRIPT OF ALL THREE

Vaticanus Latinus 4498

THIS MS, the only one containing all three of the Minor Works, is in the Vatican Library. It is written on parchment and is a miscellaneous MS of 150 leaves (the last five ruled but blank) gathered in quinions. The pages measure 7½ × 10¾ inches, with 32 lines to a page, ruled with dry point, double lines at the top, bottom, and sides. It is not a collection of separate MSS: paper, ink, and hand are uniform throughout. It is a beautifully made book obviously intended to have exactly the collection which it contains. There is no title page or opening title of any sort, the text beginning abruptly, *Cum omnis res ab Imperatore,* the opening words of Frontinus, *De aquaeductibus.* Frontinus occupies fols. 1–20^r. The other contents are: 20^v–35^v: Rufus, *De provinciis;* 36–45^r: Suetonius, *De grammaticis et rhetoribus;* 45^v–63^r: Pliny, *De viris illustribus;* 63^v–77^v: Tacitus, *Agricola;* 78–97^r: Tacitus, *Dialogus;* 97^v–109^r: Tacitus, *Germania;* 109^v–110^v: M. Junius Nypsus, *De mensuris;* 111–112^r: Incerti, *De ponderibus;* 112^v–118^v: Seneca, *Apokolokyntosis;* 119–145: Censorinus, *De die natali.* The name of Frontinus does not appear, nor does the Rufus have a title except by a later hand. The other items have titles in red ink. The Suetonius fragment is entitled: *C. Suetonii Tranquilli historici de Grammaticis prohemium.* The index of grammarians follows on the same page with the title and the opening of the essay. It contains nineteen names. On 42^v begins *de rhetoribus Liber ii* with an index containing sixteen names. The essay ends: *abstinuit cibo.* The title of the *Agricola* reads: *Cai Corneli Taciti de vita et moribus Julii Agricolae prohemium.* The ending is *superstes erit.* ϳελος. The title of the *Dialogus* is *C. Cornelii Taciti Dialogus de Oratoribus.* After the word *ventum* on 93^v, the remainder of the page is left blank except for the words *hic multum deficit.* The text resumes at the top of 94^r with *rem cogitare nihil.* The essay ends on 97^r with *cum arrisissent dis-*

cessimus. Finis, the rest of the page being left blank. The title of the *Germania* is *C. Cornelii Taciti de origine et situ Germanorum.* It ends: *ut incompertum in medium relinquam. Finis.*

There are collations of the *Agricola* text by C. L. Urlichs in his edition of 1875 and by G. Andresen in *Woch. f. kl. Phil.* (1900), p. 1299.

II. MANUSCRIPTS OF AGRICOLA AND GERMANIA

Aesinas Latinus 8

This is a parchment MS with pages measuring 273 × 220 mm. written in columns which measure 203 × 60 mm., with 17 mm. between the columns. It is supposed to be in the library of Count Balleani in Jesi but is now presumably held by the government in Florence. There are 76 leaves, the first two forming an independent folium and followed by six quaternions, a nonion, and a quaternion. The last leaf is blank. The MS contains: *Dytis de bello Troia* (fols. 1–51); *Agricola* (fols. 52–65); *Germania* (fols. 66–75). Forty-four leaves of the *Dictys* (5–8 and 11–50) and eight of the *Agricola* (56–63) are in Carolingian minuscule generally ascribed to the ninth or tenth century. The rest is in a humanistic, fifteenth-century hand said by Annibaldi to be that of Stefano Guarnieri of Perugia. The old parts of the manuscript have thirty lines to a page, the rest twenty-six to thirty-three. The old part of the *Agricola* is a quaternion in the middle of the nonion of the present volume. The MS ends with a quaternion of which the outside leaves (69 and 76) are the last two leaves of the old *Agricola,* cleaned and reused. This indicates that the old MS of the *Agricola* wound up with an independent folium. The *Dictys* and the *Agricola* are possibly not by the same scribe but are certainly from the same scriptorium. The title of the *Agricola,* on 52^r, is *Cornelii Taciti de Vita Agricolae Liber Incipit.* Beginning at the bottom of 65^v and continuing on 66^r appears: *Cornelii Taciti de Vita et Moribus Iulii Agricolae Li-*

ber explicit. Incipit Eiusdem de origine et moribus Germanorum Liber. The original *explicit* of the *Agricola,* on the reused page, read like the *incipit.* The old leaves of the *Agricola* contain C. 13, *impigre–*C. 40, *missum.* The MS was discovered in 1902 by Cesare Annibaldi, who published it with a diplomatic text of the *Agricola* at Citta di Castello in 1907. In 1943 Rudolf Till brought out his *Handschriftliche Untersuchungen zu Tacitus' Agricola und Germania,* Berlin-Dalhem, with a photographic reproduction of Aesinas.

Toletanus. 49. 2

This is a miscellaneous MS in the Capitular Library in Toledo, a part of the Zelada collection. It is a small folio, the page measuring 231 × 145 mm., and the writing 172 × 83. There are 223 leaves, regularly with 30 lines to the page but occasionally 29. The contents of the MS are as follows: *Germania* of Tacitus, 1ʳ–15ᵛ; *Agricola* of Tacitus, 16ʳ–36ᵛ; *Io. Antonii Campani Oratio,* 37ʳ–63ᵛ; Fragment of an oration, 64ʳ–66ʳ; Letters of Pliny, 66ʳ–221ᵛ; Fragment of an oration, 222ʳ–223. The first title is on 1ʳ as follows: *Cor. Taciti De vita Moribus et Origine Germanorum Opus Elegantissimum.* The *Germania* ends at the middle of 15ᵛ, followed by a subscription: *Fuliginiae scriptum gerente me magistratum pu scribae. Kal. Iun. 1474.* The *Agricola* has the title: *Opus eiusdem De Vita et Moribus L. Agricolae.* At its close is simply *Finis.* After the oration of Antonius on 63ᵛ there is another subscription: *Scripta per me M. Angelum Crullum Tudertem fulginii pu. Scribam Non. Decembr. MCCCCLXXIIII. Deo laus et honos.* The Pliny is signed from Perusia by M. Angelus Tuders with a date 1468, which date, however, is in a different ink and out of line with the rest of the subscription. The Tacitus material has many marginal variants by the original scribe, with occasional topical notes by a later hand. The MS was discovered in 1897. The *Agricola* was published by Leuze in *Philologus,* Supplementband 8, and the *Germania* by F. F. Abbott in *Decennial Publications, University of Chicago, 6,*

1903. The MS is almost universally accepted as a direct copy of the Aesinas. Collation by O. Leuze, *Philol. Suppl.*, 8, p. 513.

III. Manuscripts of Germania and Dialogus

Leidensis XVIII. Perizonianus, Q. 21

A small parchment folio in the University Library, Leiden. The writing is fifteenth century, and measures 152 × 95 mm. with wide margins. There are sixty leaves gathered in quinions. The sixtieth leaf (evidently blank) has been cut away. Neither leaves nor quinions were numbered, but there are catchwords at the end of each quinion, except on 30ʳ, where the *Dialogus* ends. There are twenty-two lines to a page. The contents are 2ʳ–30ʳ, *Dialogus;* 30ᵛ, blank; 31ʳ–47ʳ, *Germania;* with the Suetonius index on 47ʳ following the end of the *Germania;* 47ᵛ–59ᵛ, Suetonius, *De grammaticis.* The *Dialogus* is, therefore, contained within complete quinions, while the *Germania* ends on the recto of the page on whose verso the Suetonius begins. On the reverse of the fly leaf is this note: *Hos libellos Iovianus pontanus excripsit nuper adinventos et in lucem relatos ab enoc Asculano quamquam satis mendosos. MCCCC.LX martio mense.* This is not in the hand of Pontanus but is that of the scribe of this manuscript. The title of the *Dialogus* is *Dialogus de Oratoribus Incipit.* On 3ʳ there is a large capital N in *Nihilne* and on 13ᵛ a large capital H. There are no other large capitals and these are quite possibly due merely to their position at the beginning of the lines. On 26ʳ a space of one-third of a page is left blank after *ad veros iudices ventum.* In the margin in the scribe's own hand is written: *deerant in exemplari sex pagellae vetustate corruptae.* After the break comes *rem cogitant.* The essay ends with *finit* on 30ʳ, with 30ᵛ left blank. At the top of 31ʳ is the title: *Cornelii Taciti de Origine situ moribus ac populis Germanorum Liber Incipit.* At the bottom of 39ʳ in the lower margin is written the *Liberti* passage (which occurs wrongly on 39ᵛ) with the note: *in hoc loco potius* and a mark to indicate the place where it should have gone correctly. A large capital indicates the beginning of the special treatment of the tribes on 40ʳ. The *Germania* ends near the top of 47ʳ with *finit*. There follows immediately the index of Suetonius, the list of *Grammatici* and *Rhetores*. This index is rather squeezed on the page, as if it might have been an afterthought. The title on 47ᵛ at the top is *Caii Suetonii Tranquilli De viris illustribus liber incipit: De Grammaticis*. A long marginal note shows that this also was copied by Pontanus from the MS which Enoch of Ascoli brought to Italy shortly after the death of Bartolomeo Fazio. At the close of the Suetonius (*abstinuit cibo*) there is a marginal note: *Amplius repertum non est adhuc dest' rhetores XI*. The latter two-thirds of the page (59ᵛ) is blank. The MS was bought for the Leiden library in 1742 with money previously given by Perizonius. It never belonged to him. Its origin is unknown. A note on the reverse of the flyleaf indicates that it was at some time owned by a monastery of Saint Vincent: *Super aegros manus imponent et bene habebunt. Iesus Mariae filius mundi salus et dominus per merita B. Vincentii Confessoris sit tibi clemens et propitius Amen*. The MS is photographically reproduced by S. de Vries, *Codices Graeci et Latini Photographice Depicti*, Supplementum 4 (Leyden, 1907), with an introduction by Georg Wissowa.

Neapolitanus IV. C. 21

This MS, also called *Farnesianus*, is on parchment, measuring 8½ × 13 inches, in the Royal Library in Naples. It is written in the same hand throughout, a small, running fifteenth-century hand very slightly inclined to the right. There are 222 leaves, 30 lines to a page, gathered in quinions and ruled with dry point, with double vertical lines at the sides. The first page has an illuminated margin completely surrounding the text. On the opening pages of subsequent books of the major works the right-hand margin is not illuminated and the Minor Works have illuminated initials only. The MS contains *Annals* 11–16 and *Histories* 1–5 of Tacitus, ending with the excerpts, and followed, without subscription, by the *Dialogus* of Tacitus, the

Germania of Tacitus, and Suetonius, *de grammaticis et rhe-toribus*. The titles for the *Dialogus* and *Germania* are as follows: *C. Cornelii Taciti Dialogus de Oratoribus Foeliciter. incipit*, and *C. Cornelii Taciti de Origine et situ Germaniae Liber incipit*. Both treatises end with Τελως. The Suetonius ends with *abstinuit cibo*, followed by two unintelligible words and, in the margin, *vacat in exemplari*. There is no further subscription. Part of a page is left blank for the lacuna in the *Dialogus*, and in the center of this space is written in minute letters: *multum deficit in exemplaribus quae reperiuntur*. The text continues with *rem cogitare*. There are not many corrections, but more in the *Germania* than elsewhere. There are very few alternative readings but frequent topical notes in the margins.

Ottobonianus Latinus 1434

This is a MS on parchment with 209 leaves measuring 8¼ × 11¼ inches, in the Vatican Library. The gatherings are quinions; the final leaf of quinion 21 has been removed without loss of text. Leaves 19 and 183 were overlooked in the numbering, and there are two leaves numbered 125, so that the last leaf appears as 206. There are no titles and no annotations in the MS. The first page has an illuminated border and there are numerous illuminated initials. At the end of the MS is *Finis la. deo*. The pages are ruled, 30 lines to a page, with double vertical lines at the sides. The hand is uniform throughout; it has a definite slant to the right. There are frequent lacunae but no marginal or interlinear notes. The contents are Porphyrio on Horace (fols. 1–122^v with 123 blank); Cornutus on Persius (fols. 124–174^r); Suetonius, *De grammaticis et rhetoribus* (fols. 174^v–182^r); Tacitus' *Dialogus* (fols. 182^v–196^r); Tacitus' *Germania* (fols. 196^r–206^r). The index to the Suetonius fragment lists grammarians and rhetoricians in a single list at the beginning of the essay. It names 36. In the *Dialogus* space is left for the lacuna without comment. The MS is almost a twin of Vat. Lat. 1518, having the same contents and largely the same characteristics.

Vaticanus Latinus 1518

This is a miscellaneous MS on parchment in the Vatican Library. It has 198 leaves, 7½ × 11 inches, the last two blank, gathered in 19 quinions and 1 quaternion. There are 33 lines to a page. There is some slight illumination on the first page. The hand at the beginning is upright and square, a careful though not beautiful book hand. On 38ᵛ this hand comes abruptly to an end and is followed by a scrawly running hand which later gives way to the original book hand. At 110ʳ a different book hand begins, and also a thinner parchment is used for the rest of the book. The first fifty leaves are unlined, 51–109 are lined, the rest is unlined. The contents of the MS are as follows: Porphyrio on Horace, 1–108ᵛ; part of 108ᵛ and all of 109 are ruled but left blank; Life of Persius, 110ʳ–166ᵛ; Suetonius, *De grammaticis et rhetoribus*, 166ᵛ–174ᵛ; *Dialogus* of Tacitus, 174ᵛ–188ᵛ; *Germania* of Tacitus, 188ᵛ–198ᵛ. There are no marginal or interlinear corrections. The Tacitus titles are: *C. Cornelii Taciti dialogus de oratoribus*, and *C. Cornelii Taciti de origine et situ germanorum*. There is no colophon to the *Dialogus*. At the end of the *Germania* is *finis. θελος*. A half page (186ᵛ) is left blank to indicate the lacuna in the *Dialogus*, but there is no comment. Following the break, the text resumes: *rem cogitare*. The Suetonius index has 35 names, all in one list at the beginning of the essay.

Vaticanus Latinus 1862

This is a paper MS, 7½ × 11½ inches (the writing covers only 4¼ × 7 inches), in the Vatican Library with 48 leaves of which the last five are blank. The volume is bound in boards and red leather with the arms of Paulus V uniform with Vat. Lat. 1864 of the *Annals* and *Histories*. There are 31 lines to a page, ruled with dry point. The gatherings are 4 quinions and one quaternion. The hand is small and unprofessional. The MS contains the *Germania* of Tacitus, the *De grammaticis et rhetoribus* of Suetonius, and the *Dialogus* of Tacitus. The first page is illuminated, as are the initial letters of each essay. The title page has the following in four different hands: *Cornelius Tacitus de origine et situ germanorum. Et Suetonius Tranquillus de Grammaticis et rhetoribus. / Cornelius Tacitus De origine et situ germanorum. / Et Suetonius Tranquillus de grammaticis et Rhetoribus. / Cornelius Tacitus de Oratoribus.* The *Germania* has also a title by the scribe of the MS: *Cornelii Taciti de origine et situ Germanorum liber incipit.* Almost every sentence is a separate paragraph with an enlarged capital in the margin. Through chapter 37 there are marginal corrections to the number of nine. Beginning with chapter 38 the corrections, ten in number, are interlinear. The essay ends on 13ʳ: *Cornelii Taciti de Origine et situ Germanorum liber explicit.* On the verso of the same page the Suetonius begins with the index, ending on 23ʳ with *abstinuit cibo.* Opposite this in the margin, in the red ink used for titles, is *Non repperi ultra in exemplari.* On the verso of 23 the *Dialogus* begins with the title *Cornelii Taciti incipit Dialogus de Oratoribus.* There is one correction only in the *Dialogus,* but on 39ᵛ, in the same red ink and in the same hand as the titles and the "non repperi" note in the Suetonius essay, there is in the margin: *Hic desunt sex pagellae.* There are four lines left blank. The subscription on 43 reads: *Ego tantum repperi et meliusculum feci. Cornelii Taciti de Oratoribus explicit feliciter.* This is in red ink and in the regular hand of the scribe of the MS. In the Suetonius essay the index is at the beginning, a continuous list of 36 names.

Vaticanus Latinus 2964

This is a paper MS in the Vatican Library containing the *Germania* and, in a different hand and on slightly different paper, a part of the *Dialogus*—26. 25 to the end. In poor modern handwriting at the top of the first page is scrawled *Cornelius Tacitus de origine et situ Germanorum.* There are no other titles and no subscriptions. There are 18 leaves measuring 8¼ × 11¼ inches without catchwords to indicate the gatherings. There are 34 lines to a page, ruled with dry point, as are the single lines at the sides. The hand is uniform throughout, a running hand with thick strokes and black ink. There are wide margins on the outside and bottom, narrow margins at the top and on the inside. The *Germania* occupies 1–11^r, with 11^v left blank. The *Dialogus* occupies 12^r–16. The *Dialogus* fragment begins with the top line of 12^r, and it looks as though it might have been part of a separate MS. The binding would have to be taken apart to make sure. The text is unusual, with many careless errors. Blank lines are left between speeches. A space is left to indicate the lacuna, but there is no note. In 27. 7 *Messalla* is added: *non sum inquit Messalla offensus.* Elsewhere the speakers' names are omitted: in 28, *et Messalla;* in 33, *et Maternus;* in 42, *Finierat Maternus cum Messalla.*

Venetus Marcianus Class. XIV. 1 (MSS Lat. Collec. 4266)

This is a paper MS in the National Library of Saint Mark in Venice. It was written in 1464 at Bologna and has 224 leaves. The hand is a fair, small running hand, with thirty-eight lines to the normal page. It has an index of contents as follows:

Eneae de Picolominibus Senensis episcopi postea Pii
    Papae Secundi tractatus de ortu Gothorum.   a c.   1
Oratio eiusdem ad principes Ungariae.   a c.   42
Oratio eiusdem ad ambassiatores regis Franciae.   a c. 101
Copia cuiusdam bulae magnae eiusdem.   a c. 121
Copia brevis apostolici ad S. ducem Venetiarum.   a c. 133
Copia brevis ap. ad il. ducem Mediolani.   a c. 134
Copia brevis ad d. ducinam.   a c. 140
Copia duarum bullarum eiusdem.   a c. 145
Oratio funebris in die exequiarum cardinalis Firmani.   a c. 149
Suetonius de grammaticis et rhetoribus.   a c. 167
Cornel. Taciti de situ et origine Germanorum.   a c. 186
Tabula Flavi Josephi de bello Iudaico.   a c. 196

The handwriting of the Suetonius and Tacitus items is the same throughout, but different from that of the rest of the MS. In spite of the index, the *Dialogus* of Tacitus appears between the Suetonius and the *Germania*. The Suetonius ends two-thirds of the way down 172^v, with *abstinuit cibo* and a marginal note as follows: *non videtur integrum hoc exemplar.* Immediately after this is the title of the *Dialogus* as follows: *C. Cornelii* (*sic*) *Taciti Equitis Romani Dialogus de Oratoribus incipit*. The *Dialogus* ends on 184ᵛ with Τελως, followed by this subscription in letters approximating the capitals of the titles: *Opus absolutum Bononiae. Anno D. MCCCCLXIIII. ad petitionem Io. Marcanovae.* After a blank leaf comes the title of the *Germania: Cornelii Taciti Liber de situ et origine Germanorum.* At the end of the *Germania* the Marcanova note is repeated. At the point where the lacuna occurs in the *Dialogus* there is a marginal note opposite four lines left blank: *hic deficiunt quator parvae pagellae.* The MS was obviously made for Giovanni Marcanova and was given by him to the Augustinian monastery at Padua. In view of the fifteenth-century memoranda of Enoch's finds which mention Suetonius without naming any Tacitus items, the absence of the *Dialogus* in the index is noteworthy.

Vindobonensis Latinus 49

This is a large parchment folio in the Hofbibliothek in Vienna, a beautiful but careless copy with 236 leaves. It contains, in addition to the *Germania* (fols. 205–217) and the *Dialogus* (fols. 217–236), the *Annals* 11–16 and the *Histories* (fols. 1–204), ending with *potiorem* in 5. 23. The arms on the binding are traditionally supposed to be those of Matthias Corvinus, but of this there is considerable doubt. The volume belonged at one time to Joannes Sambucius and is sometimes called *codex Sambuci.* There are no titles or colophons except *Finis* at the end. A late hand credits the *Dialogus* to Quintilian.

Vindobonensis 711

This is a quarto MS on paper in three volumes in the K. K. Haus-Hof- und Staats-Archiv in Vienna. The three volumes have 239, 331, and 254 leaves respectively. The MS was written in 1466. Volume 1, in which the Tacitus items occur, has the following contents: *Italiae Illustratae libri* 8, fols. 1–179ʳ; Blondus Flavius, 180ʳ–194ᵛ; *Dialogus Chratonis et Mercurii* (Lucian), 195ʳ–199ᵛ; *Germania* of Tacitus, 200ʳ–211ᵛ; *Dia-*

logus of Tacitus, 212ʳ–230ᵛ; Seutonius, *de grammaticis,* 231ʳ–239ʳ. Empty leaves follow the Suetonius. The watermark of the paper is a hunting horn on a belt. The *Germania* title on 200ʳ reads: *Cornelii Taciti de origine et situ Germanorum liber incipit foelicissime.* The *explicit* is the same without the *foelicissime.* The *Dialogus* title on 212ʳ reads: *Incipit dialogus de oratoribus.* At the close of the treatise (fol. 230ᵛ) is *Cornelii Taciti de oratoribus explicit.* In the margin of 227ᵛ are the words *hic est defectus unius folii cum dimidio.* Except for these words, 227ᵛ is blank and 227ʳ is also blank except for two lines of text. There is a title for the Suetonius on 230ᵛ, and the index is there too, but on 231ʳ there is a second title. It looks as though the first title and the index had been added later, perhaps from a different source. They just fill the page. A subscription on 331ʳ of Volume 2 reads: *hugo haemste scripsit Romae Anno salutis 1466 impensis Rmi in xpo prs et dm: dm Io. dei et apostolicae sedis gratia epyscopi. Tridentini: ā.*

Huemer has a collation in *Zeit. f. d. Oest. Gymn.* (1878), p. 801. The fullest discussion of the MS is in Robinson's edition of the *Germania.* It has very short paragraphs like Vat. Lat. 1863.

Walters Gallery 466

Baltimore. This MS contains Herodotus (in Latin), fols. 1ʳ–117ᵛ; Tacitus, *Germania,* 118ʳ–135ᵛ; Tacitus, *Dialogus,* 135ᵛ–163ʳ. It is a paper MS of about 1470, measuring 21 ×14 cm. It was written in Italy by L.D. The binding is original boards with stamped calf.

IV. Manuscript of *Agricola* Only

Vaticanus Latinus 3429.

.This is a paper MS of the *Agricola* only, bound in with a copy of the *editio princeps* in the Vatican Library. The front cover of the book has the arms of Paulus V, the back cover those of Cardinal Scipio Borghesi, librarian. On the spine are the arms of Pius IX. There are 14 leaves. On the first blank page of this volume of the *de Spira* Tacitus appears: *Cornelio Tacito della Vita d'Agricola, scritto di mano di Pomponio Laeto, ligato dietri al Tacito stampato. Ful. Urs.* The title is *Cornelii Taciti de Vita et moribus Iulii Agricolae.* There are two inks employed, a black one for the text and a browner one for most of the marginal notes and topics, which are not very numerous. The hand is uniform throughout. The generally accepted belief that the title reads *Aulii* is unfounded. The *Iulii* is perfectly clear, with an apex over the initial I.

There are collations by C. L. Urlichs in his edition of 1875 and by G. Andresen in *Woch. f. kl. Philol.* (1900), p. 1299.

V. MANUSCRIPTS OF THE *Dialogus* ONLY

Ambrosianus Latinus H. 29. sup.

A large paper MS in the Ambrosian Library in Milan. It has 43 leaves and contains the Suetonius fragment (fols. 1–14) as well as the *Dialogus.* The latter is incomplete, ending about one page short, with *credite* (41. 21). Many spaces are left for words omitted in copying. There are no contemporary titles. Sabbadini gives a collation in *Studi Italiani di Filologia Classica, 11* (1903), 203 ff.

Bruxelles, 9145

This is a small fragment of the *Dialogus* in a fifteenth-century paper MS in the Bibliotheque Royale in Brussels. The number is given both as 93 and as 9155. The MS is a large miscellaneous one with 221 pages measuring 400 × 223 mm., with 35 and 36 lines to a page. It bears the arms of Cardinal Nicholas de Cues. The Tacitus fragment is on fols. 220ᵛ and 221ʳ and contains chapters 1–5, *famam*, with the title *Cor. Taciti Dialogus de Oratoribus Feliciter incipit*.

Harleianus 2639

This is a parchment MS in the British Museum, the pages measuring 230 × 120 mm. and the writing 135 × 85. There are

43 leaves, of which the Suetonius fragment occupies fols. 2–14ᵛ and the *Dialogus* fols. 15–42ᵛ. The MS has the coat of arms of John Tiptoft, Earl of Worcester, ambassador to the Pope in 1459. He was executed in 1470. No arms would have been put on after his execution. The first page is modestly illuminated. There is some doubt as to whether the titles are contemporary. They are: *Suetonii tranquilli de grammaticis et rhetoribus* and *C. Cornelii Taciti equitis Romani Dialogus de Oratoribus claris feliciter incipit.* The Suetonius ends: *Suetonii Tranquilli Finis,* and has opposite this a marginal note, *Hic antiquissimum exemplar finit quod non integrum videtur.* The *Dialogus* ends with Τελος. On the verso of the last leaf are the following distichs written fairly carefully on the lines ruled on the MS:

> Parva zebor tibi parva domus es corpore parvus
> Et brevis est tumulus et breve carmen habe.
> Mapheus Vegetus
> Furum moeror heri spes quondam gone catelle
> Hic nunc spes furum moeror herique iaces.
> L. A. 1462

On the first page of the MS is the inscription *Ambrosii Bonvici 1687.* Ambrose Bonwicke was the last private owner; the MS was sold from his estate to the British Museum, 1725.

Neapolitanus Latinus IV. B. 4. bis

This is a paper MS in the Royal Library at Naples, containing the Suetonius fragment, largely in epitome (fols. 1ʳ–6ʳ) and the *Dialogus* (fols. 7ʳ–19ᵛ), Fabius Victorinus, *Notes on Cicero,* Secco Polento, *Epitome of Quintilian, Libellus de Dialectica, Libellus de Definitione et Topicis.* This is cited by Rodney Robinson in his thesis on Suetonus, *de Grammaticis,* p. 35.

Ottobonianus Latinus, 1455

This is a paper MS with 346 leaves, in the Vatican Library. It has a parchment leaf at the front, with a list of contents as follows: Messala Corvinus, on the origin of Augustus; Suetonius, *de grammaticis et rhetoribus;* Corn. Taciti, *Dialogus;* Pomponius Mela, *Cosmography;* Cornelius Nepos, life of Atticus; Boccaccio, *Chronology;* Blondus, *Commentaries;* Leonardi Aret., life of Vergil; Poggio, *Decrees of Athens,* etc.; Blondus, *Italy Illustrated.* The book is made up of a number of MSS in different hands. The first contains the first four items and is in a running hand, small but elegant. The Messala Corvinus ends on 5^r, immediately followed on line 10 of the same page by the Suetonius with the title *C. Suetonii Tranquilli de Grammaticis et rhetoribus.* In 9^v the Suetonius ends with *deficit finis deus concedat ut reperiatur,* followed immediately by the title: *Cornelii Taciti Dialogus incipit de oratoribus,* to which a later hand has added *et poetis.* On 18^r a space is left to indicate the lacuna, and in the margin there is a note reading *hic deest multum in exemplari dicit deesse sex paginas.* The *Dialogus* has this subscription, on 19^v: *Cornelli Taciti de Orator. Dialog. explicit.*

Parisiensis 7773

In the Bibliotheque Nationale in Paris, this is a neatly written parchment MS. It is bound in eight quinions and one quaternion, 88 leaves, with catchwords at the end of each gathering. In the table of contents no mention is made of the *Dialogus,* but the Suetonius is listed. The *Dialogus* actually follows the Suetonius directly, with the title *C. Cornelii Taciti equitis Ro. Dialogus de oratoribus claris.* Peterson (ed. *Dialogus,* 1893, p. lxxvi) indicates that this manuscript is a direct copy of the Harleian 2639. There is a collation by A. E. Egger in *Zeit. f. die Alterth., 3* (1836), 337.

Syon. A 55

In M. Bateson, *Syon Monastery. Library Catalogue,* Cambridge University Press, 1898; appears on page 7: No. A 55. *Suetonius Tranquillus de grammaticis, et Rethoribus suo tempore florentibus in 2^{bus} libris. Cornelius Tacitus in Dialogo de Oratoribus claris in suis temporibus.* The editor suggests that this is either Hain 15,132 or Hain 15,219. But the catalogue of the Syon Library was made about 1500 and no separate edition of the *Dialogus* before 1533 is known. The books from the library were dispersed, and only six have ever been rediscovered.

Urbinas Latinus 1194

This is a parchment MS, 231 × 142 mm., with iii plus 198 leaves, in the Vatican Library. On the spine of the binding are the arms of Pius IX and Cardinal Angelo Mai, librarian. It has a beautifully illuminated first page, with a partial index of the contents, naming Plutarch, Demosthenes and Basilius, Lucian, Plato, and Leonardo Bruni. Aurispa and Leonardo are indicated in side medallions, but there is no suggestion of Tacitus or Suetonius. On 156^r the Suetonius fragment begins with the title *Suetonii Tranquilli Libellus de Vitis Grammaticorum*. It ends with *abstinuit cibo* on 172^v without subscription, followed immediately by the title *Corn. Taciti. Dialogus de Oratoribus*. The *Dialogus* is only a fragment, ending with *sed causas* (27). At the end of the Plutarch there is a date, 1471, and the whole MS looks fairly uniform.

VI. MANUSCRIPTS OF THE *Germania* ONLY

Ariminensis IV. D. 112

This MS is in the Biblioteca Gambalunghina at Rimini and came from the library of Giuseppi Garampi. It is a miscellaneous MS with the following contents: fols. 1–58, *Mirabilia urbis;* 59–60, *Romae mille quingente capellae;* 61–77^r, *Dicta quorundam;* 77^v–93^v, *Germania*. This last item has the title *Cornelii Taciti viri clarissimi liber de situ Germanico incipit*. The subscription reads *Scripsi Romae expedito sindicata senatus 1476 de mense martii dum exepectarem solutionem salarii et vexillum . . . cum magna mea expensa quia habebam in hospitio decem equos et totidem famulos Rainerius Maschius Ariminensis manu propria*.

Arundelianus 277

In the British Museum. There is a partial collation preserved in a Leiden MS, Vossianus 7, which indicates that the Arundel

MS was once the property of Wilibald Pirkheimer, later went to the Arundel library, and thence to the British Museum. The *Germania* is preceded by Poggio's *Liber facetiarum* and followed by miscellaneous items. It is discussed by Nolte in Jahn's *Archiv für Phil. und Paed., 19* (1853), 459 ff.

Bambergensis S. 4

This is a quarto fragment of the *Germania,* one quaternion, on paper formerly in the library at Bamberg but now in the Staatsbibliothek, Munich, No. 947, bound with a copy of the 1509 edition of the *Germania* which has in the margin Longolius' collation of the lost codex Hummelianus. This fragment comprises chapters 8 (*diu apud*) to 43 (*diffusum*) and is therefore probably identical with the so-called Kappianus, which contained the same text, was on paper, and has disappeared. It has also been called the Longolianus because of its having been bound with the Longolius copy of the 1509 edition. There is another MS which Lipsius, in the Plantin edition of 1595, cites as the codex Babenbergensis and which he says was collated for him by Franciscus Modius. It seems to be distinct from the Bamberg fragment, close to the Arundel MS, and quite certainly lost.

Cesena XVII. 2. 2

This is a MS in the Biblioteca Malatestina in Cesena, containing the *Germania* only of the works of Tacitus. This was formerly associated with the Pomponius Mela, which is now catalogued XVII 2. 1 and with a Latin translation of Ptolemy's *Geography*. The *Germania* has the title *Cornelii Taciti Germaniae Descriptio*. It is beautifully written in a small upright book hand, 32 lines to the page.

Harleianus 1895

This is a paper MS in folio measuring 210 × 290 mm. with the writing measuring 125 × 240 mm. It is in the British Museum. The contents are: *Pomponius Mela* (fols. 1–22), *Cento Probae* (23–34), and the *Germania* of Tacitus (35–42). The title is: *C. Cornelii taciti oratoris de origine et situ germanorum liber incipit.* On the first page the text is divided into short paragraphs with titles, *De Rheno fluvio,* etc. There is a commentary at the bottom of the page throughout, and it continues for a full page after the end of the text, which closes on 42ʳ with the subscription *Cornelii Taciti oratoris Eq. Ro. liber de origine et situ germanorum finitur.*

Harvard L. 25

This is a parchment MS in fifteenth-century Italic script, formerly known as Phillipensis and Cheltenhamensis and later belonging for a time to the Royal Library in Berlin. It is now in the Harvard Library in Cambridge, Mass., acquired in 1902. The MS measures 203 × 130 mm., the writing 127 × 64. There are 23 lines to a page in the *Germania.* The volume consists of two MSS preceded by four leaves added when the volume was bound. The first MS is one septenion, containing a letter from Rinucci to Poggio. The second MS consists of ten quinions, with Leonardo Bruni material preceding and following the *Germania* of Tacitus, which is on 36ʳ–55ʳ. Fols. 55ʳ–86ʳ are Bruni material; 86ᵛ–108ʳ has the *Liber Augustalis* ascribed to Petrarch but without the additions of the Stuttgart MS. Fols. 108ᵛ–113ʳ are the 14th book of Palladius on agriculture; 113ᵛ–116ᵛ, Ovid, *Heroides,* 31. 1–144; with 117–118 blank and 118ᵛ, like 1ʳ, pasted to the cover. The title of the *Germania* is *Cornelii Taciti equitis Ro. de origine et situ Germania liber incipit feliciter.* The manuscript is discussed fully by E. K. Rand in *A J P, 26,* 291 ff., with a complete collation.

Hummelianus

So far as known, this MS no longer exists. Friedrich Hummel of Altdorf published notes on its readings in his *Biblioteca Librorum Rarorum et Rariorum,* Nuremberg, 1776. Longolius made similar notes in a copy of the 1509 edition now in the library at Bamberg. In 1830 Chr. Selling used it in a program saying that he had it from one Dorfmuller. There has been no further word of it. According to Hummel it was a paper MS in quarto with fourteen folia, thirty lines to a page, written in a clear fifteenth-century hand easy to read. He adds: "Ipsi chartae pro signo officinae impressae erant duae sagittae in decusses obliquae et circulo imposita."

Laurentianus 73. 20

This is a small MS on parchment in the Laurentian Library, Florence. It has a magnificently illuminated first page with putti and birds and the Medici arms. The hand is a careful book hand. The MS is ruled for space, with wide margins, but not for lines. It is said to be by Piero Strozzi, and if the note at the back by E. Rostagno is to be trusted, it belonged to Lorenzo the Magnificent. The note is dated May 15, 1905. The MS contains first *Apicius,* which ends on fol. 45/46. There are two numbers, one at the top, one at the bottom. On the same page begins the *Germania,* with the title *C. Cornelii taciti equitis r. de origine et situ germaniae liber incipit,* in red. The *Germania* ends on 61^r with *Finis. Cornelii taciti equitis r. libellus de situ germaniae finit.* On the verso of the same page and in the same hand begins an elegiac poem to Pius II by Franciscus Aretinus introducing his Latin version of the "letters" of Diogenes, which runs through 83^r, completing the MS.

Madrid, Biblioteca Nacional, 10037

This MS was formerly in the Chapter Library of Toledo, coming from the collection of Cardinal Zelada. It contains fols. 1–46^r, Francesco Aretino, translation of the pseudo-Diogenes; 68–83^r, Tacitus, *Germania;* 83^v–84^v, Francesco Aretino, elegiac poem to Pius II.

Monacensis Latinus 5307

This is a small quarto MS on paper, containing four items: Peter the Lombard's *Compendium sententiarum,* a commentary on Holy Writ, a description of the Holy Land, and the *Germania* of Tacitus. The Tacitus is on 152–169^r, with the title *Cornelii Taciti de origine et situ Germanorum.* The *explicit* on 169^r is the same. There are thirty lines to a page on the average. The *Germania* is not in the same hand as the other two items, so that the date of the second, 1470, may or may not have importance for the Tacitus material. Each sentence of the *Germaniu* is writtcn as a paragraph. Throughout the volumc the paper used has a watermark of a scales suspended in a circle (the *editio princeps* and the Stuttgart MS have the same).

Ottobonianus Latinus, 1209

This is a MS on parchment in the Vatican Library. The pages are 160 × 248 mm. with 24 lines to a page. The gatherings are quinions. It has unusual illumination normal in form but very dark in color, and is in a remarkably clear fifteenth-century hand. There is a first blank page on which is written *Ex codicibus Joannis Angeli Ducis ab Altaemps* [cf. Ottob. Lat. 1795]. *Sallustius.* To this is added in the handwriting of Angelo Mai (died 1854), *et Tacitus de situ et moribus Germanorum.* The *Catiline* of Sallust occupies the first 43 leaves, the *Jugurtha,* 44ʳ–135ʳ, with *Finis* at the end. There are no titles or comments. The *Germania* begins without title on 135ᵛ and ends on 160ʳ with τελωσ. On the verso of 160 at the top appears *Rmi et Illmi d. B. Carolis Maphei.* There are some alternative readings throughout the *Germania.* This MS was first published by Felix Grat in 1925 in *Mélanges d'archéologie et d'histoire, 42.* He did not note the fact that Angelo Mai had already handled it. He does call attention to the fact that the clause and sentence divisions are wholly irrational, indicating a scribe who did not understand what he was writing and who may have had an uncorrected manuscript from which to make his copy. There is a long and important review of Grat by L. A. Constans in *Rev. des Etudes Lat.* (1926), p. 259.

Ottobonianus Latinus 1795

A small (4¼ × 5¾ inches) MS on paper in the Vatican Library. It is a miscellaneous MS with only a fragment of the *Germania.* On the flyleaf is written *ex codicibus Ioannis Angeli Ducis ab Altaemps.* The Ottoboni Collection was bought by the duke, Giovanni Altemps, on the death of Cardinal Colonna in 1611. There is a catalogue of the Duke's books in

MS Vat. Lat. 7252, fol. 49. The present volume, bound in boards covered with red Morocco, exhibits the arms of Pius IX. There are four items included in the volume, separated by blank leaves, each in a different hand and all of them poor. The items are listed on the fly leaf: *De Primis Italiae Regibus; Corn. Taciti de situ ac moribus Germaniae; Higinii de Astris; Opusculum de Orthographia et figuris.* The *Germania* begins on 24ʳ with the title *Cornelii Taciti viri cons. De situ ac moribus Germaniae libellus incipitur.* It is written in a very careless hand, 22 lines to a page. It ends on 30ᵛ, *et ipsa plerumque* (chapter 13), and the following five leaves are left blank and unnumbered.

Parisiensis. 1180

This is a miscellaneous parchment MS in the Bibliotheque Nationale in Paris, containing the *Germania,* going through *utilitas* in 44. 15. There are 41 leaves in the MS, which measures 270×200 mm., the writing itself, 180×120 mm. The first page has miniatures and the arms of a former owner, an eagle holding a shield with a branch on it, and above, *Vicissim.* On the second page is the name *Comes Hercules Silva.* Fols. 1–32 contain *Pomponius Mela,* 33–40 the *Germania* fragment, and 41ʳ a news item of January 19, 1454, which seems to be a copy. The MS is carefully written and corrected by the original scribe. A later hand has added some changes and marginalia. The title is also by a later hand: *Cornelius Tacitus de situ germaniae et moribus germanorum.* Both *situ* and *moribus* are in erasures. There is a collation by R. Wuensch in *Hermes, 31,* 42.

Pesara

A *Germania* in the Sforza library was burned in 1514 (see Annibaldi (1910), p. 15). It is said to have been associated with an Apicius and a pseudo-Diogenes.

Riccardianus 158

This is an elegant parchment MS in the Biblioteca Riccardiana in Florence. There are no titles. The contents are as follows:

fol. 1, translation of pseudo-Phalaris by Francesco Aretino; 56, translation of the letters of pseudo-Brutus by Rinuccio da Castiglione; 71ᵛ, translation of the epistles of pseudo-Diogenes by Franccsco Aretino, with the dedicatory poem to Pius II; 96ᵛ–112, the *Germania* of Tacitus.

Romanus Angelicus Fondo Antico 1172. S. 4. 42

This is a paper MS in the Biblioteca Angelica of the Augustinians in Rome. The contents are: 1–23ᵛ, *Germania;* 23ᵛ–57, Francesco Aretino, dedicatory poem to Pius II, followed by a Latin version of the letters of pseudo-Diogenes. At the bottom of 57 is *finis 1466*. There is a partial collation by R. Wuensch in *Hermes* (1897).

Stuttgartensis, Hist. Q. 152

A paper MS of 140 leaves, written at Naples in the fifteenth century, now in the Landesbibliothek at Stuttgart. It is a miscellaneous MS with the following contents: fols. 1–75, epitome of Livy by Lucius Florus; 77–89, Petrus Candidus Decembrius, *de rebus gestis populi Romani, scripsit nostro tempore Neapoli;* 90ᵛ–99ᵛ, Ruffus Sextus; 100ᵛ–119, Augustalis Benevenuti; 120ʳ–134ʳ, Cornelius Tacitus *de gestis et moribus Germanorum;* dates of the popes; tree of the dukes of Austria. The handwriting of the first five items is the same throughout. The list of dates indicates that the MS was probably written between 1457 and 1466. The *signum* on the *Germania* sheets is the same as that on the Munich MS, scales suspended in a circle, and the same as that in the *editio princeps*. The *Germania* has the title *C. Corn. Tacit. de origine situ et moribus Germanorum feliciter incipit*. Before *Haec in commune,* chapter 27, is a red title, *Liber secundus* and another in chapter 41, *Tertia pars operis*.

This MS was one of the 150 MSS which were transferred from Komburg to Stuttgart in 1803 when the Ritterstift at Komburg was secularized. It was probably bought at Bamberg on the order of Modius: see Modius, *Nov. Lect.,* Letter 115, and Graeter in Bragur, *8* (1812), 249.

Turicensis C. 56

A late paper MS in the Zentralbibliothek in Zurich. It was written in 1502. The contents are as follows: fols. 1–5ᵛ, Giasone del Maino, *Epithalamium;* 5ᵛ–6ᵛ, Sebastian Brant, *Epithalamium;* 6ᵛ–8, Jacob Wimpheling, *Distichum in Blancam Mariam;* 9–14ᵛ, Tacitus, *Germania;* 16–131, Conrad de Mure, *Fabularius.* There is a colophon to the volume: *Transcriptum manu Petri Numagen Treveren. Capellani sancti Leonardi prope Turegum Anno domini millesimo quingentesimo secundo. Die XII. mensis Iunii.* The title of the *Germania*, which lacks 8 (*longi*) to 16 (*solent*), is *Cornelii Taciti illustrissimi historici de situ moribus ac populis Germaniae libellus aureus.*

Urbinas Latinus, 412

This is a parchment MS in the Vatican Library, containing *Annals* 11–16 and *Histories* 1–5 of Tacitus, fols. 2–201ᵛ, followed by the *Germania,* 204–214ᵛ. The pages measure 8 × 12½ inches and have 34 lines to a page. The beginning of the MS is beautifully illuminated, and the hand is remarkably clear, but the copyist seems to have been careless. There are many corrections and a few variant readings. The historical books are followed by the excerpts, after which nearly five pages are left blank; on 204ʳ the *Germania* begins with the title *Cornelii Taciti de Situ Germaniae Liber incipit.* At the end there is a simple *Finis.*

15. MANUSCRIPT AFFILIATIONS OF THE MINOR WORKS

I T SEEMS safest on the whole to consider the MS tradition of the Minor Works essay by essay before attempting any conjecture as to a common source of the whole corpus. This procedure may involve some repetition but should make for greater clarity.

The *Agricola* survives in four MSS. Aesinas contains one quaternion in Ninth Century Carolingian minuscule and therefore in all probability represents a complete text of that period (this does not necessarily mean that the *Germania* is from the same MS). Toletanus is a direct copy of Aesinas and may therefore be dropped from consideration. Vat. Lat. 4498 is a miscellaneous MS of the fifteenth century, containing among numerous other items the Suetonius fragment, *De grammaticis et rhetoribus,* and the *Agricola, Dialogus,* and *Germania* of Tacitus in that order. Vat. Lat. 3429 is a MS written by Pomponius Laetus and bound into his copy of the *editio princeps* of Tacitus, which did not include this essay.

All three MSS derive from a common archetype already in error in numerous readings. In chapter 7, for example, all three read *intemplo,* which seems to stand for *Intimilium.* In chapter 28 all three read *ut illa raptis secum,* which editors have been unable to agree about. *Ut illa* is generally taken to be a corruption of *utilia,* and it seems probable that words have dropped out in what follows. In chapter 36 there is much confusion: *Egra diu aut stante* may represent *aegre clivo adstantes,* but there is even less certainty as to the reading *equestres ea enim.* In chapter 46 all three MSS have *temporalibus* for *immortalibus* and *multum* (or *militum*) *decoremus* for what was probably *similitudine colamus.*

At the same time the two Vatican MSS have numerous readings and omissions in common, which indicate that they do not derive directly from Aesinas: *senectutis* for *servitutis* (3.

17); *suis* for *ipsius* (9. 21); *dubiis* for *subitis* (18. 19); *paratu magno* for *magno paratu* (25. 15); omission of *felicibus* (15), *ingeniis* (16), *se victos* (27), *ulla* (30). Inversions like *cantu fremituque* (33) for *fremitu cantuque* are not uncommon and suggest a choice of position for a marginal addition in the source. Other readings suggest a choice of alternative readings in the source. For example, in 12 Aesinas reads *pecudumque* with *fecundum* in the margin, while the Vatican MSS read *fecundum*. In 16 Aesinas reads *facta exercitus licentia ducis salute*, with a marginal alternative, *pacti exercitus licentiam dux salutem*. Vat. 4498 has the text reading, Vat. 3429 the marginal reading. These alternative readings are not conclusive but tend to confirm the impression made by the other evidence. Vat. 4498 has many single words omitted, which makes it impossible to consider it the source of Vatican 3429. It also has unique readings, such as *luxuriae* (6) for *rationis, nostrae* (45) for *longae*. The reverse (that 3429 cannot be the source of 4498) cannot, I think, be proved. But *rationis* for *luxuriae* (6), *patientia* for *sapientia* (15), *tranvex* for *tranare extra* (18), and *longae* for *nostrae* (45) make Laetus' MS an improbable immediate source of 4498. Also the more archaic spelling of 4498 argues in the same direction. It is a striking fact that in 1, Vat. 4498 reads *infelicia* against all the MSS, which have *infesta*. If this is not merely an error by the scribe of 4498, it would suggest for that MS a source other than the Monte Cassino copy which Peter used.

In general it seems probable that the Vatican MSS derive from a common ancestor somewhat removed from the immediate ancestor of Aesinas, a conclusion quite in accord with what we know of the history of the *Agricola* text before the fifteenth century. At the same time it is impossible to rule out the chance that the Vatican MSS *could* derive from Aesinas.

It is essential, therefore, to review the currently accepted theories about the Jesi MS. They are all based on the assumption of a single MS coming from Hersfeld (or Fulda) to Rome in the fifteenth century. Annibaldi, Wissowa, and Robinson all work on this assumption and reconstruct a Hersfeld original from the evidence found in the Jesi MS. But what are the facts as distinct from hypotheses? The Jesi MS contains the *Bellum Troianum* of Dictys (fols. 1–51), the *Agricola* of Tacitus (fols. 52–65), and the *Germania* of Tacitus (fols. 66–76). The bulk of the Dictys material and ten leaves of the *Agricola* are ninth century, written in Carolingian minuscule. The rest of the MS, including all of the *Germania,* is in a fifteenth-century hand ascribed by Annibaldi to Guarnieri. Of the Dictys material, the outer leaves of the first (original) quaternion are cleaned and used again as a union at the beginning of the MS. This seems to be due to the degeneration of the first leaf. The last two leaves of the *Agricola,* which have continuous text and must therefore have formed a union, are similarly cleaned and used again in the *Germania* portion of the MS. Leaves 2 and 7 of the Dictys are lost and replaced. If there had been no Hersfeld romance to confuse matters, there could hardly have been any hesitation in assuming that here we had the remains of a ninth-century MS containing Dictys and the *Agricola,* the first and last pages of which were in bad condition. The measurements of the two parts are exactly alike and the palaeographers agree that Dictys and *Agricola* come from the same scriptorium and from the same period. Only the pressure of a preconceived theory could make anyone doubt that they could come from the same MS, for the alternative is to assume that Guarnieri (or whoever made up the Jesi codex) found and combined two ninth-century MSS (both multilated) of exactly the same mechanical characteristics. The difficulties that have arisen are due to the attempt to reconcile these facts with the knowledge we have of a MS which Decembrio saw and which for convenience we may continue to call the Hersfeld MS. They are far greater than the only difficulty which really remains with regard to the Dictys-*Agricola* ninth-century MS. This difficulty is merely how to explain the disposition of the lost material between the sixth quaternion of the Dictys and the surviving quaternion of the *Agricola.* This consists in the Jesi codex of one leaf of the Dictys and four leaves of the *Agricola.* The most obvious assumption would be that this was contained

in a single gathering, either ternion or quaternion, with some
space left blank between the two essays. Robinson (p. 20)
says: "The complete silence of Panormita, Poggio, Niccola
and Decembrio regarding the Bellum Troianum militates
against the assumption that both works were originally in the
same codex, but does not entirely preclude it." The simpler
view would be that, with all the evidence in favor of the two
works forming a single codex, the inference to be drawn from
the silence of these scholars is that they were considering another MS, a view reinforced by the fact that they all do refer
to three other items of which there is no trace in the Jesi MS.
For this MS has no *Dialogus* and no Suetonius, and its *Germania* is entirely in the fifteenth-century hand which has restored the ninth-century Dictys and *Agricola*. No fragment of
a ninth-century *Germania* remains. It is a strain on one's credulity to believe that Guarnieri discarded the Tacitus material at
hand, sought out an identical MS of Dictys with which to replace it, and then copied a *Germania* from a different source to
go with them. For Robinson (p. 350) agrees with Schoenemann that the Jesi *Germania* was not copied from the same MS
from which come the ancient parts of the *Agricola*.

Furthermore, if the *Agricola* of the Jesi MS was once a part
of the Hersfeld MS, it would have come between the *Germania*
and the *Dialogus*. Why, then, were the last two leaves bound
separately as a *unio,* and why had they degenerated to the extent of having to be cleaned and rewritten? They should have
been well protected in the center of the codex, and the make-up
of the Jesi MS shows that Guarnieri did not object to irregular
gathering.

The assumption that Guarnieri removed the *Agricola* from
the middle of the Hersfeld codex or found it removed and
combined it with a *Bellum Troianum* which was essentially a
twin is a cumbersome assumption. It is required only by the
Hersfeld romance. The only supporting evidence is the fact
that the text is written in columns and occupies fourteen leaves
and that these characteristics agree with the evidence in regard
to the Hersfeld codex. But MSS in columns were no rarity but

rather the rule in the ninth-century Carolingian minuscule MSS, as Robinson points out (p. 24), and a short essay like the *Agricola* would not vary to any great extent in different MSS in the matter of total number of pages. Furthermore, we do not know how many leaves actually composed the *Agricola* in the ninth-century MS, for the beginning is lost.

If, then, we dispense with the tradition that identifies Jesi with the Hersfeld MS, we·have the following evidence with regard to the *Agricola*. There exists a ninth-century MS in Carolingian minuscule identical in characteristics with a MS of Dictys with which it is joined in the Jesi MS. The lost parts are restored in a fifteenth-century hand. We know also that there was in Rome in the middle of the fifteenth century a MS that came from Germany and was seen by Decembrio which contained the *Germania, Agricola, Dialogus,* and Suetonius, *de grammaticis et rhetoribus.* Finally, we know that there was an *Agricola* at Monte Cassino in about 1135, quoted from by Peter the Deacon (cf. Herbert Bloch, in *Classical Philology, 36,* 185). The precise and extended quotation by Peter necessitates reconsideration of another generally accepted conclusion.

The catalogue of MSS copied in the monastery of Monte Cassino about the year 1100 (*Mon. Germ. Hist.,* Scriptores *7, 746*) contains the entry *Historiam Cornelii cum Omero.* The combination seems as odd as, but no more odd than, *Oratium cum Geometria* a little later in the list. The catalogue enumerates first theological works, then historical, then literary. The two entries cited would seem to indicate an item considered of first importance within its category, with indication of another item bound with it. Following the lead of E. A. Lowe, scholars have in general assumed that *Historiam Cornelii cum Omero* referred to the Latin rendering of Dares purporting to be by Cornelius Nepos. But this is by no means a foregone conclusion. The item appears in a list which would make Tacitus at least as probable a Cornelius as Nepos: *Historiam Anastasii; Historiam Langobardorum, Gothorum et Wandalorum; Historiam Jordanis episcopi de Romanis et Gothis; Historiam Greg-*

orii Turonensis; Josephus de bello Judaico; Historiam Cornelii cum Omero, Historiam Erchamporti. Furthermore, with the parallelism of *cum Geometria* it is safe to infer two items as clearly indicated.

It is true that the so-called second Medicean MS of the Major Works of Tacitus was copied at Monte Cassino in the twelfth century, but it is hard to account for the *cum Omero* if this is the MS referred to in the list. There would be less difficulty if the entry referred to a MS containing Tacitus material combined with something on Troy. Such would be the ninth-century Carolingian MS of Dictys and the *Agricola*. Fulda, to which Robinson assigns the script of his Hersfeld MS, was a Benedictine monastery in close touch with Monte Cassino and furnished it numerous texts. It is becoming constantly more evident that Tacitus was known at Fulda, although it has not, I think, been noted that the *Agricola* was known there. In the third paragraph of the *Annals of the Church of Hamburg* (Migne, *146*, 457 ff.) Adam of Bremen writes: "Quaerentibus autem qui mortales ab initio Saxoniam coluerint vel a quibus haec gens primo finibus egressa sit, compertum est nobis ex multa lectione veterum, istam gentem sicut omnes fere populos qui in orbe sunt occulto Dei judicio non semel de regno ad populum alterum fuisse translatos; et ex nomine victorum provincias quoque vocabula sortitas." Migne notes as a source of one phrase in this paragraph Sallust, *Jugurtha*, 13: *sed qui mortales initio Africam habuerint.* But this is to overlook *Agricola*, 11: *Ceterum Britanniam qui mortales initio coluerint, indigenae an advecti, ut inter barbaros, parum compertum.* Undoubtedly Tacitus borrowed from Sallust, but the *coluerint* and *compertum* are sufficient evidence that Adam borrowed from Tacitus. The last phrase may echo the *Germania* (2): *ut omnes primum a victore ob metum, mox etiam a se ipsis invento nomine Germani vocarentur.* At any rate, the *Agricola* was known in the neighborhood of Fulda in the eleventh century, fifty years before Peter cited it at Monte Cassino. Whether Adam used it himself or borrowed the phrase from Einhard makes little difference. He acknowledges his indebtedness to the ninth-century writer, and the probability is that it was he who knew the *Agricola*. At any rate there is no inherent difficulty in the passage of the MS from Fulda to Monte Cassino. The removal from Monte Cassino need cause no more surprise than the removal of the second Medicean by Boccaccio. It is not, therefore, difficult to believe that an *Agricola* did come to Rome from Fulda and was seen and described by Decembrio, while another had long been in the monastery of Monte Cassino.

The remaining tradition with regard to the *Agricola* brings us immediately into contact with the tradition of the *Germania* and *Dialogus*. For, in their search for MSS, Poggio and the rest always had their eye on a German MS reported by a monk of Hersfeld which contained the three Tacitus items and Suetonius, *de grammaticis et rhetoribus*. Decembrio saw this MS in Rome in 1455. In his description of the *Agricola* he quotes the last two sentences: "Nam multos veluti inglorios et ignobilis oblivio obruet, Agricola posteritati narratus et traditus superstes erit." All four MSS of *Agricola* have *veterum* after *multos*. This has induced editors (all of whom accept the *veterum*) to change *obruet* to *obruit*. Certainly, if Tacitus meant to contrast the fate of Agricola's future fame with that of heroes long before him, the change of tense is essential. If their names had lived down to the writer's day, the comparison would not hold: it would have to be some new factor which consigned them to oblivion in the future and not the fact that they lacked a biographer. But if there were no word *veterum* in the text and the contrast was intended to be between Agricola and other contemporaries who lacked eulogists, then the future tense, *obruet*, would be correct. The contrast hardly calls for the sudden introduction of the ancients and, since all the MSS have *obruet*, it seems not wholly improbable that *veterum* was an unhappy gloss which crept into the text. Decembrio would then be quoting a text independent of the source of our four MSS. This possibility receives some confirmation from a consideration of the quotations made by Decembrio from the *Dialogus* and the Suetonius. In the former he reads *cogitare* and *nihil* with all the MSS except Leidensis and Vat. Lat. 1862, which read *cogitant* and *vel*. No one can say which is right. In the Suetonius, Decembrio reads correctly *proconsulem* and *conspectu* with all the MSS except Leidensis and Vat. Lat. 1862, which have the errors *personalem* and *ipseum*. Leidensis and Vat. Lat. 1862 are the only MSS of which we can say positively that they come from a different source from that of Decembrio's citation, for they carry a note which definitely aligns them with the MS brought to Rome by Enoch of Ascoli and which did not contain an *Agricola*. We are then forced to the conclusion that for some reason the *Agricola* of the Decembrio MS disappeared and produced no descendants. This appears a less startling conclusion when we consider that only one existing MS contains all of the items mentioned by Decembrio and that such MSS as we have of the *Agricola* are either MSS of the *Agricola* alone or offer no proof of original association with the other Tacitus MSS. Vat. Lat. 4498 has all three Tacitus items and in addition the Frontinus associated with these in the Decembrio tradition. But the Frontinus has the books in the correct order, and the Tacitus items are in a different order from that of Decembrio and separated by other material from the Suetonius essay as well as from the Frontinus. The contents of Vat. Lat. 4498 are Frontinus, Suetonius, Pliny, *Agricola, Dialogus, Germania,* M. Junius Nypsus, etc., and at the end of the MS are eleven pages ruled but blank. It is obviously a miscellaneous collection. It certainly did not copy the MS which Decembrio saw, for the various items are copied continuously and their order cannot be the result of rebinding.

So far as the *Agricola* of the Decembrio tradition is concerned, therefore, the most probable conclusion is that it disappeared after the dismemberment of the MS. But there is the possibility that the *Agricola* of 4498 is from it, although the probability is rather that 4498 and the copy of Pomponius Laetus both came from the other tradition with the reading *veterum*.

Before trying to follow the other parts of the Decembrio MS, it will be better to turn to the MS brought by Enoch of Ascoli to Rome about 1455 or 1456 but retained by him until his death. It will be remembered that this contained no *Agricola* (or Frontinus) and that the note in the Leidensis indicates that it was copied by Pontanus. From Pontanus' copy came Leidensis and Vat. Lat. 1862, both of which have readings disagreeing with Decembrio and all other MSS in both the Suetonius and the *Dialogus*. All editors of these two essays agree in differentiating these two MSS sharply from the rest. The same is true of editors of the *Germania* except that Robinson, while putting them in a group by themselves, associates them more closely than other editors with certain MSS of the *Germania* alone. It should be borne in mind, in confirmation of this separation of Leidensis and 1862, that Leidensis alone in its title and in one of the Pontanus notes refers to the Suetonius item as *De viris illustribus*. This is what it is called in the Enoch tradition as against the *De grammaticis et rhetoribus* of the Decembrio tradition. It seems safe to assign Leidensis and Vat. Lat. 1862 to the Enoch tradition and to conclude that Pontanus made a copy of the complete MS represented now by these two MSS only.

In view also of the fact that Aeneas Silvius Piccolomini sought out and saw the Enoch MS of the *Germania,* it is significant that certain of our MSS show Piccolomini affiliations: the family arms, the dedicatory poem to Pius II (Piccolomini), and so on. These MSS belong to a group sharply differentiated by readings from all the rest and having no signs of conflation (see Robinson, pp. 221–2) but with innumerable errors that come from the misinterpretation of abbreviations. The most obvious explanation is that they come from a copy hastily made by Aeneas Silvius in which he abbreviated generously to save time. The errors coming from misunderstanding of a Gothic hand, if Robinson is right in seeing these, would then be mistakes made by Aeneas Silvius in copying Enoch's MS, which would then be shown to be in Gothic script. This group consists, of course, of MSS of the *Germania* only, without the *Dialogus* or Suetonius.

There are also six MSS that have Suetonius and *Dialogus* only, without the *Germania*. The order is always Suetonius first. Except for Ottob. 1455, they are all grouped together and apart from the MSS with all three essays by editors both of Suetonius and of the *Dialogus*. The order of the essays and the presence of Leonardo material (so frequently associated with Aeneas Silvius) in three of the codices of the group make this look like an Enoch group. With them must be classed the Suetonius-*Dialogus* portion of Venetus Marcianus, a MS made in 1464 for Marcanova, a friend of Aeneas Silvius. There is a dated subscription at the end of the *Dialogus* (Suetonius and *Dialogus* are continuous) and another at the end of the *Germania*, suggesting different sources rather than a common one.

In the MSS which have all three essays it has never seemed possible to find significance in the order of the separate items. But it is interesting to note that Pontanus copied them early in 1460. Neapolitan interests had been working to get Enoch's MS for some time. Aeneas Silvius had seen it and probably copied the *Germania* in 1457 or 1458. If he detached the *Germania* from the rest with which it was rejoined but in first position and the MS was then sold to Naples, Pontanus would have the order G S D. As a matter of fact, the *Germania* of Leidensis is self-contained and has a blank leaf at the end, while the Suetonius-*Dialogus* portion is continuous. Rebinding may have changed the order. Vat. 1862 has the order G S D, confirming somewhat this hypothesis. Under the circumstances the derivation of Leidensis and 1862 from the Enoch MS is consistent with the other evidence. The other "Enoch" MSS that we have discussed are therefore of value largely in support of these two.

The remaining MSS of the Minor Works may fairly be assumed to come from some other source than Enoch's MS. The question of whether they derive from a single common source or not will have to be postponed for the moment while we consider the remaining MSS of the *Dialogus*. Except in Vind. 49 and the closely related *editio princeps,* the Suetonius fragment always appears with the *Dialogus*. The incomplete character of this fragment and the existence of a considerable lacuna in the *Dialogus* point to a single imperfect ancestor, alike for

Manuscript Affiliations of the Minor Works

Manuscript Affiliations of the Minor Works 289

these MSS and those deriving from Enoch. On the basis of readings there is general agreement that S D of Vind. 711 and Ottob. 1455 are closely related and differentiated from all the other MSS. These others fall into two groups, the first consisting of Vat. 1518, Farnese, and Vat. 4498, the second of Vind. 49, with the *editio princeps*. Gudeman quite correctly considered as practically worthless the group which I have assigned to the Enoch tradition and without further analysis put them in a leftover group with Vind. 49. The essential and important points are, first, that in the *Dialogus* and in the Suetonius fragment, Leidensis and 1862 form a group independent of all the rest; and, second, that there are three groups, as indicated in the second family. There are minor bits of corroborative evidence. Vind. 711 and Ottob. 1455 are the only two that contain collateral material by Blondus. Vat. 4498, which comes nearest to reproducing what Decembrio saw, contains the two books of Frontinus.

When we turn to the *Germania,* general agreement has not been so nearly attained. Up to the latter part of the nineteenth century there was an accepted tradition that held Leidensis and 1862 to be representative of one (the X) family and put all the rest in the second or Y family. A growing skepticism as to this division came with the work of Muellenhoff, Wuensch, and Schoenemann, and a third family gradually developed to which Toletanus and Aesinas, on their discovery, gave confirmation. In general this three-family division has remained intact. Because of MSS which were not considered worth including, it is quite possible to make a better analysis today of the non-Enoch MSS, and a four-family division would probably be more generally acceptable. But in 1935 Rodney Robinson published the most exhaustive work to date on the *Germania,* presenting a meticulous study of *all* the MSS. His book will be in the future the source for all further work on the *Germania.* His conclusion, however, is not only revolutionary but to me unconvincing. He makes Vind. 711 and its relative Monacensis the sole representatives of one family; his second family with four branches includes all the rest. Only Vind. 711

has independent value. Robinson had already put forward the theory that for the Suetonius fragment, Vind. 711 and Ottob. 1455 similarly constitute an independent direct line from the Hersfeld archetype, reducing Leidensis and 1862 to a definitely subordinate position. His position on the *Germania* problem is this: Vind. 711 (with Monacensis and the lost Hummelianus) forms an "ultimate" group contributing directly to the reconstruction of Hersfeld. There is only one other line by which, through three stages of lost MSS, all our other codices come. The theory is dependent wholly on his conviction that the Hersfeld archetype, the common ancestor of all MSS, is represented by the ninth-century leaves of the *Agricola* in the Aesinas MS of Jesi. On this he bases his claim that the spelling of Vind. 711 is that of Hersfeld, and he uses Aesinas to establish almost all of the details of his demonstration. With at least a reasonable doubt existing as to whether Aesinas does alone represent the Hersfeld archetype, it would seem necessary to find confirmation of Robinson's theory on other grounds. These are lacking. Vind. 711 adds almost nothing independently to the text of the common archetype, unless we are prepared to accept Robinson's preferences for certain readings: *signatque* as against *significatque* (28. 8), *saepius* for *saepe* (38. 8), *contacti sunt* for *contacti* (10. 13), *incolatur* in preference to *incolitur* (3. 12). This last Robinson admits is unexpected and hard to defend. His one change in the text on the evidence of Vind. 711 alone (*et hic* for *hic* in 31. 10) has to be explained by the assumption of a lacuma of which there is no evidence. The passage has not been considered "unintelligible" by other editors. It seems reasonable on the whole, therefore, to return to the old method of classifying our MSS by the readings.

There is no incontrovertible proof that all our *Germania* MSS do come from a common archetype. The *Dialogus* with its lacunae, the Suetonius fragment with its same extent in all MSS, the *Agricola* with at least four passages garbled alike in all the codices—all of these clearly derive from ancestors already characteristically mutilated. For the *Germania* we have no such evidence. All that we can positively say is that on the basis of common errors the MSS fall into certain groups. There is general agreement on what these are and the evidence is available in Robinson's edition. Leidensis and Vat. 1862 are closely related and to some degree at least separated from the rest. So are Vat. 1518, Farnese, and Vat. 4498; so are the MSS which I have listed as connected with Aeneas Silvius; so are Aesinas, with its copy Toletanus, Ottob. 1209, Ottob. 1795, Vat. 2964, Rimini, and the Munich fragment; so are Vind. 49, the late Turicensis, and the *editio princeps;* so are Venetus Marcianus and Paris; and so are Vind. 711, Monacensis, and Hummelianus. On the basis of readings the group of *Germania* MSS associated with Aeneas Silvius is furthest from the rest, but this is explained by the external facts, if we accept them, regarding the hasty copying and the use of abbreviations by Aeneas Silvius. Apart from these the family commonly called Y, consisting of Vat. 1518, Farnese, and Vat. 4498, is furthest from Leid, and Vat. 1862. Between these two groups and nearer to the latter is the group including Aesinas, while the remaining MSS fall generally together nearer to Vat. 1518. These seem to fall into three related groups, Vind. 711 and Mon. forming one, Stuttgart (perhaps with Hummelianus) a second, and Venet. Marcianus, Parisiensis, Vind. 49, and Turicensis the third.

In summary it seems possible (a possibility that may disappear any day with the discovery of new evidence) that our MSS of the Minor Works all derive from the codex from the neighborhood of Hersfeld, most probably from Fulda. A ninth-century copy of the *Agricola* of this codex joined with a Dictys went as early as the twelfth century to Monte Cassino and later appeared in fragmentary form, with the *Germania* added from a separate source. From this, Toletanus was copied. Another copy, or very likely the original, came to Rome previous to 1455; this, Decembrio saw. It was presumably dismembered in copying and the *Agricola* lost, unless the *Agricola* of Vat. 4498 is a copy. At about the same time Enoch of Ascoli brought to Rome a copy that he had made of the *Germania* and

Dialogus along with the Suetonius fragment. He retained this until his death, trying to profit by disposing of it to the scholarly group at Naples. Aeneas Silvius saw it while it was in the custody of Nardini and probably copied the *Germania* in which he was primarily interested, in all likelihood detaching the essay. Copies of his transcript were made, as well as of the Suetonius-*Dialogus* section. Leidensis and Vat. 1862 were the result of a copy made by Pontanus of all three essays. He could probably have had access to it as well as Aeneas Silvius (although his copy is at least two years younger), especially as he was one of the group of Neapolitan scholars who were angling for it, or he may have made his copy from the two separate parts, which then disappeared.

A tentative classification of the MSS on the basis of the preceding discussion is shown in Chart 1. The Stuttgart MS seems to have been primarily of the Enoch group but definitely written with a MS of the Decembrio group before the copyist who took some readings from this latter MS. The *Dialogus* MSS follow the same general classification. Urb. 1194, containing the *Dialogus* only, is incomplete. Ottob. 1455 is closely related to Vind. 711. Harl. 2639 is from the Decembrio group, and Paris 7773 is a direct copy of it.

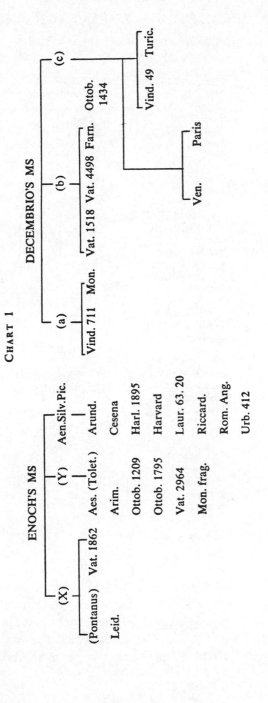

CHART 1

ENOCH'S MS

(X)   (Y)   Aen.Silv.Pic.

(Pontanus)   Vat. 1862   Aes. (Tolet.)   Arund.

Leid.   Arim.   Cesena

                 Ottob. 1209   Harl. 1895

                 Ottob. 1795   Harvard

                 Vat. 2964   Laur. 63. 20

                 Mon. frag.   Riccard.

                             Rom. Ang.

                             Urb. 412

DECEMBRIO'S MS

(a)   (b)   (c)

Vind. 711   Mon.   Vat. 1518   Vat. 4498   Fam.   Ottob. 1434

                            Ven.   Paris   Vind. 49   Turic.

Laurent. 68. 1	*Annals* 1–6
Neap. IV. C. 24	*Annals* 1 and 2
Laurent. 68. 2	*Annals* 11–21
Bodl. 27605	"
Bodl. 34372	"
Bud. 9	"
Cesena	"
Gudianus 118	"
Harl. 2764	"
Holk. Hall. 39	"
Jesus 109	"
Kop. Gl. Kgl. S. 496	"
Laurent. 63. 24	"
Laurent. 68. 4	"
Laurent. 68. 5	"
Leid. B.P.L. 16. B	"
Neap. IV. C. 21	"
Neap. IV. C. 22	"
Neap. IV. C. 23	"
Ottob. Lat. 1422	"
Ottob. Lat. 1748	"
Paris. Reg. 6118	"
Parm. 861	"
Urb. Lat. 412	"
Vat. Lat. 1863	"
Vat. Lat. 1864	"
Vat. Lat. 1958	"
Vat. Lat. 2965	"
Ven. 381	"
Vind. 49	"
Yalensis. 1	"
Yalensis. 2	"
Yalensis. 3	"
Zarag. 9439	"
Excerpt MSS	"
Rumored MSS	"

MANUSCRIPTS OF ANNALS 1–6

Laurentianus 68. 1

This MS in the Laurentian Library, Florence, is the sole source of the first six books of the *Annals*. It is often called the first Medicean. It is a folio MS on parchment, measuring 240 × 205 mm. There are 138 folia, of which the first is a recent replacement provided for the protection of the book. The last is repaired. The gatherings are quaternions, with a single duernion at the end. There are two numbering systems. On the last page of each quaternion there is an older number, the series running from I to XVII, and also a slightly younger number, this series running from XVIII to XXXIV. The natural conclusion is that the MS was at first either an independent item or the first item in a collection but was later reassembled with another item that preceded it. This item was undoubtedly the Pliny in the Laurentian (47. 36), which is uniform with the Tacitus and has quaternions numbered I to XVII.

Laur. 68. 1 is uniformly ruled with a steel point. There are twenty-four lines to the page. The hand is Carolingian minuscule, usually ascribed to the ninth century. There are numerous notes and corrections, but all are in humanistic hands. The source was presumably Córwey.

The title of the MS is *P. Cornelii Taciti Ab Excessu Divi Aug.* It ends without subscription: *suo tantum ingenio utebatur,* the close of the summary characterization of Tiberius in Book 6. Book 5 is clearly fragmentary. There are other mutilations, all of which seem to have taken place in an ancestor of Laur. 68. 1, for they are not indicated, and the numbering of the quaternions indicates that we have all the material that the MS contained.

The MS is photographically reproduced by A. W. Sijthoff, Leiden, 1902, under the direction of de Vries and with an introduction by Rostagno.

Neapolitanus IV. C. 24

A worthless sixteenth-century copy of Books 1 and 2 on heavy ruled paper 5½ × 2⅜ in., in the Royal Library in Naples.

MANUSCRIPTS OF ANNALS 11–16 AND HISTORIES

Laurentianus 68. 2

This MS is also called the second Medicean. It is in the Laurentian Library at Florence. It was probably written in the eleventh century and contains all the known material of *Annals* 11 ff. and of the *Histories,* except for one lost folio. Its format is large (270 × 339 mm.). Its material is parchment, and it is written in a Beneventan hand. It has 103 leaves (originally 105). There are thirteen quaternions and a single folium. Leaves three and six of the eighth quaternion are lost. The second leaf of the second quaternion was evidently spoiled and cut off, for, while it is missing, there is no lacuna in the text. The first page of the first leaf is blank. The MS is written in columns, with thirty-five to thirty-eight lines to a page. The Tacitus material is followed by Apuleius 104^r–125^v, *De Magia Libri* II; 126^r–184^r, *Metamorphosium Libri* XI; 184^r–191^v, *Floridorum Libri* IV. The Apuleius material was taken from an archetype made by Crispus Sallustius in the late fourth century. This is indicated by marginal notes copied by the scribe (see especially 118^r and 171^v), but there is no evidence that the Apuleius and Tacitus material came from a common source.

The MS has a covering leaf at the beginning, added for protection. On the recto of this is the present catalogue number: Pl. 68, No. 2, and on the reverse: *Cornelius Tacitus et Opera Apulegii Conventus. S. Marci de Florentia ordinis praedicatorum. De hereditate Nicolai Nicoli Florentini viri doctissimi.* The recto of the first leaf following is entirely blank, the text beginning on the verso without title and with a capital letter only slightly larger than normal, not in any real sense decorative. The opening words are *Nam valerium masiaticum.* Subsequent books have large decorative capitals and, with the exception of Books 16 and 21, a subscription, reading *Corneli Taciti Liber—explicit, incipit—.*The end of 18 and the beginning of 19 are lost with the missing folium. The manuscript ends about four-fifths of the way down column 1 of 103^v with the words *flavianus in pannia,* the first *a* being added by a later hand or, more probably, forming a ligature with the first *n,* and causing the mistaken reading of editors: *phnia.* At the end of Book 16 a little more than a page and a half is left blank, the first book of the *Histories* beginning at the top of 48^r: *Initium michi* *operis Servius Galbea.* A considerable amount of the text is illegible, and in many parts a later hand has rewritten the text between lines. End of 16: *obversis in Demetrium* (bad condition).

It is generally agreed that Laur. 68. 2 is in Beneventan script, such as was produced at Monte Cassino (cf. E. A. Lowe, *The Unique Manuscript of Tacitus' Histories,* Casinensia, 1929). The Laurentian manuscript has in the empty column of 103 the words *Abbas Raynaldus.* There were two abbots of this name at Monte Cassino in the twelfth century. The MS was used by Paulinus Venetus, Bishop of Pozzuoli before 1340 (see K. J. Heilig in *Wiener Studien, 53* (1935), 95 ff.) and was quite probably the source of Boccaccio's knowledge of the *Annals.* When it came into the hands of Niccoli is not known, but Poggio borrowed it in 1427 (See Letter III, 14). The inscriptions in the MS show that it was bequeathed by Niccoli to the library of St. Mark's in Florence whence it passed, at least before the middle of the sixteenth century, to the Laurentian. It was collated by Pietro Vittori in 1542. In the royal library in Munich is a copy of Beroaldus' edition, with collation of 68. 2. At the end is this statement (cf. Walther, *praef.,* xxxvii): *Recognovi cum vetusto exemplari litteris Langobardis scripto ne ea quidem in conlatione omittens quae corrupta aliquo pacto videbantur, ne locus coniecturae emendaturo deesset. Est autem codex e Divi Marci biblioteca. Florentiae MDXLII. Idibus Jan. P. Victorius.* The first use for an edition was by Pichena in 1607. Gronovius used it and made a new collation in 1720. The MS is reproduced: *Codex laurentianus Mediceus 68 II. phototypice editus. praefatus est Henricus Rostagno. Lugduni Batavorum,* A. W. Sijthoff, 1902.

Bodleian 27605

Now MS. Auct. F. 2. 24 in the Bodleian Library, Oxford. This MS is on parchment, in folio, $10\frac{5}{8} \times 8$ in. (writing $7 \times 4\frac{1}{2}$). It has vertical and horizontal ruling, with 30 lines to the whole page. There are 175 leaves. The first page has a magnificently illuminated border and initial capital. The binding is red leather with gold ornament, seventeenth-century English work. The hand is a fine book hand, the whole MS a de luxe item. The title reads: *Cornelii Taciti Actorum Diurnalium Historiae Augustae Liber undecimus.* The text begins, *Nam Valerium Asiaticum.* On p. 151: *obversis in demetrium,* with the marginal notation: *hic multum deest.* Book 17 begins *Initium mihi operis Servilius Galba.* Books 17 and 18 are confused. Opposite the point where they should be divided is a marginal note: *Hic incipit Lib II Historiarum in editione Gronovii.* On p. 238 at the end of the double book is the note: *decimusoctavus liber totus deest: si vis tu tibi eum quaerito.* On p. 330, at the end of Book 20: *post haec scriptum erat sed non suo ut videtur loco neque vos inpunitos patient. nisi sit hic etiam defectus textus.* On p. 343 the text of Tacitus ends, *Fabianus in Pannonia,* followed by a note: *In exemplari tantum erat. Si quispiam hinc descripserit novum sciat me quantum repperi fideliter ab ex° transcripsisse quod inter cetera non est neque pessimum neque mendosissimum   genuae pridie idus decembres anno MCCCCLX tertio.* This is followed by a letter of Pilate to Tiberius, *de Yesu Christo,* and some letters of Cicero *ad Atticum.*

Bodleian 34372

Now MS. Lat. class. d. 16 in the Bodleian Library, Oxford. The MS is on paper and measures 12 × 8⅞ (writing: 7¾ × 4¼). There are 170 leaves, the first one blank. The binding is brown calf with gilt ornament and with the arms of Pope Pius VI; it is a late eighteenth-century Italian work. This is the Phillips MS No. 3347, once in the library of Pope Pius VI, bought by Sir Thomas in the Henry Drury sale in 1827 and by the Bodleian at Sotheby's sale on December 10, 1890. The writing is 36 lines to the page in a running hand. The title is: *Cornelii Taciti Actorum Diurnalium Augustae Historiae Liber undecimus foeliciter incipit.* In the margin: *fragmentum.* The text begins: *Nam Valerium Asiaticum.* There is no illumination. On 72ʳ Book 16 ends: *obversus in demetrium* [in margin: *hic deficit*], with one and one-half pages left blank. On 73ʳ,

Cornelii Taciti Actorum Diurnalium Augustae Historiae XVII incipit. Space is left for an illuminated letter: *Nitium mihi operis Servius Galba.* Books 17 and 18 are confused with a late indication in the margin. The text ends (165ᵛ), *Fabianus in Pannonia.* In the margin, in one hand, apparently that of the scribe, *ulterius non inveni, nec puto invenietur;* in another, quite different, hand: *est autem in libris impressis defectus plus quam hic.* This would indicate that the note was written between the dates of the first and second printed editions, about 1475. Below the text, in the scribe's hand: *Explicit Anno Domini MCCCCX.* The Bodleian interprets this MCCCCX as originally MCCCCXL. At the end of Book 20 on 160ʳ, the *neque vos inpunitos patiantur* is added in a later hand. In the regular hand in the margin: *hic deficit usque ad finem.* There is, then, nearly a whole page blank but no *post haec scriptum* note. At the end of XVIII (114ᵛ): *Hic deest finis huius libri et principium sequentis: tu autem lector, cui finis rerum semper est curae indulge blasfemie: non enim potui ea scribere quae non invenni; nec puto invenietur.* In 20. 46, after *pelli poterant,* a space of several lines is left blank with *hic deficit* in the margin, and the same after *subvenere,* at the end of chapter 52. The first break is at the point where the third inversion begins. For the second there would seem to be no reason. The end of the inversion shows no such space.

Budensis 9

A parchment MS in the University Library at Budapest, of 132 folia, measuring 360 × 260 mm.; the text measures 221 × 153. There are 35 lines to a page; the hand is a professional hand, upright, very clear, of medium size. Fol. 1ʳ has elaborate marginal illumination as well as a large illuminated initial. In the marginal illumination, right margin, are two birds, a hare, and a child blowing a horn. At the bottom a circular design supported by two children, framing what I take to be the arms of Matthew Corvinus, with a crown at the top. The title is: *Cornelii Taciti Hystorigraphi Prestantissimi Fragmentorum Liber   Incip.* The next book has the title: *Cornelii Tac-*

iti Liber duodecimus incipit feliciter. The books, therefore, had their traditional numbering, but for some reason the number of Book 11 was not written in the space reserved. Book 21 lacks a title. The *Annals* have the usual beginning and ending: *Nam Valerium Asyaticum . . . conversus in Demetrium.* In the margin opposite this ending of Book 16 is *deficit.* The *Histories* begin *Initium mei operis Servius Galbea* and end with *arte navium magnitudine potiores.* The rest of 129ʳ is left blank, and on the reverse begin the two excerpts with six blank lines between them. Book 20 ends *neque vos impunitos patiantur.* At the end of all is the subscription: *Finis eorum quae Cornelii Taciti reperiuntur.* Between the last line of the text and this subscription is written in a not very careful hand: *Jo. Ar. Legi transcurrendo 1461* (or 7) *sed mansit inemendatus.* The MS has the long lacuna in Book 20 and also one from 16. 18 to 16. 26. In each instance a blank space is left and the lacuna noted. A similar blank is left at 20. 77, where there seems to be in reality no lacuna. The MS is interesting because, while it has ending II, it has all the other outstanding characteristics of the MSS with ending I. In other words, the last lines are added from a Group II MS.

Turkish inscriptions in the bottom margin of 1ᵛ and 2ʳ indicate that the MS was presented to the University at Buda in 1877 by Abdul Hamid II.

Cesena

This is a parchment MS (II. 13. 5 in the Biblioteca Malatestina at Cesena) written in an upright hand, 36 lines to the page. There are no decorations and no illuminated letters at the beginning. The title at the top of the first page is *Cornelii Taciti Actorum Diurnalium Liber XI Augustae Historiae Lege feliciter.* In the margin in an almost identical but more careless hand is *Fragmentum.* The text begins *Nam valerium Asiaticum.* Book 12 begins with an illuminated *C.* The title is *Cornelii · Taciti · Actorum · Diurnalium · Augustae · Historiae · Liber · XI · explicit · incipit · XII · feliciter.* The same style of illuminated initial is used at the beginning of 13 and the same

form of title, except that in place of XIII the MS reads TECIVS-
DECIMUS. The titles and illuminated letters continue on the
model of Book 12. The *Annals* end *obversis in demetrium.* In
the margin is *hic deficit.* Book 17 begins *Initium mihi operis
Servius Galba.* A paragraph is indicated just below by a short
space and the use of capitals, the opening line reading *Opus
aggredio plenum variis casibus* etc. In the margin is one of the
few alternative readings of this MS: *gravioribus opibus* (Harl.
reads *plenum variis casibus* but has in the margin *opimum
casibus*). At the end of Book 18 (17 and 18 are continuous
without indication of division) is the following note: *Si repperero finem septimidecimi libri et principium octavidecimi q
utraque confusa sunt cunctis in libris et varia locum annotabo.
Si lector offenderis et tu signes oro. Valeas q̄ legeris et recte
annotaveris.* (This does not seem to confirm Sabbadini in his
quae, quae rendering.) In the title of 19 the *explicit* is omitted.
The regular form is resumed at 20 but the *vicesimus* spelled
out. The title for 21 spells out both numerals and ends *Lege
feliciter.* The text ends *Fabianus in Pannonia.* In the margin:
*In exemplari tantum erat. Si quispiam hinc descripserit novum
sciat me quantum reperi fideliter ab exemplari transcripsisse.*
Sabbadini (*St. e Cr.,* p. 257) reads *ita scripsisse* but mis-
takenly. This MS has the *status mercatus* gloss at H. 3. 30 and
the "Cremona" gloss at H. 3. 34. This latter gives 1740 years
since the founding of Cremona, which is identical with Vat.
Lat. 1958, but my picture is clipped and the date of the MS
does not show. The treatment of the third inversion is identical
with that of 1958 and of Harl., and there is a lacuna indicated
that does not exist at the end of H. 4. 52 as there is in Harl.
and 1958. The note which 1958 and Harl. have at the end of
20 has been largely erased in Malat., and it is impossible from
the picture to tell which form of the note this is, *non suo ut
videtur loco,* or *non ut videtur loco.* Malat. Ces. has very few
corrections and very few alternative readings. There is a not
very extensive series of glosses, mostly topical but some of
them quotations from the poets, all of which are in Harl. and
some of them in 1958.

Gudianus, 118

In the library at Wölfenbütel, on parchment, consisting of 142 leaves bound in quinions. It bears the inscription: *Est P. Candidi. Ab eodem recognitus et emendatus. Emptus Ferrariae MCCCCLXI. die lunae XXVIII Sept. D.L.* On the first folium is another inscription: *Fransiscus Media Barba Biragus Dono Dat Literatissimo D Marquardo Gudio Domino suo colendissimo.* The title is *Cornelii Taciti Actorum diurnalium Liber XI augustae historiae.* It has the *Si repperero* note, with the readings *reperero, septidecimi,* and *que legeris.* Books 17 and 18 are continuous, without any indication of a break. This MS has the shorter form of the *si quispiam* note at the end without *novum.*

Harleianus 2764

On parchment in the British Museum. The pages are 195 × 290 mm.; the writing 110 × 200 mm. There are 168 leaves, the text ending at the bottom of the last recto. The manuscript is written in a clear but not ostentatious book hand with rather thick strokes and practically no spaces between letters, much like the hand of Bud. 9, but slightly smaller. There are many marginal notes throughout. These are mostly topical notes, but there are corrections, some alternative readings, occasional comments on the text—sometimes exclamatory, usually trite —and a few comments on the archetype. These notes are in several different hands, including that of the copyist. The first page has some rather ordinary illumination in the left-hand margin, the upper part of which has been torn away, taking with it the first letter or two of the first eight lines. This has been repaired with a large illuminated *I*, making the opening words, as they stand now, *Iam valerium asiaticum.* At the bottom of the page is a coat of arms with the fore part of a deer rising from a helmet and, above, the legend *In conctis deo gratias.* The title is *Cornelii Taciti Actorum Diurnalium Liber XI Augustae Historiae.* In the margin opposite, in what looks like the same hand, is *Fragmentum.* On 73ᵛ, Book 16 ends *obversis in demetrium*, with *hic deficit* in the margin. The next title is *Cornelii Taciti Actorum Diurnalium Augustae Historiae Liber XVI finit. Incipit XVII.* The text of 17 begins *Initium mihi operis Servius Galba.* Book 20 ends *interpretabatur* (162ʳ). In the margin opposite is this note: *Post haec scriptum est sed non ut videtur loco Neque vos impunitos patiantur nisi et hic defectus sit textus.* There is a *hic deficit* in the margin opposite 20. 77 (on 159ʳ) but no break in the text. A blank line is left at the end of 20. 52, and there is also a *hic deficit textus* in the margin (150ᵛ). This is in the third inversion, but there seems to be no omission. On 95ʳ, opposite *Struebat iam,* there is a marginal note: *hic sᵐ aliquos incipit liber decimus octavus.* Otherwise there is no indication of the division between 17 and 18. At the end of 18 is this note: *Si reperrero finem septimi decimi libri et principium octavi decimi que utraque confusa sunt cunctis in libris et varia locum annotabo. si lector offenderis et tu signes oro. Valeas qui legeris et recte annotaveris.* The MS has the quotation from the Octavia added in *Ann.* 14. 8. On 124ᵛ is the note *Status mercatus gnales nundinae ut genue allobrogum urbis hodie* . The end of the text (168ʳ) is *Fabianus in Pannonia,* with the marginal note *In exemplari tantum erat. Si quispiam hinc descripserit novum sciat me quantum reperi fideliter ab exemplari transcripsisse. Finis.* The Cremona note (125ᵛ) dates the MS 1452. The note is like that in Vat. Lat. 1958 except that it has M.DCC. and M.CCCC.LII for the two dates. The first is evidently a scribal error.

Holkham Hall, 39

This MS is listed by Seymour de Ricci, *Handlist of the MSS in the Library of the Earl of Leicester at Holkham Hall (Norfolk),* Supplement 7 of the Bibliographical Society, Oxford Press, 1932. This is said to have come from the Giuseppe Valetta collection which Thomas Coke, first Earl of Leicester, bought about 1710 in Naples, and is said to contain "Annales et Historiae" (G. Forster, *Philologus, 42* (1884), 158–67).

Jesus College 109

A small MS on parchment with 190 leaves carefully ruled throughout, 32 lines to a page. The writing measures 6¾ × 3¾ in. The MS is mutilated at the end. There is no illumination, the MS giving the appearance of having been copied for use by a professional hand, rather small and reasonably good. The title reads *Cornelii Taciti Actorum Diurnalium Augustae Historiae Librum XI. Lege Feliciter.* In the margin opposite the title is *Fragmentum.* The text begins *Nam Valerium Asiaticum.* Book 17 continues the form of the title except that it has *liber*, not *librum*, and begins *nitium mihi operis Servius Galba.* Books 17 and 18 are confused. Opposite the line where the break should come (109ʳ) there is, in the margin, *Hic incipit Lib 2 secundum edit. Lips. Gronov.* On 184ᵛ, at the end of Book 20, appears *Post haec scriptum erat sed non ut videtur loco, neque vos impunitos patiant, nisi et hic defectus sit textus.* On 191ᵛ, at the bottom, the text ends *semet in arma trusos*, which is in H. 5. 25, indicating a page lost at the end. According to a note in the handwriting of C. J. Fordyce, formerly librarian of Jesus, this MS was collated by Jacob Gronovius.

Kopenhagen, Gl. Kgl. S. 496

The Kopenhagen MS is on parchment. It has 196 leaves measuring 267 × 164 mm. It is written in a fine hand, slightly inclined to the right, which becomes less careful after fol. 90 and grows more and more careless up to the end of the book, though it is never really poor. There are 31 lines to the whole page up to 155ʳ, then 30. There seem to be several hands, but the type of writing is consistent throughout. On the blank flyleaf is written *Fridericus Rostgaard emit 1699.* The title page has a magnificent decoration, with landscape background and standing figures in the style of Mantegna. The title is *C. Cornelii Taciti Historiae Fragmentum De Rebus Gestis Imperatorum Lib. XI* (except for the *C*, this is exactly like that of Ottob 1422). The text begins *Nam Valerium Asiaticum* and ends *superstitione obnoxia*. This ending, a line and a half beyond the usual *evenerant* ending of this type of MS, seems to have been added by a later hand imitating the original. The *Histories* begin *Initium mei operis Sergius Galba,* the *Annals* having ended *conversus in Demetrium* with a note, *Hic multum deest: sequirur L. XVIII.* This error in numbering is made in spite of the fact that there is no confusion of Books 17 and 18. At the beginning of the long lacuna in 20 a later hand has added *armis oneraverat.* A blank half page follows. Book 20 ends *neque vos impunitos patiantur,* but these words are vigorously crossed out. Titles are omitted after 16. At the end of 21 is a note: *Hic aliquot libri desunt.* Then follow the excerpts, with a space, and *Hic multum deficit* between them. A colophon on 196ʳ reads *Hic liber visus et ut accuratius ex incuria temporum potuit emendatus est per me Ludovicum Regem Imolensem Anno salutis MCCCCLXXXVIII die vero XXVᵃ Septembris ///// Innocentio VIII pont. Max.* There is no lacuna in Book 16. *Deficit* notes are in all cases in a hand different from that of the text.

Laurentianus 63. 24

A miscellaneous MS in the Laurentian Library, Florence, with Valerius Maximus on fols. 1–156 and Tacitus on 157–282. The pages measure 8½ × 13½ inches and are gathered in quinions. They are carefully ruled, 36 lines to a page, with double vertical lines at the sides. Margins are wide. The hand is a fine book hand. The first page of the Tacitus material, like the first page of the MS, is superbly illuminated, with free use of heavy gold leaf. It is a sumptuous book, with the Medici arms in the illumination, and at the end: *Liber Petri de Medicis Cos. Fil.* The title is *Incipit Fragmentum. quod. reperitur. ex historiis Cornelii Taciti Feliciter.* The opening words are *Nam Valerium Asiaticum.* At the end of each book is a *finit* followed by an *incipit* for the next. Book 16 ends *obversis in Demetrium,* and four or five lines are left blank before the colophon. Book 17 begins *Initium mihi operis Servius Galbea.* There is no confusion of 17 and 18. The text proper ends with

Flavianus in Pannonia, followed, after a space of three blank lines, by the *illi veteres* excerpt, with a tiny *deficit* in the margin. There are no marginal notes or corrections with the exception of a single *aliter.* There is no lacuna in Book 20, no spaces left for omitted words, no change of hand or break at 18. 69, and no comment on the ending of Book 20, *neque vos impunitos patiantur.*

Laurentianus 68. 4

In the Laurentian Library in Florence, a parchment MS of 106 leaves measuring 8¼ × 11⅝ inches. The pages are ruled (32 lines to a page), with vertical double lines at the sides. The page numbering is modern. The MS is in perfect condition, the white parchment preserved to the very edges of the wide margins. It is written in a small book hand, upright and square. The text begins without title or illumination: *Nam valerium asiaticum.* Book 16 ends with *conversus in Demetrium,* with *hic plurimum deficit* in the margin and nearly two pages left blank. After this, with a space for the initial, *nitium mei operis Servius Galbea.* In 18. 69 the writing changes and becomes less ornamental and uniform; the page rulings cease except for one heavily ruled page. The word *audita* comes at the end of a line. The next line begins with a space into which a much later hand has written *transgressus* in a blacker ink. Then the old ink resumes and the hand is the same for *in castra ultro.* After that there is a miscellany of different hands ending (10 leaves later) *ad mutandam fidem classe ob memoriam recentis pro Othone militiae. Finis Lib. XVIII.* This is the end also of the MS and it is the only colophon or title in the whole codex. Except for half a dozen words (marginal topics), there are also no notes. There is no confusion of 17 and 18. The text does not go far enough to say whether the MS had the long lacuna in Book 20.

Laurentianus 68. 5

This MS is in the Laurentian Library in Florence and is of the fifteenth century. It is small, made of parchment and has 247 leaves measuring 9¾ × 7½ inches and gathered in quinions. It is ruled—28 lines to a page—with double vertical lines at the sides. It has a magnificently illuminated first page featuring the Medici arms. Each book has an illuminated initial. It is carefully written, in a clear, fairly large, book hand. The title is *Cornelii Taciti Fragmentum Liberi XI incipit foeliciter.* The opening words are *Nam Valeri Asiaticum.* Each book has a colophon: *Corneli Taciti Liber—explicit. Incipit—.* Book 16 ends *obversis in Demetrium,* with a small *deficit* in the margin in another hand. The next opening is *Initium mihi operis Servius Galbea.* Book 20 ends *neque vos impunitos patiantur.* Book 21 ends *Flavianus in Pannonia,* with four lines left blank at the bottom of the page. On the next page, with no further indication of a break, begin the two excerpts, *illi veteres* etc., and *toleremus* etc. Three and one-half blank lines are left between the two. At the end of the *Toleremus* excerpt is the colophon: *Cornelii Taciti Liber XXI explicit.* Occasional omissions are inserted in the margin by a later hand, but otherwise there are no notes. There is no long lacuna in this MS and Books 17 and 18 are entirely distinct. There is no indication of the provenance of the MS or of its history, aside from the Medici arms in the illumination of the first page.

Leidensis, Bibliotheca Publica Latina, No. 16 B

In the University Library at Leiden. This is a paper MS with 192 folia, with 1 blank, measuring 7⅝ × 11⅝ in., gathered in quinions. There are 31 lines to the page, ruled in ink with single lines on the sides, the margins on the right not well observed. The hand is a running, nonprofessional hand, slightly inclined to the right. The ink is faded in the *Histories,* with occasional words restored in a later hand in black ink. In the catalogue is the following statement: *Emtus e libris Roveri, cuius vid. Catal. I. p. 56, n. 245.* The text begins *Nam Valerium asiaticum* and ends *magnitudine navium potiorem,* with no note or comment of any sort. The title is *Ex Cor. Taciti libro undecimo.* Book 16 ends *conversis in Demetrium;* 17 begins *Initium mihi operis Ser. Galba.* Marginal corrections and insertions are in a minute hand made with a different pen and I should think by a different person. There are a few titular notes, which may well be by the scribe of the MS. There is a third rather scrawly hand that appears two or three times but seems to be unimportant. There are no *finis* notes and no book headings after the first title. The binding is modern brownish leather put on by the Leiden library. Book 20 ends without the *neque vos impunitos patiantur*. There is no Octavia gloss. No 3^d transposition. The MS is definitely a practical one rather than ornamental. There is no illumination. The paper has a watermark known only during the last quarter of the fifteenth century (cf. C. M. Briquet, *Les Filigrames,* 11, G–K, p. 374, No. 6599). The pages are ruled in red ink, often much faded. There are no spaces left for lacunae or omitted words.

Neapolitanus IV. C. 21

This is the MS which was called *Farnesianus* by Lipsius. It is now in the Royal Library in Naples. It measures 8½ × 13 inches, is written on parchment, has 222 leaves gathered in quinions, with dry point ruling, thirty lines to a page, with double vertical lines at the sides. The hand is a rather small, exquisite book hand with a very slight inclination to the right, the same throughout the whole text. There are occasional marginal notes in a different hand. The *Histories* are followed by the *Dialogus* and *Germania* of Tacitus and the fragment of Suetonius, *De grammaticis.* The first page is elaborately illuminated, with a border surrounding the text and the initial N showing a seated monk (front view) reading. Subsequent books, done with fine colors and good spirit, lack the figures of the first and the decoration of the right hand margin. The first title is *C. Cornelii Taciti Romanas Historias scribentis ex his qui repperiuntur Liber primus incipit. Lege feliciter.* Each book has a similar title with slight variations, the numbering of the books being 1–11 instead of the normal 11–21. At the end of each book is τελωσ. The text begins *Nam Valerium Asiaticum.* Book 6 (16) ends *conversus in Demetrium,* with nearly a page left blank except for *hic plurimum deficit.* The next book begins *Initium mei operis Servius Galbea*. There is no confusion of Books 7 and 8 (17 and 18). At Book 20. 15 two and one-half pages are left blank with the note *hic plurimum deficit*. Book 10 (20) ends *neque vos impunitos patiantur,* with the marginal note *deest hic aliquantulum.* The text proper ends with *evenerant* (20. 13), followed by three-quarters of a page blank and a marginal note, *Hic aliquot libri desunt.* Then follow the two excerpts with a blank page between them and a note, *Hic plurimum deficit.* There is no subscription. A striking characteristic of the MS is a very considerable number of spaces left for omitted words, with double rows of dots to indicate the omissions.

Neapolitanus IV. C. 22

This MS, in the Royal Library in Naples, measures 8⅜ × 12¼ inches. It is written on heavy paper in an upright hand whose long down strokes give a most unhappy effect. It is a running hand, wholly without show. There are 41 lines to a page, the pages unnumbered, gathered in quinions. The title is *Cornelii Taciti Actorum Diurnarum Augustae Historiae Liber XI incipit felicit.* This title seems to be in a slightly different hand from the text, certainly written with different ink. In the margin, in a still different hand, *Fraementum.* Book 16 ends *obversis in Demetrium,* with a marginal note, *Hic deficit non parum.* Seventeen begins *Initium mihi operis Servius Galba.* There is no confusion of Books 17 and 18. There is a marginal note, *Cremona a duce Vespasiani crematur anno CCLXXXVI° a primordio sui,* but there are none of the significant notes which appear in the "Genoan" MSS. The text ends with *magnitudine potiorem* (21. 23), followed by *Finis eius quod invenitur Cor. Taciti,* and then, in another hand, something about the Hebraei, with some Hebrew writing in the margin. The MS has many topical notes in the margin throughout.

Neapolitanus IV. C. 23

In the Royal Library in Naples; a MS on heavy paper, 8⅝ × 11⅝ inches, with large margins. It was ruled, but most of the lines have disappeared. There are 28 lines to a page, 194 folios, gathered in quinions, the last gathering a duernion. The last leaf is blank. There are no titles, no corrections, some topical notes. It has a better lettering than N. IV. C. 22 but is in a plain and unpretentious, small, square, careful hand. It begins *Nam Valerium Asiaticum.* A later hand has written above: *Cornelii Taciti Liber XI.* It ends *magnitudine potiorem,* without colophon. There is no confusion of 17 and 18. Book 16 ends *conversis in Demetrium.* Book 17 opens *Inicium michi operis sius Gabba.* At the end there is a late entry, *Antoni Scripandi ex Jani Parrhasii testamento.*

Ottobonianus Latinus. 1422

This is a small Vatican MS on parchment, 8¾ × 12½ in. The leaves are unnumbered after No. 34. There are 30 lines to a page, and the gatherings are quinions. The first page has ambitious illumination representing a monument, with the text as the inscription. There are also good illuminated initials for each book. The hand is a clear, neat, running hand, not unlike that of Vat. Lat. 1864, very legible as well as handsome. The scribe seems to have tired somewhat toward the end, and there are more corrections in the latter part of the MS. The title is *Cornelii Taciti Historiae Fragmentum de rebus gestis imperatorum Lib. XI* (cf. the title of Kop). The text begins *Nam Valerium Asiaticum.* Book 16 ends with *conversus in Demetrium.* Book 17 begins *Initium huius operis servius galba.* There is no confusion of 17 and 18. Book 20 ends *neque vos impuntios patiantur,* without comment. There is a long lacuna in Book 20 (15–62), indicated by two lines left blank and a marginal sign. The text proper ends with *evenerant* (20. 13), followed, after two blank lines, by the two excerpts separated by two blank lines. There is no indication that they are not an integral part of the text. There is no subscription of any sort. The MS has no marginal notes or topics. It has over twenty omissions, which are regularly indicated by a space left blank into which a later hand has occasionally written the word or words omitted. These omissions correspond with omissions in Ottob. Lat. 1748, of which the present manuscript might well be a copy.

Ottobonianus Latinus 1748

This MS is in the Vatican Library, on parchment, with 150 leaves, 200 × 304 mm., 34 lines to the page, gathered in quinions. The writing is in an upright, square, book hand, with topical notes in the margin in a more careless hand. On an extra page at the beginning a later hand has written *Ex codicibus Joannis Angeli Ducis ab Altaemps. De gestis Romanorum.* This is a librarian's entry referring to the purchaser of the Ottoboni collection on the death of Cardinal Colonna in 1611. There are no titles. The text begins at the top of the page, without space for title or illumination: *Nam Valerium asiaticum.* The initial letter is only slightly larger than an ordinary capital and stands in the margin. The remaining books have large illuminated first capitals, and it rather looks as though this first page had been worn out and copied or as though a decorative title page had been originally planned. Book 16 ends with *conversus in demetrium* at the bottom of 71^v; 72^r is blank except for *Hic plurimum deficit* in red; 72^v is wholly blank; and 73^r begins (with a fine initial) *Initium mei operis servius galbea.* There is no confusion of Books 17 and 18. On 137^v begins the long lacuna, with a marginal note *Hic plurimum deficit.* About two pages are left blank. Book 20 ends with *neque vos impunitos patiantur,* without comment. On 147^v the text proper ends with *concordiam pararet. evenerant.* Ten lines are left blank except for the marginal note *Hic parum deficit,* to which a later hand has added *imo aliquot libri desunt.* The *illi veteres* excerpt follows, with *Hic plurimum deficit* at the end, then five blank lines, and then˝the *toleremus* excerpt. No subscription of any sort follows this. The end of the *toleremus* excerpt is rather badly confused. There are some 21 words omitted, with space left for their insertion. These range through the whole text and the second excerpt. They are largely the same as those of 1422. In the margins many names are written in black ink in a careless hand, many (but not *so* many) topics in red ink in a careful hand. This hand has the same characteristic of writing *ci* regularly for *ti* as does the scribe of the MS.

312 *Tacitus*

Parisiensis Regius. 6118

In the Bibliotheque Nationale in Paris, to which it was presented by Carolus de Fresne in 1682. It is on paper, with 230 leaves. The title reads *C. Cornelii Taciti Historici illustris xxx librorum quos aedidit fragmenta incipiunt. primo Liber tertius decimus. vixitque sub Domitiano.* The hand is a clear running hand, carefully aligned, with the margins carefully preserved. There are many marginal notes, but these are mostly topical and of no great interest. The *Annals* begin *Nam Valerium Asiaticum,* and end *magnitudine potiorem.* A colophon reads *Finis. Laus Deo omnipotenti optimo maximo.* There are no book titles after the one with Book 12, but a space of about four lines is always left between books, and the opening words of each book are in capitals. There is no confusion between 17 and 18. The title of 12 is as follows: *C. Cornelii Taciti Fragmenta alterius libri de Agrippina secunda coniuge Claudius et suis consiliis incipiunt.* At the end of the *Annals* in the margin is *deest.* There is no lacuna either in 16 or in 20. There are no excerpts.

Parmensis 861

The information about this MS comes from Sabbadini, "Spogli Ambrosiani Latini," *Studi Italiani di Filologia Classica, 11* (1903), 203 ff.; and from Sabbadini, *St. e Cr.,* pp. 256 ff. The librarian of the Ambrosian Library in Milan, where Sabbadini says the MS is, rather violently denies all knowledge of such a MS, and I was unable to locate it. The Brera Library in Milan has no Tacitus. The MS is said to be on parchment, with 189 leaves, and was written in 1452. The title is *Cornelii Taciti actorum diurnalium liber XI augustae historiae leg. feliciter,* with *fragmentum* in the margin. The text begins *Nam Valerium Asiaticum* and ends *Fabianus in pannonia.* Book 17 begins *Initium mihi operis Servius Galba.* At the end is a note closely resembling the one at the end of Vat. Lat. 1948. It reads, in this case: *In exemplari tantum erat. Si quispiam hinc descripserit sciat me quantum reperi fideliter ab exemplari transcripsisse.* The Cremona note is a replica of that in Vat. Lat. 1958, except that the date in the present case is 1452. On fol. 134, at the end of Book 18, Parmensis has this note: *si repperero finem septimi decimi libri et principium octavi decimi, quae utraque confusa sunt cunctis in libris et varia, locum annotabo; si lector offenderis, et tu signes oro. Valeas qui legeris et recte annotaveris.* The MS has *deficit* in the margin where the inversions occur, and at 182 has this note: *Post haec scriptum erat sed non ut videtur loco. neque vos impunitos patiant: nisi et hic defectus sit textus.* These notes are all in the hand of the copyist, as are two further glosses: 14. 63 (at 57ᵛ), *nunc ischia appellatur;* and 19. 30 (at 142), *status mercatus generales nundinae ut genua allobrogum urbis hodie sunt.*

Urbinas Latinas, 412

On parchment in the Vatican Library. At the bottom of the recto of the second leaf there is a late, crude representation of the arms of Fredericus, Urbini Dux. The binding exhibits the arms of Innocent XI and Cardinal Biancati di Lauria, librarian of the Vatican. The text is on 201 leaves, 8 × 12½ in., and is followed by the *Germania* of Tacitus, beginning on 204ʳ. There is some confusion in the numbering, which is late. There are 34 lines to a page, the ruling is in ink, and the gatherings are quinions. The MS is beautifully illuminated, and the writing is a superb fifteenth-century hand. So far, however, as accuracy of copying is concerned, the MS is careless. There are many corrections in the margins by what appears to be a later hand. Part of these seem to have been intended as corrections, part as alternative readings, but all are, in actual fact, corrections. There are no further glosses or marginal notes. The title is *Cornelii Taciti Historiographi Fragmentum libri undecimi incipit feliciter.* The *Annals* begin *Nam Valerium Asiaticum,* and end *conversus in Demetrium,* with *deficit* in the margin in the original hand and not the corrector's. Six lines are left blank before the colophon, *explicit liber xvi. Inicium mei operis Servius Galbea.* At the end of Book 20, after *neque vos impunitos patiantur,* the corrector has written *hic deficit* in the margin. There is no lacuna in Book 20. There is no confusion between Books 17 and 18. The text ends *Flavianus in Pannonia.* The two excerpts, *illi veteres* and *toleremus,* follow. The corrector calls attention to their places in the text, which he has marked. He says 19th for 20th in the first case. After the second excerpt is the colophon *Cornelii Taciti liber XXI explicit foeliciter.* After four and three-quarter blank pages, the *Germania* begins.

Vaticanus Latinus 1863

A large MS (9 × 12½ in.) on fine parchment in the Vatican Library. It is bound in boards and yellow-brown leather, with the arms of Paulus V and Cardinal Scipio Borghesi, librarian, on the front and back respectively. At the bottom of page 1 are the arms of Paulus II (1464–70). There is no further illumination and no provision for an illuminated initial for Book 11. Later books have fine initials. There are 172 leaves of text; 173 and 174 have been removed, and 175 and 176 are blank. The gatherings are quinions. There are 27 lines to a page, ruled with dry point, with double lines on both sides and at the bottom. The margins are wide, and the hand is an elaborate and beautiful book hand, the lettering uniform throughout. While not always as easy to read as some others, this is perhaps the most beautiful of the Tacitus MSS for its lettering. The title is *Cornelii Taciti Liber XI,* written in red ink in the top margin. The text begins *Nam Valerium Asiaticum* and ends *navium magnitudine potiorem,* with no subscription or marginal note. Book 16 ends *conversis in Demetrium,* with *Hic deficit non parum* in the margin. With the title *Incipit liber XVII Cornelii Taciti,* the first of the *Histories* opens: *Initium mihi operis. Servius Galbea.* There is no confusion between Books 17 and 18. The end of 20 is *neque vos inpunitos patiantur,* without comment on the error. What seems to be a later hand has written *Hic deficit* opposite 20. 46 (fol. 154^r), where one of the inversions causes trouble, and there is also a *hic deficit* at 20. 77 (163^v), where there is no difficulty. There are many topical notes in the MS, some corrections, and a very few double readings. There are some ten words omitted, with spaces left blank.

Vaticanus Latinus 1864

A MS on parchment in the Vatican Library, 170 leaves, 7¾ × 11 in., gathered in quinions. There is an unnumbered page between 167 and 168, so that the last page is actually numbered 169. The volume is bound in boards and yellow-brown leather, with the arms of Paulus V and of Scipio Borghesi, librarian, front and back respectively. The first page is handsomely illuminated. The title is *Incipit Framentum Cornelii Taciti in libro XI°. Feliciter,* and the opening words *Nam Valerium Asyaticum.* The hand is an unpretentious running hand, easy to read. There are no corrections or double readings and only a few topical notes. At the end of the *Annals* (after *conversis in Demetrium*) appears *Cornelii Taciti Liber XVI explicit. Incipit XVII eiusdem secundum quosdam. Initium mei operis Servius Galbea.* Books 17 and 18 are entirely distinct, with the regular *explicit* and *incipit.* Book 20 ends *neque vos inpunitos patiantur.* On 156^r, after *pagis segnem numerum,* there is, in the margin, *hic multum deficit,* and 20. 15–62 is missing. There is a *hic deficit* in the margin on 160^v at 20. 77, but there seems to be no omission. The text ends on 166^v with *concordiam pararet. evenerant,* with *hic deficit* in the margin. The *illi veteres* and *toleremus* excerpts follow, with 1½ blank lines preceding and 2 lines blank, with *hic deficit* in the margin between the two. There is a lacuna in 16. 18–26, noted by *hic deficit.*

Vaticanus Latinus 1958

A large miscellaneous MS on parchment, 9½ × 12½ in., in the Vatican Library. The contents are as follows: 1–19^r, Pliny, *Natural History;* 19^v–22^v, ruled but blank; 23^r–40^v, Leonardo Bruni on the first Carthaginian War; 41^r–90^v, Tacitus, 11–21; 91^r–159^v, Cicero, *Epist. ad Brut.,* and Gregory of Trapezum, *Rhet.* 1–5. The volume is bound in boards and red morocco, with the arms of Pius IX and Cardinal A. Lambruschini, librarian. The hands vary in the various parts, as does also the size of the page. The Tacitus portion is in columns, 43 lines to a page, written in several small but exquisite fifteenth-century hands. The columns are ruled individually, both vertically and horizontally. The date is 1449. It has a great number of abbreviations. The title is *Cornelii Taciti historiae Augustae Liber XI actorum diurnalium.* This title is regularly repeated with each book, sometimes with change of order. At the end of Book 11 there is simply *finis XI lib.* At the end of 12: *Finis XII. die IIII° kl'as august.* There are minor additions, such as *feliciter.* Book 16 ends *obversis in Demetrium,* with a marginal note: *hic est defectus textus.* The *Histories*

begin *Initivom m̄ operis Servius Galba.* In this MS *m̄* is regularly the abbreviation for *mihi.* There is no break between Books 17 and 18, but a later hand has noted, in the proper place in the margin, *Lib. XVIII.* Book 20 ends *interpretabatur. finis vicesimi voluminis.* The regular *explicit* follows in faded red, but in the margin is *post hoc scriptum erat sed non suo ut videtur loco: neque vos inpunitos patiantur. nisi et hic defectus sit textus.* The text proper ends on 90ᵛ, line 17, *fabianus in Pannonia.* The rest of the page is ruled but left blank. In the margin opposite the next to the last line begins a ten-line note as follows (expanding the abbreviations): *In exemplari tantum erat. Si quispiam hinc descripserit novum sciat me quantum repperi fideliter ab exemplo transscripsisse quod inter cetera de quibus scitur non est neque pessimum neque mendosissimum.   die septimadecima Octobris ab ortu salvatoris nostri domini Jesu Christi anno* M.CCCC XLVIIII° *genuae pridie festum Divi lucae evangelistee.* A note at 19. 30 reads as follows: *Status mercatus. generales nundinae ut genuae allobrogum urbis hodie sunt.* There is another significant note on 78ʳ in the margin opposite 19. 34: *Cremona condita est annis* abhinc MDCC.XL. *quo etiam tempore Ariminum et Benebentum Aedificantur. hodie autem ab ortu creatoris sunt anni* MCCCCXLVIIII° *quo haec excribuntur.* The *sunt* and *excribuntur* are slightly doubtful readings. Dom Henri Quentin, *Essais de Critique Textuelle* (Paris, 1926), p. 167, argues that the scribe of 1958 was Jean Andreas de Bussi. If true, this might well account for the many "improvements" in the MS. As an editor of Pliny in 1469 and of numerous texts for Sweynheim and Pannartz, de Bussi was definitely radical.

Vaticanus Latinus 2965

This MS on paper (8¾ × 11½ in.) is in the Vatican Library. On the spine of the parchment binding are the arms of Pius VI. There are 107 leaves plus two blank leaves of the same paper and one which is doubtful. The gatherings are quinions. The number of lines to a page varies from 37 to 48. There is no ruling, and the size of the writing varies greatly. The paper is of the finest quality and in a perfect state of preservation. The writer seems to have been interested in the subject matter more than in the appearance of his copy. There is no decoration of any sort, and the hand is hardly professional. It is between a book hand and a running hand, and carelessly written. The heavy down strokes of *f* and *s* make an ugly page, and the whole is crowded irregularly. The title is *Cornelii Taciti quod reperitur*. This title may possibly be a later addition. There are no numbers to books or any other extraneous helps. The text begins *Nam Valerium Asiaticum*. There are many topical notes in Book 11 but no others except during the exchange of speeches between Nero and Seneca. The *Annals* end *conversus in Demetrium*. In the margin appears *Hic plurimum deficit*. After one and one-half blank leaves: *Initium mei operis Servius Galbea*. Nearly two pages are left blank after *Hist*. 4. 15, where the long lacuna occurs. There is no marginal comment. Book 20 ends *neque vos impunitos patiebantur*. The text proper ends *concordiam pararet. evenerant,* with *hic deficit* in the margin. After a space of five lines begins the *illi veteres* excerpt, followed by the *toleremus* excerpt, with a four-line space separating the two. In the margin opposite each set of blank lines is *hic deficit*. There is no subscription.

Venetus 381

A small parchment MS in the Biblioteca Nazionale di San Marco in Venice. The pages measure 7¾ × 10½ inches, the writing 4½ × 6⅞ inches. There are 212 leaves, the first and the last two blank. The first page has a bookplate—a lion of St. Mark with a raised sword, and the motto *custor vel ultor,* and below: *MDCCXXII. Hieronymi Venerii Equitis ac D.M. Procuratoris Praesidis Cura.* Above this plate are two inscriptions, a Latin and a Greek. The former reads *Huius libri cornelii taciti nichil plus reperitur. Caret principio et fine, ut apparet. In medio quoque non nulla deficiunt. Hic liber est mei b. Car! Tusculani bōn Legati scriptus bōn constitit ducatis quatordecim decem. Oct. 1453.* The latter part of this inscription is repeated on the last page of the MS and confirms the ownership of Bessarion: Bōn = Bononiae. Bessarion gave it to St. Mark's with his other MSS in 1468. There seems to be no evidence that it was copied, as Voigt thought, from a MS owned by Francesco Barbaro, who copied L. 68. 2 while it was in Niccoli's possession. The ending of Ven. 381 is against this theory. The MS, gathered in quinions, has 27 lines to a page, ruled in ink, with single side lines. The hand is a small upright book hand, consistent throughout. The title is *Ex Cornelii Taciti Historici Libro Undecimo.* The text begins *Nam Valerium asyaticum.* Book 16 ends *conversis in Demetrium,* and at this point, 96ʳ, there is a marginal note, *Hic non parum deficit.* Book 17 has the title *Cornelii Taciti Historiarum Liber decimus septimus. Incipit.* The book opens *Inicium mihi operis Servius Galba.* There is no confusion of Books 17 and 18. At 20. 77 there is a *deficit* in the margin. Book 20 ends *neque vos impunitos patiantur,* without comment, and the text as a whole ends *magnitudine potiorem.* There is no colophon. Some half-dozen words have been omitted, with spaces left for them; there are a very few topical notes in the margins which have been trimmed for rebinding.

Vindobonensis 49

This MS, in the Palatine Collection in the Royal Library at Vienna, contains, in addition to the eleven historical books, the *Germania* and the *Dialogus*. It is a large MS on parchment, with 236 leaves. It has had other numbers in the past (Goelzer and others cite it as 351 and Endlicher as 242), and it is often called *Sambuci*, because it once belonged to Sambucus. It is said by Endlicher to have at the front *arma regiae domus Aragonis-Neapolitanae*. Peterson (ed. *Dial.*, p. lxxii) says that it has the arms of Matthias Corvinus. These two statements are not necessarily inconsistent and may indicate a definite period of Corvinus' career. The text ends *magnitudine potiorem*. There are no titles. The hand is a handsome book hand, with almost no corrections and no marginal notes. The first page has the library citation, as follows: *No. 351 Cornelius Tacitus Eius Ab excessu Divi Augusti Annalium Lib. XI*. At the bottom of the page, upside down: *Cornelius Tacitus*. These are not contemporary inscriptions. The first leaf of text is elaborately illuminated in the tombstone architectural style but the page intrudes on this, in fact (in the photograph) looks superimposed. There are no titles or colophons except a simple *Finis* at the end. A scrawly later hand has added *Deese videntur non pauca*. The same hand also wrote in the space of four lines left blank between the *Germania* and the *Dialogus: De oratoribus suis et antiquis comparatis Quinctil*. At the end of the *Histories* the scrawly hand has written (20. 23) *desunt pauca*. The sixteenth book ends *conversis in Demetrium*, and the seventeenth begins *Initium mihi Servus Galba*.

Yalensis 1 (formerly known as Budensis)

This is a small, nearly square, MS on parchment in the Sterling Library of Yale University at New Haven. The pages measure 265 × 190 mm., the text 180 × 115 mm. The writing is humanistic Italian, a rather small book hand, square to round, not beautiful but reasonably good. There are 196 folios in 24 quaternions, with a union at the beginning and another at the end. The pages are ruled throughout. The first two folios and the last one and one-half are without writing. There are normally 28 lines to a page, but those pages with illuminated initials vary from 24 to 28 lines per page. There are no titles or colophons. Illuminated initials indicate the openings of books. This is true of Book 18, although other MSS of the same group do not distinguish Books 17 and 18. The text begins *Nam Valerium, asiaticum* and Book 16 ends *obversis in demetrium,* with a small *hic multum deficit* in the margin and a space of one line left blank. Book 17 begins *Initium michi operis servius galba.* The text ends *flavianus in Parma; gra. deo.* The MS has the Octavia gloss in Book 14. There are corrections and marginal notes by numerous hands. The binding is contemporary and elaborate, with the crow of Matthew Corvinus front and back. It is red morocco on hard wood boards decorated in part with blind tooling, in part with gold nails driven into the leather. On the first page is this inscription: *Hic liber sumptus est ex bibliotheca Budensi, jussu impensaque Matthaei Corvini Hungariae Boimiaeque Regis scriptus.* This surrounds a Corvinus coat of arms which, by its type, serves to date the MS as about 1475. The MS has the look of a commercial product and was probably made to order for Corvinus. It was used by Beatus Rhenanus in making his first scholarly edition of the *Annals* and *Histories.* Oberlin, in his edition of 1801 (Praef., p. xiv), says that it was loaned to him by a military officer named Dorsner, who had inherited it. Eventually it returned to Hungary into the possession of the Teleki family, who sold it in 1934.

Yalensis 2

This is an oblong MS belonging to Branford College, Yale University, New Haven, Connecticut. It is on deposit in the Sterling Library. The material is parchment, the pages measuring 230×316 mm., the writing 135×195. There are 205 leaves (206 is cut off), with 26 lines to the full page. The sheets are carefully ruled, the writing is a professional book hand of the fifteenth century, and the execution is consistently careful and excellent throughout. It has an eighteenth-century Italian binding. There are no titles, colophons, or illuminated initials. The MS is almost wholly unedited, showing only a very few corrections in a minute hand. There are no marginal comments or topics of any sort. *Ann.* 11 begins *Am Valerium Asiaticum; Ann.* 16 ends *obversis in demetrium, deficit multum.* This last is on 91ᵛ, the rest of which is left blank. On 92ʳ: *nitium mihi operis servius galba.* The text ends on 205ᵛ, *flavianus in parma.* It has the "Octavia" gloss complete. The so-called "third inversion" is corrected and there is no lacuna in Book 20.

Yalensis 3

This is a small volume on vellum with a modern binding, in the Sterling Library of Yale University. It has 220 leaves gathered in 27 quaternions and one duernion. The pages measure 155 mm. × 263 mm. There are 26 lines to the page, except for 23 on page one, 24 on the first page of the *Histories,* and 25 on 201ᵛ. All pages are ruled with lead, with double side rules. An illuminated border on the first page was added at a later date, as indicated by its avoidance of annotations in the margin. The border is lavish but rather poor and looks like an imitation of the much finer Florentine borders on some of the Medici MSS. The proportions and many of the characteristics of this border are reminiscent of the illumination on the first page of Budensis 9. It has been claimed as the work of Nicola Rapicano, who worked at the court of Ferdinand I of Naples until 1488. The coat of arms would seem to be that of Alfonso II, Duke of Calabria from 1448 to 1495. The title on 1ʳ is in gold capitals contemporary with the illuminated border and reads *Fragmentum. Libri. undecimi. Cornelii. Taciti. Feliciter. Incipit.* The text begins *Nam valerium asiaticum;* the *Annals* end on 82ᵛ, about the middle of the page, with *conversus in demetrium.* Fols. 83ʳ and 83ᵛ are ruled but blank; 84ʳ has two blank lines, then *Initium mei operis Servius Galba.* The volume ends on 218ᵛ, six lines from the top of the page: *flavianus in pannonia,* with a colophon in capitals: *Finis eius quod Cornelii Taciti reperitur.* The handwriting is of two sorts. Up to the middle of line 11 on 126^r it is somewhat angular, slightly reminiscent of Gothic, and is extraordinarily uniform and carefully done throughout. The rest of the MS is in the ordinary, round humanistic hand of Italy of the latter half of the fifteenth century and is less uniform and less carefully done. The space on the page occupied by writing is slightly less after the change of hand. At the bottom of 175^v the last half of the last line is left blank; at the top of 176^r the first line consists of *Hic est fragmentatus.* There is no apparent lacuna. A similar interruption occurs within a page on 205^v. Yalensis 3 has no lacuna in Book 16. At 20. 16 a line is left blank, with a note *Hic est fragmentatus,* but there is no lacuna. The same note occurs without lacuna at 20. 77. It does not have the two excerpts at the end, nor the Octavia gloss.

Zaragozza

This MS is in the Biblioteca del Real Seminar de san Carlos de Zaragozza, No. 9439. The catalogue of the library states that it is a sixteenth-century MS, 310 × 200 mm., script 198 × 106 mm. There are 393 leaves, of which 6 are blank. No complete description is available but such indications as there are suggest either a Group I MS or a mixed MS. It has a handsomely illuminated first page, illustrated in the 1943 catalogue of the library. No title appears in the illustration. The library title is *Cornelli Taciti Historiarum Libri xi usque ad XXI.*

Goettingen. Fragmentum

This is in the Morbio Collection of fragments of classical authors, Universitats Bibliothek.

       No. 2. a. 2 fols. of Plautus
              b. 1 fol. of Cicero
              c. 6 fols. of Tacitus. 295 × 190 mm.
      XV Cent. Hist. I. 81–85
              d. 3 fols. of Priscian

Bodleianus Landensis. 52

This is a miscellaneous collection of extracts in a paper MS of folio form. There are 100 folios and it was written in the fifteenth century. On fol. 91ᵛ appears *Oratio Senecae ad Neronem ex Tacito cum responsione.*

Vaticanus Latinus 5393

This is a paper MS with excerpts from Caesar and Tacitus, late fifteenth or early sixteenth century, of no value.

Ambrosianus. C. 141 inf.

This is a MS in the Ambrosian Library, Milan, from the early fifteenth century, entitled *Extractus de xiii libro Cornelii cociti.* It contains the speeches of Nero and Seneca to each other, taken from *Annals* 14. 53–56. The *cociti* is perhaps significant as indicating ignorant copying of Lombard writing.

Berlin, Royal Library MS. lat. Oct. 197. Codex Phillipsianus Cheltenhamensis 7283

Parchment with 118 leaves. The Suetonius fragment is contained in 6ʳ–19ʳ. The rest of the MS is miscellaneous but is reported to have excerpts of Tacitus.

There are scattered throughout the editions of Tacitus numerous mentions of, or citations from, MSS that no longer exist, perhaps in some cases never did exist. The MS Institutionis Oratoris Jesu in Paris, used by Dotteville and seen by Brotier, was undoubtedly destroyed by the French revolutionists. The MS Corbinelli, cited by Brotier, was a collation on the text of Beroaldus. Walther thought that it was probably one of the Vatican MSS; Brotier was inclined to think it might be the one from the Oratory. Lipsius had a collation of a MS which he called both Hispanus and Covarruviae, made for him by Andreas Schott. In 1602 there appeared a pamphlet signed Pompeius Lampugnanus (supposed to have been Marquard Freher): *Collatio notarum Justi Lipsii in Cornelium Tacituum cum MS Mirandulano. Bergami 8ᵛᵒ*. Lipsius replied to it in

1607 with a violent denunciation, holding that the writer had simply pretended to have a MS. Orelli lists a MS at Grenoble. Haekel's catalogue of the university library MSS there (p. 160) gives *Taciti Annal. lib. xi cum picturis. Sec. xvi membranaceus 4°*. The Bamberg MS cited by Lipsius seems to result from a confusion with the Bamberg fragments of the *Germania*. I. Scheykius, in commenting on Velleius in Burmann's edition, p. 504, cites a MS Herbipolensis. Oberlin tried to confirm the existence of this but was informed by the librarian of the cathedral library where it was supposed to be that there was no such MS. N. Heinsius in his notes in the Ernesti-Oberlin edition cites three times a MS Spinae. One citation is from *Hist.* 5. 25, indicating that the MS, if it was real, contained the full text. Finally, Ernesti, Croll, and Ruperti list, without comment or explanation, a MS S. Joannis in Carbonaria, which has eluded identification.

17. MANUSCRIPT AFFILIATIONS, BOOKS XI–XXI

T HE FIRST edition of *Ann.* 11–21 was printed by Spira (*ca.* 1470) from a MS very closely resembling the one now in Venice. Puteolanus followed (*ca.* 1480) with a text taken from a MS of the same sort as Vat. Lat. 1958. Beatus Rhenanus (in 1533) used the Budensis from the library of Matthias Corvinus. After his edition there was not much change in the text until the first edition of Lipsius (1574), who had the advantage of using three Vatican MSS, one of which was certainly Vat. Lat. 1864. Pichena (1607) was the first to realize the incomparable value of the so-called second Medicean (Laurent. 68. 2) and make it the basis of his text. Other MSS were from time to time used, but from Pichena's day the Medicean has been generally looked upon as the source of all the others, in spite of Ernesti's *non audeam affirmare.* The Teubner and Oxford texts are based solely on the Medicean. Some evaluation of the other MSS has been attempted, but usually as a matter of special pleading, showing the unusual value of this or that MS.

In the last generation, at least five hitherto unrecognized MSS of these books have been called to the attention of scholars, and the Budensis and Agricola after long seclusion, have been rediscovered. In publishing in 1925 two Vatican MSS that he was the first to find, Felix Grat argued for the independent value of Vat. 1958, which he believed represented a tradition not deriving from the Medicean. Dom Henri Quentin supported him in this position. Neither of them showed a comprehensive knowledge of the MSS or recognized the essential groupings, and both were much concerned over a particular method of textual criticism which is at least of limited value. But their citations did confirm to some extent the doubt which has never really died since it was expressed by Ernesti. The long lost Agricola MS has been even more convincing.

Laurentian 68. 2, better known as the Medicean, is the only extant MS older than the fifteenth century. There is general agreement that it is written in the Beneventan script characteristic of Monte Cassino in the eleventh and twelfth centuries.

There is rumor of another MS in Poggio's day. In his letter to Niccoli of Oct. 21, 1427 (III, 15), he mentions having seen another copy of this part of Tacitus in 'antique characters" (i.e. in the contemporary professional hand) and readable, which he suggests may have been written by Coluccio. Nothing further is known of it. That there were other MSS extant in 1449 is indicated by the note at the end of Vat. 1958 which says that its scribe used a text *quod inter cetera de quibus scitur non est neque pessimum neque mendosissimum,* and his original was certainly neither the Medicean nor a direct copy of it.

Today there are thirty-two known MSS of Tacitus, 11–21. They all stem from a common archetype which was written after the formation of the thirty-book corpus first mentioned by Jerome. They all begin abruptly within Book 11: *Nam Valerium Asiaticum.* They all have lost the latter part of Book 16, consistently ending this book in the middle of a sentence: *conversus* [or *conversis* or *obversis*] *in Demetrium.* They all have two misplaced passages (19. 7–9 and 19. 67–69) caused by the wrong folding of a sheet in each of two gatherings. None of them goes beyond chapter 26 of Book 21. The exact point of ending varies and furnishes a basis for grouping the MSS:

GROUP I	GROUP II
(ends *evenerant,* 21. 13)	(ends *potiorem,* 21. 23)
Budensis 9 (a later hand has extended to ending II)	Leidensis B P L. 16. B
Kopenhagen 496	Neapolitanus IV. C. 22
Laurentianus 68. 4	Neapolitanus IV. C. 23
Neapolitanus IV. C. 21	Parisiensis Regius 6118
Ottobonianus 1422	Vaticanus Latinus 1863
Ottobonianus 1748	Venetus 381
Vaticanus Latinus 1864	Vindobonensis 49
Vaticanus Latinus 2965	

GROUP III	Laurentianus 68. 2
(ends *Fabianus in Pannonia*, 21. 26)	Laurentianus 68. 5
	Malatestinus
Bodleianus 27605	Parmensis 861
Bodleianus 34372	Urbinas Latinus 412
Gudianus 118	Vaticanus Latinus 1958
Harleianus 2764	Yalensis I
Jesus College 109	Yalensis II
Laurentianus 63. 24	Yalensis III

About the MSS in Holkham Hall and Zaragozza, I have not sufficient information to make possible assignment to a group. In Group III the ending is in several cases deceptive, for four of these MSS prove on examination to be composite with sources from other groups than III. These are Laurentianus 63. 24, Laurentianus 68. 5, Urbinas 412, and Yalensis III. It might also be noted here that Laurentianus 68. 4 is listed with Group I because of its general characteristics, although it alone ends with Book 18. Also, Kopenhagen 496 agrees in readings with Group III in Books 11–13 but with group I in all other readings and in its ending.

Before proceeding to analyze the relationships between these groups and between MSS within the groups, it is necessary to take note of two MSS which in text readings show practically no affinity to one group more than another and which show at least two thousand variants from each other. These are Laurentian 68. 2 and Leidensis B P L. 16. B. On the relation between these two depends the acceptance of a single or two-fold source for our MSS and the text reading in an extensive number of instances. It will therefore be considered at considerable length.

Since 1607 when Pichena published his text of Tacitus 11–21, based on the Medicean MS, Laur. 68. 2, it has been the generally accepted doctrine that either the Medicean itself or a copy of it made before the loss of the four pages missing since the fifteenth century is the source of all our MSS of these books. This theory was the more readily accepted because the Medicean is the only MS known which is older than the fifteenth century, written as it was in the eleventh or twelfth, and the variations from it in the other known MSS are not such as to make this theory absolutely impossible. Theodore Ryck did, in the late seventeenth century, publish readings from a fifteenth century MS, once the property of Rudolph Agricola, which showed marked divergences from the Medicean but so firmly was the pre-eminence of the latter established that little attention was paid to Ryck's discovery. Even his integrity as a scholar was questioned, the suggestion gained ground that the MS was a fiction of his imagination, and the MS itself disappeared. Now it has been identified as the B P L 16. B, in the university library at Leiden, and proves indeed to show a tradition independent of the Medicean.

The most striking characteristic of Leidensis which indicates a source independent of the other MSS is the absence of what has been called the "third inversion." In Book 20 the common ancestor of all MSS except Leidensis suffered an accident by reason of which a body of text equivalent to thirty-seven lines of our Teubner edition and comprising all but nine words of chapters 52 and 53 became displaced and intruded itself between the words *pecunia* and *tanta* of chapter 46. This was evidently the result of a wrong folding of the second sheet from the center of a gathering, which produced the following order of pages for the gathering:

| 1/2 | 9/10 | 3/4 | 5/6 | 7/8 | 11/12 |

In consequence of this shift of material there were scrambled sentences at three points, obvious in the following diagram:

46. pelli poterant.   Sed
    immensa pecunia   ↑   tanta vis hominum retinenda erat.
                                        Ingressus castra—

52. sermone orasse | ferunt ne criminan- |
                    | tium . . . defuisse | dicebatur. Audita—53

The resulting scrambles were:
1. sed immensa pecunia / ferunt ne criminantium—
2. defuisse / tanta vis hominum retinenda erat.
3. sermone orasse / dicebatur. Audita—

In general, our MSS present these readings. In those of Group I the operation occurred within the text later lost in the long lacuna of that group so that only (1), preserved in the *toleremus* excerpt, appears in these MSS. Group II MSS have *fere* or *fēr* for *ferunt* in (1). The Medicean and the MSS of Group III have a fragmentary *crede* in (2) before *tanta*. It looks as though a common ancestor of this group had felt the need of a verb and had started to write *credebatur,* had noted his error but had failed to expunctuate. The MSS of the Genoan group in Class III have attempted to improve on this mistaken reading by expanding *crede* to *creditum quo.* This is the only attempt at correction (except in two Yale MSS), in spite of the fact that practically all MSS note the difficulties in the margin.

The two Yale MSS, Y¹ and Y², have restored the misplaced passage to its original location in the text but not without clear evidence that it *is* a replacement and *not* an originally correct reading. In Y¹ the first junction becomes *pelli poterant. Ingressus ob haec castra.* The *ob haec,* written above the line, but by the scribe of the MS, is obviously a conscious improvement, but *sed immensa pecunia* has disappeared entirely, as has also *ferunt.* The second junction becomes *sermone orasse dicebatur. ne criminantium,* the break having been wrongly interpreted. The third junction becomes *defuisse creditum quo tanta vis hominum retinenda erat. Audita.* Two of the three breaks have been wrongly restored. Y² attained somewhat different results. The first junction becomes *pelli poterant. Sed immensa pecunia ferme. Ingressus castra;* the second, *orasse dicebatur. ne criminantium;* the third, *defuisse tanta vis hominum retinenda erat. Audita.* The *crede* or *creditum quo* has been jettisoned, but *tanta vis hominum retinenda erat* has been misplaced, as well as *dicebatur.* The inaccuracies in the restoration seem to be in part at least due to spaces left in the Genoan source to indicate breaks in the sense.

Puteolanus' was the first printed text to restore the order of this passage, and it follows Y¹ but without including the *ob haec.* Croll, in the Bipontine edition of 1779, was the first to restore the five words *tanta vis hominum retinenda erat* from chapter 53 to chapter 46, but he retained various traces of the mutilation. It was not until Halm's edition of 1857 that the present-day reading was established. In his 1928 edition Andresen still read in a footnote *Verum ordinem praeeunte Puteolano restituit Agricola*. But Agricola died in 1485 and his MS must therefore have been written before the appearance of Puteolanus' edition.

This MS of Agricola (Leidensis) reads exactly as our printed text reads today with the single exception of *dicebatur* in chapter 53 for *credebatur*. As indicated above, *dicebatur* is probably correct. That the scribe of Leidensis should have attempted a restoration of the text, as did the scribes of Y^1 and Y^2, would not be an impossibility, though hardly consistent with his general procedure. But that either he or his source restored the passage perfectly in ·the face of the distortions which had accumulated over the centuries would be little short of miraculous. The conclusion is almost inescapable that Leidensis follows a tradition in which there had been no displacement of material in this portion of the text.

This matter of the "third inversion," while convincing, is by no means the only evidence that Leidensis represents a tradition independent of the Medicean tradition. A comparison of the readings of M. and Leidensis shows that the thousand variants listed by Ryck are less than half of the actual total. A study of Book 11 will indicate their significance. The Koestermann text is based primarily on M. Nevertheless it accepts *Italicus* (chapter 16) for *Italus* as an emendation by Agricola as well as 45 other readings of Leidensis ascribed as emendations to Puteolanus, Rhenanus, Lipsius, etc. There are in all 195 significant readings in which M. and Leidensis disagree. In 49 of these Leidensis is clearly wrong and M. clearly right; in 52, M. is clearly wrong and Leidensis right. Of the remaining 94 differences, 41 are relatively minor—matters of word order and variation between *et, ac,* and *atque,* or between singular and plural. Koestermann quite naturally accepts the reading of M. in 49 of the remaining 53 cases. But if M. had read in chapter 2, as Leidensis does, *sciscitatus* instead of *scrutatus,* the reading would have been accepted without question. Both fit the situation and both are Tacitean. Similarly, in the same chapter, *indicto silentio* and *victo silentio* are equally apt. Except for 6 passages which show major variations, the choice between M. and Leidensis is largely a question of individual preference. The 6 cases should be considered individually.

11. 4. M: *nesteris* (= *Mnesteris*); Leidensis: *Valerii.* Valerius Asiaticus is presented as a victim of Messalina. She suspects him of adultery with Poppaea. Mnester appears nowhere in the discussion and is at no time accused of improper relations with Poppaea. The reading *Valerii* seems sure.

11. 10. M: *positusque regiam;* Leidensis: *potitusque rerum.* Editors have accepted *potitus* as an emendation, which is, however, unsatisfactory, as *potior* with the accusative would be unique in Tacitus. *Regiam* would be unexpected in the context, and *rerum* is more suitable, especially as the discussion began *turbatae Parthorum res.*

11. 22. M: *velut;* Leidensis: *voluit ut.* The clause runs *donec sententia Dolabellae velut* (or *voluit ut*) *venumdaretur,* the subject of the verb being *quaestura.* The chapter began with *P. Dolabella censuit,* and the Leidensis reading gives a more suitable concluding phrase. Either reading, if it were the only one we had, would be acceptable. The constuction with *ut* does not occur elsewhere in Tacitus but does in Livy.

11. 30. This case presents a serious problem in interpretation. The marriage of Silius and Messalina is being discussed before Claudius, and Narcissus is giving his opinion of what should be done to Silius. Narcissus says that he is not going to press a charge of adultery *ne domum servitia et ceteros fortunae paratus reposceret.* M. follows with *frueretur immo his et redderet uxorem rumperetque tabulas nuptiales.* Editors have accepted Acidalius' emendation of *et* to *set* and have interpreted *ne* as *nedum.* They make Claudius or Narcissus the subject of *reposceret,* which they render as "ask back." None of this is wholly satisfactory. Leidensis reads: *cogeretur una cum his et reddere uxorem rumpereque tabulas nuptiales.* This re-

quires no emendation. The subject of *reposceret* is Silius, and its meaning is that which Tacitus gives it in all six passages in which he uses it, "to demand as a right." The contrast between *adulteria* and *uxorem* is made sharper.

11. 31. M: *quis fatentibus certium ceteri circumstrepunt.* Leidensis: *quibus dubitantibus et incertis ceteri circumstrepunt.* It is obvious that *certium* in M. is wrong, and Puteolanus changes it to *certatim* as read by Koestermann. The situation is the inquiry by Claudius into the wedding of Silius and Messalina. Two witnesses have been called on from the council of friends summoned. If they "confess," it can only mean that they confirm the charge against Silius. They have nothing to confess on their own part. The Leidensis reading, presenting them as hesitating to give evidence which must be distasteful to the emperor, gives a better contrast with *ceteri circumstrepunt* and requires no emendation.

11. 35. M: *custodem a Silio Messalinae datum;* Leidensis: *custodem Silio et Messalinae dat.* Titius Proculus is the person referred to. By the reading of M. he is included among the victims, although he has given evidence. The logic of the situation favors Leidensis.

In addition to these cases in which both readings are possible but that of Leidensis seems preferable, chapter 18 offers two widely different readings between which it is difficult to choose. M: *feruntque militem quia vallum non accinctus atque alium quia pugione tantum accinctus foderet morte punitos.* Leidensis: *erantque milites quia vallum non accincti foderent morte puniti.* It is possible that *atque alium . . . accinctus* dropped out because of the repetition of *accinctus,* but it is also possible that it represents a marginal note which crept in. In either case the tradition which did not have it in the text diverged radically at some stage from the tradition which had it.

The cases in which M. is most seriously wrong and in which Leidensis offers a solution are the following. In each instance (with the exception of *quemque* in chapter 31, already accepted as a conjecture of Agricola) the reading of Leidensis settles a difficulty still present in our accepted text.

11. 1. M: *contionem;* Leidensis: *in contione.* The reading of the Medicean makes no sense. Andresen read *contionem in,* after Nipperdey, who compared the postpositive use of the preposition with *unum intra damnum* in 3. 72. There are better examples of the usage in Tacitus, but none with *in.* Leidensis furnishes the solution.

11. 6. The question of fees for counsel is under discussion. M. reads: *quodsi in nullius mercedem negotiantur* [*ur* is erased] *pauciora fore.* To satisfy the need of a noun editors have read *negotia tueantur.* Leidensis furnishes a different and better solution: *quodsi in nullius mercedem negotiantur pauciora fore crimina.*

11. 7. The reading of M., *tacere,* is impossible, because what they say follows immediately. Leidensis reads *dicere.*

11. 7. In the same chapter the need of a verb after *pecuniis* has always been recognized. Koestermann retains the *posuit* of Andresen, but Orelli had conjectured *statuit,* which proves to be the reading of Leidensis.

11. 10. M: *et recuperare Armeniam habeat.* To make sense Lipsius changed *habeat* to *avebat,* which still persists, but Leidensis offers the more probable *in animo habebat.*

11. 14. The reading of M., *publico dis,* makes no sense, but if the original was *publicandis,* as given in Leidensis, it is not difficult to understand the scribe's mistake: he took *publico* with *aere* and changed *fixis* to *fixo* to agree, thus leaving *dis plebiscitis,* with no meaning, to be bracketed in modern editions.

11. 16. M: *Augustus,* quite impossible and caused by the carelessness of the scribe who wrote *Caesar Augustus pecunia* for *Caesar aggesta pecunia,* which appears correctly in Leidensis.

11. 22. M: *desenoni,* with a short space following. This has led to the ingenious suggestion *de se non infitiatus,* but Leidensis shows that the actual reading was *de se confessus.*

11. 28. The confusion in this case is more extensive. M: *dum histrio cubiculum principis exultabero.* The impossible last word is surely a corruption of *adulterio.* Tacitus makes a contrast between the secret disgrace of adultery in the emperor's home and public revolutionary action against the throne. *Histrio* would refer to Mnester, neatly contrasted with *iuvenem nobilem* in what follows. This very neatness evidently induced the reading, for Leidensis, with the conviction that goes with the harder reading, has what seems to be correct: *dum inservit cubiculum principis adulterio.*

11. 30. M: *quod ei cis vetticis plautios dissimulavisset.* This meaningless scramble is straightened out by the reading of Leidensis: *quod cicios vectios plautios dissimulavisset.* Confusion of *c* and *t* is not uncommon in Leidensis, nor the oratorical plural in Tacitus. Narcissus is defending himself for not having informed about *Titius* Proculus (35), and *Vettius* Valens (31), and *Plautius* Lateranus (36).

11. 31. M. omits the essential *quemque* in *tum potissimum ⟨quemque⟩ amicorum vocat.* Leidensis produces it.

11. 35. Leidensis furnishes a reasonable sense for the last four words of the sentence: *Eadem constantia et illustres equites Romani cupido maturae necis fuit.* The brackets may now be removed: *equites Romanos cupidos maturae necis fecit.*

Leidensis has readings which are surely wrong but indicate a different tradition: 11. 1, *emptos* for *coeptos;* 3, *imperio* for *impetu;* 29, *per potentiam* for *peritus et potentiam;* 31, *qua non alia* for *non alias;* 32, *auspicia marito* for *aspici a marito;* 38, *om. Epulanti,* which may conceivably be a gloss that has slipped into the text of the other tradition.

A selection of readings from the other books will be sufficient to confirm the conclusions which seem already clear.

In the account of Agrippina's death, in 14. 8, Anicetus has just broken into her room to carry out Nero's instructions to murder his mother. Our text, with the Medicean MS, reads *protendens uterum "ventrem feri" exclamavit multisque vulneribus confecta est.* As the last words of an important character, this quotation is extremely bald, wholly lacking in both distinction and significance. Leidensis reads *protendens uterem "hunc" exclamavit "hunc feri monstrum qui tale tulit" multisque vulneribus confecta est.* Of the last words of Agrippina this is certainly a more notable version. It comes closer also to Dio Cassius' report (61. 13): καὶ τὴν γαστέρα ἀπογυμνώσασα, παῖε ταύτην, ἔφη, παῖε, ᾿Ανίκητε, ὅτι Νέρωνα ἔτεκεν. Furthermore, it preserves the dramatic force of the words without directly naming Nero. Agrippina has pretended up to this point that she did not believe that her son was the guilty party, revealing her real conviction in these last words, mildly cryptic in the Tacitean version. One group of MSS has incorporated in the text at this point a long quotation from the "Senecan" *Octavia* which was presumably a marginal gloss and which would be much more readily suggested by the Leidensis reading than by the Medicean.

In 14. 32, M. reads perfectly clearly exactly what our texts have: *visamque speciem in aestuario Tamesae subversae coloniae.* Leidensis reads: *visamque speciem noctu motam esse subversae coloniae.* If the split in tradition originated when the text was written continuously, probably in capitals— INESTUARIOTAMESE—the first step may have been *in aestu motam esse,* or, as some MSS show, *mestu notam esse.* If all our MSS derive from M., it is hard to understand such a confusion as this.

In 15. 2, M. reads *in absitium suum,* which is obviously corrupt. Koestermann reads *in exitium suum,* which is attractive because of *numquam ipsis prospere lacessitam,* preceding. But *absitium* from *exitium* is not easy. Leidensis reads *obsidium.* In 11. 10 Tacitus uses *obsidium* to mean "hostageship," and in our present case it has just been remarked that the Romans did not lead the incursion under discussion but that it was *temeritate obsidis per tot annis inter mancipia habiti.* If the archetype had the word *obsidium* in this unusual sense, the mistake of M. is more understandable and Leidensis may well be correct.

The text of M. in 15. 14 has never been questioned: *illum locum tempusque consilio destinatum quid de Armenia cer-*

*nerent adiecisse deos dignum Arsacidarum simul et de legioni-
bus Romanis statuerent.* Editors have changed *et* to *ut* and
have noted that nowhere else does Tacitus use *dignus* with the
genitive. The reading of Leidensis solves both difficulties: *locum illis tempusque consilio designatum quo de Armenia cernerent quod. se fastigioque dignum Arsacidarum.* The phrase
Arsacidarum fastigium occurs in 15. 1 and is in character for
Vologeses. The awkward *quid cernerent* is gone and the syntax
with *dignum* made normal. And yet it is hardly conceivable
that even a clever scribe should have rewritten the sentence in
this fashion.

19. 13 has always led editors to emendation. M: *postquam
domos hortos opes principi abstulerint etiam militibus principem auferre litem.* The simplest change is to delete *litem,* as
does Koestermann. Leidensis, however, offers a more extensive
and understandable improvement: *etiam militibus principem
auferre, principi militem.*

One of the most vexing passages in the *Histories* is 20. 77.
M. reads *pars montibus alii alii viam inter Mosellamque flumen tam improvisa adsiluere.* Many attempts have been made
to restore the sentence, attempts in which all editors have accepted *improvisi* as an emendation of Agricola. Leidensis
shows that the Agricola MS had a readable text in thoroughly
Tacitean Latin: *pars montibus alii viam inter Mosellamque
flumen dispositi per pontem tam improvisi assiluere.*

At the end of Book 20 M. and all other MSS except Leidensis have four words making no sense at this point, repeated
for some unknown reason from chapter 77: *neque vos impunitos patiantur.* A clever scribe might well have deleted these
words, but it is a striking fact that only in Leidensis are they
missing and without comment.

One more instance of textual improvement as a result of
the reading of Leidensis will probably suffice. In 21. 8 Jerusalem is named as the capital of Judea. The next sentence reads
in M. *illic immensae opulentiae templum et primis munimentis
urbs de ingia templum intimis clausum.* Much ingenuity has
been expended on this passage without conspicuous success.

Modern editors, assuming that the whole of Jerusalem is being described—citadel, palace, and temple—have revised the text as follows: *illic immensae opulentiae templum, et primis munimentis urbs, dein regia, templum intimis clausum.* Leidensis holds the key—only the temple is under consideration at the moment: *illic immensae opulentiae templum ex primis munimentis urbis alienigenis templum interius clausum.*

It is clear that the old theory of a single MS tradition stemming from M. or a copy of it can no longer be held. Leidensis represents a second tradition which contributes extensively to our reconstruction of the text (on Leidensis, cf. *A J P, 72, 4; 75, 3*).

GROUP I

Ignoring for the moment the composite MSS which have a strong affiliation with Group I, the most obvious characteristics of the group are a long lacuna in Book 20. 15–62 and identical excerpts from this passage appended to the end of each MS. The ending of these MSS with *evenerant, 21. 13,* is highly characteristic, indicating the loss of chapters 13–23. The appearance of *fragmentum* or *quod reperitur* in the titles is also significant. At the end of Book XVI they all read *conversus in Demetrium* as opposed to *conversis* or *obversis.*

The excerpts which are characteristic of Group I MSS each contain material comprised in the Teubner text in approximately 102 lines (*Illi veteres* is just under, *toleremus* just over). The space between them comprises 307 Teubner lines of content. This would seem to indicate a quinion of 511 Teubner lines of content of which the excerpts occupied folios 1, 2 and 9, 10 respectively. It has generally been assumed that this quinion was lost and only the excerpt folios preserved but this leaves the problem of the lacuna unsolved with one hundred Teubner lines of content at one end and three hundred at the other unaccounted for. Rather, we should assume that the two sheets containing the excerpts became detached in copying and were bound in at the end of the volume. The quinion gathering we have assumed would provide two gatherings from the end of the *toleremus* passage to 21. 13, leaving 13–23 on a final duernion, which was presumably lost in the rebinding after copying, which placed the excerpt duernion in its place. In a subsequent copy there would be two gatherings of 700 Teubner lines of content, one 20. 15–62, minus the excerpts, the other 20. 62–21. 13. The former was lost. The process is of no great importance. The MSS of Class I are definitely distinguished by the resulting state of affairs, whatever the process.

The following distinctive readings are representative of a large group which confirms the independence of Group I.

GROUP I		OTHERS
11. 3.	inde	dehinc
11. 3.	calliditate Tiberii	Tiberii calliditate
13. 2.	meritis	matris
14. 4.	quo more	quorum more (quo rumore)
15. 2.	ipsi rupere	ipsis prospere
15. 14.	et Scipiones	et si quacisa
19. 2.	feratam	reseratam
20. 22.	om. copiae	
20. 53.	signanter	gignuntur (M. = signuntur)
21. 1.	superior omnibus	superiori unam, imperio dignum, etc.

One case of obvious error is of particular importance. In 14. 4, all of the Group I MSS read *moestam misellam,* a not too surprising mistake considering the situation, for *gestamine sellae,* the reading of all other MSS except Leidensis which has both readings with *moestam misellam* expunctuated.

Within Group I, Vat. Lat. 1864 and Bud. 9 are shown to come from a common ancestor by the omission in each of Book 16. 18–26. This close relationship is borne out by variant readings common to these two MSS. Ottob. 1422, Ottob. 1748, Vat. Lat. 2965, and Neap. IV. C. 21 form another closely related group within the class, as indicated by many omissions in common. Spaces are usually left for the omitted words. In 14. 65 all four read *magna moles dein prospera* for the strikingly Tacitean *magna moles et improspera.* Yalensis 3 and Kopenhagen have long omissions in common in 17. 9 and 18. 27, but one of these appears also in 1422 and 2965, the other in 1864. In 17. 76 Yal. 3 and Kop. agree in omitting a long phrase, and in 18. 62 in omitting *itineribus.* Yal. 3 and L. 68. 4 show close similarity down to 18. 69, at which point both MSS have a change of hand. Two words at the juncture are omitted by 1422, 1748, 2965, and Kop. The MSS of Group I would seem to be divided into two sections:

Vat. 1864	Neap. IV. C. 21
Bud. 9	Ottob. 1422
L. 68. 4	Ottob. 1748
Yal. 3 (to 18. 69)	Vat. Lat. 2965

As a rule, Urb. 412 and Kop. in their Group I parts fall into the first section.

GROUP II

The MSS of this class show no striking external characteristics apart from their ending in 21. 23. It is noteworthy, however, that they lack formal titles. The following readings will indicate the independence of the Group.

	GROUP II	THE REST
11. 7.	qui a re publica	quieta republica
13. 3.	amens	annis
13. 55.	postulabant	orabant
14. 2.	amore	ardore
14. 28.	frisoribus	fratris opibus (I Leid.)
		fratris sororibus (III)
17. 2.	in	in hos *or* in Rhosolanos
18. 79	v° non in nomen	v° non *or* in nomen
19. 8.	cunctum	ceterum
20. 23.	pendebant	haerebant
20. 66.	tumultus	om
21. 2.	sumitur	petitur
21. 20.	uno die	modis, modie, etc.

As against III, in 21. 13–23, material lost in Group I:

	II	III
13.	in altitudine	magnitudine
15.	om. ferocissimo	
16.	correpto (corrupto)	porrecto
	ferebatur	sperabatur
17.	materiam	victoriam
	et astan arari venisse	et hosti contraria evenisse
	medias	noxias
18.	nubibus	imbribus
20.	om. quibus ob	
22.	om. donum Veledae	
	biremem	triremem
23.	completque biremes	complet quod biremium
	fere	ferunt, serunt, etc.

These are representative of over ninety similar cases in these eleven chapters.

Within Group II there is a sharp division between Vat. Lat. 1863 and Venetus on the one hand, and Vind. and Paris on the other. The following readings from the first seven chapters of 11 are typical:

1863 VEN.	VIND. PAR.
coeptos	emptos
victo	indicto
reus	Asiaticus
esse me	me esse
subditos	subditis
pet (= petra)	praeter
evinctum	cinctum
gravitatem	caritatem
praevaricatione	prava ratione
tacere	agere

The readings *emptos* and *indicto* are given as alternative readings in 1863 and Ven. and are supported by Class I and Leidensis. 1863 and Ven. also have the careless reading *assenessentiam* for (*as*) *sentiam* which emphasizes their close relation. (M. has the same!) The impression is definitely left that Vind. and Paris derive from a more careless and less valuable copy of the common archetype than 1863 and Ven.

GROUP III

Group III has one characteristic common to all its members, the fact that they all contain the "complete" material—that is, they end in 21. 26 with *Flavianus in Pannonia* or some variation of this phrase. L. 63. 24 and L. 68. 5 are evidently composite, because this ending is followed by the excerpts characteristic of Group I. They should probably be treated separately, like Urb. 412 and Yal. 3. The evidence for a common archetype for M., Yal. 1, Yal. 2, and the "Genoans" lies (apart from the endings) in certain significant readings. Of these a few indicate a variant choice in dividing words in a continuous script. 19. 57, *Tum forte Minturnis* is, in the other MSS, *tum fortem in turmis;* 15. 3, *tumultuarium,* is elsewhere *tum multo variam.* Others indicate either misinterpretation by some scribe or choice between alternative readings: 13. 55, *orabant* as against *exorabant* or *postulabant;* 11. 8, all others omit *et ad praesentiam;* 21. 16, *porrecto* as against *correpto;* 11. 18, *feruntque militem* as against *erantque milites.* It is not wise, however, to try to force M. into close relations with the rest of Class III. True cohesion is limited to the Genoan group and Yale 1 and Yale 2. These are marked by the Octavia gloss in 14. 8 as well as by *Claudius* (12. 41), *druidibus* (12. 42), and *preces effundere* (13. 17), none of which appears elsewhere. At the same time they omit 21. 23, *et simul captae luntres sagulis versicoloribus,* which all other MSS have, and also 12. 68, *quae . . . forent* and 17. 45, *ad prohibendum . . . poterat.* They alone have *Posthumiam stupro cognitam* in 20. 44, while all others read *positam in astu procognitam* (M. reads *anstu*). Also, 14. 7, *illos in brevi die,* as against *illos invidiae* (M. = *inbidie*); 11. 22, *de se Novius,* as against *desenoni* (L. = *de se confessus*); 13. 1, *invito,* as against *inulto* or *multo.*

There seems to be more than a probability that the two Yale MSS and the Genoans have a common ancestor which was not shared by the rest. But it is even more certain that they form two groups which divided later. The Yale MSS are without titles; they end *Flavianus in Parma;* in 11. 10 they both omit about two lines. All other MSS have these, as they do also lesser omissions by Yale 1 and 2: 11. 1, *fateri;* 13. 25, *permissa;* 14. 7, *experiens;* 15. 7, *arsere;* 15. 10, *constantia,* and numerous others. They have in 19. 20 the gloss which the Genoans omit: *machinamenti . . . factum.* They are the only two MSS which have attempted to set straight the "third inversion." On the other hand, the Genoan MSS all have titles which include the phrases *Actarum Diurnarum* and *Historiae Augustae,* they close with *Fabianus in Pannonia,* and they have a series of marginal notes in common, one of which dates each MS. There are a great number of distinctive readings in the Genoan MSS, a considerable proportion of which indicate efforts to improve the text, e.g. 17. 70, *in alpe Graia* for *in alpentrianna;* 17. 2, *Rhosolanos* for *in* or *in nos.* All of the Genoans confuse Books 17 and 18—that is, there is no break—no title or number—for 18 and at its end, with the next book numbered 19, there is a note indicating the state of affairs.

Chart 1, while not offered as proof of the MS relationships which have been indicated above, has a certain value in confirming visually some of those relationships. The chart is based on the variant readings in the first 7 chapters of Book 11. There are 57 variants in all, and the chart shows the number of agreements between any two of the MSS presented. The fact that Laur. 68. 2 and Leidensis show no more than 35 and 38 agreements respectively with *any* MS indicates that they represent stages in the tradition considerably earlier than the rest do. The low number of agreements between the two indicates that the split in the tradition probably occurred well before the date of 68. 2. The chart indicates the relatively high number of agreements within the groups and also the subdivisions within the groups.

TABLE 1

	Laur. 68.2	Leidensis	Bud. 9	Vat. 1864	Yale 3	Urb. 412	Vat. 1863	Venetus	Vindob.	Paris	Yale 1	Yale 2	Vat. 1958	Cesena	Harl.	Kop.	Ed. prin.
Laur. 68.2	—	24	22	23	27	23	35	34	18	18	33	31	27	26	29	22	28
Leidensis	24	—	38	32	37	33	30	31	27	27	28	28	31	31	32	33	31
Bud. 9	22	38	—	46	48	40	26	34	21	22	27	26	20	16	17	20	28
Vat. 1864	23	32	46	—	47	45	28	34	21	19	27	27	17	16	18	21	26
Yale 3	27	37	48	47	—	43	44	36	28	—	27	25	26	26	27	30	—
Urb. 412	23	33	40	45	43	—	29	30	21	22	23	24	18	15	15	20	22
Vat. 1863	35	30	26	28	44	29	—	47	31	31	32	33	29	26	27	27	39
Venetus	34	31	34	34	36	30	47	—	31	31	31	31	29	24	25	29	41
Vindob.	18	27	21	21	28	21	31	31	—	52	24	27	23	20	19	25	36
Paris	18	27	22	19	—	22	31	31	52	—	25	27	21	22	21	26	33
Yale 1	33	28	27	27	27	23	32	31	24	25	—	48	34	33	35	31	32
Yale 2	31	28	26	27	25	24	33	31	27	27	48	—	36	37	35	34	33
Vat. 1958	27	31	20	17	26	18	29	29	23	21	34	36	—	42	43	43	25
Cesena	26	31	16	16	26	15	26	24	20	22	33	37	42	—	55	53	25
Harl.	29	32	17	18	27	15	27	25	19	21	35	35	43	55	—	51	25
Kop.	22	33	20	21	30	20	27	27	25	26	31	34	43	53	51	—	27
Ed. prin.	28	31	28	26	—	22	39	41	36	33	32	33	25	25	25	27	—

From the foregoing evidence Chart 2 shows most feasible tentative stemma for the MSS of Books 11–16.

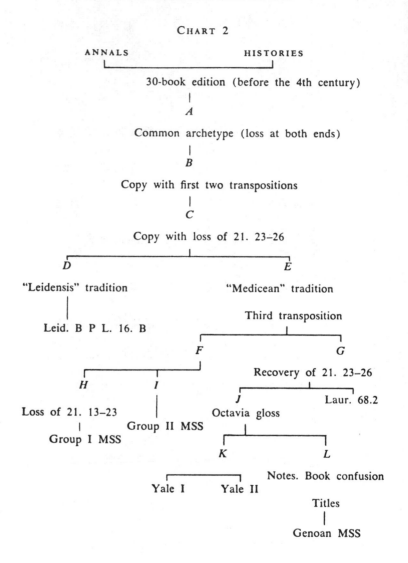

CHART 2

ANNALS   HISTORIES

30-book edition (before the 4th century)

A

Common archetype (loss at both ends)

B

Copy with first two transpositions

C

Copy with loss of 21. 23–26

D   *E*

"Leidensis" tradition   "Medicean" tradition

Leid. B P L. 16. B   Third transposition

F   *G*

Recovery of 21. 23–26

H   *I*   *J*   Laur. 68.2

Loss of 21. 13–23   Octavia gloss

Group I MSS   Group II MSS

K   *L*

Yale I   Yale II   Notes. Book confusion

Titles

Genoan MSS

THE MANUSCRIPT tradition of the Major Works is not consistent in the matter of title. Medicean I has the title *Ab excessu divi augusti,* and as there is no previous reference of any sort to the books contained in this MS, that is the only traditional title for the first six books of what are known now as the *Annals.* But Books 11–16 are included under the same title as the *Histories* in the remaining MSS, so that the question even for the *Annals* is not a simple one.

Pliny clearly referred to the work in which Tacitus was engaged as *Historiae: Auguror nec me fallit augurium Historias tuas immortales futuras (Ep.* 7. 33. 1). It is not clear whether the term was a specific one or simply referred to the general category of historical writing. The material to which Pliny refers, the eruption of Vesuvius, would have been in the *Histories.* Tertullian (*Adv. gentes* 16, and *Ad nationes* 1. 11) cites the *Histories,* using the term as a title: *in quinta Historiarum.* It should be noted that this reference is to the "separate" tradition, not to the thirty-book tradition, so that *Historiae* are the *Histories* as we name them now.

Vopiscus was the first to use another form of this title: *Cornelium Tacitum scriptorem historiae Augustae (Life of Emperor Tacitus* 10). Jornandes (*De rebus Gothicis* 1. 2) and Cassiodorus (*Getica* 2. 13) used *annalium scriptor,* and Ruodolfus, in the *Annals of Fulda,* speaks of Tacitus (*Mon. Germ. Script.* 1. 368) as *scriptor rerum a Romanis . . . gestarum.*

Historiae, Annales, Res gestae are all possible titles for a history. The MSS vary in their choice. Some of the best MSS (e.g. L. 68. 2, Vat. Lat. 1863) have either no title or only *Cor. Taciti Libri.* The most used MS title is *Actionum Diurnalium Augustae Historiae* (So Vat. 1958, Gudianus, Neap. IV. c. 22, etc.), a few have *Historiae* (e.g. Laur. 63. 24, Neap. IV. c. 21), and one at least (Ottob. 1422) has *Res gestae.*

One thing is certain. Tacitus would not have used any form

of *acta diurna,* for in *Ann.* 13. 31. 1 he makes the rather scathing remark: *cum ex dignitate populi Romani repertum sit res illustres annalibus, talia diurnis urbis actis mandare.* This statement also gives weight to the argument that Tacitus himself may have thought of *Annales* as the title of at least part of his work. In 4. 71. 1 he states his purpose to write chronologically, and in two further instances he seems to refer to his own work as *Annales:* 3. 65. 1: *quod praecipuum munus annalium reor, ne virtutes sileantur;* and 4. 32. 1: *nemo annales nostros cum eorum contenderit qui veteres populi Romani res composuere.* These citations from Tacitus, taken in conjunction with the fact that Livy called his own work *Annales,* led Beatus in his edition of 1533 to adopt this title for all the historical books of Tacitus. This met with general acceptance until Lipsius in 1574 (Simar in *Musée Belge,* 1907, gives Vertranius Maurus, 1569, as the originator) suggested a distinction between the books dealing with the period after Nero, the first published by Tacitus, and those dealing with Tiberius, Gaius, Claudius, and Nero. For the former he proposed to use the term *Histories* and for the latter *Annals.* His practice has been followed ever since, not because of any conviction that Tacitus intended such a distinction (although Lipsius evidently felt that the evidence favored two titles rather than one) but for convenience and in accord with what is indicated by Servius as Roman practice. In his comment on *Aeneid* 1. 373 he says: "inter historiam et annales hoc interest: historia est eorum temporum quae vel vidimus vel videre potuimus: annales vero sunt eorum temporum quae aetas nostra non novit, unde Livius ex annalibus et historia constat."

At the same time, there was another theoretical distinction which Aulus Gellius quotes from Sempronius Asellio, *Res gestae,* Book 1 (Aul. Gell. 5. 18. 7): "Verum inter eos qui annales relinquere voluissent et eos qui res gestas a Romanis perscribere conati essent, omnium rerum hoc interfuit. Annales libri tantum modo quod factum quoquo anno gestum sit, ea demonstrabant, id est quasi qui diarium scribunt quam Graeci 'εφημερίδα vocant. Nobis non modo satis esse video, quod factum esset, id pronuntiare, sed etiam quo consilio quaque ratione gesta essent demonstrare." A little further on he said: "Nam neque alacriores ad rem p. defendundum neque segniores ad rem perperam faciundam annales libri commovere quicquam possunt. Scribere autem, bellum initum quo consule et quo confectum sit et quis triumphans introierit ex eo bello, quaeque in bello gesta sint, non praedicare aut, interea quid senatus decreverit aut quae lex rogatiove lata sit, neque quibus consiliis ea gesta sint, iterare: id fabulas pueris est narrare, non historias scribere." On such a basis, the title *Annals* could not be applied to either of the major works of Tacitus, nor could any distinction be made between the two.

With regard to the title of the *Agricola,* the only doubt is raised by the fact that Aesinus reads *De Vita Iulii Agricolae,* while the evidence of the other MSS is all in favor of *De Vita et Moribus Iulii Agricolae.* The latter was very likely, as Wölfflin contends (*Hermes, 11*), the more generally used form in Roman biography, but there is not sufficient evidence for venturing any conclusion.

For the *Dialogus,* the simple title *Dialogus de Oratoribus* seems altogether probable. The Harleian MS adds *claris* and the Vindobonensis 49 suggests the comparison of new and old orators. The *editio princeps* used the form *oratoribus claris.* The alternative title *an sui* etc. was added by Puteolanus in his first edition.

The *Germania* offers more of a problem if we try to determine what title Tacitus actually gave to the essay. By all means the commonest title in the MSS is *de origine et situ Germaniae.* But there is by no means complete consistency. *Germanorum* often takes the place of *Germaniae; de situ ac moribus* occurs in Ottob. 1795; *de situ* alone in Urb. 412; *de origine et moribus Germanorum* in Aesinus; *de gestis et moribus Germanorum* in Stuttgartensis; and finally, in Leidensis, *de origine situ moribus ac populis Germanorum.* The *editio princeps* reads *de situ moribus ac populis Germaniae libellus aureus.* The last two words do not occur in any MS except Turicensis, which was written in 1502, long after the printing of Spira's text. The

evidence of Niccoli and of Decembrio confirms the simple titles
so far as the MS in which they were interested is concerned:
*De vita Iulii Agricolae, Dialogus de Oratoribus, De origine et
situ Germaniae.* Niccoli read *Germanorum,* but the more exact
Decembrio had *Germaniae.* Decembrio also added *soceri sui*
to the *Agricola* title, and it is possible that this represented an
original title, but the probability is that it was an explanatory
addition by Decembro. Wölfflin (*Hermes,* 11) discussed at
length the title of the *Germania.* He is undoubtedly correct in
assigning the *de situ* to the geographical tradition represented
by titles from Mela, Pliny, and Seneca. Sallust recognized this
in *Jugurtha* 17. 1, stating that he was going to write about
situm Africae et . . . gentes. This ethnographical addition is
expressed in the epitome of Livy, 104, *situm Germaniae moresque. Pliny (NH* 3) has *situs, gentes, maria, oppida,* etc.
Tacitus himself, in *Agricola* 10, speaks of *Britanniae situm
populosque.* Wölfflin thinks that the geographical, ethnologi-
cal combination is not properly represented by the common
title *de origine et situ.* It is, however, as he admits, exactly what
Ammianus uses in 27. 4. 1. He calls attention to the phrase in
Germania 27: *de omnium Germanorum origine ac moribus,*
and thinks that the title in Leidensis was the result of interpo-
lation from this passage, the *Germanorum* coming along with
the *moribus.* His conclusion is that the title should be *de situ
ac populis Germaniae.* But Decembrio gives clear evidence
that one of the two sources of early tradition had *origine et
situ.* The evidence of Aesinus and Toletanus is somewhat dis-
turbing but in neither of them does *populis* occur, and the
Germania of these MSS has no outstanding value. That word
appears only in Leidensis, causing at least the suspicion that it
was a conscious elaboration on the part of Pontanus. On the
whole, the traditional title, *De origine et situ Germaniae* seems
most likely to have been the original one.

19. HISTORY OF THE PRINTED TEXT

THE FIRST printed text of Tacitus was made, according to an elegiac colophon at the end of the *Dialogus*, by one Spira:

> Caesareos mores scribit Cornelius. esto
> Iste tibi codex: historiae pater est.
> Insigni quem laude feret gens postera: pressit
> Spira premens: artis gloria prima suae.

The work is certainly not the first publication of the first Spira. Johann von Speier received from Venice in 1469 the privilege of being sole printer in the town for a period of five years. The granting of this privilege seems to have been practically coincident with the printing of his limited edition of the *Epistolae ad Familiares* of Cicero. The colophon to this volume is as follows:

> Primus in Adriaca formis impressit aenis
> Urbe libros Spira genitus de stirpe Johannes
> In reliquis sit quanta vides spes lector habenda
> Quom labor hic primus calami superaverit artem.

This, then, was the first product of the press. Johann lived but a short time after its appearance. He published a Pliny and started a *De civitate Dei*. In the colophon to the latter, his brother Wendelin announces Johann's death and his own continuance of the work of the press. The privilege expired with Johann. Wendelin published from 1470 to shortly before his death in 1478, but in 1473 his presses were taken over by Jean de Cologne and Johann Wanthen. It is often assumed that the Tacitus is the first thing that he printed entirely on his own responsibility after his brother's death, but the phrase *gloria prima* might equally well be interpreted to mean the finest work that he had produced up to that time. It is not therefore certain to what exact date between 1470 and 1473 the *editio princeps* should be ascribed. The use of *primus* by the elder

349

brother lends some confirmation to the assumption that the younger uses *prima* in the same way and that his Tacitus appeared in 1470. There is no doubt as to its being the earliest of the known editions, for the first Puteolanus refers to it in the introductory letter and the second Puteolanus is dated 1497.

The *editio princeps* (Hain-Copinger, No. 15,218) is a folio volume of 178 folios measuring 27½ cm., with 1, 152^v, 162, 177^v, and 178 left blank. It has no signatures and no numbers on the pages but has catchwords on each left-hand page, probably the first in the history of printing. It opens without title: *Nam Valerium asiaticum.* There are no book headings and no spaces left until the end of Book 16. At that point, after *conversis in Demetrium,* there is half a page left blank. On the verso begins *Initium mihi operis Servus Galba,* without title. The *Histories* end with *arte navium magnitudine potiorem* at the bottom of 151^r, with the verso blank. On the next page (152^r): *Cornelii Taciti illustrissimi historici de situ moribus & populis Germaniae libellus aureus.* On 161^v is the word *Finis,* and one and one-half pages are left blank. Fol. 162^r has *Cornelii taciti equitis Romani dialogus de oratoribus claris.* The *Dialogus* continues to 175^r to about the middle of the page, where there is *Finis Deo laus* and the metrical colophon. In the Vatican copy which belonged to Pomponius Laetus and into which he bound a MS copy of the *Agricola,* the order of the items is changed. The *Dialogus,* with the colophon, follows the *Histories* and is in turn followed by the *Germania.*

Books 17 and 18 are perfectly distinct. Book 18 begins with an illuminated letter.

The copy of the *editio princeps* in the Yale Library has colored paragraph marks, alternating red and blue, at the beginning of nearly every sentence, as if the manuscript from which it was printed had been one like Vat. Lat. 1862 of the Minor Works or Monac. 5307 of the *Germania.*

The watermark on the paper is a scales suspended in a circle, which is also the watermark of Monac. 5307.

In the *Dialogus*, at chapter 3, line 3, there is a paragraph indention, with space left for the initial letter of *Tum Secundus*. The preceding paragraph ended at the left-hand end of the line. At the extreme right-hand end of the line is *Dialogus*. What preceded was evidently considered a prooemium.

The second edition of Tacitus is also without date or place. The editor is Puteolanus, and the usual assumption is that the book was printed at Milan by Antonius Zarotus between 1475 and 1480, although the British Museum catalogue (*6*, 719–20) lists it as 1487 (Hain-Copinger, No. 15,219; Proctor, No. 5838). It has 188 folios and is 31 cm. tall. Fols. 160, 175ᵛ, 176, 187ᵛ, and 188 are blank. There is no title or flyleaf. This edition adds *Histories* 5. 23–26 and the *Agricola* to the Tacitean corpus. The first page begins with a letter from the editor, Franciscus Puteolanus, to Jacobus Antiquarius, ducal secretary. On the second page of this letter Puteolanus lists what he plans to print: "Cor. Taciti equitis romani historicorum omnium gravissimi disertissimique quicquid incuriosae vetustati superfuit. i. fragmenta ex actionibus diurnalibus augustae historiae: De moribus et situ germaniae: de genere eloquentiae non corruptae: cui operi a quibusdam titulus de claris oratoribus inscribitur: Vitam Iulii Agricolae soceri." He then states that Berardinus Lanterius of Milan helped him, and he gives his reason for printing Tacitus: "Veneti enim Impressores adeo inculcaverant ac foedaverant hoc divinum opus ut non modo Cornelienae facundiae maiestas inquinarent sed vix sensus ullus coniectari posset. Quid ego effeci iudicent docti sed collatis exemplaribus."

This edition introduces titles for the books of the major works. The first printed page begins *Cornelii Taciti Historiae Augustae Li. XI. Actionum Diurnalium. Am Valerium Asiaticum* etc. There is no initial letter indicated. Book 16 ends *obnersis in Demetrium,* followed by the title of Book 17, which has *actorum* for *actionum,* as do the remaining books of the *Histories.* The book opens *Initium mihi operis Servius Galba* etc. Books 17 and 18 are printed continuously without break,

ending *Septimusdecimus et octavusdecimus confusi simul expliciunt*. The *Histories* end *Fabianus in Pannonia* without *Finis*
or colophon.

Puteolanus corrects the third inversion. This would seem to
indicate a Genoan MS of the Y 1 type. But he has no *Ob haec*,
which would suggest that this was an addition by the scribe
of Y 1 and that Puteolanus used the immediate ancestor of
Y 1. Here also would be the explanation of *Fabianus* as against
the *Flavianus* of Y 1, and *Pannonia* as against *Parma*.

The end of the *Histories* comes at the bottom of the last
page of a quaternion. On the next recto: *Cornelii Taciti illus-
tissimi historici de situ moribus et populis Germaniae libellus
aureus*. The *Germania* ends with *Finis* in the middle of the last
verso of the gathering. On the next recto: *Cornelii Taciti
aequitis romani dialogus an sui saeculi oratores antiquioribus
et quare concedant*. The *Dialogus* ends a folio short of the end
of the gathering. At the beginning of the next gathering. *Iulii
Agricolae vita per Cornelium Tacitum generum castissime
composita*. The *Agricola* ends with *Finis* only.

In the *Dialogus* there is a paragraph division at the third
line of chapter 3, *Tum Secundus*, the only paragraph division
in the essay. This is exactly like the *editio princeps*.

Lipsius cites an edition of 1494 at Venice. See Ruyschart,
p. 24.

The first dated edition is also by Puteolanus and was made
in Venice in 1497. It has 114 folios, with 1^v and 114^v blank.
It is 32 cm. tall (Hain-Copinger, No. 15,222; Proctor, No.
5,315). On the title page is printed *Cornelii Taciti Historiae
Augustae*. The letter to Jacobus Antiquarius appears at the
beginning, with a few minor changes, most interesting of which
is the change of *Veneti enim impressores* to *veteri enim impressores*, due no doubt to the fact that the present edition was
printed in Venice.

The titles are the same as those of the first Puteolanus edition except that the change from *Actionum* to *Actorum* comes
with Book 19. There is the same confusion of 17 and 18, with
the same colophon. *Obnersis in Demetrium* is corrected to

Obversis. The *Germania* and *Dialogus* do not begin on new gatherings but follow the preceding material immediately with the page. At the end of the *Dialogus* is a colophon: *Cornelii Taciti historiae augustae nec non de situ moribus et populis germaniae libellus ac de oratoribus dialogus foeliciter expliciunt. Venetiis fideliter Impresi ac diligenter emendati per Philippum pinci sumptibus nobilis viri dni Benedicti fontana. Anno dni MCCCCXCVII. Marcii. Imperante Sapientissimo dno Augustino Barbadico prudentissimi ac Invictissimi Senatus Venetiarum duce serenissimo.* The register follows: 12 quaternions, 1 quinion, with the printer's device on the verso. The *Agricola* follows, a complete and separate quaternion with its own colophon: *Finis. Venetiis per Philippum Pinc: sumptibus dni Benedicti fontana. Anno dni MCCCCXCVII die XXII martii.* In the *Dialogus* there is the same paragraph device as in the first Puteolanus and in the *editio princeps.*

In 1512 another edition appeared without adding any new material to the corpus. The title page reads *Cornelii Taciti Historici gravissimi disertissimique fragmenta securate recognita ac nova censura castigata. Joannes Rivius recensuit.* The book is a tall folio (31½ cm.) of 233 pages, very handsomely printed and evidently intended to outshine the Puteolanus editions. On the verso of the title page is first a letter to the reader explaining his motives, and then a very short life of Tacitus in which the editor confuses the Pliny reference to a Tacitus in Belgic Gaul, making it apply to the historian. He states in the letter that he has made more than a thousand improvements in the text but does not give his source if he had any outside his own ingenuity. The text begins on the recto of the second page at the top: *Liber XI. Cornelii Taciti Historiae Augustae Liber Undecimus Actionum Diurnalium incipit. I am Valerium Asiaticum* etc. There are printed topics in the margin throughout. Book 12 begins with the obvious mistake *Rede Messalinae.* The end of the *Annals* is *obversis in Demetrium. Finis Sextidecimi Libri.* The seventeenth book follows immediately with the regular title: *Initium mihi operis Servius Galba.* The seventeenth and eighteenth are still confused, and the statement is the same: *Septimusdecimus et octavusdecimus confusi simul expliciunt.* Books 20 and 21 have *actorum* in the title. On the verso of q III the *Histories* end with *Fabianus in Pannonia. Finis XXI. Libri.* and immediately after comes *Cornelii Taciti Illustrissimi Historici de Situ Moribus et populis Germaniae Libellus Aureus.* The *Germania* ends, *in medium relinquam,* on the recto of r. After *Finis,* the title of the *Dialogus* follows immediately: *Cornelii Taciti aequitis Romani Dialogus an sui saeculi oratores antiquioribus et quare concedant.* There is the same paragraph indication in chapter 3 that appeared in the earlier editions. The *Agricola* begins at the top of the verso of f I with a double title: *Iulii Agricola* on one line, and beginning on the next, *Iulii Agricolae vita per Cornelium Tacitum eius generum castissime composita.* There is a paragraph and a decorated initial at *Cn. Iulius Agricola.* The essay ends at the bottom of the last recto of signature S with *Finis,* followed by the colophon: *Impressum Venetiis per Ioannem Rubeum Vercelensem. Anno domini. M.CCCCCXII. Die. XX. Mensis Iulii.* Then follows the register. There are sixteen ternions and two quaternions.

The biggest advance in Tacitus publication after the *editio princeps* came in 1515, when the first five books of the *Annals,* recently acquired by Pope Leo X, were added to the corpus in a rather badly printed folio edition edited by Beroaldus. There are 388 pages, the first 73 leaves only being numbered. There are catchwords on the left-hand pages and leaf numbers on the right. The height is 30½ cm. The title page reads: *P. Cornelii Taciti Libri quinque noviter inventi atque cum reliquis eius operibus editi.* Beneath this is the Papal copyright: *Ne quis intra decennium presens opus possit alicubi impune imprimere aut impressum vendere gravissimis edictis cautum est.* On page 2: *Philippus Beroaldus junior Academiae Romanae praepositus Leoni. X. Pont. Max. Sal.* There is an address in highly flattering terms to the Pope, recounting his enthusiastic search for MSS: *Quae venatio Cornelii Taciti hos primos quinque libros qui per longum seculorum ambitum latuerant, in saltibus Germaniae invenit: quam tu praedam ad te allatam ac magna mercede comparatam* etc. Most of the letter is rather fulsome praise of Leo for his generous attitude toward letters. It is followed by a short epistle to the reader saying that Beroaldus has made what corrections of errors in the MS he could, marking the more hopeless passages with asterisks. On page 4 begins the text, with the title *P. Cornelii Taciti ab excessu Divi Augusti Historiarum Liber primus.* The separate books always begin on a new page. Book 5 ends on the recto of 73 with a colophon: *P. Cor. Taciti Liber quintus finit ad laudem omnipotentis dei et Leonis. X. Pont. Max.* At the top of the verso: *Ph. Beroaldus Lectori. Hi sunt Cornelii Taciti Quinque Libri nuper in Germania inventi et auspiciis Leonis X Pont. Max in lucem ad usum bonorum editi.* In this letter the editor explains the asterisk system again and gives conjectures for some of the corrupt passages. The last paragraph explains out-of-date spellings. This matter occupies altogether two pages, and a third is taken up with printer's errata. This is the end of the new material.

On the recto of the page with signature O begins the letter of Puteolanus to Jacobus Antiquarius, the *Veteri* form of it, taken from the edition of 1497. The eleventh book begins at the top of Oii and the titles keep the original form. With the thirteenth book the individual books no longer always begin at the top of a new page. Book 16 ends *obversis in Demetrium,* without a *Finis.* Book 17 begins *Initium mihi operis Ser Galba.* There is one line left blank where Book 18 should begin, and there is the regular colophon to the combined seventeenth and eighteenth: *confusi simul expliciunt.* There is no *Finis* to 19. Book 21 ends in the middle of a quaternion at the bottom of a page, with the colophon *Cornelii Taciti Historiarum Libri. XXI. imperfecti et reliquorum qui ad hunc diem reperiuntur Finis.* On the next page: *P. Cornelii Taciti Historici de Situ moribus et populis Germaniae Libellus.* There is no *Finis* to the *Germania,* which is followed immediately by the *Dialogus* with the title *Cornelii Taciti equitis Romani Dialogus an sui saeculi oratores antiquioribus et quare concedant.* There is the same paragraphing in chapter three that appeared in the earlier editions. A space of one word is left at the lacuna, exactly like other spaces: *ventum est   rem cogitare.* At the end of the *Dialogus* is simply *Finis,* followed by a letter from Leo to Beroaldus complimenting him highly and including an interdict against reprinting the text. It is dated as follows. *Datum Romae apud sanctum Petrum, sub annulo piscatoris die XIIII. Novembris. M.D.XIIII. Pontificatus nostri anno Secundo. Ia. Sadoletus.* This letter takes two pages. The next page contains errata, the register, and a colophon. The register indicates 35 ternions, with a quaternion preceding and following and a duernion near the middle, followed by a single folio. The colophon reads: *P. Cornelii Taciti Equitis Ro. Historiarum libri quinque nuper in Germania inventi ac cum reliquis omnibus eius operibus quae prius inveniebantur Romae impressi per Magistrum Stephanum Guillereti de Lothoringia Tullen. dioc. Anno. M.D.XV. Kl. Martii Leonis. X. Pont. Max. anno secundo.* On the reverse of this page are the papal arms, with an offer of reward for new MSS. A separate quinion follows, containing the *Agricola,* headed *Vita Agricolae,* and with the title *Iulii Agricolae vita per Cornelium Tacitum eius generum Castissume composita,* ending with a simple *Finis.*

A curious but not very important edition, the first in a small format, appeared in 1516 in Milan. It is a pirated edition printed from the sheets of the 1515 Beroaldus as they were received at Milan. The title page is a reproduction even to the printing of the papal interdict. There are ten preliminary leaves, 235 numbered leaves, and 25 supplementary pages. The height is 20 cm. The only new material in the volume are some notes by Alciatus at the end. It begins (signature a ii) with a nine-page letter headed *Cornelius Tacitus Sebastiano fererio. S.* There is a certain facetious air about this. Tacitus is presented as telling about his return, ceasing to be *tacitus,* and commending Minutianus to Ferarius on the ground of his being vouched for by Grolierus. The letter is dated *Med. M.D. XVII postridie cal. Octobris.* The six-page letter of Beroaldus to Leo is then reprinted, followed by the heading *Alexander Minutianus Lectori.* What comes under this is practically the notes of Beroaldus on the starred passages and spellings, although Minutianus makes slight and unimportant changes. At the close of Book 5, with the same ending as in Beroaldus, comes the Puteolanus letter to Jac. Antiquarius. There are no notes; Book 11 begins on the next page. The *Germania, Dialogus,* and *Agricola* follow consecutively with the usual headings, and *Finis. Ex officina Minutiana MD. XVII.* at the close. On the next page is the letter from Leo to Beroaldus which preceded the *Agricola* in the 1515 edition. On the page following begins an exchange of letters between Minutianus and the Vatican, in which, under date of March 31, 1516, he begs indulgence for pirating the edition, saying that he received the sheets one by one and did not see the papal interdict. The Pope, under date of September 7, 1516, allows him to continue, Beroaldus concurring. The Pope's letter is signed *Bembus.* On a separate quinion following is printed the Alciatus material, headed *Andreas Alciatus Iuriscons. Galaecio Vicecomiti V.C. et Eq. S.P.D.*, containing a short essay on history writing in antiquity and on Tacitus in particular, and seven and a half pages of notes on corrupt passages. This is the only really new material in the edition, which is badly printed throughout in small italics (except for the introductory epistle), with frequent mistakes in page order, numbering, and so on.

In 1519 Frobenius at Basel printed a de luxe edition in folio (33 cm.). There are 14 preliminary leaves and 380 pages. The title page has a highly ornamental border, with pictures of Arminius and Quintilius Varus fighting, of Temperance, Justice, Truth, Ignorance, Calumny, etc., signed 1517 AH (Ambroise Holbein). The chief value of the edition, however, is the editing of the *Germania* by Bilde von Rheinau (Beatus Rhenanus).

Within the pictured frame the title page reads: *P. Cornelii Taciti Eq. Ro. Historia Augusta actionum diurnalium: additis quinque libris noviter inventis. Andreae Alciati Mediolanensis in eundem annotationes. De Situ, moribus et populis Germaniae libellus: eodem Cor. Tacito autore. Eiusdem Dialogus: an sui seculi oratores antiquioribus, et quare concedant. Cn. Iulii Agricolae vita, per eundem. Apud Inclytam Basileam, ex officina Io. Frobenii.* On the reverse of the title page: *Elenchus in Historiam Augustam Cor. Taciti: qui ea potissimum indicat, quae ad res Germaniae pertinent, hactenus a multis incuriosa lectione transmissa, per Beatum Rhenanum Selestadiensem, opera cursim et carptim evoluto, congestus.* There are nine pages of this index, followed by a list of errata for the whole volume and the register indicating 30 ternions and 3 quaternions. On the following page begins the Alciatus material taken from the pirated Milan edition. This occupies eleven pages, and is followed by the letter from Beroaldus to Leo X taken from the 1515 edition with his explanation to the reader, his *castigationes,* and his remarks on obsolete spelling. Then the text begins, the first page having a decorated border and the title *P. Cornelii Taciti ab excessu Divi Augusti Historiarum, Liber primus.* There are catchwords and numbers on both right- and left-hand pages. There is still no indication of the sixth book, the "fifth" ending on page 111 and followed on page 112 by the Puteolanus letter from the 1497 edition. The eleventh book begins on page 114. The titles change on page 116 to *P. Cornelii Taciti Historiae Augustae Liber decimusquartus Actionum Diurnalium.* Books 17 and 18 are still *confusi,* though there is a line left blank where eighteen should begin. The *Histories* end on page 330 in the middle of a quaternion. Page 331 has an elaborate border, including Frobenius' printer's device. Within the border the *Germania* begins, with the heading *P. Cornelii Taciti eq. Ro. de situ moribus et populis Germaniae libellus, a prodigiosis mendis repurgatus per Beatum Rhenanum, beneficio codicis vetustioris.* The *Dialogus* follows directly after the *Germania* and the *Agricola* after the *Dialogus.* The *Agricola* ends on page 379 with *Cn. Iulii Agricolae Vitae, per P. Cornelium Tacitum Eq. Ro. Compositae, Finis.* On the reverse of this page is the printer's device and *Basileae apud Ioannem Frobenium Mense Augusto, Anno, MDXIX.*

The first Juntine edition in 1527 added nothing to the tradition of Tacitus texts. It was published in small format (16 cm.) with 366 pages, evidently as a handy volume, and followed Beroaldus closely. The title page reads: *P. Cornelii Taciti ab excessu Divi Augusti Historiarum Libri quinque nuper inventi atque cum reliquis eius operibus maxima diligentia excusi.* The printer's device is below this. On the reverse of the title page is a one-page letter: *Ant. Franc. Varchiensis Studiosis S.* The editor commends the work of Beroaldus, which he claims to have reviewed. Of some interest is his explanation of why he is editing Tacitus in the midst of wars and troubles in Italy. It is because he fears that all good disciplines may take flight to the other hemisphere. He reprints Beroaldus' letter to Leo before the first five books and his explanation of corrupt passages and spellings after. The *Germania* and *Dialogus* follow Book 21, with the usual titles. Six or seven lines of the *Dialogus* are omitted at the end, which concludes *magnam famam et.* This is on page 363, on the reverse of which is the register and this colophon: *Florentiae per haeredes Philippi Iuntae. Anno Domini M.D.XXVII. Mensis Maii. Die. XXII. Clemente Pontifice Max.* On the reverse of the next and final page is the printer's device. There is no *Agricola.*

The year 1533 is a landmark in the history of the Tacitus text. The corpus had already been completed. Certain corrupt passages had been noted by editors with some slight effort at explanation. An index of a sort had been provided. This was the work of Spira, Puteolanus, and Beroaldus. Beatus Rhenanus had begun his critical work on the *Germania.* Now, in 1533, he produced as editor the second of Frobenius' editions, with far-reaching results. He introduced the Codex Budensis to assist in the construction of the text; he established the title *Annales* for the historical books; he published a considerable body of critical notes; he eliminated the confusion of Books 17 and 18; he made a study of Tacitean usages with reference to Livy; he raised the question of the Tacitean authorship of the *Dialogus.* It will be necessary to quote at considerable length from the remarks of Rhenanus throughout the volume.

The edition of 1533 has 36 preliminary leaves and 516

pages, and measures 29½ cm. The title of the volume is extensive: *P. Cornelii Taciti equitis Romani Annalium ab excessu Augusti, qui vulgo receptus titulus est, libri sedecim qui
supersunt, partim haud oscitanter perlecti, partim nempe
posteriores ad exemplar manuscriptum recogniti magna fide
nec minore iudicio per Beatum Rhenanum. Nihil hic fingi do-
cebunt castigationes suis quaeque libris additae. Libellus de
Germanorum populis, Dialogus de oratoribus, denique Vita
Iulii Agricolae, non solum emaculatius prodeunt sed et expli-
catius adiunctis in hanc rem scholiis. Super haec omnia acces-
serunt in initio operis Thesaurus constructionum locutionum-
que et vocum Tacito sollennium citatis etiam ex Livio plerumque testimoniis, ac in calce rerum memorabilium index
copiosissimus. Nec desunt aliorum in hunc autorem ante aedi-
tae annotationes praefationesque sive Beroaldi seu Alciati.*
The printer's device follows, and below it: *Basileae in officina
Frobeniana Anno* MDXXXIII. The reverse of the title page is
blank.

On the following page is a dedicatory epistle, *Amplissimo
Patri et Principi D. Bernardo Episcopo Tridentino ac S. R. E.
Cardinali, etc. Beatus Rhenanus S. D.* This three-and-a-half-
page letter, after eulogies of literature and of the cardinal, proceeds: *Nam cum accepissem futurum ut Annales Cornelii Taciti denuo typis informarentur, primum experiri libuit an operae
pretium esset vulgatum aeditionem conferre cum manuscripto
codice quem nactus fueram iampridem ex bibliotheca Budensi
cuius autor Vngariae rex Matthias ille Corvinus Martis et Pal-
ladis studiis inclytus, donante Iacobo Spiegellio amico ac cive
meo charissimo. . . . Deinde quum succederet negotium, hoc
est infinita loca foeda depravata, quod nemo credidisset, hac
opera restituerentur, a labore coepta non destiti, donec uni-
versum volumen a capite ad calcem haud oscitabunde contulis-
sem. Quid autem effecerim, castigationes libris praefixae doce-
bunt. In quinque voluminibus quae reperta apud Corbeiam in
Saxonibus, paulo post Romae evulgata sunt, item in libello
Germanorum, Oratorum Dialogo, Agricolaeque Vita, defuere
quidem scripti codices cum quibus conferrem, caeterum ipse*

aeditionem vulgatum percurri non prorsum indiligenter, ac loca quaedam accuratius excussi. The epistle ends with a fine appeal for good textual construction: *Sed deterret plerosque non imperitia, verum labor gloria carens, et reprehensioni indoctorum etiam obnoxius. Quidam rident tantum, levius ferendi, quidam nec a conviciis absitinent. Et tamen non est alia via succurendi veterum scriptis nisi haec, nempe et primum conferantur attente exemplaria manuscripta, dein iudicium adhibeatur.* The letter is dated *Selestadii Nonis Decembribus, An. MDXXXII.*

There follows next: *Annalium Inscriptionis Reddita Ratio,* of a little more than two pages. Rhenanus notes Puteolanus' change from *actionum* to *actorum,* and the title used by Beroaldus: *Ab excessu divi Augusti historiarum libri.* He continues: *In codice Corbeiensi titulum hunc repererit, an excogitarit ipse, incertum. Meum certe volumen Buda allatum ἀνεπίγραφον erat.* Vopiscus, he notes, calls Tacitus *historiae Augustae scriptor.* Beatus himself chooses the title *Annales,* because of four passages from Tacitus' own writings in which he not only repudiates the title *Acta Diurna* but, in Beatus' estimation, implies the title *Annales.* Jornandes is cited as speaking of Tacitus as *annalium scriptor,* and it is pointed out that Livy used *Annales* for his own history and that Tacitus makes frequent use of the annalistic phrases, *eodem anno, principio veris, per idem tempus, fine anni,* etc. Beatus thinks that there was some confusion and loss in the Tacitean tradition evidenced by Tertullian's calling the twenty-first book the fifth. But he expresses wonder that the devotion of a few interested monks preserved the classics at all, and winds up with another reference to Laur. 68. 1: *Sic nobis priores quinque Taciti libros Corbeia Visurgi fluvio vicina, Benedictorum monasterium est, conservavit, proximis annis illinc ad Leonem X. Pont. Max. allatos.*

The next page presents the thesaurus of Tacitean usage, which is sixty pages long and discusses such characteristic phrases as *circuli, componere pro sepelire, humilia pro vili, qua proximum, sesquiplaga, suam pro eius.*

After the thesaurus comes the letter of Beroaldus to Leo,

with his explanation to the reader and his note on spelling. Then the text begins, the title being *P. Cornelii Taciti Ab Excessu Divi Augusti Annalium Liber primus.* This type of title is used consistently throughout. On page 122, the end of "Book V" (there is still no indication of a sixth book), Beatus explains that even without the Córwey MS he has been able to make some corrections in the text, and these he lists as *castigationes.* There are about twenty for each book and they are on the whole of a conservative character. Beginning on page 127, he reprints the letter of Puteolanus to Antiquarius, and then, on 129, again addresses the reader to explain his task of restoring the later books by means of his MS, which he calls *recentior,* saying that it was given to him by Spiegel and that it was written in Italy at the expense of Corvinus. He lists his changes for Book 11 as *castigationes,* then prints the book, and so on through 21. There are about four pages of notes per book. At the end of Book 16 he writes *Hic multa desunt,* which has the look of coming from the MS. The *Histories* begin *Initium mihi operis Ser. Galba,* and end *Fabianus in Pannonia.* There is no sign of the confusion of 17 and 18 which occurs in earlier editions.

The beginning of the *Germania* (p. 421) is of interest because of the light it throws on the earlier edition. It follows directly after the *Histories,* with this note introducing eleven pages of *castigationes: Denuo relegi hoc de Germanis opusculum, quod anno 1519 contuleram cum exemplari non scripto, sed impresso tantum. Id tum communicavit mihi Hieronymus Artolphus medicae rei consultus et profuit locis non paucis. Addidi rursum quaedum ex annotationibus illis collati quondam codicis. De quibis hic statim admonebitur lector.*

The introduction to the *Dialogus* (p. 445) is even more interesting. *Beatus Rhenanus Lectori S. Hunc dialogum vix crediderim esse Taciti. Quamquam autor quisquis fuit eius eruditissimi seculi, testatur se disertissimorum hominum sermonem repetere, quem iuvenis admodum audiverit. . . . Sane fit hic anni mentio Vespasiani principatus, quo tempore iuvenis fuit admodum Tacitus. Fit et mentio Mutiani senatorumque elo-*

quentium, Eprii Marcelli ac Crispi Vibii, quorum Tacitus quoque meminit in libris Annalium. Nec Iustus Fabius cui inscribitur opusculum ex Plinii Caecilii epistolis ignotus est. Sed haud me latet quaedam etiam apud veteres tam apte conscripta, ut antiquiora videri queant quam sunt. He refers to the Gallic origin of some of the speakers and then drops the question, using the traditional title: *P. Cornelii Taciti Eq. Ro. Dialogus, an sui seculi oratores antiquioribus et quare concedant.*

On page 469 he states that he had no MS of the *Agricola* but that he had made some improvements, and he gives five pages of notes, preceding the text, after which come the letter and notes of Alciatus and finally the *elenchus* or index. At the end of this, on the final page, is the colophon: *Basileae in officina Frobeniana per Hieronymum Frobenium et Nicolaum Episcopium, An. M.D.XXXIII.* The register, or, as he calls it, *Index ternionum,* follows, indicating 49 ternions. On the verso is the printer's device.

It should perhaps be noted that this edition of 1533 has marginal topics like those of Rivius.

The Aldine edition appeared in 1534. It is larger than the "pocket" editions, 19 cm., with 544 pages. It is an edition for use and not intended to add to the advance of Tacitean scholarship. It accepts the title *Annales* and, after a half-page appeal to students not to scorn the style of Tacitus, and a 22-page index, prints the text consecutively in small italic without interruptions. After the end of the *Agricola* come selections from the notes of Beatus and the complete Alciatus material. Then follows the register, showing 33 quaternions and 2 duernions, followed by the colophon: *Venetiis, in aedibus Haeredum Aldi Manutii Romani, et Andreae Asulani soceri. Mense Novembri. MDXXXIIII.* On the verso is the anchor device and the date, MDXXXIIII.

The first Gryphius edition, printed at Lyons in 1542 (the notes have the date 1541), added some annotations by Ferretti but was otherwise of no importance except as the first of a long series of handy Tacitus texts from a French press. The title page indicates only the historical works—*P. Cornelii Taciti equitis Ro. Ab excessu Augusti Annalium Libri sedecim. Ex castigatione Aemylii Ferretti, Beati Rhenani, Alciati, ac Beroaldi.* But after a dedicatory letter from Ferretti to Cardinal Francisco à Turnone, the texts of the *Annals, Histories, Germania, Dialogus,* and *Agricola* are printed consecutively. There are 768 pages, 17½ cm. tall. It is printed in italic type, with topical notes in the margins. The title *Annalium* is carried through the sixteen books. The page numbering stops with the end of the *Agricola,* page 710. The next page begins the *Elenchus in Annales reliquosque Libellos Cornelii Taciti, non omissis his quae prius addiderat Beatus Rhenanus.* In several instances long notes are inserted in the index taken from the *Res Germanicae* of Beatus. After the index there is a new title page, with the printer's device repeated: *In Cornelii Taciti Annalium libros Aemylii Ferretti Iurisconsulti Annotatiunculae. Lugdunum apud Seb. Gryphium, 1541.* After the blank verso of this title page there is a letter of one and a half pages from Thomas Sertinus to the reader, explaining that Tacitus is very useful to men of the day because of the similarity of his times to theirs, because of his *gravitas sententiarum,* and because of his knowledge of courts and royal ways. At the same time, inasmuch as Tacitus is difficult to read, the writer has gotten the eminent scholar Ferrettus to write the notes which he is now publishing. This section has a new numbering which goes through page 52. The next page has *errata* and is blank on the verso. The page following is blank on the recto, with a griffin and crab on the verso.

Croll, in the Bipontine edition, says that Brubach printed Tacitus in 1542 at Frankfurt, but I find no copy of this edition anywhere,[1] nor of the Gryphius editions of 1543 and 1554. The Gryphius Tacitus was reprinted without essential changes in 1551, 1559, 1576, and 1584. In 1544 a second edition of Beatus appeared from the press of Frobenius. It is practically a

---

1. Schweiger gives this, too, with the title: *Cornelii Taciti Historiae Augustae libri XVI, libellus de moribus et populis Germaniae, vita J. Agricolae, dialogus de claris oratoribus Francfurt ex off. P. Brubachii 8vo 1542.*

reprinting in new type. No essential improvement in the editing of Tacitus occurred until the first Plantin in 1574, edited by Justus Lipsius.

The first Plantin edition is a small volume, 17½ cm., with 768 pages, published at Antwerp. Lipsius prints royal and imperial privileges and a papal sanction, and opens the volume with a dedicatory epistle to the emperor Maximilian II, rather fulsome in its flattery and expounding the usefulness of Tacitus. The title page reads: *C. Cornelii Taciti Historiarum et Annalium Libri qui exstant, Iusti Lipsii studio emendati et illustrati ad Imp. Maximilianum II. Aug. P.F. Eiusdem Taciti Liber de Moribus Germanorum. Iulii Agricolae Vita. Incerti Scriptoris Dialogus de Oratoribus sui Temporis. Ad C.V. Ioannem Sambucum. Antverpiae, Ex officina Christophori Plantini, Architypographi Regii, M.D.LXXIV.* After the royal and imperial sanctions comes *C. Cor. Taciti Vita, Res gestae et scripta,* followed by *Veterum Scriptorum De Tacito Testimonia vel eiusdem Fragmenta.* Lipsius cites Pliny, Orosius, Vopiscus, and Sidonius. On page 15 begins the text of Books 17–21, which, however, appear now as Books 1–5 of the *Histories: P. Cornelii Taciti Ab Excessu Neronis Historiar. Lib. Primus. Initium mihi operis* etc. These end on page 214, *Fabianus in Pannonia,* followed on page 215 by *P. Cornelii Taciti ab excessu Divi Augusti Annalium Liber Primus.* Book 5 is indicated as a *fragmentum.* The *Annals* end with *obversis in Demertium* on page 559. The following page is blank and on 561 is a dedication of the Minor Works to Sambucus. These begin on page 562 with the *Germania, P. Cornelii Taciti de Situ, Moribus et populis Germaniae Libellus.* On page 583 is *Iulii Agricolae Vita Scriptore Cor. Tacito,* and on page 609 the interesting title: *Fabii Quinctiliani, ut videtur, Dialogus; an sui saeculi oratores antiquis, et quare concedant: Cor. Tacito falso inscriptus.* The *Dialogus* is followed by Lipsius' notes, preceded by an explanation to the reader, containing much of significance. First, as to his sources for improving the text: *Usus sum Romae tribus cod. mss. Bibliothecae Farnesianae primus fuit, quem beneficio C.V. et humanissimi Fulvii Ursini sum aptus; duo alii promti ex illo Thesauro Musarum, Vaticano. Sed alteri ex his duobus neque aetas neque bonitas eadem fuit: alter ex interiore et arcana bibliotheca, admirabile dictu est, quas notas boni et sinceri codicis saepe praetulerit. Eius argumentum, quod pleraque in eo more antiquo descripta, Anquiro, Cludo, Escendo, et alia quae opportune commemorabo. His tribus accessit editio Veneta vetus, anni (1494) quam adhibere vice libri scripti ideo non piguit, quod inter studiosos harum rerum constet, Taciti manuscripta exemplaria spissa et vix in Europa inveniri.*

In the next place, Lipsius explains his new division into *Histories* and *Annals*. The separation of the last five books he justifies by the fact that Tacitus makes a distinct beginning at the opening of the so-called Book 17, *Initium mihi operis,* by the citation of the fifth book of the *Histories* by Tertullian, and by the fact that the Farnese MS calls the eleventh book Book 1, while the Vatican has the phrase *Incipit XVII secundum quosdam.* The actual name, *Historiae,* he takes from the references in Pliny, Vopiscus, Tertullian, and Sidonius. He adopts the title *Annales, vel distinctionis causa vel quia Tacit. ipse aliquot locis sic appellat.* The notes extend from page 647 through page 750. He says that he adopts the name C. rather than P. because of the testimony of Sidonius and the Farnese MS. He reads T. Vinius for T. Iunius because of the evidence of a Roman inscription.

There are but two pages of notes on the *Germania,* with some readings from the Farnese MS, such as Bistonem, Barditum, ἀσκιπύργιον, Fluriniam. The *Agricola* has three pages of notes; then he comes to the *Dialogus,* with his doubt of the authorship. He claims to have done much for the *Dialogus,* which was in worse shape than the other essays. Hence the eight pages of notes. *Admirable dictu est quantum a Farnesiano codice (nam a Vaticanis aberat) in eo sanando simus adiuti. Multae lacunae expletae: verba et lineae integrae insertae et supra sexcentos locos, (Latine hoc non oratorie dico) emendati.* He concludes his general comments on the *Dialogus* with this: *Superest ut de scriptore huius libri verbo admoneam.*

*Quem Tacitum non esse tam certum apud me est quam si
Apollo respondisset. Argumentum eius rei firmum et apud
doctos unicum phrasis erit. Inclino ut Quinctiliano tribuam,
primum quia ipse fatetur lib. VI. initio, libellum a se editum
De caussis corruptae eloquentiae. . . . Deinde argumento
styli. . . . Convenit et ratio aetatis.*

The edition by Lipsius became from this time on for a hundred years the foundation for the text of Tacitus. There were
nearly a score of editions from the Plantin Press itself, most
of them sumptuous folios. At the other extreme were the Elze-
virs and other popular editions, all using the Lipsius text. Only
one important contribution was made, that of Pichena in his
edition of 1607.

*C. Cornelii Taciti Opera Quae Extant Iuxta veterrimos
Manuscriptos emendata, Notisque auctioribus illustrata per
Curtium Pichenam. Francofurti MDCVII.* This is a quarto
volume of 548 pages with 162 pages of notes. The notes have a
separate title page and separate numbering, although the regis-
tration is continuous. In a note to the printer Pichena implies
that the notes have been separately published previously.
Pichena is far more modest than Lipsius about his own work
and strongly commends his predecessor's notes to his readers.
About his own he is somewhat diffident, making no claim to
scholarship. Nevertheless it was he who first appreciated the
pre-eminent value of the two Medicean MSS and made them
(with the Puetolanus printed edition of 1497) the basis for
his text. Although he does not comment on the fact, his is the
earliest edition to have the modern chapter divisions. He was
deceived by the colophon in Med. II and believed that his MS
was written in 395.

In 1621 Elzevir presented the Lipsius text to the public in
pocket form, 13 cm. tall. In view of the modern notoriety of
Elzevir products it is worth while to note what the publisher
says to the reader in a preliminary letter: *Ut in exigua hac
forma, sine ambitione consulamus tibi, visum fuit . . . ut in
mole hac exigua nullum sentias incommodum . . . Minor
enim est, ni fallor, quam ut esse possit oneri: maior autem,*

quam ut occulos offendat. The volume, in octavo, has 218 pages and includes Lipsius' judgment on Tacitus, the life of Tacitus, and the ancient *testimonia.* There are also summaries at the beginning of books and a few notes at the end of each. Primarily it is merely a low-priced, handy copy of Tacitus for convenient reading. About twenty editions followed, as well as imitations from the presses of Hack, Blaeu, Janson and others of less repute. None of them adds anything to the body of Tacitean knowledge.

Various editors produced what amount to variorum editions in the first half of the seventeenth century without making any scholarly contribution to the tradition. Jan Gruter edited Tacitus in octavo at Frankfort in 1607, the same year in which Pichena's edition appeared. Gruter, like Pichena, has the modern chapter numbers. Jacob Mycillus made an edition in 1612, also octavo and also printed at Frankfort, and accompanied the text with a German translation. In 1638 Matthew Bernegger published his Tacitus, an octavo volume printed at Strassburg. It had an introduction by Freinsheim, has had considerable attention, and ran through several editions, but added nothing new in the way of Tacitean scholarship. In 1643 M. Z. Boxhorn did a similar edition for the Jannsen Press.

The Gronovius editions have had a greater reputation than they really merit. Johann Frederich Gronovius was a thorough scholar and deep student of Tacitus. He did not publish his own work. His son Jacob, however, in 1672 published a two-volume edition with some of his father's notes, in addition to a selection from those of all previous editors. Elzevir was the printer, but this was not one of his pocket editions. It is a good-sized octavo, 20 cm. high. In 1721 Jacob Gronovius published an edition in quarto (2 vols., 25½ cm.) at Trajecti Batavorum which is largely an improved edition of his earlier work. Such value as the two have lies in the fact that the father and son had had the use of a MS in Oxford which must have been the Bodleian 27,605 as is indicated by the letter from Pontius Pilate at the end, cited by Gronovius. This is a beautiful MS but it added nothing to the text because it belonged to the same closely related group of MSS of which one was the basis of the Puteolanus edition.

The Delphine edition by Julian Pichon, with its running interpretation, was simply a de luxe item in four volumes quarto.

Theodore Ryck in 1686–87 was the first to contribute further to the real study of Tacitus. His small edition (15½ cm.) in two volumes, one with the text (688 pp.) and one with notes (323 pp.) was published by Hack at Leyden. He made some use of Medicean II and corrected the error with regard to its date. In addition he used somewhat the Parisiensis Regius. He himself had access to Beroaldus' edition and also to that of Rivius, and he borrowed Puteolanus from a friend in Venice. He worked with J. F. Gronovius and Henry Savile. For the latter's attack on Tacitus for hostility toward the Christians, Ryck felt deep shame. The importance of Ryck's edition is the use he made of a MS which had belonged to Ruodolphus Agricola, who died in 1471. This MS subsequently lost, would seem to have been of great importance. Ryck was a man of high integrity, and his citations in themselves give evidence of soundness. And yet in numerous instances they are quite out of line with the generally accepted tradition and would seem to indicate a MS independent of the immediate source of Medicean II.

In 1752 the first attempt at a critical edition was made by Ernesti. The program which he laid down was decidedly modern in its method but unfortunately under the conditions of the day could not be lived up to. Ernesti could not personally see or check up the MSS which he listed. His edition, published by Weidmann at Leipzig, was in two volumes (20 cm., octavo). In the preface he points out the necessity of giving more complete collations of MSS used and of valuing an edition for its MS source rather than for the name of the editor. This leads to an enumeration of the MSS known up to his time and a review of the important editions based on them. A fair complaint is voiced that none of the editors had ever given any real description of the MS or MSS which he used. Ernesti thinks that

Spira may have used a Venetus MS for his *editio princeps*, Puteolanus a MS like Ernesti's Gudianus. In the latter supposition he was undoubtedly correct; the former involves a difficulty. Ernesti bases his guess on a comment of Victorius on a Venetian MS in the Library of St. Mark, calling it *antiquus*. This, Ernesti claims, could not have been Venetus 381, which was written in 1453 and therefore was not *antiquus*. But *antiquis litteris* means a fifteenth-century hand, and the text of Spira corresponds to the class to which Ven. 381 belongs. At the same time it should not be forgotten that there was at one time confusion between St. Mark's at Venice and St. Mark's at Florence, where 68. 2 once resided, and this may have some bearing on Victorius' remark.

Ernesti accepts Lipsius' low estimate of Rhenanus' Budensis with slight modification, notes Lipsius' use of two Vatican MSS and the Farnese, rather scorns the Agricola MS of Ryck, but does not feel that its existence can be denied. He notes Ryck's use of Parisiensis Regius. He credits the Gronovius editions with the first use of the Jesus College MS and Bodleian 27,605. Finally he mentions as MSS that he has heard of Laur. 68. 3, 68. 4, 68. 5 (68. 3 is actually a copy of the *editio princeps*), Venetus 381, an Ottoboni MS in the Vatican, another MS at Naples, one at Cesena, one that he actually used at Wölfenbuttel (Gudianus 118), and one in S. Joan. in Carbonaria. About this last I can find no further information. In spite of this impressive survey, Ernesti did not make use of any MS except the Gudianus. The importance of his edition lies largely in his insistence on study, description, and use of the MSS and his reasoned rejection of the term *lectio vulgata* (*sive recepta*). In spite of his excellent precept, he gives little description of his Gudianus MS, though the citations of readings in his notes are fairly constant.

In 1771 after much advertising and delay there appeared from the press of Delatour in Paris the most sumptuous edition of Tacitus since the great Plantin folios. This was the four-volume edition by Gabriel Brotier in large quarto with wide margins and excellent paper. Brotier's only real addition, if such it should be called, to the tradition of Tacitus was that of the Supplements which Brotier wrote to complete the histories of Tiberius, Gaius, Claudius, and Nero. His text, however, served as that of the finest printed edition of Tacitus' Works, the three-volume 1795 Bodoni. It was pirated for printing in Edinburgh under its own title, and it served as the text of Homer's sumptuous but otherwise worthless London edition of 1790–94 and of many French and Italian editions with and without translations.

G. C. Croll was editor of the Bipontine Tacitus which appeared in 1779. This was revised in a second edition by F. C. Exter in 1792. Aside from the convenient lists of MSS, editions, and translations known to the editors, this edition is of no particular value.

Much more important was the revision of Ernesti published in 1801. This had been begun by Frid. Aug. Wolf but all save a minor portion of the work was done by J. J. Oberlin, the rediscoverer of the Budensis MS which Beatus Rhenanus had used in making his edition of 1533 and which had afterward disappeared. Oberlin states that it was given to him by a strenuous military officer named Dorsner, who had inherited it. Undoubtedly Oberlin had an exaggerated idea of the value of the Codex Budensis, but it enabled him to improve the text of Ernesti, and in his description of his MSS Oberlin follows the injunctions rather than the practice of his predecessor.

Almost immediately following the appearance of Oberlin's revision of Ernesti, G. A. Ruperti published an annotated edition of the *Annals* (Göttingen, 1804), which was followed by his complete edition of the Works in 1832–39. Carson, in his text edition (Edinburgh, 1818) says that he made primary use of Ruperti, whose work he dates 1801. Possibly Carson used only the Ruperti *Annals* or possibly Ruperti published in separate parts of which I have found no record. At any rate, Ruperti in the 1832 preface evaluates the work of Oberlin, whom he passes by rather scornfully; of C. H. Weise, whose text made for Tauchnitz in 1825 he characterizes correctly as a repetition of Oberlin; of Weikert (Leipzig, 1813–16), a mere school edition, not the work of a scholar; of Bekker (first edition, 1801, second and chief edition, Berlin, 1825) as a rehash of Lipsius, Heinse, Ernesti, and Wolf (Bekker leaned heavily on the text of Ernesti); and of Walther (Halle, 1831–33), which he admits to following largely in his text. Ruperti gives the most complete conspectus up to his time of the Tacitean MSS. He lists twenty-two of the thirty MSS now known and in addition the Bambergensis, Agricola, Orat. Jesu, Hispanus vel Couvarouviae, Spina, Mirandulanus, P. Victorii in St. Mark's at Venice, Herbipolensis, and S. Johannis in Carbonario. In addition Ruperti gives a good bibliography of Tacitus and has an extensive *annotatio perpetua* with his text. He made no attempt to group his MSS into families, and his evaluation of them shows no great advance over his predecessors.

Walther, already mentioned as the source of Ruperti's text, produced a four-volume edition in 1831–33, first dividing the MSS into "Genoan," "Roman," and "Miscell." Lünemann had already edited a school edition in 1825 and Bach produced another, 1834–35, as did Fr. Ritter in 1834–36. This last-named edition was succeeded by Ritter's more ambitious text in 1848, in which he has a good account of the origin of Medicean I and II. Doederlein produced for Bernhardy's Bibliotheca still another school edition in 1841–47. Orelli, in 1846–48, produced a complete text based on a collation of the two Medicean MSS, made for him by I. G. Baiter. This text was not in any major sense an improvement on Ruperti's. The text of the *Agricola* was based on readings from Wex, that of the *Germania* and *Dialogus* on Tross' readings of Leidensis. The introductory essays and the commentary accompanying the text are largely, almost completely, borrowed from Ernesti, Walther, and other sources. The emphasis on the Medicean MSS had its important value, but the edition was hardly a credit to Orelli. When only the first volume had appeared, Nipperdey wrote a devastating review in *Die Allgemeinen Literatur-Zeitung* (Halle, 1847), *1, 161*. Orelli undertook a revision as early as 1859 and completed the *Annals*. The rest was brought out by Schweizer-Seidler, Andresen, and Meiser in 1877. It was perhaps as an answer to Nipperdey that Orelli says in his preface to the revised edition that it is intended for the really cultured nations who had appreciated his Horace— the English, French, and Italian. Nipperdey himself made an excellent text with *apparatus criticus* for Weidmann in 1871– 76, to supersede their Haase stereotype edition of 1855 without apparatus, itself the successor of a similar text by Bekker (1831). He based his text on Ritter, but his apparatus gave ample readings from the Medicean MSS and selected emendations of previous editors.

The modern text really begins with the Teubner edition by Karl Felix Halm in 1850–51. This went through many printings, appeared in a second edition in 1857, a third in 1874, and a fourth in 1883, the year after Halm's death. A fifth edition entirely revised by G. Andresen came out in 1926–28, and a sixth, further but less successfully edited by Köstermann, appeared in 1934–37, followed by a seventh, also by Köstermann, in 1949–50. Andresen had also revised Nipperdey's text for Weidmann (1892–1904). Several other modern text editions should be noted: the Oxford text, with Minor Works by Furneaux (1899), *Annals* (1906) and *Histories* (1910) by C. D. Fisher; and the Budé text by Goelzer, consisting of the *Annals* (1923–25), with a French translation, and the Minor Works (1923). But Goelzer published an edition of the *Histories* in 1920 for the Libraire Hachette with text and commentary. Editiones Helveticae (Frauenfeld) published an excellent text of the *Annals* in 1949, edited by Harald Fuchs.

Meanwhile interest had grown in the making of good annotated editions for use in schools and universities. Emile Jacob edited the *Annals* in this fashion at Paris in 1875–77, with a second edition in 1885–86. Holbrook did a fine college edition of the *Annals* for Macmillan in 1882, and Furneaux for the Oxford Press two years later. Carl Herraeus produced a school edition of the *Histories* in 1864 and Spooner a college edition (Macmillan) in 1891. Goelzer published a two-volume edition of the *Histories* with commentary for the Libraire Hachette in 1920, followed by the *Annals* with introduction, text, apparatus, and translation for the Libraire Budé in 1923–25, and the Minor Works (text, introduction, and apparatus) in 1923.

GERMANIA

Rodney Robinson, in his edition of the Germania (*Am. Phil. Ass.*, 1935) gives an excellent account of the *Germania* editions. The treatise was published at Bologna separately from de Spira's text in 1472. In 1473(?) and 1474 respectively separate editions of the *Germania* alone were published at Nüremberg and Rome by the Creussner and Gensberg Presses. These were based either on two separate unknown MSS or on two independent recensions of a still unknown MS. At Venice two separate editions of the *Germania* made from the text of de Spira appeared in 1476 and 1481. A Vienna edition in 1500 (?) was issued from the Winterberg Press and was reprinted at Paris in 1511. This was taken from an unknown MS and the text of the Puteolanus edition of the collected works. Puteolanus was the sole source of two Leipzig editions (1502 and 1509) and one at Erfurt (1509). The Vienna text of 1515 used both Puteolanus and the Vienna edition of 1500.

The first really scholarly attempt to establish a text of the *Germania* was made by Beatus Rhenanus. He published a separate *Germania* in 1519, using the Nüremberg edition as well as the known MSS. This was the established text down to 1574. The second period, that of the Lipsius text, produced no separate edition of the *Germania,* and neither Gronovius nor Pichena did anything important for the *Germania* text.

With Brotier's edition of 1771 began a period in which the various *Germania* MSS were given more careful attention. Kapp at Leipzig in 1788 first used the reading of the lost Hummelianus and was followed by Passow (1817), largely by Orelli (1819), who used Turicensis, by Gruber (1832), who made the first attempt at MSS classification, by Bach (1834), who used Venetus and Stuttgart, and to a lesser extent by Gerlach (1835). Gerlach cited eighteen MSS and had borrowed collations of Massmann; his idea was excellent but his execution bad.

A new period began with Tross in 1841. He discovered the

Leidensis and based his text on it; he was the first to learn about Enoch of Ascoli and the Hersfeld correspondence. Massmann was even more epoch-making. In 1847 he published his edition, for which he used complete collations of twenty MSS. His text is still to a large degree definitive. Tagmann did not make an edition but published in 1847 his *De Taciti Germaniae Apparatu Critico*. He had access to Massmann's material and made the first great attempt to group the MSS. He conceived of two classes, the second derived from the first, and divided his first class into two sections with Farn., Vat. 1518, Stuttgart, and Hummelianus in one group and Leidensis, Vat. 1862, Monacensis, and Vat. 2964 in the other. Leidensis held its own as the best MS through the editions of Orelli (1848), Haase (1855), Ritter (1848), Halm (1850–1), Haupt (1855), and Kritz (1860).

Reifferscheid, in 1867, published his *Coniectanea in Taciti Germaniam*, beginning a new period in which Vat. 1862 took the place of Leidensis as the best MS. He was followed in Schweizer-Seidler's second edition of Orelli-Baiter (1877) by Halm in his third edition (1874) and by Müller in 1887. Meiser in the meantime (1873) had gone back to Leidensis, and Nipperdey (1876) to the pre-Tross era. Hirschfelder (1878) in the fourth edition of Kritz used Stuttgart in addition to the four great MSS.

In 1878 Holder produced the history of a *Germania* tradition represented by Hummelianus, Monacensis, and Stuttgart. The other MSS came from Enoch's apographa and are inferior Italian products. His second edition appeared in 1882. Wünsch combated the theories of Holder in a dissertation in 1893 but did not produce an edition.

With the publication of Toletanus by Abbott in 1903 and of Aesinus in 1907 by Annibaldi all the traditions seemed for the moment to be threatened; but Andresen in 1914 returned to comparative simplicity, accepting the X and Y families as represented by the four main MSS and the Z family represented by Aesinus. He was followed by Wolff (1915) and by Gudeman (1916 and 1928). Annibaldi (n.d.) used his Aesinus almost exclusively and was followed in this by Valmaggi in 1924. In 1935 Robinson published an edition with a complete study of all the MSS and with text, apparatus, and annotations, as well as a history of the printed text, a monumental contribution to the study of the *Germania* (*Am. Phil. Ass.,* Middletown, Conn., 1935). In 1949 Jacques Perret added a *Germania* with French translation to the Budé series.

AGRICOLA

The Life of Agricola was not included in the *editio princeps* of Tacitus but was added to the corpus by Puteolanus in his first edition. There would seem to have been no separate edition of the *Agricola* until 1637, when it was printed in a 295-page octavo volume by M. Virdung at Nüremberg. With only two known MSS of the essay and these two probably copies of the same archetype, there was less incentive to produce new editions than in the case of the *Germania* with its numerous MSS representing different lines of tradition. Boxhorn edited the *Agricola* at Leyden in 1642, Sibaldi at Edinburgh in 1711, M. I. Soergel at Limoges in 1772. Foulis printed an *Agricola* from the text of Jacob in 1777. Editions were produced by Dronke (Coblenz, 1824, 1844), Becker (Hamburg, 1826), Peerlkamp (Leyden, 1827, 1864), and Walch (Berlin, 1828). This last edition was strongly denounced by Wex as not only bad but a real detriment to the critical tradition. Roth (Nüremberg, 1833) and Nepveu (Paris, 1840) added nothing to the knowledge of the text or its interpretation, and the same is almost true of Dübner (Paris, 1843). Of course, the *Agricola* had appeared in the editions of the collected works, but little was done for its clarification until Wex published his edition at Braunschweig in 1852.

This edition by Wex established the text for years to come. He gave a thorough re-examination to the two MSS, presented essays on the composition of the essay and on the Romans in Britain, and gave an excellent bibliography on the work done on the *Agricola* to date. His list of editions is admirably complete.

Following Wex came a stream of annotated editions of the

Agricola. Between 1852 and the end of the century more than thirty such publications appeared, of which perhaps the most notable are the following: Kritz (Berlin, 1859, 1874), Quicherat (Paris, 1867, 1879), Draeger (Leipzig, 1869, sixth edition 1905), Tuecking (Paderbour, 1869), Gantrelle (Paris, 1875, 1880), Urlichs (Würzburg, 1875), Peter (Jena, 1875), Henry (Paris, 1876, 1909), Prammer (Vienna, 1880), Cornelissen (Leyden, 1881), Jacob (Paris, 1881 with nine later editions), Schoene (Berlin, 1889), Pichon (Paris, 1895), Furneaux (Oxford, 1898, 1922), Nemethy (Budapest, 1899).

In 1903 F. F. Abbott published the MS recently discovered at Toledo which represented a different tradition from that already known. Editions by Stuart (New York, 1907) and Sladovich-Sladoeievich (Zagreb, 1910) were the most notable results.

In 1916 C. Annibaldi published the Jesi MS, giving a definitely greater interest to the *Agricola* than it had previously possessed. Editions followed by Spinelli (Citta di Castello, 1914), Ramorino (Bologna, 1917), Smolka (Leipzig, 1919), Anderson (complete revision of Furneaux in 1922) and E. de Saint-Denis (Collection Budé, Paris, 1948).

DIALOGUS

The *De oratoribus* was first printed separately by Beatus Rhenanus in a 22-page quarto volume at Paris in 1539. Rhenanus made use of the Farnese MS for the first time, the earlier texts (in editions of the collected Works) having been based on a MS like the Venetus. I can find no trace of an independent *Dialogus* between 1539 and 1706, although the essay appeared regularly in the editions of Tacitus. It was also edited by P. Pithou and published as the work of Quintilian in the edition of his *Declamationes* (Paris, 1580, 1594, 1618, 1641, 1665) and with his *Institutio* at Geneva in 1604, 1618, 1641. In 1665 the *Dialogus* was included in the edition of Quintilian's *Opera* published by the Hack Press at Leipzig; in 1675 it formed part of the Oxford edition of Quintilian's *Declamationes* and in 1696 of Obrecht's edition of the same at Strassberg. In the *editio princeps* it is entitled *Dialogus de Oratoribus Claris.* Puteolanus gave it the more extensive title, *Dialogus an sui saeculi oratores antiquioribus et quare concedant.* Beatus Rhenanus in his edition of 1533 expressed serious doubts as to whether Tacitus was the author of the *Dialogus,* although he uses the traditional title of Puteolanus. Lipsius declared flatly against the Tacitean authorship, inclining to ascribe it to Quintilian and using the title *Incerti Scriptoris Dialogus de Oratoribus sui Temporis.*

The separate edition of 1706 by Benzel at Uppsala was overshadowed by the better one of Heumann, Leipzig, 1719. Heumann definitely ascribed the *Dialogus* to Quintilian. In 1788 Schulze issued his first edition at Leipzig and designated the *Dialogus* as erroneously ascribed to Tacitus. There followed editions by Homer (London, 1789), Seebode (Goettingen, 1813), Dronke (Coblenz, 1828), Osann (Giessen, 1829), Boetticher (Berlin, 1832), Ritter (Bonn, 1836), and Pabst (Leipzig, 1841), none of which made marked advance in the development of text or commentary. In 1841 Hess published an edition at Leipzig, bringing in the readings of the Vienna MS (Vind. 49) and Tross another at Hamm with a collation of Leidensis. After minor editions by Nicolas at Paris in 1845 and by Orelli at Zürich in 1846, Michaelis made the next and most distinguished contribution by awarding first place among the MSS to Vat. 1862. Since Michaelis there have been many editions, of which the most comprehensive and useful is probably that of Gudeman, Leipzig, 1914. The others are: Andresen (Leipzig, 1872), Peter (Jena, 1879), Deltour (Paris, 1879), Weinkauff (Cologne, 1890), Baehrens (Leipzig, 1881), Dupuy (Paris, 1881), Goelzer (Paris, 1877), Wolff (Gotha, 1890), Valmaggi (Torino, 1890), Peterson (Oxford, 1893), Gudeman (Boston, 1894), Bennett (Boston, 1894), Nicolas (Paris, 1894), Forest (Paris, 1896), John (Berlin, 1899), Schoene (Berlin, 1899), Longhi (Milano, 1899), Constans (Paris, 1899), Manoni (Palermo, 1902), Dienel (Leipzig, 1908), Roehl (Leipzig, 1911), Wick (Torino, 1919), Goelzer and Bornecque (Collection Budé, Paris 1947).

SELECTED BIBLIOGRAPHY

ANYTHING like a complete bibliography of the published work on Tacitus would consist of so many thousands of items as to defeat its own purpose if included in such a book as the present one. All that is attempted here is reference to some of the most significant and fundamental publications, including the more recent books, pamphlets, and articles in the main fields of Tacitean study.

I. General Introduction

Schanz-Hosius is basic for any work in the general field of factual investigation and furnishes a good selective bibliography.

Gaston Boissier's *Tacite* (Paris, 1903; 6th ed. Paris, 1926) with an American edition (*Tacitus and Other Roman Studies,* G. P. Putnam, 1906) still furnishes one of the best introductions to Tacitus and his work studied with reference to his life and environment.

Other convenient sources of collected information with useful summaries of the essential material are Dubois-Guichan, *Tacite et son siècle,* 2 vols. Paris, 1861; G. Unita, *Vita, ingegno e pensiero politico di Cornelio Tacito, con uno studio sulla lingua e lo stile,* Rome and Milan, 1935; and C. Gierratano, *Cornelio Tacito,* Rome, 1941.

On the historical side, one of the best approaches is by way of J. Asbach, *Roemischen Kaisertum und Verfassung bis an Trajan. Eine historische Einleitung zu den Schriften des P. Cornelius Tacitus,* Cologne, 1896. This may well be supplemented by the following books on special periods: F. B. Marsh, *The Reign of Tiberius,* Oxford University Press, 1931; V. M. Scramuzza, *The Emperor Claudius,* Harvard University Press, 1940; B. W. Henderson, *The Life and Principate of the Emperor Nero,* London, 1903; and B. W. Henderson, *Civil War and Rebellion in the Roman Empire,* London, 1908.

For the *Agricola* the best introductory material is that dealing with the literary form of the essay. F. Leo, *Die griechische-roemische Biographie* (Leipzig, 1901) is fundamental but should be supplemented by G. L. Hendrickson, *The Proconsulate of Julius Agricola in Relation to History and Encomium,* University

379

380   *Bibliography*

of Chicago, Decennial Publication, Chicago, 1902. The archaeological background is of less general importance and is scattered
through many books, mostly English, dealing with the antiquities
of Britain. An adequate account of what is relevant to the *Agricola*
may be found in Furneaux's introduction to his edition.

The student of the *Dialogus* will naturally go to R. Hirzel, *Der
Dialog* (Leipzig, 1895) and to E. Norden, *Die antike Kunstprosa*
(Leipzig and Berlin, 1909) for an understanding of the form. For
other matters the best summaries are to be found in the Prolegomena to Gudeman's German edition, Leipzig and Berlin, 1914.

For introductory material to the *Germania,* E. Norden, *Die
germanische Urgeschichte in Tacitus' Germania* (2d ed. Berlin
and Leipzig, 1922) covers one side, and Rodney P. Robinson's
edition (No. 5 of the Philological Monographs of the American
Philological Association, 1935) the rest.

II. Life of Tacitus

Gaston Boissier, "Comment Tacite est devenu Historien," Revue
    des deux mondes, 2 (1901), 277.
E. Paratore, *Tacito,* Milan, 1951.
Mary L. Gordon, "The Patria of Tacitus," *Journal of Roman
    Studies* (1936), p. 145.
P. Fabia, "La Carriere senatoriale de Tacite," *Journal des Savants*
    (1926), p. 193.

III. Religious and Philosophical Bias

J. D. M. Cornelissen, *Hooft en Tacitus,* Nijmegen, 1938.
Nils Eriksson, *Religiositaet och Irreligiositaet hos Tacitus,* Lund,
    1935.
P. Fabia, "L'Irreligion de Tacite," *Journal des Savants* (1914),
    p. 250.
Robert von Poehlmann, *Die Weltanschauung des Tacitus,* 2d ed.
    Munich, 1913. Extensively reviewed by P. Fabia, in *Journal
    des Savants* (1914), p. 250.
A. Sizoo, "Paetus Trasea et le Stoicisme," *Revue des études Latines*
    (1926), p. 229.

IV. Historical Method

P. Fabia, "Le Regle annalistique dans l'historiographie romaine,"
    Journal des Savants (1900), p. 433.

M. A. Levi, *Nerone e i suoi tempi,* Milan, 1949.

F. Marx, "Untersuchungen zur Komposition und zu den Quellen von Tacitus' *Annalen," Hermes* (1925), p. 74.

F. G. Moore, "Annalistic Method as Related to the Book Divisions in Tacitus," *Transactions of the American Philological Association* (1923), p. 5.

F. Pfister, "Tacitus als Historiker," *Woch, f. kl. Phil.* (1917), pp. 833, 899.

R. L. Roberts, *Tacitus' Conception of the Function of History* Greece and Rome, (1936), p. 9.

G. H. Stevenson, "Ancient Historians and their Sources," *Journal of Philosophy* (1920), p. 204.

B. Walker, *The Annals of Tacitus. A Study in the Writing of History,* Manchester, 1952.

A. Walser, *Rom, der Reich und die Fremden Voelker in der Geschichtschreibung des Fruehen Kaiserzeit,* Baden-Baden, 1951.

V. Sources

C. Baier, *Tacitus und Plutarch. Progr.,* Frankfurt a/m, 1893.

O. Clason, *Tacitus und Sueton,* Breslau, 1870.

D. Detlefsen, "Ueber des aelteren Plinius' Geschichte seiner Zeit und ihr Verhaeltniss zum Tacitus," *Philologus* (1875), p. 40.

E. Egli, *Feldzuege in Armenien von 41–63 n. Chr.,* Leipzig, 1868.

P. Fabia, *Les Sources de Tacite dans les "Histoires" et les "Annales,"* Paris, 1893.

A. Gudeman, "The Sources of the Germania of Tacitus," *Transactions of the American Philological Association* (1900), p. 93.

P. Keseling, "Tacitus und Seneca," *Ph. Woch.* (1932), p. 1461.

F. B. Marsh, *The Reign of Tiberius,* Oxford, 1931. The best discussion of the sources of *Ann.* 1–6, superseding Sievers and Freytag.

J. Martin, *Zur Quellenfrage in den "Annalen" und "Historien." Hosius Studien zu Tacitus,* Stuttgart, 1936.

F. Marx, "Die Quellen der Germanenkriege bei Tacitus und Dio," *Klio* (1933), p. 323.

F. Marx, "Tacitus und die Literatur der exitus illustrium virorum," *Philologus* (1837–38), p. 83.

T. Mommsen, -"Cornelius Tacitus und Cluvius Rufus," *Hermes* (1870), p. 295.

T. Mommsen, "Das Verhaeltniss des Tacitus zu den Acten des Senats," *Sitz. der kgl. Preurs. Akad. der Wiss. zu Berlin* (1904), p. 1146.

E. Norden, "Josephus und Tacitus," *Neue Jahrb. f. d. kl. Alt.* (1913), p. 637.

R. Raffay, *Die Memoiren der Kaiserin Agrippina,* Vienna, 1884.

W. Schur, "Die Orientpolitik des Kaisers Nero," *Klio,* new Ser. 2, Supplement 15 (1923).

F. Walter, "Zu Tacitus und Seneca Rhetor," *Berl. Phil. Woch.* (1918), p. 237.

F. Walter, "Zu Tacitus und Valerius Maximus," *Phil. Woch.* (1918), p. 789.

VI. Literary Characteristics

C. G. Cole, *The Poetical Qualities in the Diction and Style of Tacitus,* New York, 1910.

O. Clason, *De breviloquentiae Taciteae quibusdam generibus,* Leipzig, 1881.

E. Courband, *Le Procédés d'art de Tacite dans les "Histoires,"* Paris, 1906.

J. Couisin, "Histoire et Rhetorique dans l'*Agricola*," *Revue des études Latines* (1936), p. 326.

F. Degel, *Archaistische Bestandteile der Sprache des Tacitus,* Nurnberg, 1907.

A. Gunz, *Die deklamatorische Rhetorik in der Germania des Tacitus,* Diss., Lausanne, 1907.

G. L. Hendrickson, *The Proconsulate of Julius Agricola in Relation to History and to Encomium,* University of Chicago, Decennial Publication, Chicago, 1902.

P. Kegler, *Ironie und Sarkasmus bei Tacitus,* Diss., Leipzig, 1913.

F. Krohn, *Personendarstellungen bei Tacitus,* Diss., Grosschoenau. i. Sa., 1934.

A. Salvatore, *Stile e Ritmo in Tacito,* Naples, 1950.

G. Soerborn, *Variatio Sermonis Taciti,* Diss., Uppsala, 1935.

E. Wolfflin, "Schriften ueber den Taciteischen stil und genetische Entwicklung derselben," *Philologus* (1867), p. 126.

VII. Syntax

A. H. Draeger, *Ueber Syntax und stil des Tacitus,* 3d ed. Leipzig, 1882.

J. Gantrelle, *Grammaire et style de Tacite,* 2d ed. Paris, 1882.

Articles on the details of syntactical usage are too numerous for citation. Useful summaries are to be found in the introductions to the editions of the *Annals* by Furneaux and the *Dialogus* by Gudeman.

VIII. Lexicography

P. Fabia, *Onomasticon Taciteum,* Paris, 1900.

A. Gerber and A. Greef, *Lexicon Taciteum,* Leipzig, 1903.

IX. Reliability

E. Bacha, *Le Genie de Tacite,* Paris, 1906.

J. de Boisjoslin, "De l'Authenticité des *Annales* et des *Histoires* de Tacite," *Revue de la Société des Ét. Hist.,* 4th Ser. 2 (1898), p. 155.

E. G. Hardy, "Tacitus as a Military Historian in the *Histories,*" *Journal of Philology, 61* (1940), 123.

H. Naumann, "Die Glaubwuerdigkeit des Tacitus," *Bonn. Jahrb.* (1934), p. 21.

G. Vogt, "Tacitus und die Unparteilichkeit des Historikers," in *Hosius Studien zu Tacitus,* Stuttgart, 1936.

The books by Ross, Hochart, Wiener, and Jerome, now chiefly known as literary curiosities, are discussed in the chapter on the Reliability of Tacitus.

X. Survival

E. Cornelius, *Quomodo Tacitus, historiarum scriptor, in hominum memoria versatus sit usque ad renascentes litteras saeculis XIV et XV,* Wetzlar, 1888.

L. Delamare, *Tacite et la littérature française,* Paris, 1907.

M. Lehnerdt, *Enoch von Ascoli und die Germania von Tacitus,* Berlin, 1895.

C. W. Mendell, "Leidensis B P L. 16. B," *AJP, 75* (1954), 250.

P. de Nolhac, "Bocace et Tacite," *Mel. d'Arch. et d'Hist.* (1892), p. 130.

L. Prelle, *Die Wiederentstehung des Tacitus,* Fulda, 1952.

F. Ramorino, *Cornelio Tacito nella storia della coltura*, Milan, 1898.

R. Sabbadini, *Storia e critica di alcuni testi Latini*, Florence, 1890.

G. Toffanini, *Macchiavelli e il "Tacitismo,"* Padua, 1921.

XI. Manuscripts

1. REPRODUCTIONS

Laur. 68. 1 and Laur. 68. 2 were published in photographic reproduction by A. W. Sijthoff at Leyden in 1902 with an introduction by H. Rostagno.

Leidensis 18, of the minor works except the *Agricola*, was similarly published by Sijthoff at Leyden in 1907 with an introduction by G. Wissowa.

Aesinas 8, of the *Agricola* and *Germania*, was photographically reproduced by Rudolf Till in 1943 in his *Handschriftliche Untersuchungen zu Tacitus' "Agricola" und "Germania,"* Berlin and Dahlem.

Photostatic copies of some of the less important manuscripts (Budensis 9; Cesena Malatestinus; Harleianus 2764; Kopenhagen; Paris Regius 6118; Vaticanus Latinus 1863, 1864, 1958; Vaticanus Urbinas 412; and Venetus Marcianus XIV. 1) are available at the Sterling Library of Yale University.

2. MAJOR WORKS

G. Andresen, *De Codicibus Mediceis Annalium Taciti. Progr.*, Berlin, 1892.

F. Grat, "Nouvelles Recherches sur Tacite," *Mélanges d'Arch. et d'Hist.* (1925), p. 31.

M. Lehnerdt, "Zur Ueberlieferung des Tacitus," *Hermes* (1900), p. 350.

C. Meiser, "Zur Handschriftlichen Ueberlieferung der Historien des Tacitus," *Neue Jahrb. f. Phil.* (1882), p. 133.

C. W. Mendell, "Manuscripts of Tacitus XI–XVI," *Yale Classical Studies, 6* (1939), 39.

C. W. Mendell, "Leidensis B P L IV B," *AJP, 75* (1954), 250.

3. MINOR WORKS

The discovery of the Aesinas MS in 1910 made practically all previous work on the *Agricola* out of date. The introduction to the edition of J. G. C. Anderson is perhaps the best basis for work on the *Agricola*. For the *Dialogus,* Michaelis is basic, Gudeman's the best recent summary. Robinson's edition of the *Germania* is indispensable for any work on that essay.

W. Aly, "Zur Ueberlieferung des Dialogus," *Rhein. Mus.* (1913), p. 636.

G. Andresen, "Zur Handschriftlichen Ueberlieferung des Taciteischen Agricola," *Woch. f. kl. Phil.* (1900), p. 1299.

G. Andresen, "Zur Handschriftlichen Ueberlieferung des Taciteischen Dialogs," *Woch. f. kl. Phil.* (1900), pp. 641, 697, 778, 1210.

C. W. Mendell, "Manuscripts of Tacitus' Minor Works," *Memoirs of the American Academy in Rome,* 1949.

J. Perret, *Recherches sur le texte de la Germanie,* Paris, 1950.

R. Reitzenstein, "Zur Textgeschichte der Germania," *Philologus* (1898), p. 307.

F. Scheuer, "De Tacitei de Oratoribus Dialogi Codicum Nexu et Fide, *Bresslauer Phil. Abhandl.,* 1891.

A. Schoenemann, *De Taciti Germaniae Codicibus Capita duo,* Halle, 1910.

R. Till, *Handschriftliche Untersuchungen zu Tacitus' Agricola und Germania,* Berlin and Dahlem, 1943.

INDEX

CHAPTERS 14 and 16 are not indexed because the manuscripts described in them are presented in alphabetical order. Chapter 19 is not indexed; the editions listed in it are in chronological order.

Acilius, C., 32

Acta Diurna, as source material, 212

Acta Senatus, as source material, 212

Acte, characterization of, 153

Adam of Bremen, knowledge of Tacitus, 235

Adua River, 174

Aemilius Scaurus, autobiographical material, 34

Aeneas Silvius Piccolomini: use of *Germania* by, 287; knowledge of the MSS of Enoch, 250

African War, 187

Agricola: a eulogistic biography, 26; change in style from *Dialogus,* 25; character drawing in, 138 f.; MS at Monte Cassino, 283 ff.; political implications of, 69; so-called Hersfeld MS of, 280 ff.; sources of, 214 ff.; style of, 81 ff.

Agricola, Rudolph, 328

Agrippa, Menenius, 44

Agrippa Postumius, death of, 126

Agrippina, commentaries of, as source for Tacitus, 204

Agrippina the Younger, how presented, 148 ff.

Albiganum, 170

Albinus, Postumius, A., 32

Alfonso of Naples, MS transactions of, 244

Alimentus, Cincius, 32

Ammianus Marcellinus, probable knowledge of Tacitus, 228

Annales, as title for Tacitus' writings, 346

Annales Maximi, 31

Annals: different material from *His-* *tories,* 102 f.; distinction between *Histories* and *Annals,* 346; efficient motivation in, 102; foreign events treated as interludes in, 119 f.; increased dramatic tension, 108; mature bitterness in, 28 f.; stylistic change in later books, 109 ff.; summaries of minor events in, 119; violations of annalistic order in, 119 ff.

Annibaldi, Cesari, discovered Jesi MS, 253

Annius Bassus, admired by Pliny and Tacitus, 17

Anteius Rufus, P., as possible source for Tacitus, 214

Antias, Valerius, 33

Anti-imperialism, 68

Antipater, Coelius, 33

Antipolis, 170

Antistius, pamphlets as source material, 212

Antistius Sosianus, how presented, 145

Antonius, 179

Antonius Julianus, as possible source for Tacitus, 214

Apollinaris, Sidonius, knowledge of Tacitus, 3, 229 f.

Appius Claudius, 44

Aquileia, 170, 175, 178 f.

Aquilius Regulus, M., as possible source for Tacitus, 214

Archaeological remains, as source material, 213

Aristocracy, change in first century A.D., 42 f., 48 f.

Armenia, 185

Arminius, 183

387

Arruntius, L., 127 ff.
Artificiality, in first-century literature, 44
Arulenus Rusticus: as possible source for Tacitus, 214; obstinate opponent of emperors, 47; victim of Domitian, 18
Ascoli, Enoch of, 5, 248 ff., 286
Asinius Bassus, friend of Pliny and Tacitus, 18
Asinius Gallus, 127 ff.
Asinius Pollio, 43 f.
Asinius Rufus, friend of Pliny and Tacitus, 18
Asselio, Sempronius, 33
Ateius Capito, M., 127 ff.
Attilio Hortis, the books of Boccaccio, 240 n.
Aufidius Bassus, 47, 214
Augsburg Chronicle, cites Enoch, 254
Augustus, peace policy of, 40
Aulus Gellius, 77
Aurispa, connection with Hersfeld MS, 242, 249
Autobiography, in early Roman literature, 33 f.
Avitus, Junius, friend of Pliny, 17

Bacha, E., author of *Le Genie de Tacite*, 220
Bassus, Asinius, 18
Bassus, Aufidius, 47, 214
Bassus, Saleius, dramatic productions of, 106
Batavians, Island of, 180
Beatus Rhenanus: first editor to use Yale MS, 325; questions authorship of *Dialogus*, 5
Beccadelli, Il Panormita, connection with Hersfeld MS, 250
Bedriacum: campaign of, 170 ff.; sources for first campaign, 176
Beroaldus, first editor of Tacitus, 239
Bias, republican, 45
Bilde von Rheinau, questions authorship of *Dialogus*, 5

Biography, in early Roman literature, 33
Blaesus, uncle of Sejanus, 183, 187
Boccaccio: knowledge of Tacitus, 237; connection with second Medicean MS, 240
Boissier, Gaston, author of *Tacite*, 220
Boudicca, 185
Bracciolini, Poggio: in reference to *Dialogus*, 5; knowledge of Tacitus, 237; transactions with Niccoli, 241 ff.
Britannicus, characterization of, 160
Brixellum, 173 f.
Bruni, L., knowledge of Tacitus, 237
Bruttidius Niger, 45
Brutus, cult of Brutus and Cassius, 19, 45, 67
Burrus, characterization of, 160

Caecina, advance on Italy from Germany, 168 ff.
Caesar, Julius: as author of *Commentaries*, 37; as military historian, 168; digressions on Gaul and Germany, 190; source for *Agricola*, 215 f.; source for *Germania*, 216
Callistus, Pallas, Narcissus, composite characterization of, 160 f.
Calpurnius Piso, L., 32
Camillus, 187
Capito, Ateius, M., 127 ff.
Capito, Titinius, as source for Tacitus, 213
Capra, Bartolomeo, the trade in MSS, 243
Cassiodorus: knowledge of Tacitus, 232; title of Tacitus' works, 345
Cassius, Dio, knowledge of Tacitus, 226
Cassius Hemina, L., 32
Cassius Severus, pamphlets as source material, 212
Castra Vetera, 180
Cato: as historian, 32; Stoic hero, 67 f.

Catulus, autobiographical material, 34

Celsus, 171, 173

Chance and fate, in first six books of *Annals,* 57 ff.

Cicero: on the annalists, 32; on the oratorical nature of history, 34; stylistic comparison with Tacitus, 97; stylistic source for *Dialogus,* 71 ff.

Ciceronian revival, 73

Cincius Alimentus, 32

Civilis, revolt of, 179 ff.

Claudian, knowledge of Tacitus, 229

Claudius, Appius, 44

Claudius: autobiography as source material, 212; lost works of, 46

Claudius Pollio, Ti.: as possible source for Tacitus, 214; friend of Pliny, 17

Cluvius Rufus: as source for Tacitus, 208, 213; writer of history, 47

Coelius Antipater, 33

Cörwey, MS of Tacitus at, 237

Collatio, comparison of sources, 200

Commentarii Agrippinae, as source material, 212

Commentarii Corbulonis, as source material, 212

Commentarii principum, as source material, 212

Composite characterization, of freedmen, 160 f.

Conjunctions, use of, in Tacitus, 94

Corazzini, the MS of Boccaccio, 240 n.

Corbulo: biographical characterization, 153 ff.; Roman general, 183

Cordus, Cremutius, 45

Cornelius, Emmerich, knowledge of Tacitus in Middle Ages, 225

Cornelius Sulla, how presented, 146

Cornutus Tertullus, friend of Pliny, 17

Correlia, intimate of Pliny's mother, 16

Correlius Rufus, friend of Pliny, 17

Corvinus, Messalla, cited as source, 52, 202

Courbaud, on Tacitus' method, 117

Cousin, J., on Tacitus' style, 89

Cremona, 170 f., 174, 179

Cremutius Cordus, 45

Curtius Rufus, 47 f.

Dasumius, Lucius, will of, 16 f.

Decembrio, Pier Candido: note on MS of minor works seen in *1455,* 247 ff.; testimony on minor works tradition, 285 ff.

Dictys of Crete, knowledge of Tacitus, 233

Dialogus: authorship, 5 f.; character sketches in, 97; Ciceronian style of, 72; date, 6; dramatic characterization in, 138; general spirit of, 22 ff.; non-Ciceronian traits in, 75; post-Augustan uses in, 75; role of the author in, 97; *Sententiae* in, 76; sources for, 216 f.; style, 74 ff.; stylistic criticism in, 79 ff.; variety, brevity, and pungency in, 76

Digressions: as footnotes, 197; biographical, 195 f.; comparative use in *Histories* and *Annals,* 198; death notices in, 195; for personal comment, 197; irrelevant, 196; nature and importance of, 189 f.; on Jewish history, 190; on sources, 194; on Stoic ethics, 193; summary characterization in, 195

Dio Cassius, knowledge of Tacitus, 226

Diodorus Siculus, use of prologue, 112

Dionysius, use of prologue, 112

Documents, public, as source material, 204, 207

Dolabella, 188

Domenico di Bandini, knowledge of Tacitus, 237

Domitian: advances Tacitus in office, 6; source of Tacitus' bitterness, 142

Draeger, on Tacitus' style, 89
Dramatic devices, applied to history, 96
Dramatic element: definition, 105; in *Annals,* 97 ff.; in *Histories,* 99

Egyptian priests, cited as source, 202
Einhard of Fulda, knowledge of Tacitus, 234
End of year summaries, in *Annals,* 59 ff.
Enoch of Ascoli: MSS finds of, 5; his MS of the minor works, 241 f., 248, 286 f.; notes about, in Leiden MS, 251
Eulogistic biography, 44
Eumenius, knowledge of Tacitus, 227
Euphorion, 44
Exitus Clarorum Virorum, as source material, 213
Exitus Virorum Illustrium, 47
Eye-witnesses, as source material, 213

Fabia, Ph., theory of single source, 211
Fabius Justus, friend of Pliny and Tacitus, 17, 19
Fabius Maximus, 32
Fabius Pictor, 32
Fabius Rusticus: as general source for Tacitus, 208 f., 213; as source for *Agricola,* 215; friend of Pliny, 17
Fabricius Veiento, author of gossip book, 207
Fannia, wife of Helvidius Priscus, 18
Fannius, C., as source for Tacitus, 213
Fate and chance, in first six books of *Annals,* 57 ff.
Fazio, Bartolomeo, connection with Hersfeld MS, 242
First-century literature, characterization of, 49

First Medicean MS, discovery and publication of, 239
Foreign affairs, treatment of, in *Annals,* 119 f.
Fortuna, Tacitus use of (stylistically), 124
Freytag, on dependability of Tacitus, 220
Frontinus, Julius, friend of Pliny and Tacitus, 19
Fronto, 77
Fugitive literature, as source material, 212
Fulda, Einhard of, knowledge of Tacitus, 234
Fulda, Tacitus MSS at or near, 235
Fundanius, Minicius, friend of Pliny and Tacitus, 17
Furneaux, on style of Tacitus, 89

Galba, character of, in *Histories,* 140
Gallus, 170, 173, 181
Gaza, Teodoro, about Enoch's finds, 249
Gellius, Aulus, 77
Gellius, Cn., 33
Germania: MSS of, 289 ff.; satiric qualities, 28, 87; sources for, 216; style, 86 ff.; traces of bitterness, 27
Germanicus, 130 ff.; 183 f.
Gods: casual reference to, in *Histories,* 56; vengeance of, 55
Goldman, A., the books of Boccaccio, 241 n.
Grat, Felix, argues independence of Vat. Lat. *1958,* 325
Guarino, connection with Hersfeld MS, 242 ff., 324, 326
Guarnieri, writer of part of Jesi MS, 253
Gudeman, A., date of *Dialogus,* 9
Guibert de Nogent, knowledge of Tacitus, 236
Guglielmo da Pastrengo, knowledge of Tacitus, 237

Hardy, E. G., on Tacitus as military historian, 167

Hecataeus, use of prologues, 111

Hegesippus, knowledge of Tacitus, 229

Heilig, K. J., on Paulus Venetus and the Second Med. MS, 240 n.

Helvidius Priscus, victim of Domitian, 18

Hemina, Cassius, L., 32

Henderson, B. W.: on Otho's strategy, 170; on Tacitus as military historian, 166

Hendrickson, G. L., date of *Dialogus*, 6, 9

Herennius Senecio, 18, 47; as possible source for Tacitus, 214

Herodotus, use of prologue, 110

Hersfeld, 280 ff.; reputed source of MS of Minor Works, 242 ff.

Histories: different material from *Annals*, 102 f.; distinction between *Histories* and *Annals*, 346; character of Galba in, 140; dramatic tendencies in, 99, 107; minor characters in, 140; program laid down, 51; summary character sketches in, 141; twofold prologue, 107

History: in category of oratory, 34; types of, ancient and modern, 166

Hochart, P., on authenticity of Tacitus, 219

Hordeonius, 181 ff.

Hortis, Attilio, 240 n.

Hostilia, 174, 179

Inscriptions, as source material, 212

Interamna, 4

Intermediate characters, presentation of, 153

Intimilium, 170

Island of the Batavians, 180

Jean de Montreuil, knowledge of Tacitus, 237

Jerome, knowledge of Tacitus, 228

Jerome, T. S.: attack on Tacitus' honesty, 220; treatment of treason cases, 133

Jesi MS of *Agricola*, 280 ff.; not same as MS at Monte Cassino, 253 f.

Jordanes, knowledge of Tacitus, 232

Jornandes, title of Tacitus' writings, 345

Josephus, use of prologue, 111

Journals, private, as source materials, 212

Julianus, Antonius, 214

Julius Caesar, as source in *Agricola*, 215 f.

Junia Silanus, how presented, 146

Junius Avitas, 17

Junius Mauricus, victim of Domitian, 18

Justus, Fabius, friend of Pliny and Tacitus, 17, 19

Justus, Minicius, friend of Tacitus, 16

Koestermann, use of Med. and Agricola MSS, 330

Lactantius, knowledge of Tacitus, 227

Lamola, Johannes, MS deals of, 244

Landolfus Sagax, knowledge of Tacitus, 232

Leiden, MS of Minor Works at, 251 f.

Leidensis, readings of, showing independent sources, 330 ff.

Leo X, Pope, connection with First Med. MS, 239

Leo, F., date of *Dialogus*, 8

Lepidus, M., 127 ff.

Lex maiestatis, 133 ff.

Libertas vs. *vetus res publica*, 64

Liberty, personalization in *Annals*, 108

Licinius Macer, factional history, 34

Licinius Sura, in will of Dasumius, 17

Linguet, expansion of Voltaire's attack on Tacitus, 219

Lipsius, Justus: first editor to use Vatican MS, 325; questioned authorship of *Dialogus*, 5

Livy, 36, 40, 41; as source for Tacitus in *Agricola*, 215; as source for Tacitus in *Germania*, 216; comment on digressions, 191; lack of geographical digressions, 190; story more important than characters, 138; use of prologue, 112

Locus Castrorum, 171

Loefstedt, on Tacitus' style, 89, 91

Lowe, E. A., on Second Med. MS, 240 n.

Lucan, 55

Lucian, theory of source use, 201

Macer, Licinius, factional history by, 34

Macer, Marcius, 171

Manitius, on Einhard, 234

Manni, the books of Boccaccio, 240 n.

Manuscripts: *Agricola,* affiliation of, 279 ff.; *Agricola* only, description of, 267 f.; *Agricola, Germania, Dialogus,* description of, 257 f.; *Agricola* and *Germania,* description of, 258 ff.; *Dialogus,* affiliations of, 288 f.; *Dialogus* only, description of, 268 ff.; *Germania,* affiliation of, 289 ff.; *Germania* only, description of, 271 ff.; *Germania* and *Dialogus* description of, 260 ff.

MAJOR WORKS. Argument for single source of, 326; characteristics of Group I, 337 ff.; characteristics of Group II, 339 ff.; characteristics of Group III, 341 ff.; chart of, showing agreements, 343; composite, 339; description of, 294 ff.; excerpts in Group I,

338; fragmentary, 322 f.; "Genoan" group, 342; grouping by endings, 326 f.; list of, 294; lost, 323 f.; rumor of unknown, 15th century MS, 326; tentative stemma of, 344; two classes of, in Group III, 341.

MINOR WORKS. Affiliations (apart from Jesi MS), 285 ff.; chart of, 293; classification of, 293; Decembrio's description of, 285 ff.; Enoch tradition, 286 ff.; list of, 256; tentative classification, 293

Maps, lack of, in Roman times, 168

Marcius Macer, 171

Marius, autobiographical material, 34

Marsh, F. B.: on dependability of Tacitus, 220; on Tacitus' use of sources, 211

Martial, on dramatic production, 106

Martin, on Tacitus' style, 89

Marx, F. A., on sources of Tacitus, 213

Mauricus, Junius, victim of Domitian, 18

Maximus, Fabius, 32

Medici, Carlo di, letters about Enoch's finds, 249 ff.

Meister, on the Dictys, 233

Memoirs of Suetonius Paulinus, as source material, 212, 215

Memoirs of Tiberius, as source material, 212

Menenius Agrippa, 44

Messalla Corvinus, 45

Messalla, Vipstanus, 44, 47 f., 202, 213

Military accounts, function in political history, 166 f.

Minicius Fundanus, friend of Pliny and Tacitus, 17

Minicius Justus, friend of Tacitus, 16

Minor characters, in *Agricola,* 139

Mommsen, on Tacitus as military historian, 167

Monarchy, effect on literature, 46

Monte Cassino: *Agricola,* known at, 253; MS of *Agricola* at, 283 ff.; Tacitus known at, 236

Motive for writing, change in 1st century A.D., 43

Motive for writing history, Tacitus', 193

Mylasa inscription about Tacitus, 4

Musonius Rufus, friend of Pliny praised by Tacitus, 18

Mutiny in Pannonia, 183 f.

Naevius, 31

Napoleon, attempt to discredit Tacitus, 219

Narcissus, Pallas, Callistus, composite characterization of, 160 f.

Narratio, legal and historical, 100

Nauportus, 183

Nepos, 36, 39

Nero, characterization of, 161 ff.

Niccoli, Niccolo: handled books of Boccaccio, 241; knowledge of Tacitus, 237; memorandum of MSS, 5; transaction with Poggio, 241 ff.

Nicholas V, Pope, sends Enoch for MSS, 248

Nicolo da Montefalcone, relation to second Med. MS, 240

Niger, Bruttidius, 45

Nonianus, Servilius, as source for Tacitus, 46, 213

Octavia, characterization of, 160

Octavius Sagitta, how presented, 146

Omens: dramatic use of, in *Histories,* 55; in histories, 51 ff.; in last six books of *Annals,* 61 ff.; Livy's use of, 121; summary account of, in *Histories,* 53; Tacitus' use of, stylistically, 121 ff.

Orosius, knowledge of Tacitus, 230 ff.

Otho: futility in campaigning, 169 f.; movements of his fleet, 170

Paetus Thrasea: characterization of, 156 ff.; fanatic opposition to Empire, 18 f.

Pallas, Narcissus, Callistus, composite characterization, 160 f.

Panaetius, 33

Panormita, Il: letter about Tacitus MSS, 5; letter to Guarino, 242, 244

Paratore, Ettore, on authorship of *Dialogus,* 5

Parthia, 185 f.

Parthian Wars, treatment of, by Tacitus, 185 f.

Paterculus, Velleius, possible source for Tacitus, 45 f., 214

Paul, correspondence of Seneca and St. Paul, 233 f.

Paulinus, Suetonius, 156, 171 ff., 184 f.

Paulinus Venetus, knowledge of Tacitus, 236, 240

Peace policy of Augustus, 40

Perret, J., on Tacitus' style, 89

Peter of Blois, knowledge of Tacitus, 237

Peter the Deacon, knowledge of Tacitus, 236

Peterson, on style of Tacitus, 94

Petrarch, possible knowledge of Tacitus, 237

Piccolomini, Aeneas Silvius, 250, 287 f.

Pichena, first editor to use second Med. MS, 325

Pictor, Fabius, 32

Pierre de Nolhac, on Boccaccio and Tacitus, 240 n.

Piso, L., 127 ff.

Piso, Calpurnius, L., 32

Pizzolpasso, Francesco, Archbishop of Milan, search for MSS, 246

Placentia, 170

Planta, Pompeius, possible source for Tacitus, 214
Plautus, Rubellius, presentation of, 146
Pliny the Elder, 47; as source for Tacitus, 202, 207 ff., 213
Pliny the Younger: as source for Tacitus, 210; calls Tacitus' work *Histories*, 345; estimate of Tacitus, 15; literary interests, 20 f.; on writing of history, 199 f.; position in Rome, 12 ff.
Plutarch, on Bedriacum, 173, 176
Poggio Bracciolini: in reference to *Dialogus*, 5; knowledge of Tacitus, 237; transaction with Niccoli, 241 ff.
Polento, Secco, knowledge of Tacitus, 237
Political implications in Tacitus' works, 69
Pollio, Asinius, 43 f.
Pollio, Claudius, Ti.: friend of Pliny, 17; possible source for Tacitus, 214
Polybius, 33, 35; use of prologue, 109 f.
Pompeius Planta, as possible source for Tacitus, 214
Pomponius Laetus, MS of *Agricola*, 279
Pomponius Secundus, 106
Pontanus, Jovianus: connection with Hersfeld MS, 242; copy of minor works by, 288; notes in Leiden MS about Enoch, 251
Poppaea Sabina, characterization of, 152, 159
Postumia, Via. *See* Via Postumia
Postumius, Albinus, A., 32
Pralle, Ludwig, origin of Hersfeld MS, 5
Primus, 178
Principatus vs. *res publica vetus*, 127
Priscus, Helvidius, victim of Domitian, 18

Prodigies, increased number in later books of *Annals*, 61
Prologue: conventional Greek usage, 110; historical use in general, 109 ff.; moral tone in Roman, 113; use by Tacitus in *Annals*, 116; use by Tacitus in *Histories*, 115
Ptolemy, knowledge of Tacitus, 225
Public documents, as source material, 204, 207
Puteolanus, first editor to use "Genoan" MS, 325

Quadrigarius, 33
Quentin, Dom Henri: argues independence of Vat. Lat. *1958*, 325; on Medicean MSS of Tacitus, 239
Quintilian, 46, 73, 77 f., 216; on style of Tacitus, 94; possible teacher of Tacitus, 20

Rambaldi, knowledge of Tacitus, 237
Ravenna, 177
Raynaldus, Abbas, relation to Second Med. MS, 240
Recitationes, 43
Regulus, M. Aquilius, possible source for Tacitus, 214
Restoration of Capitol by Vespasian, 52
Revolt in Britain, 184 f.
Revolt in Germany, 183 f.
Rhenanus, Beatus, 325
Rhetoric, theory and practice in 1st century B.C., 37 ff.
Robinson, R., on the MSS of the *Germania*, 290
Roman annalists, 32
Roman history, early character of, 36
Roman literature, in first century A.D., 41 ff.
Ross, W. R., author of *Tacitus and Bracciolini*, 219
Rubellius Plautus, how presented, 146

Rudolphus of Fulda, knowledge of Tacitus, 234 f.
Rufus, Asinius, 18
Rufus, Aufidienus, 183
Rufus, Cluvius, as source of Tacitus, 47, 208, 213
Rufus, Corellius, friend of Pliny, 17
Rufus, Curtius, 47 f.
Rufus, Musonius, friend of Pliny, 18
Rufus, P. Anteius, possible source for Tacitus, 214
Rufus, Verginius: friend of Pliny and Tacitus, 19; source for Tacitus, 239
Rusticus, Arulenus: possible source for Tacitus, 214; victim of Domitian, 18; writer of biography, 47
Rusticus, Fabius: friend of Pliny, 17; source for Tacitus, 207 f., 213, 215
Ryck, Th., his MS readings, 328

Sabina, Poppaea, characterization of, 152, 159
Sagax, Landolfus, knowledge of Tacitus, 232
Sagitta, Octavius, presentation of, 146
Saleius Bassus, dramatic production, 106
Sallust, 36, 39; influence on style of Tacitus, 71; limitation of influence on Tacitus, 82; model for geographical digression, 190; Stoic digression in, 193; Stoic elements in, 40; use of prologues, 113 f.
Salvatore, on Tacitus' style, 89
Satiric touches in *Germania*, 87
Scaurus, Aemilius, 34
Scholiast to Juvenal, knowledge of Tacitus, 232 f.
Scipio the Younger, relation to historical writing, 33
Scipionic circle, relation to history, 33
Sempronius Asselio, 33
Seneca the Elder, 46

Seneca: characterization of, 143 ff.; dramatic productions of, 106; correspondence of Seneca and St. Paul, 233 f.; introduction of, 143; literary style of, 76 ff.
Senecio, Herennius, 214; possible source for Tacitus, 214; victim of Domitian, 18; writer of biography, 47
Sententiae, 38; in *Dialogus*, 76
Servilius Nonianus, 46; source for Tacitus, 213
Servius, knowledge of Tacitus, 229
Severus, Cassius, 212
Severus, Sulpicius, knowledge of Tacitus, 228
Secco Polento, knowledge of Tacitus, 237
Secondary sources, general histories, 213
Secondary sources, special histories, 214
Secundus, Pomponius, 106
Sejanus, 132 ff., 187
Senate, government of, vs. imperial government, 65
Senate records, as source for Tacitus, 210
Senators, recalcitrant group of, 127 ff.
Sidonius Apollinaris, 3; knowledge of Tacitus, 229 f.
Sievers, on dependability of Tacitus, 220
Silanus, Junia, presentation of, 146
Sisenna, Cornelius, factional history, 34
Soderini, Cardinal, letter of, 3, 239
Sosianus, Antistius, 145
Sources: *Acta Diurna*, 212; *Acta Senatus*, 212; *Agricola*, 214; archaeological remains, 213; citation of unnamed, 201 f.; cited in *Annals*, 204 ff.; cited in *Histories*, 201 ff.; comparative use in *Histories* and *Annals*, 210; *Dialogus*, 216; general citation of, 209; *Germania*, 216; primary, listed, 212 f.;

Sources (*continued*)
secondary, listed, 213 f.; speeches
of emperors, 212
Speeches in historical writing, 33
Speeches of emperors, as source material, 212
Spira, first printer of Tacitus, 325
Spirito, S., recipient of books of Boccaccio, 240 f.
Spurinna, 170 f.
Stahr, on dependability of Tacitus, 220
Stoic elements in Sallust, 40
Stoic fanatics in early empire, 18 f.
Stoicism, 33; conventional in Tacitus, 63; in first century A.D., 108; so-called Stoic opposition, 66 ff.
Style, change in later books of *Annals,* 109
Suetonius, on Bedriacum, 176
Suetonius Paulinus, 156, 171 ff., 184 f.; memoirs of, 212, 215
Sulla, autobiographical material, 34
Sulla, Cornelius, 146
Sulpicius Severus, knowledge of Tacitus, 228
Summaries of minor events, 119
Supernatural, in *Annals,* 56 ff.
Supernatural, in *Histories,* 51 ff.
Sura, Licinius, in will of Dasumius, 17

Tacfarinas, 187
Tacitus: anti-imperialism of, 68; artificiality of style, 94 f.; attitude toward sources, 200 ff.; birthplace, 4; bitterness in *Agricola,* 26, 27; brevity, 84, 90, 93; code of historical honesty, 194; comments on digressions, 191 ff.; date of death, 7; desire for personal fame, 200; desire for public approval, 102; development of style, 89; discussion of previous historians, 204; familiar with dramatic production, 106; familiarity with historical writers, 101 f.; family background, 3; geographical

knowledge, 217; hatred of tyranny, 142; irony in *Dialogus,* 23 f.; lack of political trend in *Dialogus,* 24 f.; lack of Stoic digressions, 193; literary interests, 20 ff.; method in military history, 185 f.; moral note in *Dialogus,* 24; motive for writing history, 193; Mylasa inscription about, 4; name, 3; official career, 6; point of view in *Dialogus,* 22 f.; primarily lawyer or historian? 101; personal interest as against political, 70; reputation as military historian, 167 f.; use of earlier literature, 10 f.; use of new words, 75; summary of character, 29, 30; use of annalistic framework, 103, 119; use of conjunctions, 94; use of traditional methods, 103.
    STYLE. Brevity, 84, 90, 93; comparison with Cicero, 97; contrast, 85; effectiveness of presentation, 101; evidence of *Dialogus* on aims, 71 ff.; influence of Sallust on, 71; use of present participle as noun, 85; variety, 84, 93; of *Annals,* 91 ff.; of *Histories,* 89 ff.; of Major Works, 89 ff.; unique, 71
Tacitus, the Emperor, 4
Tertullian, knowledge of Tacitus, 226 f.
Tertullus, Cornutus, in will of Dasumius, 17
Third inversion: absent from Leiden MS, 328 f.; corrected by scribes of Yale 1 and Yale 2, 329; restored by Puteolanus, 329
Thrasea, Paetus: characterization of, 156 ff.; fanatic opposition of, 18 f.
Thucydides, 31, 35 f.; use of prologue, 110
Tiberius: dramatic treatment of, 126 ff.; memoirs of, 212
Tigellinus, incomplete characterization, 158 f.
Timaeus, 31

Titinius Capito, as source for Tacitus, 213
Titles: *Agricola,* 347; *Dialogus,* 347; evidence of MSS, 345 f.; evidence of Pliny the Younger, 345; evidence of Tertullian, 345; evidence of Vopiscus, 345; *Germania,* 347 f.; *Histories,* 345; *Historiae* and *Annales,* 346; *Res Gestiae* and *Annales,* 346 f.; Tacitus' own evidence, 346
Titus, advances Tacitus in office, 6
Traversari, connection with Poggio, 243, 247
Treason cases, 133 ff.

Urbinum, 178

Valens, 172, 175, 177 f.
Valerius Antias, 33
Varus, 178
Veiento, Fabricius, author of gossip book, 207
Velleius Paterculus, possible source for Tacitus, 214
Venetus, Paulinus, knowledge of Tacitus, 236, 240

Verginius Rufus: friend of Pliny and Tacitus, 19; source for Tacitus, 176
Verona, 174
Vespasian: appoints Tacitus to office, 6; attitude toward omens, 52; in relation to date of Curtius Rufus, 48; miraculous cures, 53; restores Capitol, 52
Via Postumia, 174
Violations of chronological order, 119 ff.
Vipstanus Messalla, 47; as source for Tacitus, 213
Vitellius, 168, 170, 176 f.; disregard of tradition, 52
Vocula, 181
Voltaire, attack on Tacitus, 219
Vopiscus: opinion of Tacitus, 227; title of Tacitus' works, 345

Wiener, Leo, on Tacitean forgeries, 219
William of Malmesbury, knowledge of Tacitus, 237

Xenophon, 31